Johannine Studies

✝

ANDRÉ FEUILLET

alba house
STATEN ISLAND N.Y.
A DIVISION OF ST. PAUL PUBLICATIONS

Translated from the French by
Rev. Thomas E. Crane
St. John Vianney Seminary
East Aurora, N. Y.

Nihil Obstat:
Myles M. Bourke, S.S.L., S.T.D.
Censor Librorum

Imprimatur:
✠ Francis Cardinal Spellman
Archbishop of New York

First printing - October 28, 1964
Second printing - April, 1966

Library of Congress Catalog Card No. 64-20112

Designed, printed and bound in the U.S.A. by the Pauline Fathers
and Brothers, Society of St. Paul, Staten Island, N. Y.

Contents

FOREWORD 13

PART ONE: THE FOURTH GOSPEL

CHAPTER I THE HOUR OF JESUS AND THE SIGN
OF CANA 17

1. The Hour of Jesus in the Plan of the Fourth Gospel . 19
2. The Significance of the Cana Miracle 28

CHAPTER II THE THEOLOGICAL SIGNIFICANCE OF
THE SECOND CANA MIRACLE . . . 39

1. Relation to the Preceding Context 39
2. Relation to the Following Context 44

CHAPTER III THE PRINCIPLE BIBLICAL THEMES
IN THE DISCOURSE ON THE BREAD
OF LIFE 53

1. The Manna as Symbol of Spiritual Food 58
   — Recollection of the Exodus and of the Manna . . 58
   — Jesus' Explanation of the Manna 60
   — The Synoptic Account of the Temptation . . . 64

2. Eschatological Perspective; The Messianic Banquet . 66
   — Eschatological Character of the Promised Food . 66

     — The Messianic Banquet in the Old Testament .   .   70
     — The Messianic Banquet in John VI and the
        Synoptics   73

  3. Wisdom's Banquet   76
     — The Old Testament   76
     — John VI   80
     — Literary Relationship between the Fourth Gospel
        and the Wisdom Literature   80
     — Johannine Formulas with *"Ego eimi"* .   .   .   83
     — "I am the Bread of Life"   86
     — The Allegory of the Vine   87
     — The Disciples of Christ in John, and the Disciples
        of Wisdom   89
     — Jesus and Wisdom in the Synoptics .   .   .   91
     — The Johannine Logion   98

  4. The Disciples of Christ According to the Synoptics
    and the Fourth Gospel   102
     — The Old Testament and Judaism .   .   .   102
     — The New Testament   108

  GENERAL CONCLUSIONS: UNITY OF THE DIS-
  COURSE: JOHN'S EUCHARISTIC DOCTRINE . 118

CHAPTER IV   THE COMPOSITION OF CHAPTERS
             IX - XII   129

  1. Defects of Composition; Displacements Suggested . 130

  2. Justification of the Present Order of the Text .   .   136

CHAPTER V   THE TIME OF THE CHURCH IN ST.
           JOHN   149

  1. The Fourth Gospel   151
     — The Time of the Church and Men's Relations
        with God   152

— The Time of the Church and Men's Relations
among Themselves 157

2. The Apocalypse 159
— The Presence of Christ in History 161
— The Battle between Christ and anti-Christ . . 163

CONCLUSION 166

CHAPTER VI   PARTICIPATION IN THE LIFE OF GOD
ACCORDING TO THE FOURTH GOSPEL 169

1. Johannine Mysticism and Hellenistic Mysticism . . 170

2. Johannine Mysticism and the Synoptic Gospels . . 173

PART TWO: THE APOCALYPSE

CHAPTER I   THE TWENTY-FOUR ELDERS OF THE
APOCALYPSE 183

1. The Twenty-four Elders are Glorified Men . . . 185

2. The Twenty-four Elders are the Saints of the Old
Testament 194

CHAPTER II   THE VALUE OF THE APOCALYPSE FOR
THE SOLUTION OF THE ESCHATO-
LOGICAL PROBLEM 215

1. Exegesis 215

2. Eschatological Significance of the Passage; Its Place in
the General Plan of the Apocalypse 224

CHAPTER III   INTERPRETATION OF CHAPTER XI OF
THE APOCALYPSE 233

1. The Measuring of the Temple (vv. 1-2) 235

2. The Two Witnesses (vv. 3-13) 240

3. The Third Woe and the Seventh Trumpet . . . 250

CHAPTER IV   THE MESSIAH AND HIS MOTHER
             ACCORDING TO APOCALYPSE XII .   . 257

1. Birth and Heavenly Assumption of the Messianic
   Child 258
   — Statement of the Problem; Proposed Solution .   . 258
   — Arguments for a Metaphorical Birth of the
     Messiah 260
   — A Possible Explanation: The Metaphorical Messi-
     anic Birth in Qumran 267

2. The Mother of the Messiah 270
   — The Woman; Biblical References 271
   — Basic Meaning of Apocalypse XII; its Relation-
     ship to the Woman, Mother of the Messiah .   . 277
   — The Marian Interpretation of Apocalypse XII .   . 283

Foreword

The studies in John collected in this volume have all been published before, in various periodicals, memorial volumes and Mélanges. Various times the suggestion has been forthcoming that a single collection of the studies would make them more accessible, and thereby more useful. Perhaps the reader will notice that we have made some corrections in the text, and have entered some additions.

The present study is divided into two quite unequal parts. The first, by far the more important, deals with the fourth Gospel. Johannine theology, because of its depth, differs considerably from the doctrine of the Synoptics; whereas the Synoptics wish above all to emphasize the inauguration by Jesus of the Kingdom of God, the accent in the fourth Gospel is almost exclusively on the person of Jesus, in so far as this person constitutes the great revelation made to men of the very mystery of God. As we explained in *Introduction á la Bible*, (2nd ed. vol. II, Paris, 1959, p. 673), the principal theme of John's Gospel is that the Son of God has been sent in the flesh by the Father, to reveal and communicate to men the mysterious riches of divine life. Furthermore, it is above all in the Church that these riches are to be offered to men. This Gospel is ecclesial to the same extent to which it is Christological. Jesus' public ministry, with His preaching and His miracles, is presented therein as an anticipation of the life of the Church, which will sanctify souls through the Word and the sacraments. The existence of the Church, in its turn, is seen as a foreshadowing of the Parousia.

Although the studies presented here treat only certain texts, or certain main themes, still the manner of considering them will make it possible, we hope, to form a fairly precise idea of the general structure and theological orientation of John's Gospel.

The lengthy study which we have dedicated to the Discourse on the Bread of Life has been received in a most gratifying manner, and has frequently been requested. This is part of the

reason for which we have chosen to accept the kind invitation
of Father Dejaifve, Director of the Museum Lessianum, to add
our humble effort to his collection.

The second part of the book treats the Apocalypse. One could
hardly exaggerate the momentous difficulties which hamper the
commentators who seek to unravel the meaning of John's writings.
And it is only proper to remark that the Apocalypse, difficult as
it is, tends to hold less attraction nowadays than formerly, for
exegetes. Such a state of affairs is regrettable indeed, for the
Apocalypse is the crowning finish of the entire Scripture, both
Old and New Testament. The Apocalypse is the only book of
the New Testament which proposes to explain the Christian
meaning of history. Thanks to a methodical approach and to a
Christian re-reading of ancient texts, its precious doctrine is presented as the fulfillment, in Christ, of the wonderful teachings
of the prophets of Israel. No other inspired writing expresses so
forcefully the unity of the two testaments. We hope that the
studies which we have gathered in this latter part will give some
idea of the doctrinal richness of the Johannine corpus.

The monograph of the Woman of the Apocalypse will doubtless be of interest. During recent years the twelfth chapter of
the Apocalypse has been the object of intense new study, and
has provoked new discussions. It seems to us that exegetes should
agree at least on one point; that the vision which St. John
describes deals primarily with the idealized Sion of the prophets,
and to the Church of Christ; if Mary is seen here too, as we are
sure she is, it is only in a secondary and subordinate way.

We have the most pleasant obligation of rendering our sincere
thanks, first of all to Fr. Dejaifve, who has encouraged and
supported this work. We thank also the publishers of the periodicals for their gracious permission to reproduce several articles
which they originally published.

A. F.

Part I
The Fourth Gospel

CHAPTER I

THE HOUR OF JESUS AND THE SIGN OF CANA [1]

A *Contribution to the Study of the*
Structure of the Fourth Gospel

The Wedding of Cana has called forth in recent years an extraordinary number of studies, almost all of which have been by Catholics.[2] Some of them have been excellent; others are excessively concerned with apologetics—for example, the concern to remove all trace of apparent harshness from Jesus' words to His Mother, or to eliminate the paradoxical way in which Jesus grants Mary's prayer, immediately after He has seemingly rejected her intercession.

---

1 Originally published in *Analecta Lovaniensia Biblica et Orientalia* Serie III, Fasc. 16, · 1960.

2 In addition to the standard commentaries on the fourth Gospel, there are a number of studies which have appeared since 1942. The following listing (which is not intended to be exhaustive) is in chronological order: GALLUS, *Quid mihi et tibi mulier? Nondum venit hora mea. Potestne intelligi tanquam allusio?* in *Verbum Domini*, 1942, pp. 41-50; ROSCHINI, *La vita di Maria*, Roma, 1945, pp. 245-269; LILLY, *Jesus and His Mother during the Public Life*, in *Cath. Bibl. Quart.*, 1946, pp. 52-57; 197-200; ZOLLI, *Quid mihi et tibi mulier?*, in *Marianum*, 1946, pp. 3-15; KLEIST, *Our Lady's Training for the Sacrifice of Separation*, in *Amer. Eccl. Review*, 1946, pp. 81-89; GAROFALO, *Le Parole di Maria*, Torino, Roma, 1947, pp. 131-154; VANNUTELLI, *Alle Nozze di Cana*, in *Marianum*, 1948, pp. 72 ff.; PREISKER, *Jo. II: 4 and XIX: 26* in *Zeitschr. für N. T. Wissenschaft*, 1949, pp. 209-214; SCHNACKENBURG, *Das erste Wunder Jesu*, Jo. 2, 1-11. Freiburg I. B., 1951; BRUNET, *Les Noces de Cana*, in *Études et Recherches. Cahiers de Théologie et de Philosophie*, Ottawa, 1952, pp. 9-22. VAN DEN BUSSCHE, *Het Wijnwonder te Cana*, in *Coll. Gand.*, 1952, pp. 193-225; J. LEAL, *La hora de Jesus*, in *Est. Ecles.*, 1952, pp. 357 ff.; CHARLIER, *Les Noces de Cana*, in *Bible et Vie Chrétienne*, 1953, pp. 81-86; ROBILLARD, *Le vin manqua*, in *Vie Spiritu-*

The purpose of this study is not to add another hypothesis to all those which have been proposed so far, much less to set about a critical examination of them. Rather, we shall take as our starting point the exegetical conclusions which we believe have already been established with sufficient certitude.

First of all, we are convinced, along with Gaechter,[3] Braun,[4] H. Van den Bussche,[5] and many others, that the Hour of Jesus which has not yet come, is that of His Passion and Glorification. On the other hand, even if it is true that in the Bible the phrase, "What is it to me and to thee?" can sometimes express the absence of any hostility ("What is there that makes us opposed to each other?"), still in all, the meaning of the absence of a common ground is the most current interpretation, ("What is there between us?"). This is the only meaning which the profane Greek writings know for the phrase.[6] Therefore it seems wrong to seek to exclude from Christ's reply any nuance of opposition to His Mother's implied request. The difficulty seems to be rather

---

elle, 1953, pp. 28-45; BRAUN, La Mère des Fidèles. Essai de théologie johannique, Tournai - Paris, 1953 (2e edition revue et augmentée, 1954); TEMPLE, Conversation Piece at Cana, in Dominican Studies, 1954, pp. 104-113; CONZALO MAESO, Una leccion de exégesis linguística sobre el pasaje evangélico de las bodas de Cana, in Cultura Biblica, 1954, pp. 352 sq.; TESTA, La meditazione di Maria a Cana, in Studi biblici Franciscani, 1954 - 1955, pp. 139-190; MICHL, Bemerkungen zu Joh, 2, 4, in Biblica, 1955, pp. 492-509; MICHL, Die Hochzeit zu Kana. Kritik einer Auslegung, in Theologie und Glaube, 1955, pp. 334 sq.; CEROKE, Jesus and Mary at Cana. Separation or Association, in Theological Studies, 1956, pp. 1-38; BOISMARD, Du Baptême à Cana, Paris, 1956; PEINADOR, La respuesta de Jesus a su Madre en las Bodas de Cana, in Ephemerides Mariologicae, 1958, pp. 61-104; QUIRANT, Las Bodas de Cana, in Marianum, 1958, pp. 155-189; ANZALONE, Gesu a Maria alle Nozze di Cana, in Rivista Biblica, 1958, pp. 135-146; J. GALOT, Marie dans l'Evangile, Paris-Louvain, 1958.

3 Maria im Erdenleben, Innsbruck-Wien-München, 1954, pp. 180-191.

4 La Mère des Fidèles, 2e edit., pp. 55-58. Trans., Alba House, 1965.

5 L'Évangile de Jean. Etudes et Problèmes (Recherches Bibliques sous le patronage du Collegium Biblicum Lovaniense), 1958, p. 79, note 2. Cf. the same author's work, L'attente de la grande révélation dans le quatrième évangile, in Nouvelle Revue Théologique, 1953, pp. 1009-1019.

6 Cf. M. E. Boismard, Du Baptême à Cana, pp. 144-149. The best French equivalent is "Qu'avons-nous affaire ensemble (dans cette affaire)" or "Que me veux-tu"? The nuance of resistance can have varying degrees; here the context calls for a limited emphasis.

in understanding what it was at the moment which separated them.

Since the reason for Jesus' apparent refusal is that His "Hour" had not yet come, would it not seem to be in order to define, more exactly than most do, what the fourth Gospel means by the simple phrase, "the Hour of Jesus"?

This will be the object of our first part, which will place in relief one of the most curious, and one of the least noticed, aspects of the peculiar literary and theological structure of the fourth Gospel. This part, (which seems to us to be the more important, since it calls for an understanding of the structural plan of the entire Gospel), will be somewhat brief, for even though we may need to refer to the contents of chapters 18-21, it will be out of the question to undertake a detailed exegesis here.

In availing ourselves of the clear light which the last pages of John's Gospel shed on Cana (and, for that matter, on the rest of the "Signs" of Jesus as well), we shall be able to explain in the second part what seems to us to be the profound meaning of the Cana miracle. The marian importance of the incident, which occupies (and rightly so) many commentators, will also be corroborated and explained thereby.

(1) *The Hour of Jesus in the Plan of the Fourth Gospel*

The authors whom we mentioned above have shown well that the Hour of Jesus which is mentioned in the Cana narrative is that of His Passion and Glorification. It seems unnecesary, therefore, to enter here into a detailed examination of the problem. Furthermore, it seems to be beyond question that Jesus' statement, "My hour is not yet come," is a negation, and not a question, "Has my hour come?". The two parallel passages of John VII: 30 and VIII: 20 show that the phrase is to be taken as a negation, and that the Hour of Jesus refers to His Death and Glorification.

In general, in the fourth Gospel, a person's "hour" is the time in which he does the work to which he has been specifically assigned. The hour of the woman is that of her childbirth (XVI: 21); the hour of the unbelieving Jews is the time in which God allows them to commit their crime (XVI: 3-4); the Hour of Jesus is the moment in which is definitively fulfilled the work for which He was sent into this world by the Father, that is, for His victory over Satan, sin and death (cf. especially XII: 23-24; 27; 31-32). We may compare these johannine texts also with Lk. XXII: 53, "But this is your hour, and the power of darkness," and with Mt. VIII: 29, "Hast thou come to torment us before the time?"

But it is the profound meaning of this Hour of Jesus, and of the work which it implies, which we must now attempt to determine. It is evident that all the happenings of Jesus' public life are oriented toward the Hour, as toward a point of consummation. This is particularly true of His miracles, which recall the wonders of the Exodus.[7] At the same time, however, they are made to appear as figures of the sacraments, which can become active only after Christ shall have gone away.[8] Contrary to what is usually held, the evangelist's plan is not only to prove that Jesus is the Anointed and the Son of God (which was already long known!), but rather to emphasize that there is no distinction between Jesus of Nazareth, who lived and preached in Galilee and Judea, and the Christ of faith, the Son of God, present in the Church, who continues to sanctify souls by the sacraments. We believe that this is the profound meaning of XX: 31, where, as others have said, the emphasis is undoubtedly on the word "Jesus".[9] Far from abandoning facts for the sake of engaging in theological speculation or allegory, John works rather to unite closely the faith and life of the Church with the Gospel history.

If such be the case, then it is indispensable to see underscored in chapters XVIII - XXI, the ecclesiological and sacramental meaning of the Passion and Glorification. And this will become abundantly clear in the course of our study.

---

7 Cf. Ziener, *Weischeitsbuch und Johannes - Evangelium*, in *Biblica*, 1957, pp. 396-418; 1958, pp. 37-60. Cf. also the somewhat exaggerated thesis of H. SAHLIN, *Zur Typologie des Johannesevangelium*, Uppsala - Leipzig, 1950.

8 Cf. O. CULLMANN, *Les Sacrements dans l'Évangile johannique*, Paris 1951; J. G. H. Hoffmann, *Le Jésus de l'histoire et le Christ Seigneur de l'Église*, 1952. We should be on guard in this respect against the tendency to systematize too much. Cf. J. A. T. ROBINSON, *The "Others" of John 4; 38. A Test of Exegetical Method*, in *Studia Evangelica, Papers presented to the International Congress on The Four Gospels, Oxford, 1954* (Akademie - Verlag, Berlin, 1959), pp. 510-515.

9 Cf. F. MUSSNER, *Der historische Jesus und der Christus es Glaubens*, in *Biblische Zeitschrift*, 1957, pp. 236-237.

It is common knowledge that the fundamental theme of the Jesus of the Synoptics, the Kingdom of God, is almost entirely absent from the preaching of John's Christ, which is centered squarely on His person as the revelation of the divine riches which men are invited to share. The Kingdom is mentioned only once, in passing, in the interview with Nicodemus (III: 5). On the other hand, it returns where the Synoptics do not have it at all, in the Passion narrative. And here, as one would imagine, this theme is presented in a guise which is peculiarly johannine. As has been shown elsewhere, the Passion is conceived in the fourth Gospel as a kind of epiphany of Christ the King. In John XVIII - XIX, the word occurs twelve times, compared to four in Matthew and six in Mark.[10]

During the public ministry, the transcendent character of Jesus' person is often emphasized. Jesus is not of this world; He is from on high, like divine wisdom (III: 31; VIII: 23; cf. Sirach XXIV: 3). Before Pilate Jesus says the same thing of the *Basileia* which He has come to inaugurate,[11] that it is not of this world either, but from on high. This is why the Jews, in delivering Jesus up to Pilate are guilty of such a serious sin; it would not have been so severe, had Jesus' Kingdom been of this world (XVIII: 36; XIX: 11).[12]

Why this eventual application to the Kingdom, of qualities

---

10 Cf. J. BLANK, *Die Verhandlung vor Pilatus im Lichte johanneischer Theologie*, in *Biblische Zeitschrift*, 1959, pp. 60-81.

11 C. K. Barrett observes that in the Synoptics *Basileia* is a reality of the future world (from the temporal point of view), whereas here it is presented as a reality originating in heaven (from the spatial point of view). *The Gospel according to St. John*, London, 1955, p. 447. These two concepts, however, both occur in Daniel; they need not be mutually exclusive.

12 As for XIX: 11, many exegetes are opposed to the incorrect use which is often made with this statement; they emphasize (correctly) that we should not see here a definition of the divine origin of political power, but that the text could also be interpreted thus: Because Pilate had received power from on high to dispose of Jesus, he is less culpable than the one who delivered Him up to the Procurator, i.e., Caiphas or Judas. However, this comparison of the two persons responsible for Jesus' death sentence is surprising. Further, the argument does not seem decisive, because Caiphas and Judas also acted only by virtue of a permission from God. As for Judas, it was the Savior Himself who permitted him to act: "What thou dost, do quickly" (XIII: 27). For these reasons we see in XIX: 11 a veiled profession by Jesus of His own transcendance; because He comes

which were applied at first to its Founder? It is because the Kingdom is to be the earthly continuation and representation of Jesus after He has gone. As the fulfillment of the chosen people's messianic expectations (cf. the title on the Cross, "Jesus of Nazareth, King of the Jews"), the Kingdom will be at the same time universal, for the Crucified will "draw all men to Himself" XII: 32. This explains also why John stresses the fact (XIX: 20) that the title was written in the three official languages, Hebrew (or, rather Aramaic), Latin, and Greek. Unlike the kingdom of David and Solomon, which Ahias of Shilo had predicted would be split, by tearing his new cloak into twelve parts (I Kgs. XI: 29-31), the Kingdom of Christ will never be divided This, apparently, is the meaning of the Savior's seamless garment, which was not torn into pieces (XIX: 23-24); later also (XXI: 11), the miraculous draught of fishes are to be caught in an unbroken net. In both cases the verb *schizo* is used. Cf. also the use of the same verb in VII: 43; IX: 16; X: 19.

In the Synoptics the Passion drama culminates in the Death of Jesus, amid the most shocking circumstances; from the sixth to the ninth hour of the day, darkness covers the earth; the veil of the Temple is torn in two; the bystanders are seized with terror; in Matthew the dead rise from their tombs. John omits all this and brings his narrative to its culmination in a detail which at first glance may seem to be only secondary, but which he stresses with the greatest solemnity. This is the moment in which, after Jesus is already dead, a soldier pierces His side with a lance, and blood and water flow out (XIX: 31-37).

Why the difference of emphasis? The reason seems clear, once we recall, on the one hand, the coming of Jesus by water (baptism) in the Jordan, and blood (the Passion) in I Jo. V: 6-7, and, on the other hand, the importance which the fourth Gospel assigns to the sacrament of Baptism (theme of water) and to the Eucharist (blood of the Son of Man, VI: 53-56). Add to this the

---

from above and is not an ordinary condemned criminal, a special authorization from above is necessary before men may put hands upon Him; only God could give such a power. We might repeat here St. Augustine's reflection on XIV: 11: *"Nisi se traderet Christus, nemo traderet Christum."* Thus also the one who delivered Him up to the tribunal is more guilty than if he had delivered up an ordinary innocent man. The entire context, which emphasizes strongly Jesus' royal dignity, seems to favor this exegesis. However, we hesitate to propose it as certain.

almost certain reference in XIX: 36 to Ex. XII: 46: "You shall not break any of its bones." The fourth Gospel places here the announcement of the Christian Pasch, as fulfillment of the Jewish Pasch, which characterizes the Last Supper narrative of the Synoptics.[13]

Being Himself the living sacrament, whose contact brings life to souls, Jesus is now about to separate Himself from men and return to His heavenly Father. His sanctifying action, however, will be continued by the Church, through the sacraments, especially Baptism and the Eucharist. The Church with the sacraments is born of the redemptive Passion, like the blood and the water flowing from Christ's pierced side; as long as the incarnate Logos was on earth, there was no place for a sacramental economy.

It is fitting to mention in this connection, the gift of the Spirit which coincides with the Savior's last breath, according to the probable double meaning of the formula *paredōken to pneuma*.[14] We should refer once more here to I Jo. V: 6-7: "And it is the Spirit that bears witness, because the Spirit is the truth. For there are three that bear witness, the Spirit, the water and the blood; and these three are one."

The Synoptics narrate the election of the Twelve by Jesus; they give their names and show them undergoing a sort of apprenticeship for their future apostolate, when the Master sends them out on a mission. Matthew alone has the solemn promise made to Peter at Caesarea Philippi, and a whole discourse (Ch. XVIII) on the life of the members of the future community. John leaves aside this important aspect of Jesus' public ministry. But he shows the risen Jesus conferring on the Twelve the power to *forgive or to retain* sins (XX: 22-23), and this in a declaration made up of antithetic terms, the same as the formula of *binding*

---

13 Obviously, a much longer treatment would be required in order to explain adequately all that we have said above; the significance of the water and of the blood is not explained in the same way by all commentators. Some have questioned the reference to the paschal lamb. And on this scene, cf. besides the commentaries, A. LEFEVRE, *La blessure du côté*, in *Études Carmélitaines, Le Coeur*, 1950, pp. 109-122.

14 This double meaning is admitted especially by A. LOISY, *Le quatrième évangile*, Paris, 1903, p. 882; E. HOSKYNS, *The Fourth Gospel*, London, 1947, p. 532; R. H. LIGHTFOOT, *St. John's Gospel*, Oxford, 1956, pp. 319-320.

and loosing, which is repeated twice in Matthew, the first time in the statement to Peter (XVI: 19), and again in the statement to the whole group of apostles (XVIII: 18). The terms are less strictly Jewish in John than in Matthew, but the ideas are similar in both cases, if it is true that the terms "bind and loose" refer to the disciplinary power of excommunication, which can be imposed or dispensed.[15] We see here also the plan of the fourth evangelist to give Jesus' Passion and Glorification (His "Hour") an ecclesial perspective.

In the Synoptics, physical contact with Jesus during His public ministry is important, as we see from the frequent use of the word *haptesthai.* Jesus Himself often takes the initiative in these touches, but many times it is the sick who, seek to be cured, and reach out to touch Him (Mt. IX: 20; 21; 29; XIV: 36; Mk. III: 10; V: 27-28; 30-31; VI: 50; X: 13). Luke sums up the situation thus: "And all the crowd were trying to touch Him, for power went forth from Him and healed all" (VI: 19).

John has none of this. He uses the word *haptesthai* only once, in the meeting of the risen Christ with Mary Magdalene, "Do not touch me, for I have not yet ascended to my Father" (XX: 17). This apparently means that physical contact with Jesus is neither the best thing, nor even essential. But when He shall be again with His Father, then, paradoxically, it will be possible to have the perfect contact with Him, through grace and the sacraments. Cf. the paradox of XIV: 26; "I go away, and I am coming to you."

If, a little further on (XX: 24-29) St. Thomas is invited to place his finger in the place of the nails, and his hand into the side, it is because, like the other apostles, he must be an official witness of the Resurrection. But, "Blessed are they who have not seen, and yet have believed" (XX: 29).[16] On this occasion Thomas

---

15 Cf. H. STRACK - P. BILLERBECK, *Kommentar zum Neuen Testament aus Talmud und Midrasch,* München, 1922, t. I, pp. 739-741. Regarding the relationship of Matthean and Johannine formulas to each other, cf. C. H. DODD, *Some Johannine "Herrnworte" with Parallels in the Synoptic Gospels,* in *New Testament Studies,* II, 1955-56, pp. 85-86.

16 In our opinion, the passage in Luke XXIV: 13-45 seems to confirm our exegesis, since it appears to be the exact parallel of this section. The disciples at Emmaus wish to detain the risen Christ, but at the same moment, He disappears from their sight, after having proposed to them His sacramental presence, as something much better than His physical

makes a profession of faith which is, in this Gospel, a climax
corresponding to the climax of Caesarea Philippi in the Synoptics.
However, in John, the Apostles' faith does not reach its point
of culmination until after the Resurrection.

As for chapter XXI, opinions vary as to its origin. Certain
factors have led some to see it as an addition made by a disciple
of the evangelist; for example, the phrase, "Sons of Zebedee"
(XX: 2) occurs nowhere else, and even seems to have been
avoided by John himself.[17] Other exegetes, however, stress the
fact that, except for this phrase, the chapter has a definitely
johannine coloring. The stylistic elements which convince some
have, for others, no convincing weight to support johannine
authorship; consequently these latter see this section to be the
work of the same hand as the rest of the book. Some [18] go so far
as to question whether the chapter is even an appendix, adducing
the fact that, although I Jo. V: 13, has a conclusion similar in style
to Jo. XX: 31, the author of the epistle nevertheless considered
himself free to add a lengthy passage to this apparently final
phrase (V: 14-21).

For our part, we would be willing to maintain that, aside
from the two final verses (XXI: 24-25), which are most certainly
the work of a group of disciples,[19] the rest of the chapter, appendix or not, must have the same author as the preceding chapters.
We must not be arbitrary about St. John; as a matter of fact,
we can observe the same factors as those which occur in chapters
XVIII - XX.

The Synoptics agree that Jesus promised the Galilean fisher-
men that He would make them fishers of men (Mk. I: 17;

---

presence. The breaking of bread seems to be at least a symbol of the
Eucharist if not a eucharistic act (as J. DUPONT holds in Lumière et Vie,
31 (1957) 77-92. Immediately following this incident, Luke recounts how
the risen Christ appears to the eleven, showing them His hands and feet,
making them touch Him, and eating with them, so that they can be
"witnesses for Him in Jerusalem and in all Judea and Samaria and even
to the very ends of the earth" (Acts I: 8).

17 Cf. M. E. BOISMARD, Le chapitre XXI de saint Jean, Essai de
critique littéraire, in Revue Biblique, 1947, pp. 473-500. For a contrary
opinion, cf. E. RUCKSTUHL, Die literarische Einheit des Johannes-
evangelium, Freiburg in der Schweiz, 1951, pp. 473-501.

18 Cf. E. HOSKYNS, The Fourth Gospel, pp. 561-562.

19 Cf. L. VAGANAY, La finale du quatrieme évangile, in Revue
Biblique, 1935, pp. 512-536.

Mt. IV: 19; Lk. V: 10). Luke alone describes the miraculous catch, symbol of the Church's future apostolic successes. Matthew alone records the parable of the net "that gathered in fish of every kind" (XIII: 47-50), and also the account of Peter's walking on the water, which shows the close union between the Savior and the chief of the apostolic college (XIV: 28-31). John's corresponding treatment comes only after the Resurrection, in XXI: 1-14, where he records an appearance of Christ, and an extraordinary catch of fish.

Even if the two narratives of Luke and John are too dissimilar to be understood as referring to the same event, still they have some undeniable similarities. Furthermore, the fact of Peter's jumping from the boat to join his Master recalls the first Gospel. So does the detailed reference to the 153 fishes (XXI: 11), if it is true that this detail refers to an opinion current at the time that there are 153 species of fish (cf. Mt. XIII: 47, "fish of every kind").[20]

We believe it necessary to insist on the essentially ecclesial character of Saint John's narration of this event. Although one might be tempted to see the miraculous draught as joined to the seven other miracles so as to be the eighth in a series, such is certainly not the case. The catch is not an act of Christ, but of His Church, which will have a fruitful apostolate only with the assistance of its Founder, according to His statement that "Without me you can do nothing" (XV: 7). This passage, therefore, is not a sign of the sacramental economy, nor is it certain that it is properly a miracle at all. J. H. Bernard writes: "The Sea of Galilee still swarms with fish, and it is noteworthy that this great catch is not described as a *sēmeion*, nor is it suggested that it was miraculous".[21]

---

20 Cf. M. J. LAGRANGE, *Évangile selon saint Jean,* Paris, 1927, pp. 526-527. Some hold that the reference is not to the various kinds of fishes, but to a triangular number, as a symbol of plenty. Thus 153 is the sum of the numbers 1 through 17 (1 plus 2 plus 3 etc.,) which form an equilateral triangle. Cf. E. HOSKYNS, *The Fourth Gospel,* pp. 553-554; R. M. GRANT, *One Hundred Fifty-Three Large Fishes,* in *Harvard Theological Review.* pp. 273-75; J. A. EMERTON, *The Hundred Fifty-Three Fishes,* in *Jo.* xxi: 11, in *Journal of Theological Studies,* 1958, pp. 86-89; F. C. GRANT, *The Gospel and the Epistles of John,* London, 1958, vol. II, p. 38.

21 *The Gospel according to St. John,* Edinburgh, 1942, vol. II, p. 697.

The meal which the Apostles share after the catch, and at which Jesus presides (XXI: 12-14), is not a eucharistic meal. It does not even seem to be a symbol of the Eucharist, or least not to the same degree as the miracle of the multiplication of the loaves, which was performed expressly to announce the mystery of the Eucharist.[22] Lagrange explains well the profound meaning of this meal, as a new indication of the assistance which the risen Christ will give to His Church: "Jesus will always be with His disciples in an invisible way, and here He gives them a sensible proof of this. They have worked to follow His direction, and to be united to Him. He Himself now serves them refreshment which He has prepared for them".[23]

The conferral upon Peter of the primacy in response to his triple protestation of love (XCI: 15-17) corresponds in John to Matthew's scene of the incident at Caesarea Philippi (XVI: 13-19). In both cases, Jesus addresses Peter as "Simon, son of John." John's incident is not so much a mere addition, as it is a complement to the scene in Matthew. In the one case there is an act of faith and an announcement of a future act ("I will build my Church"), whereas in the other there is an act of love and an order to be carried out immediately. In John X, Christ presented Himself as the only Shepherd of the flock; now that He is about to leave, He assigns this work to Simon Peter, *"Christus jam mox relicturus terram gregem suum totum Petro committit, pascendum et regendum; ergo eum instituit suum vicarium".*[24]

The parallel nature of the passages in John XXI: 15-17 and Mt. XVI: 13-19 is evident. However, few pay much serious attention to the close parallelism which exists between the following passages, Mt. XVI: 21-28 and Jo. XXI: 18-23. The profession of faith at Philippi Caesarea Philippi is closely followed by the announcement of Jesus' Passion, which arouses a protest on the part of Peter. The disciples too must take up their cross and "follow" their Master, who one day will judge the world; there are some present among them, who will not die until they

---

22 Syr., sin., and D add *eucharistesas* to v. 13, thereby suggesting this eucharistic interpretation. However, this is only a harmonization with VI: 11.

23 *Évangile selon saint Jean,* p. 527.

24 J. KNABENBAUER, *Commentarius in Johannem,* Parisiis, 1900, p. 597.

have seen the inauguration of His kingdom. In the fourth Gospel the announcement of the Primacy is joined to the announcement of Peter's martyrdom, which will have a similarity to the Passion of his Master. This will be the way in which Peter will have to "follow" Him ("Thou, follow me!"). The fate of the beloved disciple will be different. He will be one of those who are to "remain" until Jesus "comes." We have already shown that this last passage is related to Mt. XVI: 28.[25] The closest parallel passage is this one in Matthew, which speaks of the coming of the Son of Man, whereas Mark (IX: 1) and Luke (IX: 27) speak only of the coming of the Kingdom of God.

We certainly cannot be entirely certain about the relationship which we have indicated between the Synoptic passages and those of John, or of the explanations which we have offered. It would take us too far afield to take up a detailed discussion of each point. We must be content, therefore, merely to have shed some light on the exact meaning of Jesus' "Hour," in the thought of the evangelist.[26] From what has been said, it should be evident that John has attached systematically to Calvary and to the Resurrection, all that involves the Church and the sacraments, which are to be the earthly continuation of the Savior's life-giving act.

(2) The Significance of the Cana Miracle

We can now approach the question of the incident at Cana. It would be an error to take any point of departure other than that of seeing the scene as primarily Christological.[27] By this miracle Jesus intends to "manifest His glory" and to excite the

---

25 Cf. Le triomphe eschatologique de Jesus d'après quelques textes isolés des évangiles, in Nouvelle Revue Theologique, 1949, pp. 821-825.

26 Strictly speaking, in order to give a complete idea of Jesus' Hour, we would have to mention also the discourses after the Last Supper (XIII-XVII), which are also placed within the Hour (cf. XIII: 1), and which are full of the thought of the Church as continuing the work of Christ after His departure. Here also is a systematic arrangement like the one which we saw in Chapters XVIII-XXI. In the Synoptics, the disciples also benefit from special revelations, but these revelations are spread throughout the account. Thus Chapters XIII-XVII of John's Gospel are a synthetic presentation.

27 R. SCHACKENBURG emphasizes this well, in Das erste Wunder Jesu, pp. 25-30.

faith of His disciples. This is the intent of the final verse, (v. 11), and of the entire context, designed to show that Jesus is the Messiah who was foretold by the prophets (Servant of Jahweh; King of Israel; Son of Man; the Founder of a new era). Exegesis, therefore, should not put the primary meaning of the passage either in a sacramental explanation, or in a marian one. The situation is somewhat similar to that of the interview with the Samaritan woman, where the main theme is not that of the living water, as is often held, but rather that of the messianic dignity of Jesus, who offers the gift of life, symbolized by the water of Jacob's well (cf. IV: 10, 19, 26, 42).

Evidently the evangelist, in writing the words, "Jesus manifested His glory," interprets Jesus' first miracle in relation to His Hour. As he sees it, the glory of God (*kabod*), once present mysteriously in the Jerusalem Temple, dwells now in an incomparably superior way, in the incarnate Logos (I: 14). While the Synoptics connect Christ's glory to His appearance in the clouds, and Saint Paul sees it as beginning with His Resurrection, for John, the Incarnation already was in itself the beginning of the manifestation of His glory. It is hidden, however, perceptible only by faith. In St. Paul the Cross is the great scandal for those who do not have the faith; John sees the scandal in the fact that Jesus hides His divinity under the veil of His humanity. Properly speaking, Christ's glory will begin only when His Hour comes, and this glory will determine the time of the Church. "The originality of John's vision is in considering, with well studied logic, Jesus' life and mission in relation to His end, and in placing Christ's existence from the beginning under the sign of the *doxa* which was revealed to the Apostles only through the Resurrection and Ascension, and through the sending of the Spirit".[28]

But, while it shows the divine power of the miracle worker, the Cana miracle has a significance closely related to the messianic task which Jesus wishes to perform. A comparison of the miracle with what follows, brings out a significant difference. In other instances emphasis is placed upon the manner in which the miracle is worked; e.gr., the second Cana miracle becomes

---

28 W. GROSSOUW, *La glorification du Christ dans le quatriéme évangile*, in *L'Évangile de Jean. Études et Problèmes*, p. 140.

effective the moment in which Jesus says, "Thy son lives," which puts in bold relief the life-giving power of Jesus' word (cf. IV: 46-53). Here, however, we have not a single detail of this kind. The evangelist seems interested primarily in the material change of the water into wine; for him it has a great symbolic importance.

In order to appreciate the symbolism without allowing ourselves to be deceived by a false dichotomy between historicity and symbolism, (as often happens with regard to this passage) we should link this symbolism more closely than most do, with Jesus' own messianic consciousness. We must bear constantly in mind, with regard to this fourth Gospel, that whenever one approaches Jesus about material things, He invariably responds by working to bring His hearer to a higher plane.[29] He passes from the material Temple of Jerusalem to the temple of His Body; from the water of Jacob's well to the living water which is the Spirit; from the manna of the desert to an imperishable heavenly food. Mary Magdalene seeks to touch Him; He responds by speaking of a kind of contact which transcends the senses (XX: 17). Following Father Bouyer,[30] we might add the journey up to Jerusalem (VII: 1-10). Jesus seems unwilling to do this act, "wishing to do it only in a way that will give it a meaning other than that which one might humanly expect." In Luke II: 48-49, Jesus responds to Mary, who speaks to Him of His earthly father, by alluding to His Father in heaven.

The same is the case here. Without explicitly asking a miracle of her Son, but impelled by the hope that he might intervene, (otherwise she would hardly have told the servants, "Do whatever he tells you.") Mary simply informed Him of the embarrassment facing the bridal couple, "They have no wine." But Jesus is of a world other than that of men, even of saints; this is one of the marks of His transcendence, which the evangelist wishes to emphasize. The perspective here is primarily Christological. *To forget this is to lose sight of the structure of the Gospel.* Any attempt to minimize the abrupt character of the Savior's response to His mother would be regarded by St. John as a restriction on His transcendence.[31]

---

29 Cf. R. LAURENTIN, *Structure et Théologie de Luc I-II*, Paris, 1957, pp. 170-173.

30 *Le quatrième évangile*, Paris - Tournai, 1955, pp. 82-83.

31 The following are a few attempts of this kind: According to M.

Jesus' response brings to mind the wine of the new Covenant, which He is charged by God to inaugurate. In the Scripture, of course, wine is a figure of the benefits which will flow from the messianic covenant (Is. XXV: 6; Jer. XLIX: 11-12; Joel IV: 18; Cant. I: 2; II: 4). The same symbolism occurs in the Synoptics (Mk. XI: 22 and parallel texts), where Jesus opposes old wine and new (the old and new covenants), just as in our narrative (II: 10) John speaks of poor wine and good wine. We can recall also the chalice of the Last Supper, which is linked to the inauguration of the new Covenant.

Jesus declares that His Hour is not yet come. As we have already said, the simple fact that elsewhere in the fourth Gospel (VII: 30; VIII: 20), the figure of the "Hour of Jesus" has not yet come refers to the Passion and Glorification, indicates that the same should be the case here. Some object that it is incorrect to relate Jesus' "Hour" with His Passion and Glorification, unless this is indicated by the immediate context. As far as we can see, such an argument has no force in the light of the literary structure of the fourth Gospel, and of the precise doctrinal plan which John is following. Given all that we have said above, there should be no doubt as to the exact meaning of Jesus' reference to His Hour; it refers to the Cross, upon which the Church will be definitively founded, and which will administer the sacraments, thereby dispensing the new wine of the messianic era.

These points of explanation shed a great deal of welcome light. Because Jesus, seeing everything from the point of view of the mission which His Father has entrusted to Him, interprets His mother's intervention as a request for the messianic wine,

---

PEINADOR (*Ephemerides Mariologicae,* 1958, pp. 61-104). Jesus' words mean, "What is there to separate us? We are fully agreed; has my hour (the hour of my being manifested by miracles) not come?" J. C. QUIRANT (*Marianum,* 1958, 155-189) says that Jesus would not reproach His mother for asking a miracle but that He would for not asking it with greater confidence. Thus He would suspect that she is not as forthright with Him as she used to be. Thus He asks: "Why this change? What has come between us? I am still your Son. The hour of my Passion, in which I will no longer be able to work miracles, is not yet here." According to DOM DELATTE (*L'Évangile de N.S.J.C.,* Tours, 1943, tome I, pp. 115-119), Mary urges Jesus to show Himself by a miracle, but He protests in a filial way, hesitating to have to separate Himself from the happiness of His private family life. V. ANZALONE, follows this explanation in *Rivista Biblica* (1958), pp. 135 ff.

He could only consider it premature, "You are asking for something which I do not yet intend to give; my Hour is not yet come." But this does not mean that he blames her in any way. How could He blame her for not having intimate knowledge of God's secret design? He does not blame her, but, by using enigmatic language, he excites her faith.

Mary does not consider herself at all rebuffed, but she merely turns to the servants and directs them to do whatever He tells them. As at the finding in the Temple, (Lk. II: 48-50), she does not understand her Son's words; but she trusts Him. Just as she has presented to Christ the poverty of men so that God may give His riches ("They have no wine"), so now she presents Christ to men, this time expressing the pure graciousness of this act in their behalf ("Do whatever He tells you"). And Jesus performs the miracle.[32]

In the light of what we have seen, it is clear that this miracle is much more than a material favor for a bridal couple in need of wine. It is fundamentally something different from what Mary could ask or wish, even if one were to hold that she did ask Her Son for a miracle of the messianic order.

In order to avoid the inconsistency of a request repulsed and then immediately granted, many modern authors, following some of the Fathers, have had recourse to a different translation, "Has my Hour yet come?", which is unnatural. However, in the narrative as we understand it, there is no inconsistency, because what Jesus does does not correspond to what was expected. As H. Van den Bussche [33]remarks, "No miracle in the fourth Gospel corresponds exactly to the request. The Synoptics recount several miracles in which the suppliant receives his favor on condition that he have faith. John, on the other hand, prefers to leave the working of the miracle to Jesus alone. In other cases the miracle takes place without being requested (II: 3; V: 7; VI: 5-9; IX: 6-8; 17; 36-38), or else where it is asked, Jesus always grants it in a way of which the petitioner had not thought (IV: 47; XI: 3; 21; 24; 32; 39). This latter case is that of John's narrative of the Cana miracle. At Cana, human lack gives way in an unforeseen manner to abundance, indicated by the generous amount and extraordinarily good quality of the wine (II: 6-10).

---

32 L. Bouyer, *Le quatrième évangile*, pp. 82-83.

33 Structure de Jean I-XII, in *L'évangile de Jean, Études et Problèmes*, pp. 78-79.

The wine is not only for the benefit of the wedding guests, but it is also to serve as a sign of the richness of the messianic era. John could have added an observation after II: 4, as he did after II: 21: "But He was speaking of the wine of the new era."

Even in giving gifts of the material order, Jesus was not at all willing to pose as a dispenser of temporal benefits, such as the Jews were expecting (cf. ch. VI—the Discourse on the Bread of Life). Thus He gives to His miraculous acts a meaning which is imperceptible to most of those who witness them, even to those who, like Mary, believe in a spiritual Messiah. Those who read the Gospel can now appreciate this profound significance in the light of later understanding. At Cana they can see that He who makes excellent wine out of water destined for Jewish purification rites, will one day change the institutions of the old Covenant into something incomparably better. In ordinary weddings, "Every man at first sets forth the good wine, and when they have drunk freely, that which is poorer" (v. 11). God's salvific plan, however, works in inverse order; the better Covenant comes last.

The context immediately following suggests this exegesis. The expelling of the buyers and sellers from the Temple (II: 13-22) suggests the perfect temple, which will be the Savior's glorified Body. The interview with Nicodemus (III: 1-21) treats explicitly of the new birth in the order of the Spirit. The Baptist's second testimony shows Jesus as the bridegroom of the new Covenant. Finally, in the conversation with the Samaritan woman (IV: 1-42), the contrast between the water of Jacob's well and that which Jesus will give, suggests the contrast between the regime of the Mosaic law (which long before was compared to a well of living water in the Damascus Document (VI: 5; XIX: 34; Cf. Sirach XV: 3; XXIV: 25-27), and the rule of the Spirit, which is nothing other than the Christian dispensation, source of the new worship in spirit and truth.[34] Add to this the fact that the designation of Christ as "Lamb of God" (I: 29-36) and it becomes clear that the first narratives of John's Gospel are all closely connected with Jesus' "Hour," just as we defined it in the beginning of our treatment.

In other words, Cana is a sign, a symbol of the new Covenant, or more precisely, of the eucharistic wine which Jesus will give

---

34 Cf. F. M. BRAUN, *L'arrière-fond judaïque du quatrième évangile et la communauté de l'alliance*, in *Revue Biblique*, 1955 pp. 24-26.

to men once His Passion is completed.[35] And the sign which opens
His public ministry, and justifies the faith of His disciples
(II: 11) is granted through the intercession of Mary, who thus
represents the Church, and is intimately associated by Her Son
with the work of establishing the new Covenant between God
and men.[36]

Many commentators abstract completely from Mary in explaining the theological significance of Cana. We think they are
wrong, for two reasons. First, Jesus' strange reply to His Mother
allows for the understanding that Mary too is to have her hour.
The Woman's hour will come (XVI: 21) when Jesus' hour comes.
Besides, the account of the miracle is brief and schematic. It
omits a number of details on which we would like to be informed,
how Jesus performed the miracle, how the bridal couple reacted,
the impression made upon the servants, and upon the guests,
etc. In a narrative so selective in details, Mary's presence is
mentioned three times, and it is emphasized.

---

35 It is possible that this mention of the "third Day" at the beginning
of the account may be more than a mere chronological indication; it may
be designed to direct the reader's attention to the hour, especially to the
Resurrection (the "third day"), which is the supreme manifestation of
Jesus' glory, of which Cana is only a prelude. This is, of course, not certain,
but it is accepted by M. E. BOISMARD, *Du Bapteme à Cana*, p. 136;
R. H. LIGHTFOOT, p. 105.

36 Our exegesis is similar in this respect to that of H. SAHLIN (*Zur
Typologie des Johannes - Evangelium, Uppsala - Leipzig*, 1950, pp. 9-10)
and to that of A. G. HERBERT (*The Virgin Mary, Daughter of Sion* in
Theology, 53, 1950, pp. 403-413, tr. by R. FORET in *Vie Spirituelle*,
85, 1951 pp. 127-135.) These authors see Mary at Cana as the daughter
of Sion, whose eschatological hope is fulfilled in Jesus. It is certain that
the Christian Church sees itself as the continuation of the Sion of the
prophets, and that the Woman of Apocalypse XII is first and foremost
the ideal people of God of the Old Testament, and then the Church
(cf. Part II, Chapter IV). Still, we hesitate to affirm that Mary's statement,
"They have no wine" expresses her desire for the messianic renewal which
is characteristic of the daughter of Sion, and that Jesus reproaches her
for her impatience, because His hour has not yet come (cf. *Vie Spirituelle*,
art. cit. p. 136). To bring a symbolic meaning to Mary's words, instead
of seeing it as coming *only* from Jesus' own consciousness of being the
Messiah, would lead to seeing the Cana narrative as no more than an
allegorical fancy on the part of the evangelist. For the reasons supporting
the historicity of the account, cf. R. SCHNACKENBURG, *Das erste
Wunder Jesu*, pp. 3-9.

Still, Mary's words could have been omitted, and the miracle would not cease to be understandable. John's insistence, therefore, on showing Mary's role here can have no explanation other than a deliberate doctrinal intention.

This exegesis also serves, it seems to us, to clarify, most satisfactorily a point to which Schnackenburg [37] and Braun [38] have called attention. This is the clear line of separation which Jesus drew between Himself and His human family, including His Mother, during the course of His public ministry (cf. Mk. III: 31-35 and parallel texts). When there is question of the incarnate Son of God, Jesus speaks only of His Father, who alone is Savior and Redeemer. Such is the limit which Scripture places upon mariology. On the other hand, once the Passion is over, then it is really Mary's Hour, which is also the hour of the Church and of the sacraments.

Given these clarifications, it seems to us useless to raise an objection which has often come up with regard to the marian significance of the Cana miracle. Some say,[39] for example, that in this account the evangelist is interested only in the action of Jesus, that Mary's future role is outside John's purview and Christ's as well. Otherwise, they contend, Jesus would have told her, "Your hour is not yet come!"

This objection should raise no serious difficulty, given the relationships which we have outlined above. The Hour of Jesus is the Hour of the Church and of the sacraments, and is also the Hour of the Woman (Mary, in her messianic role). In the fourth Gospel, no less than in the Synoptics, Jesus does not see His salvific action culminating in His Hour, without thinking of His Church, which is to continue this action. And at Cana, as in Apoc. XII, Mary (the Woman) and the Church are intimately associated in their soteriological function.

It follows, therefore, that Cana announces in advance the scene of XIX: 25-27, and presupposes that this last scene of farewell between Christ crucified and His mother is much more than a gesture of filial piety. In effect, Mary is united again to the Church and to the sacraments, which as we have seen, are the object of the context, both preceding and following, and she

37 *Das erste Wunder Jesu*, pp. 31-39.

38 *La Mère des Fidèles*, pp. 59-62.

39 Cf. J. Levie, in *Nouvelle Revue Théologique*, 1954, p. 432; H. VAN DEN BUSSCHE in *Collationes Gandavenses*, 1952, pp. 217s.

is here invested with the role which Jesus intends her to have.
If Mary was allowed to intervene at Cana, it is only because
this miracle is oriented toward the new dispensation, toward
the era of grace.

In our exegesis we have deliberately avoided using the word
"Woman." We are not convinced that this solemn and emphatic
title is explained sufficiently by the oriental custom of not
recognizing a female relative in public. As a matter of fact,
J. Michl says [40] that there is not a single instance of a Jew
addressing his mother in this way.

This title can be explained only by referring to the parallel
texts of Calvary and of Apoc. XII. Already at Cana this unusual
way in which Jesus addresses His mother serves to indicate that,
in replying to Mary, he intends to transcend considerably the
level of ordinary men, and to elevate His mother to this higher
plane.[41] We know now what the realities were, with which He
was dealing. As we said above, anyone who for reasons of mis-
guided piety attempts to make light of the abrupt tone of the
reply, fails to do justice to johannine Christology, and, we might
add, to mariology.

What we have said of the meaning of the Cana miracle holds
also for the other miracles in the public ministry of John's
Christ. They are all proclamations of the Hour, and an anticipation of the sacramental dispensation. The evangelist has no
need each time to stress this relationship with the Passion and
Glorification, and with the Church; he has expressed it once
and for all, on the occasion of Jesus' first "sign." It serves thus
as a key, like the clef of a musical text. This is, therefore, not
something which we invent, but something which the evangelist
seems to suggest when he explains that the Savior worked this
miracle as the first of His signs.

---

40 *Biblica,* 1955, pp. 498-499.

41 Cf. J. GALOT in *Marie Dans l'Évangile,* p. 126, in which the
author remarks, "It is the Messiah Himself who calls Mary, 'Woman,'
thereby giving this word its messianic meaning. The unique thing about
Mary's care, the reason why it must be recognized as messianic, is that
Jesus calls her "Woman,' instead of the simple term 'mother,' which would
be much more ordinary and normal. For this reason there is no validity
in the objection of some that this interpretation is impossible because all
the other instances in which Jesus uses the term "Woman" also must have
a messianic intent.

"Not merely the first sign," explains C. K. Barrett, "but a primary sign, because representative of the creative and transforming work of Jesus as a whole".[42]

We have added to this short study the subtitle, "A Contribution to the Study of the Structure of the Fourth Gospel." This shows the fact that one cannot explain properly any individual passage of this Gospel, which is, in the words of Loisy,[43] the most unified of all the New Testament writings, without placing it in its context relative to the entire Gospel, and to the very reflective theological pattern of the evangelist.

* * * * *

Some months after the completion of this study, we came upon the fine work of J. P. Charlier, "Le Sign de Cana; Essai de Theologie Johannique," Brussels, Paris, 1959). Both these studies are in agreement in essentials, and are complementary, in so far as our work defines a bit more precisely the meaning of Jesus's Hour. Also, we have felt the need for the greatest discretion with regard to the specifically marian meaning of the narrative. There is an important divergence on one point: desiring (and rightly so) to give a messianic significance to Christ's response to His mother, Fr. Charlier concludes that Mary's words, "They have no wine," are on the same level as those of Jesus. He sees Mary as making herself the "voice of Israel's anguish, intervening on behalf of her people, to beg Jesus the liberation of the Remnant, still enslaved by sin." (p. 62).

Such an exegesis would lead to seeing in this narrative of John nothing more than a purely theological presentation. We, on the contrary, have emphasized how, in the Fourth Gospel, Jesus' actions and words constantly surpass the expectation of those who witness them, because He is the Messiah. To accord to the Virgin the title of Spouse of Christ, in the sense of an aid like Himself, would not seem to be at all in accord with John's perspective.

---

42 *The Gospel According to St. John*, p. 161. Barrett quotes a similar text found in ISOCRATES' *Panegyric of Athens*, 38: *All' archēn men tautēn epoiēsato tōn euergesiōn, trophēn tois deomenois heurein.*

43 "No New Testament writing other than the fourth Gospel, is so dominated by a single idea." *Le quatrième évangile*, p. 147.

CHAPTER II

THE THEOLOGICAL SIGNIFICANCE
OF THE SECOND CANA MIRACLE [1]

(John IV: 46-54)

The second miracle of Cana, the healing of the son of a royal official from Capharnaum (John IV: 46-54), troubles many commentators. They find it difficult to place this passage in the light of the whole gospel structure. Many, as a matter of fact, have maintained that the account could be dropped without serious consequences. It is indeed an unusual section, once one recognizes how carefully the Gospel as a whole is structured. The author records only a limited number of deeds, but he then proceeds to ponder their doctrinal meaning, and establishes a close connection between them and Jesus' teachings, so much so that the miracles of the fourth Gospel have been called "parables in act" (Tatgleichnisse).[2]

In the following pages we shall attempt to determine the theological significance of Jo. IV: 46-54, by studying its relation to the context. And, since the doctrinal import of an episode can vary according to whether one attaches it to the preceding or to the following context, we must consider both of these possibilities, weighing the respective arguments in each case. Finally we shall offer our own opinion as to which solution seems to us to be best.

(1) *Relation to the preceding context*

Usually the healing of the son of the official from Capharnaum is attached to the preceding context. The strongest argument in favor of this arrangement is that, with Chapter V, Jesus' public

---

1 First published in *Recherches de Science Religieuse*. Tome XLVII, Jan. - Juin, 1960.

2 W. Lutgert, *Die Johanneische Christologie*, Gütersloh, 1916, p. 17.

ministry takes a new turn. Jesus goes up to Jerusalem, and there He cures a paralytic on the Sabbath day. This is the first occasion in which He encounters the hostility of the Jews, a hostility which will end in His death.

Another observation: up to now, Jesus, in alluding to His own divine transcendence, has revealed Himself as the Messiah awaited by the Jews and foretold by the prophets, the King of Israel, Servant of Jahweh, Son of Man, Son of God, in the broad sense, (as in Ps. II), in I: 50.[3] Furthermore, He has gone so far as to indicate that He was charged to inaugurate a New Covenant, superior to the old. In His statement to Nathaniel, "a true Israelite, in whom there is no guile," (I: 47), Jesus promises that through His mediation there will be a new Israel (the vision of the angels ascending and descending) not over any specific part of the earth, as Bethel (Gen. XXXVIII: 10-17), but above the glorified Son of man, which will be, in the Christian dispensation, the "House of God and gate of heaven".[4] The account of the wedding at Cana refers to the new covenant, and, more precisely, beyond a doubt, to the messianic wine of the Eucharist;[5] the Expelling of the buyers and sellers from the Temple suggests the perfect temple, which will be the body of the risen Christ;[6] the interview with Nicodemus reveals the new birth in the order of the Spirit; the conversation with the Samaritan woman shows the opposition between the old forms of worship and the new worship in spirit and in truth.

Now, in the discourse in ch. V, there is no treatment of this opposition between the two covenants; the person of Jesus Himself acts, not only in His messianic dignity, but in His divinity properly so called, His intimate relationship with His Father. For the first time, Jesus affirms clearly that He and the Father

---

3 Cf. M. E. BOISMARD, *Du Baptême à Cana*, Paris, 1956, pp. 104-105.

4 We consider this to be the most probable interpretation of this difficult text. Cf. also, in this sense, O. Cullmann, *Les Sacrements dans l'évangile johannique*, Paris, 1951 p. 43; Y. CONGAR, *Le Mystère du Temple*, Paris, 1958, p. 161; cf. especially I. FRITSCH, *Videbitis angelos ascendentes et descendentes*, in *Verbum Domini*, 1959, pp. 1-11.

5 Cf. our study, *L'Heure de Jésus et le signe de Cana, Contribution à l'etude de la structure du quatrième évangile*, in *Les Ephemerides Theologicae Lovanienses;* cf. also the preceding chapter.

6 Cf. X. LÉON - DUFOUR in *Mélanges Lebreton, I* (RSR), 1952, pp. 155-175.

give life. Given this, it seems normal that there should be a break between Chapters IV and V, and that the miracle of the pool in V: 1-18 should be seen as the immediate preparation for the new teaching of ch. V, which introduces a new section.

Other arguments have been proposed. If it were proven that John intended to establish a clear dichotomy between *signs* and *works*, with signs corresponding to the Jewish expectation and indicating that the Messiah has come, and works revealing the one sent by the Father, the Son of God in the strict sense, then the second miracle of Cana which is formally described as a sign (IV: 54), could not be attached to ch. V, which begins the section on works (cf. V: 20; 36) [7] Of course, we would not deny that there is a real difference in meaning between the two terms *sēmeia* and *erga*. The former term always refers to a miracle, the second, not necessarily so.. The former term is ordinarily used by those around Jesus or by the evangelist; Jesus Himself uses it only rarely, by exception (IV: 48; VI: 26); the second, on the contrary, is regularly on Jesus' lips (V: 20; 36; VII: 21; IX: 3ff.; X: 25; 32; 37; 38; XIV: 10-12; XV: 24).[8] Nevertheless, the distinction does not seem to be as basic as some would maintain. Both terms are used in reference to the Old Testament, especially to the signs and wonders of the Exodus period; both are done by Jahweh (cf. Ex. XXXIV: 20; Num. XIV: 22; Dt. III: 24; IV: 34; VI: 22; VII: 19; XIII: 2; XXIX: 2; XXIV: 11); cf. especially Num. XIV: 22, where, as in the first Cana miracle, the glory of God is lined to signs; *hoi horōntes tēn doxan mou kai ta sēmeia ha epoiēsa*. The second Cana miracle seems also designed to show not only that Jesus is the Messiah, but that His word has the same sovereign efficacy as that of God (see below), being thus rather a work of God.

If it were correct to say that the evangelist has divided his material according to the liturgical feast which he mentions,[9]

---

7 On this distinction cf. H. VAN DEN BUSSCHE, *Structure de Jean I-XII*, in *L'évangile de Jean, Études et Problèmes* (*ouvrage collectif*), Louvain, 1958, especially pp. 63-64, 88-90, 108-109.

8 Cf. H. H. WENDT, *The Gospel according to St. John* (translated by E. Lummis), Edinburgh, 1902, pp. 58-66; L. CERFAUX, *Les Miracles et signes et oeuvres de Dieu selon l'évangile de saint Jean*, in *Recueil Lucien Cerfaux*, Gembloux, 1954, t. 11, pp. 41-50.

9 Cf. D. MOLLAT, *L'évangile selon saint Jean* (Bible de Jerusalem), Paris, 1953, pp. 32-36.

then the beginning of ch. V, where we see Jesus, going up to Jerusalem for a feast of the Jews, would have to be the beginning of a new section. However, as we have said elsewhere,[10] a liturgical setting seems too external for a writing as full of meaning as the fourth Gospel, even if it were to seem as if the author wishes to suggest that the Christian liturgy had replaced the Jewish.

In discussing this problem, therefore, it is better to hold to the point which we made earlier; the undeniable fact that ch. V constitutes a turning point in Jesus' public activity, inclines us to join the second Cana miracle to the preceding context, rather than to the following. Given this, then what could have been the evangelist's purpose in placing the incident here? This is the difficulty which we should try to resolve. Perhaps he wished to assign to this miracle the function which the Synoptics accord to the healing of the centurion's servant (Mt. VIII: 5-13; Lk. VII: 1-10).[11] He would have shown thereby that some non-Jews align themselves with the Christ who is rejected by His own countrymen; the example of the royal official who believes "with all his household," (V: 53), would be joined to that of the Samaritan woman (or of her countrymen) to place this truth in relief.[12] The difficulty is that there is no progression from one case to the other; while the Samaritans believe without having seen the miracle, Jesus seems to berate the official from Capharnaum, for needing signs and wonders (v. 48).

Furthermore, even though this account offers a good example of passing from imperfect faith, founded on the extraordinary as such, is the incident told just to introduce a new type of believer (a pagan, after Nicodemus and the Samaritans)? Rather than this, the whole ending of the section (vv. 50-53) suggests that the purpose is to emphasize the life-giving power of Christ's word. In general, the basic theme of the fourth Gospel

10 Cf. *Introduction à la Bible*, t. II, *Nouveau Testament*, Paris, 1959, pp. 623-624.

11 The delicacy of the problem concerning the relationship between these two events is well known; even the Fathers, beginning with Irenaeus, held them to be identical.

12 Cf., for example, R. H. LIGHTFOOT, *St. John's Gospel*, Oxford, 1956, p. 128; R. H. STRACHAN, *The Fourth Gospel, Its Significance and Environment*, London, 1947, pp. 161-162; H. VAN DEN BUSSCHE, L'évangile du Verbe (Jean 1-4), Bruxelles - Paris, 1959, pp. 74-75.

is the manifestation of the incarnate Son of God, the Light and
Life of men. Important as it is, the reaction of belief or unbelief
which this manifestation evokes, is not the main point.

Some exegetes [13] have seen this incident as a complement to
that of the Samaritan woman. After promising the living water,
Jesus gives life to the sick. However, there does not seem to be
any connection at all between the living water (the Holy Spirit)
and the miraculous healing. Besides, the central theme of IV:
1-42, is not the iving water, but the revelation of Jesus as the
Messiah.[14]

If one would wish to see the second Cana miracle connected
to the preceding context, the best reason for its presence here
would doubtless be that the author wished to establish, in a
Semitic way, an inclusion of this miracle with that of the water
changed into wine. This would explain v. 54, which recalls II: 11.
But this reference to the first miracle of Cana could also come
from the identical structure of the two accounts,[15] as well as
from a desire to indicate that the second miracle begins a new
phase of Jesus' public ministry,[16] especially after the proclamation
in IV: 42, that Jesus is the "Savior of the world."

In any case, relating the second Cana miracle to the preceding context explains only imperfectly the meaning of the
incident, which is manifestly foreign to the basic theme of the
first four chapters, the establishment of a higher dispensation
in place of the old.

---

13 Cf. par exemple C. K. BARRETT, *The Gospel according to St.
John*, London, 1955, p. 206; L. BOUYER, *Le quatrième évangile*, Tournai -
Paris, 1955, p. 110.

14 Cf. H. VAN DEN BUSSCHE, *Structure de Jean I-XII*, pp. 85-87.

15 W. BAUER notes this structural identity; in each of the two cases,
he says, there is a prayer, and at least apparent refusal; perseverance,
and a granting of the request (*Das Johannes - Evangelium*, Tübingen,
1932, p. 78).

16 In this sense cf. B. F. WESTCOTT, *The Gospel According to
St. John*, London, 1937, p. 79; A. SCHLATTER, *Der Evangelist Johannes*,
Stuttgart, 1918, p. 139. R. H. LIGHTFOOT (St. John's Gospel, p. 128)
thinks that after the first manifestation of Christ's glory at the miracle
of Cana, the healing of the royal official's son could be already a foretelling of the supreme revelation of Christ's glory (before the Passion and
Glorification), which will occur at the raising of Lazarus.

(2) *Relation to the following context*

The fact that at the end of ch. IV Jesus is in Galilee, and that at the beginning of ch. V He goes up to Jerusalem inclines some to link the second Cana miracle with that of the pool, which occurs in the Holy City itself. It is surprising that this connection has not so far found many supporters.[17] Nevertheless, one could adduce some solid arguments in favor of this hypothesis.

First of all, there is a short preface (IV: 43-45), which the author has placed before the second Cana miracle, and which shows Jesus going to Galilee, adducing as a reason the dictum that a prophet has no honor in his own country. What does this mean? It seems to us that this could make no sense at all, if Galilee is to be taken as Jesus' country, because in the very next verse, the Galileans receive Him well. Any commentary on this text which would remark simply that Jesus bypasses these outpourings of enthusiasm, would be an arbitrary distortion of its meaning.[18] The evangelist, knowing that Jesus was born in Bethlehem (Cf. VII: 41-42), and referring to Judea as *ta idia* in relation to Christ, and to the Jews as *hoi idoi*, must surely have considered Judea to be Jesus' country.[19] Dodd, in referring to this passage, says rightly that, in the fourth Gospel, Jerusalem is Jesus' true country (*idia patris*); He teaches mainly there; He is rejected there; and the proverb (IV: 44) becomes here equivalent to I: 11; He comes among his own, and they do not receive Him. John wishes, therefore, to say that, if Jesus absents Himself now from Judea, it is

---

17 Cf. E. C. HOSKYNS, *The Fourth Gospel,* London, 1957, p. 249; G. H. C. MACGREGOR, *The Gospel of John,* 1949, distinguishes "*The relation of the New Gospel and the Old*" (from II to IV: 42) and "*The Appropriation of the New Gospel*" (IV: 43 - VI) pp. 1-2: 117; C. H. DODD, *The Interpretation of the Fourth Gospel,* Cambridge, 1953, pp. 318-319, offers some convincing arguments in favor of this connection.

18 J. H. BERNARD, *The Gospel According to St. John,* Edinburgh, pp. 164-165, speaks of a gloss, inserted either by John or by a later redactor. Such a gloss, however, is not proven, and would render the text incoherent.

19 In favor of this interpretation, cf. J. C. BELSER, *Das Evangelium des heiligen Johannes,* Freiburg-i-B., 1905, p. 149; H. H. WENDT, *The Gospel according to St. John* p. 30, note 1; P. SCHANZ, *Das Evangelium des heiligen Johannes,* Tübingen, 1885, pp. 222-223; B. F.

because of the hostility of the Jews toward Him. (This interpretation seems to be required all the more, given the similar reflections in IV: 1-3 and VII: 1.) The evangelist would wish to contrast the ill will of the Judeans and the favorable reception accorded to Jesus by the Galileans.

The surprising thing is that, immediately afterwards, Jesus seems to treat the officer from Capharnaum, a pagan,[20] who manifests faith in Jesus, as the incarnation of the faithless Jews, who seek signs and wonders; "Unless you see signs and wonders, you do not believe" (IV: 48). This apparent inconsistency can be explained, we think, as follows: from the beginning of his narrative, John is aware of the violent opposition which Jesus is going to encounter in the Holy City. The preface, in vv. 43-44, indicates this. The exclamation in v. 48 is addressed to the Jews, through the personage of the official. This is why Jesus' unexpected remark is not a reproach, but a test, designed to purify the man's faith, lifting it from a desire for novelty and sensation, to the simple acceptance of the Word, which does not insist on seeing new signs.[21] The official rises to the higher level of faith, and thus becomes the living antithesis of the

---

WESTCOTT, *The Gospel according to St. John*, p. 77; E. C. HOSKYNS, *The Fourth Gospel*, p. 252; F. C. Grant, *The Gospel of John*, New York - London, 1956, vol. I, p. 33; C. H. DODD, *The Interpretation of the Fourth Gospel*, p. 352; C. K. BARRETT, *The Gospel according to St. John*, p. 206. This interpretation is not at all excluded by I: 46 or VI: 41; 52, because it is clearly suggested in VII: 42 (cf. BARRETT ad loc.), that Jesus was born not in Galilee, but in Bethlehem of Juda, according to the prophecy of Michea (VI: 1). In IV: 44, John is careful to place the adjective *idios* as modifying *patris*, as if to distinguish Jesus' real homeland from the supposed one. The same saying is applied to Nazareth in the Synoptics (cf. Mark VI: 4; Luke IV: 24; Matthew XIII: 57). However, in these accounts the adjective *idios* is missing (except in some MSS of Matthew and Mark, in which it was added, doubtless in imitation of the johannine account).

20 J. A. T. ROBINSON proposes that the official is not a pagan but a Herodian, hence a Jew; this would explain better the language which Jesus addresses to him (*New Testament Studies* VI, 1960) p. 120.

21 In the fourth Gospel Jesus often puts his hearers to the test by using language which tries their faith and by inviting them to rise higher. This would explain Christ's reply to His Mother at Cana (II: 4), without the necessity of seeing it as a reproach.

authorities in Jerusalem, who, after the miracle of the pool, close their eyes to the light.

Another and more pressing reason for attaching the second Cana miracle to ch. V, is that it seems designed to inculcate the great soteriological theme of the fourth Gospel, mainly that the Son of God has come into this world to give eternal life to men. As F. Muszner [22] has shown, although eternal life is proper to the world above and belongs only to God, the Incarnation of the Logos resulted, in John's view, in the descent of this eternal life into the world below, which, failing to recognize God (to know God is to live; not to know Him is to be condemned to death), was destined for death, living before God in a constant state of sin (cf. I: 29, in the singular, the "sin of the world"), and was subject to the dominion of the Devil, the prince of this world (XII: 31; XIV: 30; XVI: 11). For John there is only one kind of existence which can be called "life," i.e., eternal life. Where he speaks of this life, he always uses the terms *zoē, zōn, zēn, zōopoiein;* so when these terms are present, it is always eternal life that is in question.

There is a single exception to this rule, and it is precisely here, in the second Cana miracle, where the verb is used three times in succession (vv. 50, 51, 53), to indicate the son's return to ordinary physical life. And for that matter, as H. Pribnow explains very well,[23] this exception ceases to be such if we compare the episode with that of the raising of Lazarus. When Jesus brings Lazarus back to physical existence, it is to illustrate His saying, "I am the resurrection and the life" (XI: 25). In other words, this miracle is designed to show that Jesus has the double power to enable men to pass from now on from death to eternal life, and to raise them on the last day.

It could be held that the second Cana miracle has a similar doctrinal import. The son of the official from Capharnaum was at the point of death (V: 47: *ēmellen apothnēskein*). Jesus snatched him from it. The narrator is most aware that this idea if *life re-found,* as is evident from the triple repetition of the formula, "thy/his son liveth/is cured"; (cf. Num. XXI: 8). It

---

22 *Die Anschauung von Leben in vierten Evangelium, unter Berüksichtigung der Johannesbriefe, München,* 1952.

23 *Die Johanneische Anschauung von Leben, Greiswald,* 1934, pp. 154-155.

may be interesting to note, with Bultmann,[24] that the same phrase, "Thy son liveth," occurs also in the account of the raising by Elias of the son of the widow of Sarepta (I Kgs. XVII: 23). In any case, it seems unlikely that such an emphatic statement should be devoid of any connection with the leitmotiv of the Gospel, i.e., is the giving of eternal life to men, which will develop at the end of time into a glorious resurrection.

It is worth recalling here that the symbolism of sickness and healing is deeply rooted in biblical tradition. In the Old Testament the word "sickness" is often used metaphorically to designate the sins of the people or the calamities which result from them as a punishment from God (Ex. XXV: 6; Dt. XXXII: 39; Osee V: 12-13; VI: 2; Is. I: 5-6; XXXVIII: 13; LIII: 4; Jer. VIII: 21-22; Prov. XXIX: 1; Job II: 18). Healing, on the other hand, is a common figure for salvation, especially for eschatological salvation (Gen. XX: 17; Osee VI: 23; VII: 1; XIV: 5; Is. VI: 10; LIII: 5; LXI: 1; Jer. III: 22; VIII: 22; XVII: 14; XXX: 17; Ps. VI: 3; XXX: 3; XLI: 5; CIII: 3, etc.).[25] In the Synoptics Christ says, "It is not the healthy who need a physician, but those who are sick," (Mk. II: 17 and parallel texts). He is using here a current figure of speech to refer to the era of grace, suggesting thereby that it has come.[26]

If such be the symbolic meaning of the second miracle of Cana, then it follows that we must see in it a sort of parable in act preparatory to the great discourse of ch. V. In effect, the first part of the discourse (vv. 19-20) attributes to the Son of Man a double resurrection: on the one hand the spiritual resurrection of the faithful, which will take place above all in the Church, but which is already inaugurated in Jesus' public ministry (V: 25; "The hour is coming and is now here");[27] on the other hand, there is the resurrection of the body, which is to occur at the end of the world's history (V: 28-29).

---

24 *Das Evangelium des Johannes, Göttingen*, 1950, p. 155, note 2.

25 Cf. J. HEMPEL, *Heilung als Symbol und Wirklichkeit im biblischen Schrifttum*, Gottingen, 1948; TWNT., III, art. *hiaomai* (Oepke), pp. 202-204.

26 Cf. J. JEREMIAS, *The Parables of Jesus* (translated by S. H. Hooke, London, 1955, pp. 97-100.

27 On the ecclesial outlook present throughout the fourth Gospel, cf. A. CORELL, *Consummatum est, Eskatologi och Kyrka i Johannesevangeliet*, Stockholm, 1950, especially Chapter IV, pp. 92-134.

An even closer relation could be established between IV: 46-54 and V: 24-29. As Loisy [28] saw well, one of the characteristics of the second Cana miracle is to place in relief the life-giving power of the word of Jesus, which, like that of Jahweh Himself, does instantly and by itself, what it signifies, even at a distance. Jesus pronounces the simple words, "Thy son liveth," and the evangelist dedicates all the remainder of the account to emphasizing that the healing took place at the exact hour in which Jesus spoke the words.[29] And in ch. V the two resurrections promised to humanity, that of the present and that of the last day, are likewise attributed to the "voice of the Son of God" (vv. 25-29). The hour is coming and now is, when whoever hears (with docility) the word of Christ shall escape the judgment, and pass from death to life (V: 24). This resurrection will be spiritual (V: 25). The hour is also coming, and will be at the end of time, when the same word of Christ will bring the dead out of their tombs. Therefore, the hour in which Jesus says, "Thy son liveth," is a foretelling of these two hours, of the two epochs in the religious history of humanity, both of them determined by the word of the incarnate Son of God.

As for attaching this second miracle to the context following, one could make the point that thus the account seems to serve a double purpose, along with the curing of the paralytic at the pool, and that furthermore this healing was the occasion of the discourse. These difficulties are both far from insurmountable. As for the latter, it is true enough that the discourse of ch. V follows chronologically after the miracle of the pool. However, the chronological succession of facts is one thing, and John's theological plan another.[30] As for the presence of two accounts leading to a single discourse, the same phenomenon occurs in

---

28 *Le quatrieme evangile*, Paris, 1903, pp. 377-378. It seems better to us to remain within the limits of the text. Some say that the fever left at the seventh hour because the number seven is a symbol of the Resurrection (cf. W. WILCKEN, *Die Entstehungsgeschichte des vierten Evangeliums*, Zollikon, 1958, p. 43). Such a hypothesis lacks evidence.

29 This is in contract to the great wonder-workings of some Old Testament prophets; examples, the son of the widow of Sarepta returns to life at the call of Eliseus. However, it is Jahweh who performs the miracle at the prayer of Elias.

30 Cf. our remarks in *Mélanges Robert*, Paris, *La Composition littéraire de Jo.*, 9-12, p. 486. Cf.

other places; in Ch. VI the two miracles of the multiplication of
the loaves and of the walking on the water both serve to introduce the Discourse on the Bread of Life.

The analogy between the two chapters might be pressed
still further. In ch. VI the multiplication of the loaves heralds
the basic theme of the Discourse (VI: 26-58), i.e., that the Son
of Man is the true heavenly food which God has given to men.
As for the walking on the waters, the manner in which John
narrates it [31] seems designed to suggest that Jesus is a divine
being independent of the laws of matter, who, like Jahweh,
"treads upon the crests of the sea" (Job IX: 8). This suggests the
end of Ch. VI, where, in response to the objections of his hearers,
Jesus stresses that the eating of the Eucharist concerns a being
who does not belong to the world of earth when they see the
Son of man returning to where He was before, then they will
understand His heavenly origin and His divine nature.[32] Likewise,
it seems that, if the second Cana miracle is linked principally
with the first part of the discourse of ch. V, which promises the
double resurrection, then the healing of the paralytic at the pool,
with its specific quality of obedience to the word of Jesus, seems,
in spite of the law of Sabbath rest [33] to prepare more especially
for the second part of the same discourse (vv. 31-47), in which
Jesus laments that He has not found among the Jews that humble
docility which would win for them the way to eternal life. The

---

31 In Mark (VI: 48) Jesus stands on the shore, sees His disciples
weary from rowing, and comes to their aid. In John's Gospel this human
element is missing from the incident (cf. H. STRATMANN, *Das Evangelium
nach Johannes*, Göttingen, 1955, p. 115). From the fourth Gospel alone
we would not see Jesus boarding the boat, or the effect which the
miracle had on the souls of the disciples. John stresses only one fact;
Jesus walked on the water.

32 Cf. J. LEBRETON, *La vie et l'enseignement de Jésus-Christ
Notre-Seigneur*, Paris, 1951, t. I, p. 372; W. HEITMÜLLER, *Die Schriften
des Neuen Testaments*, Göttingen, 1920, t. IV, p. 135; C. H. DODD,
The Interpretation of the Fourth Gospel, p. 344-345.

33 C. F. DODD, *Interpretation of the Fourth Gospel*, p. 318, seems
to exaggerate in saying that the healing becomes effective only when the
paralytic obeys the Savior's command by taking up his pallet and walking.
According to BARRETT (*Commentary*, p. 213) the words, "Sin no more,"
imply not that moral evil was the cause of the man's physical sickness,
but that both have been cured together; this suggests that man can receive
divine life only by removing the obstacle of sin and resistance to God.

paralytic, whom the Sabbath law forbids to obey Jesus, acts completely contrary to the Jews, whom a misunderstood attachment to the Mosaic law prevents from coming to Christ. (Of course, we present this latter explanation merely as a hypothesis).

If it is true that the exegesis of the fourth Gospel is dominated by the idea that one has of its structure and plan, then the problem which we have discussed is of primary importance. We have presented as objectively as possible each of the two alternative positions. It would serve no purpose, however, for us to conceal that the second of these, although up to now the less popular of the two, seems preferable to us. In John's Gospel, Jesus' words and acts explain each other. Now, attaching the healing of the official's son to ch. V has the advantage of relating it to a discourse which can serve as a commentary on it. The resemblance between IV: 43-54 and VII: 1-9 is remarkable. The two passages, of which one is the beginning, and the other the conclusion of the Galilean ministry, explain why Jesus has not spent more time in Judea (cf. IV: 43-45 and VII: 1). Each describes a Galilean scene, but only as prelude to events which take place in Jerusalem.

Throughout this study we have preferred to avoid discussing the hypothesis of an accidental transposition of ch. V and VI, which has been defended by a considerable number of commentators.[34] Let us say simply that even if one were to show the necessity of maintaining this inversion, we would still insist on seeing the second Cana miracle as a point of departure rather than as a conclusion. In effect, the theme of Christ as life-giver (first by His word, then by His flesh and blood) continues all through ch. VI.

We are of the opinion, along with many recent commentators on John's Gospel,[35] that given the absence of any justification

---

39 OLIVIERI, *RB*, 1926, p. 392; LAGRANGE, *RB*, 1926, p. 396; MEINERTZ, *Biblische Zeitschrift*, 1917, p. 228-249; Bernard, de Grandmaison, Prat, Jouon, Bultmann, all admit this inversion.

35 Cf. the commentaries of Hoskyns, Mollat, Dodd, Barrett, etc. The Bodmer Papyrus II, recently published, offers no support to the transpositions proposed by the critics. Van den Bussche says, "It seems to me that modern exegesis is more demanding with those authors who defend the present order of the text, than of those who specialize in rearranging it!" (*Structure de Jean I-XII*, p. 62).

for this hypothesis in the manuscripts and versions, it is better not to attempt to change the text. Although the hypothesis is inviting at first glance, still it runs at once into a serious obstacle, in so far as, if we join ch. V and VII, then, at the beginning of ch. VII, Jesus would be coming from the Holy City, which makes it difficult to see why His "brethren" urge Him to go and show Himself (VII: 3-4).

CHAPTER III

THE PRINCIPAL BIBLICAL THEMES IN
THE DISCOURSE ON THE BREAD OF LIFE [1]

One could hardly overestimate the doctrinal importance of
John's treatment of the Discourse on the Bread of Life (VI:
24-71), which brings us right to the heart of Christianity. Aside
from the many controversies about the interpretation of it, the

1 * First published in *Nouvelle Revue Theologique*, tome 82, nos.
8-10, 1960.

We have consulted and used the following works on the fourth Gospel:
Commentaries: Godet (1865), B. Weiss (1893), Loisy (1903 and 1921),
Wellhausen (1908), Spitta (1910), Lagrange (1925), Durand (1927),
Bornhauser (1928), McGregor (1928), Odeberg (1929), Tillmann (1931),
Bauer (1933), Buchsel (1934), Braun (1935), Hoskyns (1947), Wilken-
hauser (1948), Schlatter (1948), Strathmann (1951), Mollat (1953),
Bultmann (1953), Dodd (1953), Barrett (1954), Bouyer (1955), Lightfoot
(1955), Grant (1956). Monographs: T. Philips, *Die Verheissung der
heiligen Eucharistie nach Johannes*, Paderborn, 1922; J. M. VOSTE,
Studia Joannea, Rome, 1930; E. JANOT, *Le pain de vie*, in *Gregorianum*,
1930, pp. 161-170; W. GOOSSENS. *Les origines de l'Euchariste, sacrement
et sacrifice*, Paris - Gembloux, 1931; P. Gaechter, *Die Form der eucharis-
tischen Rede*, in *Z. kath. Theol.*, 1935, pp. 422-424; W. MICHAELIS,
Die Sakramente im Johannes - Evangelium, Berne, 1946; J. TEMPLE,
The Eucharist in St. John, in *Cath. Bibl. Quart.*, 1947, pp. 442-452;
E. Ruckstuhl, *Die literarische Einheit des Johannesevangelium*, Fribourg
en Suisse, 1951 (pages 220-271); J. SCHNEIDER, *Zur Frage der
Komposition von Joh. VI, 27-58 (59)*, in *In Memoriam Ernst Lohmeyer*,
Stuttgart, 1951, pp. 132-142; O. CULLMANN, *Les sacrements dans
l'évangile johannique*, Paris, 1951; E. SCHWEIZER, *Das johanneische
Zeugnis vom Herrenmahl*, in *Ev. Theol.*, 1952-1953, pp. 358-363; J.
JEREMIAS, *Jo. 6, 51c-58 redaktionell?* in *Z.N.W.*, 1952-1953, pp. 256-
257; G. BORNKAMM, *Die eucharistische Rede im Johannesevangelium*,
in *Z.N.W.*, 1956, pp. 161-169; J. LEAL, *La promesa y la institucion de la
Eucaristia. Sus Coincidencias de forma y fundo*, in *XII Sem. Bibl. Esp.*,
Madrid, 1953, pp. 339-358; D. MOLLAT, *Le chapitre VI de saint Jean*,
in *Lumiere et Vie*, 1957, no. 31, pp. 107-119; W. WILKENS, *Das
Abendmahlzeugnis im vierten Evangelium*, in *Ev. Theol.*, 1958, pp. 354-

general structure of the Discourse seems determined by Christ's
progressive revelation of the mystery of the Bread of Life.[2]

After a short introduction indicating the setting of the hearers,
(vv. 22-25), Jesus, in the first part, excites the faith of His audience, seeking to awaken their deepest religious aspirations (cf. the
conversation with the Samaritan woman), by contrasting perishable material nourishment with a mysterious kind of food which
"remains"; such as the Son of Man will give. (This is why,
paradoxically, the basic work which He expects of men is to
believe in Him). This food is the true heavenly bread, not the
manna of Moses' time. His puzzling words lead them to reply,
"Lord, give us always this bread." In v. 32 the adjective *aléthinos*
contrasts with the figures of the Old Testament and the fulfillment in the New, a typical biblical idea. But it seems to us that
He is also contrasting perishable material nourishment with the
eternal realities of God, an idea well known to the biblical
authors (cf. Is. XL: 8; LI: 6), but which also links them to the
Greek thought pattern.[3]

In the second part (vv. 35-47), Jesus, descended from heaven
and made man, identifies Himself with the true heavenly bread
which is capable of providing eternal life for those who believe
in Him. The Jews, acquainted with Jesus' family background,
cannot accept His claim to a heavenly origin. To these Jews,
who are proud of their knowledge of the Law, Jesus answers

370; H. SCHURMANN, *Joh. 6, 51c, ein Schlüssel zur johanneischen
Brotrede*, in *Bibl. Zeitschr.*, 1958, pp. 254-262; X. LÉON -DUFOUR,
Le Mystère du Pain de vie, in *RSR.*, 1958, pp. 481-523; F. J. LEENHARDT,
La structure du chapitre 6 de l'évangile de Jean, in *Revue d'Hist. et de
Phil. Rel.*, 1959, pp. 1-13; B. GÄRTNER, *John 6 and the Jewish Passover,
Coniectanea Neotestamentica*, XVII, Lund - Copenhagen, 1959; E. J.
KILMARTIN, *Liturgical Influence on John 6*, in *Cath. Bibl. Quart.*, 1960,
pp. 183-191.

2 This structure is proposed by J. M. VOSTÉ, S. LÉON - DUFOUR,
H. VAN DEN BUSSCHE, in *L'Évangile de Jean, Études et Problèmes*,
Paris, Bruges, 1958, pp. 94-96. A glance at the commentaries and monographs cited above should suffice to show that there are a number of
other ways of understanding the structure of the discourse, Schneider
(art. cit.) distinguishes three parts, each introduced by a mention of the
conduct of the Jews (vv. 28, 41, 56), and each expressing the same
fundamental ideas. Cf. still another idea on this question, in the remark
at the end of this chapter.

3 Cf. DODD, *The Interpretation of the Fourth Gospel*, p. 139.

that faith in Him is possible only through a free gift and an interior instruction (*Torah*) from the Father (as the prophets had said). Only thus can they come to Him who reveals the mysteries of God. We shall have occasion later, to show that this prophetic and sapiential theme of an instruction given directly by God is much closer to the mystery of the Eucharist than one might be inclined at first to imagine.

After this digression, more apparent than real, occasioned by the objections of the Jews, Jesus returns, in the third part (vv. 48-58) to His basic statement, that He is the bread of life which they must eat. Now He adds that this bread is His flesh, delivered up for the life of the world, and that they must eat His flesh and drink His blood in order to have eternal life. The verb trogo (vv. 54; 56; 57; 58) and the phrases *alethes* (not *alethinos*), *brosis*, and *alethes posis* seem to exclude a purely metaphorical interpretation. The last part of the Discourse (vv. 59-71) is designed to describe the division which occurred then among the disciples, and the Faith of the Twelve. The statement that, "It is the spirit that gives life, the flesh profits nothing," (v. 63) causes some surprise, coming in the wake of what Christ has said about the necessity of eating His flesh. This verse has been understood in various ways; the flesh of Christ would profit nothing without the Spirit of God which animates it (Lagrange, Cullman, Braun); or else, by seeing the word, "flesh" as not referring to the flesh of Christ. Thus it would mean that man, reduced to his natural powers, (the flesh), can find no sense in Jesus' words, which, being "Spirit and Life," require the action of the Spirit in order to be accepted. According to this latter exegesis (which we consider preferable),[4] v. 63 is better understood as a response to the objections raised by the Jews in the second part of the Discourse.

Although apparently quite self-evident, the Discourse on the Bread of Life presents serious problems for the commentators, as it has done since antiquity. Some of the Fathers of the Church, including Clement of Alexandria, Origen, and Saint Augustine,

---

4 Cfr. J. PASCHER, *Der Glaube als Mitteilung des Pneumas nach Jo. VI, 61-65*, in *Theol. Quartalschrift*, 1936, pp. 301-321; L. TONDELLI, *Caro non prodest quidquam*, in *Biblica*, 1923, pp. 320-327; M. MEINERTZ, *Theologie des Neuen Testaments*, Bonn, 1950, II, p. 299; H. VAN DEN BUSSCHE, *L'attente de la grande révélation*, in *N.R.Th.*, 1953, pp. 1016-1017.

were inclined to interpret the Discourse in a purely spiritual
way (eating by faith), in order to avoid any idea of material
eating of Christ's flesh (which might seem too banal). St.
Augustine places a relationship between John VI and the Eucharist, but he offers spiritual explanations which fail to convince.
One such is the following: *"Facinus vel flagitium videtur jubere;
fugura est ergo praecipiens passioni dominicae communicandum,
et suaviter atque utiliter recondendum in memoria quod pro
nobis caro ejus crucifixa et vulnerata sit."* (*De Doctrina Chris-
tiana,* III: 16 P. L., XXXIV: 74-75). The great Doctor of Hippo
had great influence on the medieval writers, and, later, on Cajetan,
who saw in this exegesis a good way to refute the Hussites'
teaching that all Christians should communicate under both
species. The Council of Trent (Session XXI, July 16, 1562) preferred not to choose between spiritual and real exegesis, and
managed to express the view that Christ had both meanings in
mind.[5]　Today, perhaps more than ever, the controversy continues, as to whether the Discourse is to be understood entirely
of faith or entirely of the Eucharist. Would it not be possible for
us to see here the two themes developed in succession, that of
faith, and then that of the Eucharist? And at just what point
does the treatment of the Eucharist begin? Or again, would it
not be possible to see in the last part of the Discourse, (vv. 51-58,
which many consider the only really eucharistic part), either
a Christian interpolation, or else a pre-johannine homily, which
the redactor of the Gospel inserted here? These are typical of
the questions which have been raised in the past, and which
are still debated today.[6]

In addition to these exegetical problems, there is another,
in the historical order. Is such a Discourse likely on the lips of

---

5 Cfr. F. CAVALLERA, *L'interprétation du chapitre VI de saint
Jean, Une controverse exégétique au Concile de Trente,* in *Rev. d'Hist.
eccl.,* 1909, pp. 687-709.

6 For the opinions of the critics, of the beginning of the article
of X. LEON - DUFOUR, cited above (p. 54). Among the defenders of
a purely objective intrepretation are F. Godet; B. Weiss; K. Bornhauser;
H. Odenberg; A. Schlatter; H. Strathmann; defenders of a purely eucharistic
interpretation are A. Loisy; O. Cullmann; T. Philips; E. Janot; W. Goosens;
H. van den Bussche, and many others. Among those who distinguish two
successive themes are M. J. Lagrange; D. Mollat; E. Gaugler, E. Schweizer,
P. H. Menoud; those who favor the hypothesis of a Christian addition of
vv. 51-58 are J. Wellhausen, F. Spitta, J. Jeremias, the Bible de Jérusalem.

the historical Jesus? How could Christ's hearers have comprehended it? And if we can wonder whether John VI was influenced by the primitive eucharistic liturgy, then was it also influenced by the Jewish paschal liturgy, and to what extent?

We do not intend to offer in these pages a detailed answer to all of these questions. We merely think that a careful examination of the principal biblical themes used in John VI could offer valuable helps toward a solution. Furthermore, such research can be of great interest on the strictly theological level. In instituting the Eucharist, Christ created a ritual, which was entirely new, but the Old Testament, with its mysterious preparations, helps to make its real sense, profoundly spiritual as it is, more intelligible. (The two exegeses, the spiritual and the real, are not so far apart as might seem). Here the paradox of the two Testaments is abundantly evident; Jesus' most original institutions are linked in innumerable ways to the religious notions of the Old Testament. And the fourth Gospel brings out this point more strongly than the others. It has been said that this Gospel, more akin to the Greek world than any of the other New Testament writings, is at the same time "the most Hebraic, with the possible exception of the Apocalypse".[7]

Such a study is doubly interesting, because it is new. As a matter of fact, with the exception of the commentaries, so many writings have come out treating the questions which we considered above, that this one has been considerably neglected. It has been approached only indirectly. We are sure that there are a number of citations made, which permit us to take note of the close connection linking the two Testaments together.

There are three biblical themes, otherwise closely united, and which we separate only for the sake of analysis, which seem to us to be at the base of the Discourse on the Bread of Life: the manna, symbol of spiritual food; the Messianic Banquet; and Wisdom's Banquet. We shall come to the following conclusions: these themes are present throughout the Discourse taken as a whole, and not merely in one or other part of it. More or less developed in the Old Testament, these themes are also familiar to Christ as we know Him not only from the Fourth Gospel, but from the Synoptics as well.

---

7 This expression is from J. B. Lightfoot; J. A. T. ROBINSON quotes it and agrees with it in *The Destination and Purpose of St. John's Gospel*, in *N. T. Stud.*, 6 janvier 1960, p. 118.

This study of the hidden links between John's doctrine and the synoptic tradition will lead us to deepen some very important concepts. In a last section (ch. III, section 4), we shall examine the gospel idea of "disciple of Christ" (Christ who at this point unites His disciples to His person, and feeds them on His own substance). This biblical notion is one of the richest that one can imagine, and one of those which show best the hidden harmony between John and the other evangelists, and also the depth of the preparatory function of the Old Testament.

Finally, we shall formulate the conclusions which seem to us to flow from these observations, as regards the origin and true meaning of the Discourse on the Bread of Life. We shall also attempt to show precisely the principal characteristics of John's doctrine on the Eucharist, by comparing it to that of the Synoptics and of St. Paul.

(1) *The Manna as Symbol of Spiritual Food*

RECOLLECTION OF THE EXODUS AND OF THE MANNA

The Discourse of John VI refers obviously to the crossing by God's people of the Sinai desert. The murmuring of the Jews (*goggyzein* vv. 41, 43, 61) may be an allusion to the incessant murmurings of the Hebrews in the desert, which are also described by the words *goggyzein, goggysmos,* (Ex. XVI: 7; 8; 9; 12; XVII: 3; Num. XI: 1; XIV: 27; 28; XVI: 41; XVII: 5; 6; 10). In any case the bread of life refers to the manna. This wonder is recalled in all the parts of the Discourse, in vv. 31; 32; 49; 50; 58. The statement of v. 50 recalls that of Ex. XVI: 15; "This is the bread which the Lord has given you to eat." However, the manna is presented in different ways in the Old Testament and in Jewish tradition. It is important, therefore, to indicate exactly which interpretation Jesus follows in His teaching.

Most often, in the Old Testament, the manna is described without more ado as bread from heaven (Ex. XVI: 4: "I will now rain down bread from heaven for you"; Neh. IX: 15: "Thou gavest them bread from heaven in their hunger"; cf. Ps. CV: 40; Ps. LXXVIII: 24). In this latter Psalm, the manna occurs also in the following verse as the bread of the mighty (*lehem 'bbirim*); the LXX translate this (correctly) as "the bread of angels." The same reference to "bread" or "food of angels" occurs in Wis. XVI: 20 and 4 Esd. I: 19.[8]

In the same way, in Jo. VI, Jesus' hearers turn their attention to the manna. V. 31 shows this: "Our fathers ate manna in the desert, even as it is written, 'Bread from heaven He gave them to eat'." Otherwise it is not easy to determine which passage of the Scripture is in question. It could be either Neh. IX: 15 (*kai arton ex ouranou edōkas autois*), or Ps. LXXVII: 24 (*kai ebexen autois manna phagein kai arton ouranou edōken autois*). The word *phagein* of the Gospel passage seems to recall the Psalm verse; on the other hand, the phrase *ek tou ouranou* suggests the text in Neh.[9]

Later Judaism did not content itself with merely recalling the manna of the past. It looked forward to the messianic era and the renewal of this wonder. In the Syriac Apocalypse of Baruch we read "And he will come in the same time as when the manna will come down again from above, and they will eat of it" (XXIX: 8). According to the Sybilline Oracles (VII: 148-149), manna is to be the food of the members of the messianic kingdom. Cf. also Pesiqta XLIXa; Midrash Ruth II: 14. In the rabbinic tradition Moses is sometimes the type of the Messiah; like Moses, the Messiah will feed with manna and living water the people of the messianic era.[10]

The same sort of ideas seem to be present in John VI, in the Dialogue between Jesus and the Galileans. To feed a crowd which has followed Him to the desert (cf. Mk. VI: 31 and parallel texts),[11] Jesus has multiplied five barley loaves and two fishes. The

---

8 In late Judaism, angels have no need of food (cf. Tob. XII: 19). The rabbis held that the devils eat, drink, and reproduce themselves, but not the angels. Cf. BONSIRVEN, *Le Judaïsme palestinien au tempis de Jésus Christ*, Tome I, Paris 1935, p. 237. Interventions of God in human history are easily attributed to angels, cf. BONSIRVEN, ibid., pp. 231-232. This last sense is doubtless the one which applies to the expression "bread or food of angels" (i.e., "The food which angels bring"). Cf. J. WEBER, *Le Livre de la Sagesse*, in *La Sainte Bible of Pirot*, tome VI, Paris, 1943, p. 510. In Wis. XVI: 20, the manna is called not only but also, i.e., not the "substance of God" but the means of subsistence which God provides through the ministration of angels.

9 Cfr. C. K. BARRETT, *The Gospel according to St. John*, London, 1955, p. 240.

10 Cfr. R. BLOCH, *Moïse dans la tradition rabbinique*, in *Moïse homme de l'alliance, Cahiers Sioniens*, 1954, pp. 156 (274), 160 (278).

11 Not in the desert strictly speaking (there is no desert at the shore

crowd are thrilled, and want to proclaim Him king (VI: 15); they cry, "This is indeed the prophet who is to come into the world" (VI: 14), that is, the prophet like Moses, foretold in Deut. XVIII: 15. [12]

Still, the Galileans remember that in the Sinai desert Moses gave the Hebrews manna. Now they see the multiplication of the loaves as a wonder inferior to that act of Moses. If Jesus, who now pretends to give an imperishable food (cf. VI: 17), wishes to be accepted as the Messiah, then let Him perform a miracle as great as that of the manna; "What sign then, dost thou, that we may see and believe thee? What work dost thou perform? Our fathers ate manna in the desert even as it is written, 'Bread from heaven He gave them to eat'" (VI: 30-31).[13]

JESUS' EXPLANATION OF THE MANNA

The misunderstanding between Jesus and His hearers comes from the fact that He presents an explanation of the manna entirely different from the one which they are accustomed to hear presented, and much more profound as well. In conformity with the prophetic manner of seeing religious history, especially the era of grace, not as a mere material reproduction of the

---

of the lake, but in a desert place, i.e., in a remote place, a place apart. Cf. LAGRANGE, Évangile Selon Saint Marc, Paris, 1942, pp. 165-166.

12 In I: 21 this prophet is clearly distinguished from the Messiah. As a matter of fact, in the writings of later Judaism, the prophet of Dt. XVIII: 18 is not identified with the Messiah. The Qumran community awaited "the coming of the Anointed ones of Aaron and of Israel" (IQS IX: 10-11). It is generally admitted that these two Anointed ones are two distinct Messiahs. Messiah of Aaron is the priest-Messiah; the Messiah of Israel is the traditional Scion of David. Jo. VI: 14-15 seems to present the popular expectation of a prophet, Messiah, who would be proclaimed king in order to serve as the instrument of nationalistic aspirations. Cf. M. E. BOISMARD, Du Baptême à Cana, Paris, 1956, p. 32. J. GIBLET, Le Messianisme prophétique in L'Attente du Messie, Desclée De Brouwer, 1954, especially pp. 107-108.

13 This situation can be compared with the one described in Matthew XVI: 1-4 and Mark VIII: 11-12. After the second multiplication of the loaves, the Pharisees call for a sign from heaven, Jesus replies with a refusal (in Mark) and with a reference to the sign of Jona (in Matthew). In John, after the multiplication of the loaves, the Galileans call for a sign comparable to the miracle of the manna; Jesus replies that He Himself is the sign, the bread from Heaven.

privileged experiences of the past, but as a progressive spiritualization, Jesus sees in the manna, (as He does in the loaves which He has multiplied) an imperfect image of the only true heavenly food, which God is to give to the world through the mediation—or better,—in the very person—of the Messiah.[14] This is the basic theme which unites the various parts of the Discourse. Jesus reproaches His hearers for limiting themselves to a comfortable material view of life, instead of seeking to discover the spiritual meaning of the multiplication of the loaves, which is a "sign" (*sēmeion*) no less than the other miracles.

The miracles of the fourth Gospel are essentially signs which should be seen in relation to those of the Old Testament, especially to those of the Exodus. That is to say, they are, as are the miracles of the Exodus, a revelation of the living God and of His all powerful intervention in history. Christ's signs are not only His credentials as envoy of the Father, corresponding to what Bultmann calls the "Legitimationsfragen";[15] they announce and prefigure the messianic salvation which Jesus is charged to bring

---

14 In *Golgotha* (Leipzig, 1926, pp. 83-84), J. JEREMIAS observes the parallelism between VI and VII: 37-40. In both cases the crowd hails Jesus as the new Moses, the eschatological prophet of Dt. XVIII: 15. (Cf. VI: 14 and VII: 40); in both cases also Jesus identifies Himself with two of the miracles of the Exodus, the manna and the rock of Horeb (ex. XVII: 6; Num. XX: 11) (if it is true that in this latter passage Jesus really is the spiritual rock announced by the Scripture, from which the living waters are to come).

15 *Das Evangelium des Johannes*, Göttingen, 1950, pp. 87 sq.

16 On the notion of sign in the Old Testament, cf. especially C. A. Keller, *Das Wort 'oth als Offenbarungszeichen Gottes*, Bale, 1946. On *sèmeion* in John, cf. especially CERFAUX, *Les Miracles, signes messianiques de Jésus et oeuvres de Dieu selon l'évangile de S. Jean*, in *Recueil Lucien Cerfaux III*, Gembloux, 1954, pp. 43-46; D. MOLLAT, *Le Séméion Johannique*, in *Sacra Pagina, Miscellanea Biblica Congressus Internationalis De Re Biblica*, Paris - Gembloux, 1959, vol. II, pp. 193-198. Note that in the Synoptics the word *sēmeion* is applied only by exception to Christ's miracles (the only case is Luke XIII: 8 in which Herod hopes to see the *sign* from Christ). In the Synoptics *sēmeion* is a sign indicating the end of time (Matthew XXIV: 3, 30; Mark, XIII: 4; Luke, XXI: 7; XX: 25). Otherwise, in the Synoptics Christ proposes His miracles as signs of the presence of the Kingdom, but without using the word *sēmeion* (Luke XI: 20; Matthew XII: 28; Luke VII: 22; Matthew XI: 4-5).

to the world.[16] Like the miracles of the Synoptics, these miracles are not merely so many interruptions in the course of nature; rather, they are prophecies of a new world, ruled by new laws.[17]

Only in this light can we appreciate the meaning of VI: 26-27: "You seek me not because you have seen signs, but because you have eaten of the loaves and have been filled. Do not labor for the food that perishes, but for that which endures unto life everlasting, which the Son of Man will give you" (or "gives you"; see below). "For upon Him the Father, God Himself, has set His seal." He thus opposes the two foods, and, indirectly, also the two kinds of life which they bring. Bodily food can bring only perishable life; the food which Christ brings, which is His very self, gives a life which remains, which is eternal. As for the seal which the Father has set upon Jesus, it is doubtless the power which He has given Him to perform miracles.

Here a number of observations are in order. In seeing the manna as a symbol of a higher gift, and of a heavenly food, Jesus follows the most authentic tradition of the Old Testament. According to Deuteronomy, the real purpose of the miracle of the manna was not to provide material food, but to teach the Hebrews that the word of God and His commandments are also food. "Remember how for forty years now the Lord, your God, has directed all your journeying in the desert, so as to test you by affliction and find out whether or not it was your intention to keep his commandments. He therefore let you be afflicted with hunger and then fed you with manna, a food unknown to you and your fathers, in order to show you that not by bread alone does man live, but by every word that comes forth from the mouth of God" (Dt. VIII: 2-3).

Cazelles,[18] whose translation of Dt. occurs in the *Bible de Jerusalem*, comments there; "There is an alliteration here; Jahweh, who can create by His Word, has the means to give life to men. He gives life to the Israelites by His divine commandments (*Mitzwah*), which comes from His mouth (*Motzah*)." The LXX emphasizes this beautiful thought: *ouk ep'arto mono zesetai ho anthropos, alla epi panti rhemati to ekporeuomeno dia stomatos Theou zesetai ho anthropos.* In other words, the same word of God which created the manna, is present in the commandments;

---

17 Cfr. J. COMBLIN, *La résurrection de Jésus-Christ*, Paris, 1958, pp. 72-73.

18 *Le Deutéronome* (Bible de Jérusalem), Paris, 1950, p. 49, note a.

thus the commandments are real food for those who observe them.

We saw above that the Alexandrian author of Wisdom called the manna the bread of angels; he also sees its purpose to be the spiritual formation of the children of God: "That your sons whom you loved might learn, O Lord, that it is not the various kinds of fruits that nourish man, but it is your word that preserves those who believe you!" (XVI: 26).

This passage is obviously inspired by Deuteronomy. What is new here, is that the life of the believer, which is preserved by the Word of God, must be more than mere earthly life. It seems that we should see here the eternal life which is promised in the first pages of the book. This explains the suppression of the adjective *monos* (does not live on bread alone) and the emphasis on the contrast between the two kinds of life. Obviously, material food, of whatever sort it be, is incapable of nourishing eternal life.[19]

The Discourse of John VI is in the same line as these two texts from Deuteronomy and Wisdom. Jesus' reason for performing the miracle of the loaves was to show that His Word, His teachings, are food, on condition that one be united to Him by faith, and to show even more clearly that He, who is called in the Prologue to the Gospel, the Word of God, is the true bread which came down from heaven.

As for the Book of Wisdom, we generally can see in it a continual shifting from the natural level to the transcendent order of the spirit. The material benefits which Jahweh granted to Israel at the time of the Exodus are a guarantee of the transcendent spiritual benefits which He grants to the faithful in all times.

It is certainly in order, to challenge certain exaggerated relationships which some exegetes have seen between the fourth Gospel and the Exodus events; [20] John's attitude toward these events is the same as that of the Alexandrian author of Wisdom. He recalls them, either directly, as in III: 14 (the brazen serpent), or indirectly, as the multiplication of the loaves as a recollection of the manna, in order to suggest, as did the Wisdom author,

19 Cfr. G. ZIENER, *Weisheitsbuch und Johannesvangelium*, in *Biblica*, 1957, esp. pp. 406-408.

20 We have in mind here especially H. SAHLIN, *Zur Typologie des Johannes-evangeliums*, Uppsala, 1950.

this passing to the transcendent order. The material life given by the manna or by the loaves which Jesus multiplied, is merely an imperfect image of the eternal life which will be given by the true heavenly bread, the Son of man, come down from heaven.

Furthermore, the idea that God's Word or His Commandments are spiritual food for those who accept them, occurs elsewhere in the Scripture. This idea is present in all the Old Testament teachings on the sovereign efficacy of the Word of Jahweh; word and act go together, as fire, sword, and hammer against the enemies of Jahweh, and bringing unlimited blessings to the just. All these qualities place this Word infinitely above that of man.[21]

We need cite only a few texts on this point; Amos VIII: 11: "Yes, days are coming, says the Lord, God, when I will send famine upon the land; not a famine of bread or thirst for water, but for hearing the word of the Lord." Cf. Jer. XV: 16: "When I found your words, I devoured them; they became my joy and the happiness of my heart." Ps. CXIX: 103: "How sweet to my palate are your promises, sweeter than honey to my mouth." In a vision Ezechiel is invited to eat a book of oracles. "I ate it, and it was sweet as honey in my mouth" (III: 3; cf. Apoc. X: 9). In the fourth Gospel Christ says, "I have a food to eat of which you do not know ... my food is to do the will of Him who sent me, to accomplish His work." Also, later Judaism described the Torah as life-giving bread; "God gave it to His people, both as bread and as a rod; if they do not use it as bread, then they shall be struck by it as a rod".[22]

THE SYNOPTIC ACCOUNT OF THE TEMPTATION

It is important to stress that the idea of the manna, as well as that of spiritual food which John attributes to Jesus, in the Discourse on the Bread of Life, are also closely related to the

---

21 On this question cf. especially L. DURR, *Die Wertung des göttlichen Wortes im Alten Testament und im antiken Orient*, Leipzig, 1838.

22 J. BONSIRVEN, *Le judaisme palestinien au temps de Jésus-Christ* T. I, p. 203; cfr. also STRACK - BILLERBECK, II, pp. 483 sq.; H. ODENBERG, *The Fourth Gospel interpreted in its relation to Contemporaneous Religious Currents in Palestine and the Hellenistic - Oriental World*, Stockholm, 1929, p. 241 sq.; R. BULTMANN, *Das Evangelium des Johannes*, p. 165, note 9.

Christ of the Synoptics. The Synoptics tell how Jesus was led by the Spirit into the desert, where He remained for forty days and was tempted by the devil. These elements recall most strikingly Deut. VIII: 2: "Remember how for forty years now the Lord, your God, has directed all your journeying in the desert, so as to test you by affliction and find out whether or not it was your intention to keep His commandments." In both passages we notice three identical elements: the desert, the number forty, and the testing.[23]

When Jesus is in the desert, as were the Jews of the Exodus period, and suffers from hunger, as they did, but, unlike either the Hebrews of the Exodus period or the Jews of John VI, does not make the slightest murmur, the devil challenges Him to prove that He is the Messiah by working a miracle like that of the Manna, thereby establishing Himself as a temporal and earthly Messiah. "If thou art the Messiah, command that these stones become loaves of bread" (Mt. IV: 3). Jesus' answer comes quickly, borrowing from the Deuteronomy passage cited above, which explains the spiritual meaning of the manna: "Not by bread alone does man live, but by every word that comes forth from the mouth of God" (Mt. IV: 4). The parallel to the scene in John VI is evident, with the difference that in John VI it is the Galileans who tempt Jesus, whereas in Matthew's passage it is the devil.[24] In either case, Jesus is faced with a purely material understanding of His mission. In either case, the Savior's reaction springs from the same principle; the manna, and all material food, is infinitely inferior to the spiritual food which is the Word of God.

We do not at all mean to infer that John's account is historical

---

23 Cfr. M. SABBE, *De tentatione Jesu in deserto,* in *Collationes Brugenses,* tome L, 1944, pp. 461-462. Cfr. also J. DUPONT, *L'arrièrefond biblique du récit des tentations de Jésus,* in *N. T. Stud.,* II, 1956-1957, pp. 287-304.

24 In general the temptations of Jesus as they are described in Matthew and Luke are closely related to His public ministry. The episode of the temptations brings us not only to penetrate Christ's most intimate thought, but also to have an awareness of the spirit which animates Him. It is, as it were, a kind of "prologue, on the level of the invisible, of what is to take place on earth" (Lagrange, *Évangile selon Saint Matthieu,* Paris, 1911, p. 63).

25 This is the position maintained by H. PREISKER, *Zum Charakter des Johannesvangeliums,* in *Luther, Kant, Schleiermacher in ihrer Bedeutung*

and that the Synoptic temptation narrative is mere myth.[25] Let us say rather that Jesus' reference to the text of Deut. VIII: 3, which is made evident by His reply to the devil in the Synoptics, inclines us to have confidence in John's account, when he shows Jesus using this situation as a point of departure to prepare souls for the mystery of the Eucharist.[26]

(2) Eschatological Perspective; the Messianic Banquet

ESCHATOLOGICAL CHARACTER OF THE PROMISED FOOD

The perspective which Jesus establishes of a spiritual food, of which the manna is but a symbol, is not an atemporal promise, valid for all time without distinction. Even if it is to be related to the ideas of Deuteronomy and of Wisdom ("Man does not live by bread alone"), still it is not exactly the same.

In v. 27, after the words, "which endures unto life everlasting," we must choose one of two readings; "which the Son of Man *gives* you *didōsin*, (2), or "which the Son of Man *will give* you." The present tense expresses an eschatological gift, the definitive revelation brought by the Messiah, the Son of Man. As for the future tense, which is probably the authentic reading, it must refer to the sacrament of the Eucharist, which will be

---

für den Protestantismus, Forschungen und Abhandlungen Georg Wobbermin dargebracht, 1929, pp. 379-384.

26 In Matthew VI: 11 (and Luke XI: 3) it is impossible to determine the exact meaning of *epiousios*, an adjective virtually unknown in Greek, cf. T.W.N.T. II, pp. 587-596, (FOERSTER). Some relate it to *epi tēn ousan* (*hēmeran* implied), hence the present day, today; others relate it to *epiousa*, participle of *epienai* hence the day to come, (i.e., tomorrow). In any case, Jesus, who said in Matthew (VI: 34) "Sufficient for the day in its own trouble," would be contradicting Himself by recommending now that we be concerned for tomorrow's sustenance. The text should be: "give us today's bread today." Cf. Lagrange, *L'Évangile Selon Saint Matthieu,* Paris, 1941, p. 130; H. VAN DEN BUSSCHE, in *Bible et Vie Chrétienne,* Mars-avril, 1960, pp. 42-46; J. DeFraine's article *Oraison Dominicale* in *S. D. B.,* cols. 795-799. Whatever may be the outcome of this philological problem, the *Pater Noster* could be an allusion to the Manna, which would thus be a new manifestation of Jesus' relationship to this theme; the redundant phrases of the *Pater Noster* could be seen as related to Ex. XVI: 4: "Each day the people are to go out and gather their daily portion; thus will I test them" (LXX: *syllexousin to tēs hēmeras eis hēmeran, hopōs peirasō autous*). Cf. J. DE FRAINE, art. cit. col. 798.

the product of Christ's redemptive Passion (cf. VI: 51: "The bread that I will give is my flesh for the life of the world").

We also have other indications of this eschatological perspective. The account of the multiplication of the loaves, which prepares the way for the Discourse, is related to the theme of the Messianic Banquet (cf. below); furthermore, it is situated near the Jewish Passover (IV: 4). For John this is a way of suggesting that Jesus is preparing to replace the Pasch of the Jews with a Christian Pasch. This miracle completes that of Cana, in which Jesus has already suggested that, when His Hour comes, He will give to humanity the messianic wine promised in the ancient prophecy.[27] Generally speaking, all the miracles presented in the fourth Gospel have a soteriological meaning. Chosen, perhaps, for the purpose of recalling in detail the great wonders of the Exodus,[28] they announce the definitive salvation of the era of grace, and the sacramental dispensation, through which this salvation is to be communicated to men.. In particular, the loaves which Jesus multiplies miraculously and distributes to the crowd, show the bread of life which is Himself, and which will be given to men, once His Passion shall have been accomplished.

---

27 Cfr. our article *L'Heure de Jésus et le signe de Cana, Contribution à l'étude de la Structure du quatrième évangile*, in *Eph. Theol. Lov.*, 1960, I, pp. 5-22 et above, pp.

28 According to G. ZIENER (*Biblica*, 1957, p. 405) there would thus be in the fourth Gospel a systematic recollection of the miracles of the Exodus, not according to their chronological order, but according as they are listed in Wisdom. The first miracle, of Cana, would thus correspond to that of the water from the rock (Wis. XI: 4-14); the second Cana miracle and the paralytic at the pool would correspond to the brazen serpent (Wis. XVI: 5-13): the multiplication of the loaves, to the Manna (Wis. XVI: 20-26); the healing of the man born blind, to the light granted to the Israelites while the Egyptians were lost in the darkness (Wis. XVIII: 1; cf. Ex. X: 23); the raising of Lazarus, to the delivery of the Israelites from death at the word of Aaron (Wis. XVIII: 22; cf. Num. XVII: 13). These resemblances are, of course, subject to the greatest reserve. The certain similarity between Wisdom and John's Gospel is in the way in which they both treat the Exodus events as figures of the final salvation event. Wis., for example, says of the brazen serpent, "He who turned toward it was saved, not by what he saw, but by you, the savior of all" (XVI: 7), which recalls John III: 14-17, in which, as Osty says, "the brazen serpent and God's plan of universal salvation are joined in one context" (*Livre de Sagesse*, Bible de Jérusalem, Paris, 1957, p. 96, note f).

We should note the expression, "the bread of life" (*ho artos tēs zōēs*), the bread which gives life, in relation to the "light of life" of VIII: 12; the "word of life" of I Jo. I: 1; the "water of life" of Apoc. XXI: 6 and XXII: 1. This expression is borrowed from a biblical tradition on the manna, which is thoroughly familiar with this manner of speaking. On the contrary, it recalls also the tree of life in Paradise (*to xylon tes zoes*; cf. Gen. II: 9; III: 22-24; cf. Prov. III: 18; XI: 30; XIII: 12; XV: 4), symbol of the immortality which man could have enjoyed, had he not sinned. The promises of vv. 51 (*ean tis phage ek toutou tou artou zēsei eis ton aiōna*) and 58 (*ho trōgōn touton ton arton zēsei eis ton aiōna*) serve to counterbalance the sentence passed by God against man in expelling him from the garden of Eden; *Kai nyn mēpote ekteinē tēn cheira kai labē tou xylou tēs zōēs kai phagē kai zēsetai eis ton aiōna* (Gen. III: 22. John's Apocalypse shows that this relationship, already indicated by Schlatter,[29] is not arbitrary. The letters at the beginning of the Apocalypse promise, like two practically equal benefits, the eating of the fruit of the tree of life (Apoc. II: 7) and the eating of the hidden manna (II: 27). Of the former text, Swete says: "Man's exclusion of the tree of life (Gen. III: 22 ff.) is repealed by Christ on condition of a personal victory over evil".[30]

The immortality which Jesus attaches in John VI to the eating of the Eucharist has nothing to do with the immortality of Plato, which is limited to a dualistic concept of man. It is never called, interestingly enough, *athanasia* or *aphtharsia*.[31] Rather, it is the eschatological restoration of the primitive privilege which was

---

29 *Der Evangelist Johannes*, Stuttgart, 1948, p. 177.

30 *The Apocalypse of St. John*, Londres, 1909, p. 30.

31 Basically, *John does the opposite of Paul*. Paul freely uses the words *athanasia* (I Cor. XV: 53-54) and especially *aphtharsia* (I Cor. XV: 42; 50; 52; 54; cf. Rom. I: 23; II: 7; Eph. VI: 24). However, in I Cor. XV we see that these words refer to the state of risen Christians. Paul, writing to a Christian community, adopts a terminology with which they are familiar and which they will be willing to accept, baptizing it, in a way, and changing its meaning completely, since he obviously makes no concession at all to the Greek doctrine of immortality, which is based upon the metaphysical dualism of body and soul. Even more than Paul, John should be led by his theology to use the terminology of immortality (*athanasia, aphtharsia*); but he never does. Thus many authors are in error in seeing Greek ideas here. (Cf. *Introduction à la Bible*, ROBERT - FEUILLET, *tome II*, (*Nouveau Testament*), Tournai, 1959, pp. 910-911).

originally an essential part of God's plan (Wisdom II: 23: "God formed man to be imperishable"), but was lost because of man's sin. The manna in the desert could not effect this restoration; it had to come through the work of Jesus. This is why Jesus could say, "Your fathers ate the manna in the desert, and have died. This is the bread that comes down from heaven, so that if anyone eat of it, he will not die.... He who eats my flesh and drinks my blood has life everlasting, and I will raise him up on the last day." (VI: 48; 54; cf. 58).[32] In other words, unlike the manna, the eucharistic food is to put the believer in possession of eternal life, over which physical death will have no power, and which should grow and develop until the glorious resurrection at the end of time. The intrinsic unity established between the immortality which is granted beginning now, and the final resurrection, shows well the biblical and eschatological character of the benefits thus given.[33]

---

32 LAGRANGE (Évangile selon Saint Jean, Paris, 1927, p. 182) describes a difficulty arising from VI: 49-50-58: "The fathers ate manna and died; now, are those who eat the bread of life to be freed from natural death? And if it is a question of a spiritual death, then Moses and his people must not have suffered it. St. Augustine recognized this difficulty, and was less inclined to stress the difference between the Manna and the bread from heaven, than he was to distinguish good dispositions from evil ones. However, it should suffice for us to follow the literal sense, understanding natural death in the first case, and death, or rather, spiritual life, in the second. "Basically, for both John and Paul, Christ alone has changed the meaning of death, which is in itself a curse, being the sign of spiritual death. Cf. our article Mort du Christ et mort du chrétien d'après les épîtres pauliniennes, in R.B., 1959, pp. 481-513.

33 The thought of resurrection of the body has a principal place in the fourth Gospel. Far from being a later correction by the Church, or an accomodation to the language of primitive Christianity, it is the high point and culmination of Christ's salvific work. This is what is emphasized by the raising of Lazarus, which, like the other miracles of John's Gospel is a sort of parable in act (Tatgleichnis, to use the word of W. LUTGERT, Die Johanneische Christologie, Gütersloh, 1916, p. 17). Jesus wishes to show that He is now the source of divine life and of supernatural resurrection for all men, although He is performing a physical resurrection at the moment. This means that the divine life which the Savior offers now to men, will eventually find its necessary fulfillment in the glorious resurrection of the body. Thus the promise of resurrection is linked to the promise of the Eucharist. In effect, if the glorified Son of Man, whose flesh is vivified by the Spirit of God (VI: 63), is to feed men with His flesh

THE MESSIANIC BANQUET IN THE OLD TESTAMENT

In the Old Testament the first prediction of the eschatological destruction, of death and of the resurrection of the dead, occurs in the Apocalypse of Isaia,[34] in which this announcement is closely linked to that of the Messianic Banquet. This text is of considerable importance:

> On this mountain the Lord of hosts will provide for all people a feast of rich food and choice wines, juicy, rich food and pure choice wines.... (Is. XXV: 6)
> He will destroy death forever.... (XXV: 8)
> But your dead shall live, their corpses shall rise;
> Awake and sing, you who lie in the dust. For your dew is a dew of light, and the land of shades gives birth. (XXVI: 19)

The theme of the Messianic Banquet seems to have had more than one source. On the one hand, the Jahwist narrative of the conclusion of the Sinai covenant attaches it to a meal held in the presence of God by Moses, Aaron, Nadab, Abihu, and sixty-six of the elders of Israel (Ex. XXIV: 9-11). On the other hand, while the Hebrews were crossing the desert, God gave them the manna, and also water from out of the rock. Finally, there is the Jewish tradition of "The sacred meals taken within a holy place, (Gen. XXXI: 54; Ex. XVIII: 12; I Sam. IX: 12, ff.; Osee VIII: 13; Amos II: 8). The Law of Deuteronomy, of course, attaches importance to this practice (Deut. XIII: 7; 15; XIV: 23; XV: 20; XVII: 7). Fermented liquors were permitted on these joyous occasions (Dt. XIV: 26); the pious Israelite, accustomed to having little meat, was to eat here the flesh of the victims, after a part had been offered to Jahweh. We can also recall here that Jahweh, dwelling in His holy place, would receive at His

---

and blood, the salvation which He offers must affect their whole being, body as well as soul. Thus Jesus describes Himself as the resurrection and the life of men (*ego eimi hē anastasis kai hē zōē*), implying thereby that the divine life which He gives now will eventually be fulfilled in a resurrection of life (*anastasis zōēs*). Cf. F. MUSSNER, *ZŌĒ, Die Anschauung vom Leben im vierten Evangelium unter Berücksichtigung der Johannesbriefe*, Munich, 1952, pp. 140-144.

34 The dating of this text is disputed, but it is undoubtedly late. Cf, on this point D.B.S., art. *Isaïe*, col. 682-684; cf. also *Introduction à la Bible*, t. I, p. 571.

table those who came to render Him their homage, a notion symbolic of the union between the God of the Covenant and the faithful Israelites.[35]

The waiting for the messianic banquet is mentioned quite often in the Old Testament, and under various forms. One reference to it is in Deutero-Isaia's prediction that those returning from Babylon, during the crossing of the desert, will receive food and drink miraculously from God, as did their ancestors in the time of the Exodus:

> They did not thirst when he led them through the dry lands; water from the rock he set flowing for them; he cleft the rock and the waters welled forth. (Isaia XLVIII: 21)
> Along the ways they shall find pasture, on every bare height shall their pastures be.
> They shall not hunger or thirst, nor shall the scorching wind or the sun strike them; for he who pities them leads them and guides them beside springs of water. (XLIX: 9-10)

As is his custom, Trito-Isaia picks up these eschatological promises in order to apply them to the just of the divided post-exilic community:

> Therefore thus says the Lord God: Lo, my servants shall eat, but you shall go hungry; my servants shall drink but you shall be thirsty; my servants shall rejoice, but you shall be put to shame. (LXV: 13)

If the Canticle of Canticles is, as we suppose it to be, an allegory celebrating in terms of human love (although as an ideal much more desired than attained) the loving friendship of Jahweh and Israel, then it is the Messianic Banquet which is described in V: 1. Like the banquet of Isaia XXXV: 6, it takes place on the "hill of incense" (Cant. IV: 6), which can mean only the site of the Temple: [36]

---

35 A. ROBERT, *Les attaches littéraires de Prov. I-IX*, in *R. B.*, 1934, pp. 375-376.

36 Following Jewish exegesis (*Targum, Rashi*), many interpreters see the "Mountain of Myrrh" and the "hill of incense" as an allusion to the

I drink my wine and my milk. Eat, friends; drink freely
of love! (Cant. V: 1)

The figure of wine and milk occurs again in relation to water
and wheat, in the invitation to the Messianic Banquet which
we read in Isaia LV. Here, however, it is clear that this food,
opposed to illusory pleasure, has a metaphorical meaning, referring to the material and moral happiness of the messianic
era, promised to those who listen to Jahweh:

> All you who thirst, come to the water!
> You who have no money, come, receive grain, and eat;
> Come without paying and without cost, drink wine and
> milk!
> Why spend money for what is not bread; your wages for
> what fails to satisfy?
> Heed me, and you shall eat well, you shall delight in
> rich fare.
> Come to me heedfully; listen, that you may have life.
> I will renew with you the everlasting covenant, the bene-
> fits assured to David. (Isaia, LV: 1-3)

We find the same imagery in Psalm XXIII in which the
author, actualizing the eschatological promises, especially that
of the good shepherd and that of the Messianic Banquet, pictures
to himself under the image of a finely spread table, God's friendship, which he enjoys:

> The Lord is my shepherd; I shall not want. In verdant
> pastures he gives me repose.... You spread the table
> before me in the sight of my foes. (vv. 1-5)

Temple of Jerusalem. Cf. P. JOUON, Le Cantique Des Cantiques, Paris,
1909, pp. 267-268. One of the most recent commentators on the Canticle,
H. RINGGREN, affirms that this is the normal literal meaning of these
phrases. (Das Hohe Lied, Klagelieder, Das Buch Esther, Göttingen, 1958,
p. 19). We are happy to announce the forthcoming publication of a commentary on the Canticle by A. ROBERT, in the collection Études Bibliques.
Robert shows that the interpretation of the Canticle in terms of the prophetic literature is fully justified. Other exegeses almost always require
transpositions or corrections in the text, which are nothing short of arbitrary.

THE MESSIANIC BANQUET IN JOHN VI AND THE SYNOPTICS

It would be superfluous to demonstrate, after what we have shown, that the traditional theme of the Messianic Banquet is at the base of John's treatment of the Discourse on the Bread of Life, and that it is linked there, as it is in the Apocalypse of Isaia, to the eschatological destruction of death and to the resurrection of the dead. Situated, as we have seen, in an essentially eschatological context, the promise of a food which will bring eternal life, lends itself well to this theme. Like the meals taken in the holy place, which the messianic banquet suggests, the eucharistic eating will be of Christ, the victim immolated on Calvary for the salvation of men; "The bread that I will give is my flesh, delivered up for the life of the world" (VI: 51). The assurance that, "He who comes to me shall not hunger, and he who believes in me shall never thirst" (VI: 35), goes back explicitly to many of the texts which we have cited above, especially Isaia XLVIII: 21; XLIX: 9-10; LV: 1-3; LXV: 13.[37] Jesus' quotation from the Scripture in VI: 45; "They shall all be taught of God," is taken from Isaia LIV: 13, an oracle which in itself suggests Jer. XXXI: 31-34, where for the first time we see the extraordinary idea of a new covenant, much more interior than the old, because it will be written in men's hearts by God Himself. Now it is immediately after He had said, "All your sons shall be taught by the Lord," that Deutero-Isaia issues his invitation to the Messianic Banquet (Isaia LV: 1, ff.). The similarity between this context and that of John VI is nothing short of remarkable. The reciprocal formula, "He who eats my flesh and drinks my blood abides in me and I in him" (VI: 56), appears to be an interiorization of the traditional formula of the covenant; Israel is the people of Jahweh; Jahweh is the God of Israel (cf. Osee II: 25; Jer. XXXI: 33, etc.), an interiorization in keeping with the general character of the covenant.[38]

---

37 This is one more of many indications of the close relationship between the fourth Gospel and the Apocalypse; VII: 7 refers, evidently, to Is. II: 10; cf. also XXI: 1; XXII: 17.

38 Rather than emphasize the distance between this concept and the hellenistic mysticism in which the initiate is considered to be made identical with the god ("Thou art I and I Thou"), we prefer to relate VI: 56 to the reciprocal phrase of X: 14: "I am the good shepherd, and I know mine and mine know me," in which this mutual knowing (the semitic

That Christ has in effect promised the gift of the Eucharist in relation to the messianic banquet, becomes all the more credible in the light of the synoptic tradition, which stresses this theme quite a bit. It seems to be already implied in the means which Jesus shares with publicans and sinners, a gesture of mercy signifying that the messianic healing has come for the sick and for sinners, and that therefore God has decided to resume with them a relation of friendship, because He calls them to take part in the eschatological banquet.[39] In any case, it is surely presupposed by the saying about the new wine which needs new wine skins, a saying common to all three Synoptics (Mk. II: 22; Mt. IX: 17; Lk. VI: 37-39).[40]

At the time of Jesus, one of the symbols commonly used to designate the future kingdom of God was that of the banquet, which helps us to understand the words of one of Jesus' hearers, "Blessed is he who shall feast in the kingdom of God" (XIV: 15). It also explains why Jesus Himself often refers, especially in the parables, to the banquet image to indicate the future kingdom of God, either under the terrestrial aspect (the Church) or under its completed aspect (the Heavenly reward): Luke VI: 21 (and Mt. V: 6): the beatitude of those who hunger and thirst (thirst in Mt. only);[41] Mt. VIII: 11-12 (and Lk. XIII: 28-29): those who will come from the East and from the West, and will feast with Abraham and Isaac and Jacob; Lk. XIII: 16-24 (and Mt. XXII: 2-10): those who fail to come to the feast; Lk.

sense) is allied to the eschatological theme of the good shepherd, as in the oracle of Ezechiel regarding the new Covenant, "Thus they shall know that I, the Lord, am their God, and they are my people, the house of Israel. . . . You, my sheep, you are the sheep of my pasture, and I am your God, says the Lord God" (XXXIV: 30-31). We would also invoke the covenant formula and the shepherd theme to explain the famous verse of Cant. II: 16; "My love belongs to me and I to him; he browses among the lilies."

39 Cfr. in this sense E. Lohmeyer, *Das Evangelium des Markus*, Göttingen, 1951, p. 56; Y. De MONTCHEUIL, *Mélanges Théologiques*, Paris, 1956, p. 39.

40 Cfr. J. JEREMIAS, *The Parables of Jesus* (tr. by S. H. HOOKER, London, 1955, p. 95.

41 While the formulation of the Beatitudes in Luke is concerned primarily with the material, Matthew's account starts off immediately on the spiritual plane. However, the fulfillment promised in Luke is evidently Messianic, and has therefore the broad meaning of the messianic promises,

XII: 35-37: the servants who are served by their master; Mt. XXII: 11-13: the wedding garment; Mt. XXV: 1-13: the ten virgins. The formula (found only in Matthew) of "the darkness outside" (VIII: 12; XII: 13; XXV: 30), presupposes "a banquet taking place in a brightly lighted room.[42] Cf. Apoc. III: 20: the banquet of the friends of Christ; XIX: 9: the wedding banquet of the Lamb.

In the Synoptics, the institution of the Eucharist in the setting of a holy meal, which probably was the Paschal meal,[43] fits quite naturally into this general context. It is quite normal, then, that in John VI Jesus should make use of this traditional treatment, to prepare His hearers for the institution of the sacrament.

It might be helpful to note here a number of remarkable parallels between John VI and the narratives of the Last Supper. John probably had them in mind as he wrote. In our conclusion we shall come again to the twin phrases, "eat my flesh," and "drink my blood" (VI: 53; 54; 55; 56). This is a repetition, or, according to some authors, the original form, of the words of the Last Supper about Christ's body and blood. At the Last Supper, Christ must have said, "my flesh," not "my body".[44]

Furthermore, in this johannine Discourse, as at the Last Supper, the drama of Calvary is announced in terms suggesting the sacrifice of the Servant of Jahweh in Isaia LIII. "My flesh which I will give for the life of the world" (VI: 51), is related to "My body which is given for you," of Lk. XXII: 19. The two formulas, as well as "My blood which is being shed for many," (Mk. XIV: 24 and parallel texts), recall the Servant given up for the sins of many (i.e., the multitudes; in Hebrew, as in Aramaic, "many" is not partitive, but expresses a multitude which

---

according as the Old Testament was well aware of spiritual fulfillment; Cf. e. gr., Ps. XVII: 15. Lagrange says of Luke VI: 21, "Most agree that there is room here for a sense higher than the literal" (*L'Évangile Selon Saint Luc*, Paris, 1927, p. 187). In Matthew, hunger and thirst after justice seems to be not the desire for a higher perfection, but the messianic expectation of God's gift of justice. In the Old Testament, metaphorical hunger and thirst always refer to spiritual blessings given by God, and never to the justice which man must practice.

42 P. JOUON, *L'Évangile de Notre Seigneur Jesus Christ*, Paris, 1930, pp. 47-48.

43 This discussion still goes on. Cf. the recent position of P. Benoit regarding Mlle. JAUBERT'S work on the date of the Last Supper (*R. B.* 1958, pp. 590-594).

may or may not be the whole). The mention of Judas' betrayal
is in both the Discourse on the Bread of Life (VI: 70-71) and
the Synoptic accounts of the Last Supper.

There are some other similarities, somewhat less obvious.
In the Discourse on the Bread of Life, the person of Moses, the
mediator of the first covenant, is recalled consistently, so much
so that v. 50: "This is the bread *houtos estin ho artos* that comes
down from heaven," imitates the language of Moses in Ex. XVI:
15: "This is the bread *houtos ho artos* which the Lord has given
you to eat." The same holds true for the Last Supper. In effect,
the words of Jesus, "This is my blood (the blood of the covenant),"
recalls Moses' statement at the conclusion of the Sinai covenant:
"This is the blood of the covenant which the Lord has made
with you" (Ex. XXIV: 8). In speaking at the Last Supper of the
new Covenant, Jesus alludes to Jeremia's great announcement
of a new covenant (*diatheke kaine*), to be written by God Himself in men's hearts (Jer. XXXI: 31-34). Cf. also the allusion
to Isaia LIV: 13 in John VI: 45.

(3) Wisdom's Banquet

Wisdom's Banquet, as we shall see, is basically nothing but
a variation of the Messianic Banquet. Still, because this theme
is of considerable importance, and also because of the complexity
of the problems which it raises, we shall divide this third part of
our study into three stages: the Old Testament; the sixth chapter
of St. John's Gospel; and the Synoptic Gospels. The whole question is ultimately one of johannine Christology and its sources,
which we shall be drawn to consider.

THE OLD TESTAMENT

The oldest biblical text treating of Wisdom's Banquet is that
of Prov. IX: 1-6. It is said therein that Wisdom has built herself
a house, and set up for it seven columns.[45] In this lovely house

---

44 Cfr. J. BONSIRVEN, (*Hoc est corpus meum*), *Récherches sur
l'original araméen*, in *Biblica*, 1958, pp. 205-219.

45 Most translators (including the Bible of Jerusalem) follow the LXX
rendering, "She has set up her seven columns." The Masoretic Text rendering
is correctly kept in the *Bible de la Pléiade* (Dhorme): "Wisdom herself
is a cutter of stones." Many of our translations are from the *Bible de la
Pléiade*. (The CCD version here is comparable to that of the B. J. - Tr.)

she prepares a banquet, "dressed her meat, mixed her wine, yes, she has spread her table." Now she sends her servants to the heights out over the city, to call the inhabitants and to invite them to her banquet.

> Let whoever is simple turn in here; to him who lacks understanding, I say, "Come, eat of my food and drink of the wine I have mixed! Forsake foolishness that you may live; advance in the way of understanding! (*Prov.* IX: 4-6)

A. Robert, who has produced a most profound work on Prov. I-IX,[46] has expressed perfectly the meaning of this allegory. Like Jahweh Himself, Wisdom has her house (cf. Sirach XIV: 23-25), her holy place, in which she offers a holy meal. This metaphorical temple is to be identified with the collection of *mashals* (*meshalim*), which Prov. I-IX introduces. One might say she has formed her sages whose maxims are preserved in the Book of Proverbs.

The bread and wine which she offers in her banquets are nothing else than these *mashals*, which men are invited to eat, as a heavenly food, because they are a true sharing in God's own wisdom. "We are amazed," writes Robert, "to see affirmed in these texts such a precise foretelling of the dogma of the Eucharist".[47]

This allegory, of course, cannot be separated from the banquet which the prophets foretell for the messianic era, as is evident from the similarity of vocabulary. The passage most similar in this regard is Isaia LXV: 11-13,[48] except that, whereas the prophets looked to the future, the author of Prov. I-IX sees these prophetic promises actualized. From this point on, Wisdom's faithful disciples are, to a certain degree, admitted to the eschatological benefits which the prophets describe in terms of banquet images. At a time in which men are tiring of their

---

46 *Les attaches littéraires de Prov. I-IX*, in R. B., 1934, pp. 42-68; 172-204; 374-384; 1935, pp. 344-365; 502-525.

47 *R. B.*, 1934, p. 379.

48 Cf. *R. B.* 1934, pp. 376-377. From the point of view of the literary form, Is. LV: 1-3 would be closest to Prov. IX. Dhorme says (*Bible de la Pléiade*, tome II, p. 194, note) that the style and imagery of this prophetic oracle are related to the sapiential literature.

long and, apparently, vain wait for the Messiah, the author of
Prov. I-IX proposes to show them that, from this point on, divine
Wisdom, without being the Messiah, nonetheless fulfills his func-
tions in a marvelous manner.[49]

The invitation to the banquet has several parallels in the
early chapters of the Book of Proverbs itself. In Prov. VIII
divine Wisdom praises herself, vaunting the excellence of the
benefits entrusted to her, and boasting proudly that she was a
co-worker with God in the work of creation. The end of this
beautiful section (vv. 32-36) shows that it has but one purpose;
to gain men's confidence and to bring them to enroll themselves
in Wisdom's school. Another appeal from Wisdom is I: 20-33,
with the promise that "Lo, I will pour out...my spirit" [50] upon
those who come, threatening at the same time to wreak terrible
punishments upon those who refuse. She will abandon them
"When distress and anguish befall you. Then they call me, but
I answer not; they seek me, but find me not" (vv. 27-28). We
must not overlook the invitation in the Book of Baruch to seek
true wisdom (III: 9; V: 9). All Israel's woes are due to the
fact that "You have forsaken the fountain of wisdom (III: 12),
i.e., the fountain of life. Wisdom belongs only to God; no man
of earth knows it (III: 15-28). "Who has gone up to heaven
and taken her, or brought her down from the clouds?" (III: 29).
But God Himself "has given her to Jacob, His servant, to Israel,
His beloved son. Since then she has appeared on earth, and
moved among men (vv. 37-38). The conclusion is obvious:
"Turn, O Jacob, and receive her; walk by her light toward splendor!" (IV: 2).

Wisdom's Banquet recurs in Sirach XXIV, the highpoint of
the book, which obviously depends on Prov. VIII-IX. Once

---

49 Cf. H. CAZELLES, *L'enfantement de la Sagesse*, in *Sacra Pagina*,
1959, vol. 1, pp. 511-515. At the time (shortly after the exile) in which
the Davidic dynasty no longer existed, God Himself was the object of
Messianic hope. Divine Wisdom possesses qualities which Isaias recognizes
as God's gifts to the Messiah (v. 15, cf. Is. XI: 1 ff). Wisdom is possessed
of a royal investiture (v. 23, *nissakti* "I have been invested," not to be
corrected, as many versions propose, into "I have been established or
founded").

50 The normal translation of v. 23b is, "Behold, I shall pour out my
Spirit upon you," not "Behold, I shall pour out my heart for you" (B. J.).
Wisdom and Spirit are closely related concepts in the Bible.

again Wisdom states her titles of nobility; She existed with God before the creation of the world, issuing from the mouth of the Most-High. She dwelt on the heights; her throne was on a cloud. She surveyed the entire world, from the vault of heaven down to the abyss (vv. 3-5). She sought a resting place to put up her tent, and God gave her a dwelling place in Israel (vv. 7-11). She is now firmly rooted, like a tree; six tree images (cedar; cypress; palm; rosebush; olive; plane) express her mysterious greatness; her penetrating power and beneficence are pictured as seven aromatic plants (cinnamon; balm; myrrh; galbanum; onycha; spice; incense). She spreads her branches wide, like a terebinth, and buds forth delights, like a vine, and produces fruits fair and rich (vv. 12-13). The fruit images naturally suggest eating; here again, as in Pr. VIII-IX, it is evident that Wisdom's plan is to gain men's confidence, and to bring them to follow her teachings:

> Come to me, all you that yearn for me, and be filled with my fruits; you will remember me as sweeter than honey, better to have than the honeycomb. He who eats of me will hunger still, he who drinks of me will thirst for more; he who obeys me will not be put to shame, he who serves me will never fail. (Sir. XXIV: 18-21).

The import of this passage is that, to listen to Wisdom's teaching is the same as to eat of her fruits. As is said in Sir. XV: 3, divine Wisdom feeds men on the "bread of understanding" and the "water of learning." "She inebriates men with her fruits" (I: 14). "As though plowing and sowing, draw close to her; then await her bountiful crops. For in cultivating her, you will labor but little, and soon you will eat of her fruits" (VI: 19-20).

Wisdom shares her own privileges with her faithful disciples. We can relate Sir. XXIV: 6-10 to IV: 14-15: "Those who serve her serve the Holy One; those who love her the Lord loves. He who obeys her judges nations; he who hearkens to her dwells in her inmost chambers." Wisdom will dress her followers in her own royal and priestly robes: "Her fetters will be your throne of majesty; her bonds, your purple cord. You will wear her as your robe of glory, bear her as your splendid crown" (VI: 30-31).

In the light of these prerogatives of Wisdom, which are offered to men, we might well add to these references that of the man who is filled with divine Wisdom, and invites others to come and hear:

> When I was young and innocent, I sought wisdom before all else. In prayer I begged for her, and from my youth I followed after her. She was rich like ripening grapes; in her was my heart's joy. My feet were steadfast in her path; thus I attained to her at last. For a short time I paid heed, and I acquired great instruction.... (Sir. LI: 13-16)

> Come to me, you who need instruction, and take your place in my school; how long will you be deprived of what you need, how long will your souls remain so sorely parched?... gain, at no cost, wisdom for yourselves. Submit yourselves to her yoke, let your souls bear her weight, for she is close to those who seek her. (Sir. LI: 23-26)

It seems hardly necessary to remark that this passage is obviously inspired by the description of the Messianic Banquet of Isaia LV: 1-6. This passage of Isaia was the source of the images of thirst (v. I), of receiving without money (v. 2), and of God who is close and may be found (v. 6).

The Alexandrian Book of Pseudo-Solomon (Wisdom) is in the same tradition, except that the author combines the praise of Wisdom and of himself. His repeated invitations to kings,[51] "Hear; learn; hearken; desire my words" (VI: 1; 2; 11) are based on two points: the sovereign excellence of divine Wisdom, depositary of all blessings, and also the fact that Wisdom has been given to him, and has given him universal knowledge.

JOHN VI

LITERARY RELATIONSHIP BETWEEN THE FOURTH GOSPEL AND THE WISDOM LITERATURE

Because there is such a close relationship between the fourth Gospel and the Wisdom Literature, we might be led *a priori* to suspect that there would be a connection between John's Discourse on the Bread of Life and the sapiential tradition.

---

51 The author (or pseudo-author), being a king himself, can address himself to kings as to equals.

If the Prologue is to be explained at least in part by the Old
Testament theology of the Word of God, and by primitive Christianity's treatment of the Word which comes from Jesus and has
Jesus for its object; then it is at least equally correct, if not more
so, to think of the development by the wisdom writers, of
divine Wisdom, personified, and, as it were, hypostatized, medi-
ating in the work of creation, and of the salvation of men. Prov.
VIII, Sir. XXIV, and John's Prologue, have the same general
structure; the pre-existence of Wisdom, or of the Logos; their
role in creation and their soteriological role. Wisdom plants her
tent in Israel (Sir. XXIV: 8: *en Iakōb kateskēnōsen*); the incarnate Word dwells amongst us (*eskēnōsen en hymin* I: 14). When
John contrasts the Law and the Logos incarnate (I: 17), could
we say that he is correcting Sirach, which identifies Wisdom and
the Law (XXIV: 23)?[52]

It is beyond dispute that there is a sapiential character to
the Christology of John's Discourse account. Thus the sending
of the Son by the Father, rarely mentioned in the Synoptics,
but common in John, recalls the sending of Wisdom in Pseudo-
Solomon (IX: 9-10).

Like divine Wisdom, (Sir. XXIV: 3; cf. Ep. of St. James, III:
15; 17), Jesus is from on high, (cf. III: 31; VIII: 23, and perhaps
also XIX: 11.[53] There is considerable controversy [54] over the
meaning of the antithesis of heavenly things-earthly things in
III: 12. However, it seems good to maintain, with Lagrange,[55]
that it is related to Wis. IX: 16-17, which mentions the revelation
which Wisdom has brought to the world: "And scarce do we
guess the things on earth, and what is within our grasp we

---

52 Cfr. C. SPICQ, *Le Siracide et la structure littéraire du prologue
de saint Jean*, in *Mémorial Lagrange*, Paris, 1940, pp. 183-195; F.
BÜCHSEL, *Johannes und der hellenistische Sinkretismus*, Gütersloh, 1928,
pp. 30-36.

53 Perhaps we could interpret XIX: 11 thus, "Thou wouldst have
no power over me, if it were not given thee from on high" (implying
"because I am from on high"). Cf. our study, *L'Heure de Jésus et le
Signe de Cana*, in *Eph. Theol. Lov.*, 1960, p. 9, note 11; cf. also above,
ch. I, note.

54 H. VAN DEN BUSSCHE sees in this antithesis the traditional
opposition between the present realities already revealed at the moment
in which Jesus speaks, and the eschatological realities, *Évangile Du Verbe*,
(*Jean* 1-4). Brussels - Paris, 1953, p. 64.

55 *Évangile selon saint Jean*, Paris, 1927, p. 79.

find with difficulty; but when things are in heaven, who can search them out? Or who ever knew your counsel, except you had given Wisdom, and sent your holy spirit from on high?" Baruch asks: "Who has gone up to the heavens and taken her, or brought her down from the clouds?" (III: 29), and Jesus tells Nicodemus: "No one has ascended to heaven except him who has descended from heaven; the Son of Man who is in heaven" (III: 13). In Jo. VII: 34 (also in VIII: 21) the words: "You will seek me and will not find me" are, as Mollat says,[56] nothing more than the repetition of a threat against the chosen people. The contrary of this theme occurs in the prophetic writings (Osee III: 5; V: 6; 15; Jer. XXIX: 13; Is. LI: I; LXV: I; Zach. VIII: 21-22; cf. also Mt. VII: 7-8), and comes up in the Canticle of Canticles, of which it is one of the basic themes. The phrase is reproduced in Prov. I: 28, in the passage in which divine Wisdom personified plays the role of a prophetic preacher, threatening to abandon to their hate her rebellious hearers. The context, therefore, is entirely similar to that of John VI.

It is with the same presuppositions that we should read the reply made by Christ a little farther on (VIII: 25), to the Jews who ask Him who He is: *Tēn archēn ho ti kai lalō hymin.* This text has been translated a number of different ways.[57] When we recall that the word *archē* taken from the sapiential texts, has an important function in johannine Christology (John I: 1-2; I Jo. I: I; II: 13-14), we may be tempted to see here a Christological teaching of the same kind, but veiled, like a sort of enigma, of which there are so many in the fourth Gospel, i.e., those texts of which the meaning becomes clear only with the later development of revelation ("I am" since the beginning,

56 *L'évangile et les épîtres de saint Jean,* Paris, 1953 (*Bible de Jérusalem*), p. 109, note b.

57 Many authors suppose that Jesus is speaking as if to ask whether He must continue the conversation, "Must I speak to you?" or "Why must I speak to you?" Such a translation is possible, but it would presuppose a Greek nuance quite unlikely in John, and the use of *archēn* in the sense of *holos,* which does not occur in the Bible. The better thing seems to be to depart from the Greek of the LXX, in which there are at least four instances of *tēn archēn* meaning "in the beginning" or "at first," Gen. XLI: 21; XLIII: 18 (17); 20 (19); Dan. IX: 21; cf. also Dan. VIII: 1 in the version of Theodotion. Cf. E. Hoskyns, *The Fourth Gospel According to St. John,* pp. 283-284.

that is, from always, who speak to you, cf. Wisdom, existing from the beginning, Sir. XXIV: 9 and Prov. VIII: 22).

As for the Discourse on the Bread of Life, it is good to note that Jesus insists therein on describing Himself as one descended from heaven, (vv. 33; 38; 41; 42; 50; 51; 58). Outside of ch. VI this occurs only in III: 13. What is the origin of this expression? The Synoptics do not have it explicitly. It is not because Jesus is the true manna that He can say He is descended from Heaven. The exact contrary is true; it is the descent from heaven of the Son of God by the Incarnation which justifies His being called the heavenly bread. It is true that Christ, bread of life, does not call Himself only Son (VI: 40), but that He takes to Himself the apocalyptic title of Son of Man, borrowed from Daniel, which was current in the Synoptic tradition. Although in the apocalyptic literature the eschatological realities come down from heaven, Daniel does not say that this is to be the case with the "Son of Man," who advances on the clouds toward the Ancient of Days. On the contrary, in the sapiential tradition, which we are sure is related to Daniel's apocalyptic Son of Man,[58] divine Wisdom comes down from the heights of heaven to dwell among men, and to guide them, especially Israel (cf. Sir. XXIV: Bar. III: 29-38; Wis. IX: 1-18).

JOHANNINE FORMULAS WITH "EGO EIMI"

Now we arrive at the question most closely related to our subject, that of the Johannine formulas with *"ego eimi,"* followed

---

58 Cfr. our study, *Le Fils de l'homme de Daniel et la tradition biblique,* in R. B., 1953, pp. 170-202 et 321-346. Cfr. in the same sense P. J. DE MENASCHE, Daniel (*Bible de Jérusalem*) 2d edit. Paris, 1958, pp. 21-22; R. LAURENTIN, *Structure et Théologie de Luc I-II*, Paris, 1957, pp. 132-133. A. Robert was very much inclined to interpret the Messianism of Daniel in this way, showing that it was well founded in later tradition, beginning with Henoch (the Son of Man in Henoch is obviously a heavenly being whose pre-existence is described as like that of Wisdom in Prov. XIII: 22 ff.; cf. esp. XLVIII: 3). Cf. A. Robert and A. Tricot, *Guide to The Bible*, (tr. by Arbez-McGuire), Paris, Tournai, Rome, New York, 1960, p. 512. The objections raised against this position by H. Kruse (*Verbum Domini* 1959, pp. 208-209) do not seem valid to us, since they tend toward a real misunderstanding of the profound

by some designation.[59] They proclaim eloquently Jesus' divinity, the ultimate source of men's salvation: "I am the bread that has come down from heaven" (VI: 35; 41; 48; 51); "the light of the world" (VIII: 12; IX: 5); "the door of the sheep" (X: 7; 9); "the good shepherd" (X: 11; 14); "the resurrection and the life" (XI: 25); "the true vine" (XV: 1-5).

Since this type of phraseology has no parallels in the Synoptic gospels, some have considered it as borrowed from hellenism or from the oriental religions, in which gods, kings and prophets emphasize their dignity by *ego eimi* followed by an attribute. We can cite as an example the hymn in honor of Isis, doubtless of Alexandrian origin,[60] and which Diodorus Siculus mentions in the inscription on the tomb of Isis and Osiris "in Arabia."

> I am (*ego eimi*) queen of all this region, taught by Hermes; there is none who can undo the laws which I have imposed. I am the beloved, the daughter of Kronos, youngest of the gods. I am the daughter and wife of King Osiris. I am the first to give fruit to men. I am the mother of King Horus. I am she who rises in the constellation of the Dog. (*Bibliotheca Historica*, I: 27).[61]

There are also the inscriptions and poems in honor of Isis on the islands of Ios,[62] on Andros,[63] and at the Egyptian sanctuary of Kyme on Eolis;[64] the prayer to Isis in *Papyr. Oxyr.* XI: 1380; the opening words of *Poimandres* "I am Poimandres, the *Nous*

---

relationship existing between the sapiential literature and traditional Jahwism, especially prophetic teaching. Cf. A. ROBERT, *Le Yahwisme de Prov. X: I XXII: 16; XXV-XXVI*, in *Mémorial Lagrange*, pp. 163-182.

59 On these phrases cfr. especially *T.W.N.T.* II, art. *egō* (Stauffer), pp. 341-349, E. SCHWEIZER, *Ego Eimi, Die religionsgeschichtliche Herkunft und theologische Bedeutung der johanneischen Bildreden, zugleich ein Beitrag zur Quellenfrage des vierten Evangeliums*, Göttingen, 1939; R. BULTMANN, *Das Evangelium des Johannes*, p. 167, note 2.

60 Cfr. P. ROUSSEL, *Un nouvel hymne à Isis*, in *Révue des Études*, Grecques, 1929, p. 144.

61 Cf. the original text of this inscription in A. DEISSMANN, *Lich vom Osten*, Tübingen, 1923, pp. 110-111. The author's French translation is that of LAGRANGE, *L'Évangile Selon Saint Jean*, p. CXLV.

62 Cf. DEISSMANN, op. cit., pp. 111-112.

63 Cfr. P. FOUCART, *Les Mystéres d'Éleusis*, Paris, 1914, p. 71.

64 Cfr. P. ROUSSEL, *Révue des Études Grecques*, 1929, p. 145.

of the absolute rule" (I: 12). Other examples of the same genre
of autodoxology exist in the Egyptian, Sumerian, Akkadic, and
Babylonian worlds.

There is plenty of reason for believing that John wishes to
reach the Greek world, or, as C. H. Dodd puts it, "the varied and
cosmopolitan society of a great Hellenistic city such as Ephesus
under the Roman Empire".[65] We can also agree with A. T. Robinson [66] that John writes, if not exclusively (which seems an exaggeration), at least principally, to bring the Faith to Jews of Greek
culture living in the Diaspora. Could one doubt that John's
repeated use of the *"ego eimi"* phraseology on the lips of Jesus,
is due to some sort of influence of the Hellenistic milieu, in
which he is living and to which he is directing his gospel?

Whatever be the answer to these questions, the idea is the
important thing, and there can be no doubt that it is basically
and specifically biblical. Against Norden, K. Kundsin [67] has
shown that the discourses which reveal John's Christ are distinguished by their structure from all parallels in the oriental
religions. Instead of having as their only purpose the glorification
of the one speaking them by accumulating grandiose titles of
honor, the *"ego eimi"* formulas and other related phrases in the
fourth Gospel, all of them strikingly brief, are intended only as
a basis for the promises of salvation. This is why they are usually
followed by a second proposition, often the principal one, indicating the condition on which salvation is offered to the believer
(VI: 33; 51; VIII: 12; X: 9; XI: 25; XV: 25; XVIII: 37). Here
too are the structured developments of the Old Testament on
Wisdom personified, Prov. VIII: 12-21; Sir. XXIV: 1-21. They
also have no purpose other than to make men desire a share in
the salvific blessings which Jahweh offers them through the
mediation of His Wisdom.

Possibly Kundsin exaggerates the contrast between the sapiential and Johannine texts, and the autodoxologies of the hellenistic and oriental cults, in which there is often mention, although

---

65 *The Interpretation of the Fourth Gospel,* p. 9.

66 *The Destination and Purpose of St. John's Gospel,* in *N. T. Stud.,*
January 6, 1960, pp. 117-131.

67 *Charakter und Ursprung der Johanneischen Reden,* in *Acta Universitatis Latviensis. Theologijay Fakultates Serija,* Riga, 1939, t. I,
No. 4, pp. 185-293.

only in a secondary way, of the good of men.[68] For our purpose
there it is important simply to note the presence in the fourth
Gospel of a style of revelation already characteristic of the wisdom literature.

"I AM THE BREAD OF LIFE"

We should pay special attention to the three *"ego eimi"*
formulas in the Discourse on the Bread of Life (VI: 35; 48-50; 51).
They are all accompanied by an invitation to believe in Jesus,
to come to Him, to eat of this heavenly bread, which is Himself.
In this way they resemble closely the development of Prov.
VIII: IX and Sir. XXIV, where the praise which Wisdom makes
of herself (Prov. VIII: 12; 17; Sir. XXIV: 16; 17) is invariably
followed by an invitation to listen, to come to her, to be fed by
her. "So now, O children, listen to me" (Prov. VIII: 32); "Come
to me, all you that yearn for me, and be filled with my fruits"
(Sir. XXIV: 18). Bultmann sees the johannine phrase "come to,"
which he also relates to Sir. XXIV: 18, (cf. IV: 15; VI: 18) as
the typical way in which Jesus calls to souls.[69] The phrase is frequent in John VI (vv. 35; 37; 44; 65). Cf. also Peter's question
in v. 69, "Lord, to whom shall we go?"

Christ's words in v. 35, "I am the bread of life; he who comes
to me shall not hunger, and he who believes in me shall never
thirst," recall especially Sir. XXIV: 18-20: "Come to me, all you
that yearn for me, and be filled with my fruits"... He who eats
of me will hunger still; he who drinks of me will thirst for more."
Although at first glance there might seem to be an opposition
here, there clearly is no contradiction; Wisdom's followers will

---

68 Cfr. H. BECKER, *Die Reden des Johannesvangeliums und der
Stil der gnostischen Offenbarungsrede*, Göttingen, 1956, pp. 48-49, note.
R. Bultmann's book is partly intended to be a refutation of the thesis
of K. Kundsin. Bultmann supposes that the fourth Gospel is made up
from various sources, among which are a collection of signs (Sēmeia-
Quelle), and of revelation discourses (Offenbarungsreden). H. Becker,
who writes to justify the existence of this latter collection, offers some
valid points, although his thesis is dubious in itself. Especially pp. 41-59
propose an analysis of the revelation discourses of Prov. and Sirach. Becker,
who cites and discusses the studies of A. Robert, recognizes also the
striking similarities between these Old Testament discourses and the fourth
Gospel.

69 Cfr. *Das Johannes-Evangelium*, p. 168, note 4; p. 228, note 7.

always hunger and thirst because it offers a food which never satisfies. Jesus' followers will have no hunger or thirst, because their Master, giving them Himself, in the mystery of the Eucharist, is capable of satisfying all their religious aspirations.

A further step will bring us to see the reason why the johannine formula is different from that of Sirach. It is because the johannine formula is also a recollection of Deutero-Isaia's prediction of the new Exodus, in which the repatriates will neither hunger nor thirst, an image applicable also to the Messianic Banquet (Isaia LV: I; LXV: 13).

Thus the text of John VI: 35 is, as it were, the synthesis of the complementary themes of the eschatological banquet and of Wisdom's Banquet; the complete satisfaction of hunger and thirst gives it a clearly eschatological color; it remains certain, therefore, that the nearest parallel text is Sir. XXIV: 20.

THE ALLEGORY OF THE VINE

The allegory of the vine (XV: 1ff) confirms the sapiential background of John's teaching on the Eucharist. We might go so far as to say that this allegory has a eucharistic meaning; Christ the true vine, and Christ whose blood is the wine, the drink of the new Covenant. The themes are closely related (cf. Cana; Mk. XIV: 25 and parallel texts). The mutual indwelling of Christ and His disciples, indicated by the verb *meno*, is, in VI: 56, the fruit of the reception of the Eucharist; this idea of mutual indwelling, always with *meno*, recurs often in John XV: 1-11 (vv. 4; 5; 6; 7; 9; 10), and nowhere else in the fourth Gospel. We could also mention here that the ancient eucharistic prayer of the Didache (IX: 2) thanks the Father "for the holy vine of David".[70]

The usual form of exegesis relates John's allegory of the vine with those Old Testament passages in which this same image refers to the chosen people (Is. V: 7; XXVII: 2-4; Jer. II: 21; V: 10; XLVIII: 32; XLIX: 9; Ez. XV). Quite certainly the synoptic parallels relative to the vine (the murderous vine-dressers, Mk. XII: 1-11 and parallel texts; the workmen sent

---

70 On the eucharistic significance of the allegory of the vine, cf. O. CULLMANN, *Les sacrements dans l'évangile johannique*, Paris, 1951, pp. 78-79; H. VAN DEN BUSSCHE, *Le discours d'adieu*, Paris-Maredsous, 1959, p. 102.

into the vineyard, Mt. XXI: 1-16) have this origin; like the Old
Testament texts, they too point an accusing finger at the chosen
people. Hence they are related in this way. However, Lagrange,
Bernard, Bultmann, Bauer, E. Schweizer [71] doubt that this passage, which in some ways recalls Ez. XV: 4-5 (the wood and
the vine thrown on the fire), could hardly be said to have no
source *other* than the prophetic texts mentioned above. In effect,
egō eimi hē ampelos hē alēthinē is a formula of revelation,
just as in *ego eimi ho artos tēs zōēs*. Bultmann remarks that,
given the way in which Jesus uses the vine symbol here, He
could well have said, "I am the vine of life," just as He once said,
"I am the bread of life."

In the Old Testament the vine as Israel is deliberately never
presented as the source of life. For this reason Bultmann and
Schweizer propose some Mandean parallels.[72] However, we prefer
to content ourselves with those parallels which we find within
the confines of the Old Testament. In Sirach the same image of
the vine, which the prophets used in reference to the chosen
people, is applied to Wisdom, and this in the same passage in
which we discovered a remote foretaste of the mystery of the
Eucharist:

> I bud forth delights like the vine, by blossoms become
> fruit fair and rich. Come to me, all you that yearn for
> me, and be filled with my fruits; you will remember me
> as sweeter than honey, better to have than the honey-
> comb. He who eats of me will hunger still; he who drinks
> of me will thirst for more. (Sir. XXIV: 17-20)

---

71 Cf. Lagrange, *Évangile selon saint Jean*, p. 401; BERNARD, *The
Gospel according to St. John*, vol. II, pp. 477-478; Bultmann, *Das Evangelium des Johannes*, pp. 406-407; Bauer, *Das Johannes-Evangelium*,
p. 189; Schweizer, *Egō Eimi*, pp. 39-40.

72 On these proposed mandaean parallels, cf. the work of E. PERCY,
Untersuchungen über den Ursprung der Johanneischen Theologie, Lund,
1939. Percy examines the allegory of the vine in pp. 229-236, showing
that, if we compare the ideas carefully on both sides, the analogies with
Mandaism are practically non-existent. The book is excellent for its refutation
of apparent similarities, but questionable and even deceiving with regard
to the real sources of johannine thought. Percy has virtually no awareness
of the importance of the wisdom literature in this regard.

THE DISCIPLES OF CHRIST IN JOHN, AND THE DISCIPLES OF WISDOM

From what we have said it should be evident that for John the disciples of Christ are similar to the disciples of divine Wisdom, as they are described in the sapiential texts, even though these writings refer to the "children" of Wisdom, rather than to her "disciples."

This is true especially of Sirach (Ecclesiasticus): "This book frequently adopts metaphors related to generation, using them to describe the relationship which exists between the disciples and their master ... and between Wisdom and her disciples".[73] For disciples of Wisdom, cf. Prov. VIII: 32; Sir. IV: 11; for disciples of the master, cf. Prov. I: 8; 10; 15; III: 1; 11-21; IV: 1; VI: 18; 21; 32; X:28; XIV: 11; 24; XVIII: 15.

A. Robert [74] lists the precedents for this practice, in the deuteronomic and prophetic literature; Jahweh calls the Jews His children, especially in passages in which He is pictured as their teacher (cf. Dt. I: 31; VIII: 5; Osee XI: 1-4; Is. I: 2; Jer. III: 14-15). An interesting passage in Sirach describes the way in which divine Wisdom forms her disciples, beginning with a test, and then gradually revealing her secrets to them:

> Wisdom instructs her children and admonishes those who seek her.... Those who love her the Lord loves.... If one trusts her he will possess her; his descendants too will inherit her. She walks with him as a stranger, and at first she puts him to the test; fear and dread she brings upon him and tries him with her discipline; with her precepts she puts him to the proof, until his heart is fully with her. Then she comes back to bring him happiness, and reveals her secrets to him. (IV: 11; 14; 16; 18)

In the fourth Gospel Jesus, like Wisdom, calls His disciples His *"little children"* (XIII: 33, *teknia*; cf. I John II: 1; 12; 28; III: 7; 18; IV: 4; V: 21). According to Bultmann, this is the ordinary language which would be common between a teacher and his pupils (*die Anrede des Lehrers an die Schuler*); Bult-

---

73 *Bible de la Pléiade, Ancien Testament,* vol. II, p. 1716, note on III, 1.

74 R. B., 1934, p. 49.

mann,[75] following Strack-Billerbeck, emphasizes the point by showing parallel texts in the rabbinical literature. However, we are inclined to prefer the parallels listed above, from the sapiential and prophetic texts.

Once He has purified His disciples by His Word (XIII: 10; XV: 3), and has judged them worthy of His confidence, Jesus, like Wisdom, reveals His secrets to them, as to friends (XV: 15); this is the whole burden of the discourse following the Last Supper. To "love Wisdom" is to keep her laws (Wis. VI: 18); Jesus says the same thing in virtually the same words: "He who has my commandments and keeps them, he it is who loves me" (XIV: 21). He adds, "He who loves me will be loved by my Father." Sirach, in its turn, says, "Those who love her the Lord loves" (IV: 14). Proverbs has, "Those who love me I also love" (VIII: 17). "This beautiful thought," says A. Robert, "seems to be a foretelling of the mysticism of the fourth Gospel." Still, we need to keep in mind the limits of the Old Testament revelation, if we are to appreciate the fullness of· that of the New Testament, which John exemplifies.

As we said above, Wisdom shares with her disciples her own special prerogatives. She is like the trees and the aromatic plants (Sir. XXIV: 13-17); her disciples are like roses, opening their petals, like roses planted near running water, sending up a sweet odor like that of incense (Sir. XXXIX: 13-14). Wisdom is identified with the Law, and compared to the great rivers which give out their life-giving waters in numberless rivulets (Sir. XXIV: 25-27). Then, in the next few verses, Sirach himself, who presents himself as having attended Wisdom's school, speaks of himself as pouring out his instruction upon generations to come (vv. 30-31). The same idea occurs in John VII: 27-28, if we admit that Jesus here presents Himself as the source of living water, speaking of the streams of living water which are to flow from His disciples. We should be cautious here, however, since the interpretation of this passage remains subject to considerable controversy, even at present.[76]

---

75 *Das Evangelium des Johannes*, p. 402, note 5.

76 In our treatment in *Introduction à la Bible*, tome II, p. 897, we have preferred the interpretation according to which the living water flows, not from within the believer, but from within the Messiah, according to the promise which Jesus makes in IV: 10, 14. This exegesis is becoming more and more widespread, especially after the study by H. RAHNER,

How remarkable it is, that the God of the Judeo-Christian revelation can unite Himself to His people, in the most intimate way conceivable, without compromising in the least the basic distinction between the Creator and His creatures! Divine Wisdom also promises to reveal herself to men, and to come to dwell in their midst (Wis. I: 4; VI: 13; 16). This refers, of course, not to all men, but to those who love her; "Wisdom will not come (*ouk eiseleusetai sophia*) into an evil soul, or dwell (*ouk katoikesei*) in a body given to sin" (V: 4). Sirach says, "Wisdom shows herself to few" (VI: 22). Jesus also gives to those who love Him, a hope that He will show Himself to them (not to the world), and that He will come with the Father to dwell in their hearts (XIV: 21-23). It is precisely in this context of intimacy and mutual friendship, brought about between God and poor humans, who are to become His disciples, that we should see both Wisdom and John's Christ, promising to give themselves as the food of souls.

JESUS AND WISDOM IN THE SYNOPTICS

The Synoptics could well be a preparation bringing us to a fuller appreciation of the riches which the wisdom writings bring us to discover in the fourth Gospel. This question should be all the more interesting, since our answer to it is somewhat new. The late A. Robert used to say that Old Testament commentators have failed to appreciate the proper value of the wisdom writings.

Flumina de ventre Christi, Die patristische Auslegung von Joh. VII, 37-38, in *Biblica,* 1941, pp. 269-302; 367-403. Cf. also M. E. BOISMARD, *De son ventre couleront des fleuves d'eau* in *R. B.,* 1958, pp. 523-546. The opposite interpretation (the former cited above) cannot be based upon a parallelism with IV: 14, because in this text of Chapter IV there is question only of living water given to the believer as a powerful source "springing unto eternal life," and not as a communication to others of the living water which is identified with the Holy Spirit. Throughout the New Testament only the Father and Jesus can give men the gift of the Spirit. Neither the Hebrew nor Greek Bibles, nor the targumin give the origin of the quotation in VII: 38. Yet the origin ceases to be problematic when we consult the parallel text in Apocalypse XXII: 1ff. The river of the water of life is here clearly a reference to the river which comes forth from the Temple in Ez. XLVII: 1ff. (cf. Apoc. XII: 2) and of the living waters flowing from Jerusalem in Zach. XIV: 8 (recalled in Apocalypse XXII: 3).

One could say the same of the relationship between these texts and those of the New Testament. So far this relationship has hardly been noticed.

In particular, very few have noticed the hidden allusions in the Synoptics to the relationship between Jesus and Wisdom. The very fact that these allusions have been discussed seem to us to put the fact of their existence beyond question. However, it is certainly a matter of more than several similarities in vocabulary and themes.

We mention only in passing an obscure text of two traditions, that Wisdom is justified by her children, according to Lk. VII: 35, and, according to the best attested reading of Mt. XI: 35, by her works. We have discussed elsewhere [77] the meaning of this passage with regard to its context. It seems, as Loisy says, that Wisdom here represents Jesus; "If they are not to be formally identified, then at least Jesus is the organ of its complete manifestation".[78]

Deserving of more extended consideration are Jesus' words of woe over Jerusalem:

> Jerusalem, Jerusalem, thou who killest the prophets and stonest those who are sent to thee! How often would I have gathered thy children together, as a hen gathers her young under her wings, but thou wouldst not! Behold, your house *is* left to you desolate.[79] For I say to you, you shall not see me henceforth until you shall say, 'Blessed is he who comes in the name of the Lord!' "
> (Mt. XXIII: 37-39; Lk. XIII: 34-35)

Following Reitzenstein, Bultmann relates this passage to the one recalling the myth of divine Wisdom, which, after having dwelt among men and called them in vain, takes her leave and returns whence she came forth.[80] This myth would be associated

---

77 *Jésus et la Sagesse divine d'après les évangiles synoptiques*, in R. B., 1955, pp. 164-168.

78 *Les évangiles synoptiques*, Ceffonds, 1907, t. I, p. 679. Cfr. in the same sense *The Interpreter's Bible*, vol. VII, New York, 1951, p. 385.

79 Many texts omit *erēmos* in Matthew, but this may be an attempt to harmonize with Luke.

80 *Die Geschichte der synoptischen Tradition*, Göttingen, 1957, pp. 120-121.

with that of the *Urmensch*, because, ultimately, it is a question
of the reappearance of the Messiah, in view of the judgment:
"You shall not see me henceforth until you shall say, 'Blessed
is he who comes in the name of the Lord'."

It seems sure to us that these words of Christ recall at one
time the themes of Wisdom and of the Son of Man, synthesizing
in this way the sapiential and apocalyptic traditions.[81] However,
Bultmann has not shown at all that these could not be together
on the lips of Christ living on earth. Neither has he proven
that the biblical themes of Wisdom and of the Son of Man are
merely so many extensions of the pagan myths. He has seen at
least that this statement has an air of mystery about it, and that
He who pronounces it belongs to another world. It recalls those
Old Testament passages in which Jahweh, the savior of His
people, is compared to an eagle or a bird (Dt. XXXII: 11; Is.
XXX: 5; Ps. XXXVI: 8), and those in which Israel is threatened
with abandonment by God, e. gr. Jer. XII: 7: "I abandon my
house, I cast off my heritage." Even more, it recalls the eschatological threats uttered by divine Wisdom when she is rejected,[82]
esp. Prov. I: 24-28, which we cited above to explain John VII: 34
and VIII: 21.

> Because I called and you refused, I extended my hand
> and no one took notice; because you disdained my counsel,
> and my reproof you ignored—I, in my turn, will laugh
> at your doom; I will mock when terror comes upon you
> like a storm, and your doom approaches like a whirlwind;

---

81 Following T. ARVEDSON (*Das Mysterium Christi. Eine Studie
zu Mt. XI, 25-30*, Uppsala, 1937, p. 211), we might note that the image
of the mother hen protecting her young serves very well to describe
the maternal concern of Wisdom (cf. Sirach XIV: 26; Wis. VII: 12;
VIII: 2; 9. Luke XI: 49 seems to indicate that the words of Jesus in
Matthew XXIII: 34-36 are taken from a lost text describing Wisdom,
which would also be the source of Matthew XXIII: 37-39. Such a hypothesis would explain this image well.

82 Some authors speak of identifying Jesus with the *Shekinah*, which
goes out of the temple, leaving it deserted (which would be the equivalent
of "you shall see me no longer." However, Th. Preiss observes that
"Wisdom and *Shekinah* are rather fluid and closely related hypostases,
rather than distinct entities" (*Le Fils de l'homme*, in *Études Théologiques
et Religieuses*, Montpellier, 1953, no. 1, p. 73).

when distress and anguish befall you. Then they call me, but I answer not; they seek me, but find me not....

We find a similar element in the account of the healing of the demoniac; this time, furthermore, we have the advantage of seeing the incident related by all three Synoptics, and centered directly on the disciples, who have been unable to expel a demon: "O unbelieving generation," cries Jesus, lamenting their lack of faith, "how long shall I be with you? How long shall I put up with you?" (Mk. IX: 19; Lk. IX: 41; Mt. XV: 11; 17). Lagrange writes, "In themselves the words are not merely those of a man among men; they express the sentiment of a divine being, who, naturally, lives in heaven".[83] Windisch [84] emphasizes the distance separating the woes of the prophets, as for example, those of Elias, who, placed in a similar situation, wishes only to die (I Kgs. XIX: 4), from the woe of Christ, who comes as a stranger to our world, and wishes anxiously to return to His rightful place. Everything goes along as if He wished to return to heavenly glory which He has enjoyed on the mount of the Transfiguration (The scene to which we refer here comes immediately after that of the Transfiguration).

Windisch recalls, in this regard, Horace's second Ode, in which the poet prays that Hermes-Mercury, who has come among the Romans in the person of Augustus in order to avenge the murder of Caesar, may not be influenced by the crimes of the sons of Romulus, to return too hastily to heaven, but may continue to dwell among them:

> Serus in caelum redeas diuque
> Laetus intersis populo Quirini
> Neque te nostris vitiis iniquum
> Ocior aura tollat!   (Od. I: 2)

Rather than this pagan piece, or than the ending of Ovid's Metamorphoses (XV: 867ff.) we would prefer to cite the passage of Prov. I: 20-33, of which we have given some verses just above; Wisdom threatens to abandon those who refuse to follow her.

---

83 *Évangile selon saint Luc*, p. 277.

84 *Theologisch Tijdschrift, 1918, Urchristentum und Hermesmystik*, pp. 215-218.

We should cite again the reproaches directed toward the Jews because of their having rejected God's envoys. Jesus makes these reproaches His own. At least, this is the case in Mt. XXIII: 33-34. However, we must remember, following Lagrange, that the text appears here in a setting which is more primitive than that of Luke. In Matthew there is a reference to prophets, wise men and scribes, all of them consecrated terms among the Jews. Luke speaks rather of prophets and apostles, evincing his inclination to use a vocabulary meaningful to Christian readers.

Matthew's text is as follows: "Serpents, brood of vipers, how are you to escape the judgment of hell? Therefore, behold, I send you prophets, and wise men, and scribes; and some of them you will put to death, and crucify, and some of them you will scourge in your synagogues, and persecute from town to town." The language is surprising; Christ's envoys are associated here with the Old Testament prophets. Christ bewails the maltreatment of His apostles in terms which recall the words of Jahweh in Jer. VII: 25: "I have sent you my servants, the prophets, but you have not listened to them" (cf. also Jer. XXV: 14; XXVI: 5; XXIX: 19; XXXV: 15). Likewise, the punishment which shall come upon the persecutors of the chosen envoys recalls passages such as 2 Kgs. IX: 7-8: "And I will revenge the blood of my servants the prophets, and the blood of all the servants of the Lord, at the hand of Jezabel, and I will destroy the house of Achab."

The relationship between these Old Testament reproaches and those of the New Testament is forceful; in the Old Testament the prophets are Jahweh's servants *par excellence;* Wisdom in its turn has its servants (Prov. IX: 1-6); and, in the New Testament, the apostles are called, in their turn, servants of Jesus.

Luke's Gospel only serves to confirm this conclusion, offering, singularly enough, this same complaint, but on the lips of Wisdom personified, instead of on those of Jesus: "For this reason also the wisdom of God has said, I will send them prophets and apostles; and some of them they will put to death and persecute" (XI: 49). Many have suggested that this may be a citation from a lost Jewish text. Bultmann holds this opinion, basing it on the introductory formula and the use of the verb *eipen.* Thus Luke would be attesting the source of the quotation. Matthew, on the other hand, would offer the best preserved rendering of the primitive form. Matthew's *prophetas kai sophous kai grammateis* is preferable to Luke's future tense. Finally, the reference to Jerusalem, which we have studied above, and which Matthew places immediately after this text, would be part of the same citation. Luke's changed context is, therefore, less reliable, although Bultmann considers it possible that Jesus Himself may have made the citation.

This hypothesis, although by no means universally accepted,[85] nevertheless has merit.[86] It shows Jesus identifying Himself with Wisdom. He is the sender of the Christian missionaries, whom the Jews will persecute.[87] It also provides us with another *rapprochement* between the apocalyptic and sapiential traditions. The *sophia tou Theou* and the Son of Man, who is to return at the end of time (Mt. XXIII: 39, *ho erchomenos*) are one and the same person. It is therefore not without reason that Reitzenstein [88] thinks that there is here a perspective extending through all of Jewish history, from the beginning up to the time of Christ. It is in thinking of this part that Christ (Wisdom) could truly say, *posakis ēthelēsa episynagagein ta tekna sou.*

---

85 According to many critics the matthean text which credits Jesus Himself with sending the prophets, is so typically Jewish in form that it is very probably original. On the other hand, however, they also have great respect for Luke's placing the reproach against Jerusalem in a different context. Cf. T. W. MANSON, *The Sayings of Jesus*, London, 1954, p. 102; W. G. KÜMMEL, *Verheissung und Erfüllung*, Zürich, 1956, pp. 73-75.

86 Also favorable to this hypothesis are A. HARNACK, *Sprüche und Reden Jesu*, Leipzig, 1907, p. 72; R. REITZENSTEIN, *Das mandaische Buch des Herrn der Grösse und die Evangelienüberlieferung*, Heidelberg, 1918, p. 44. REITZENSTEIN corrected himself later on, however (cf. *ZNW*, 26, 1927, p. 55, note 1). Matthew's introduction is original, but the words have been attributed to Wisdom because they seemed strange on Jesus' lips in this circumstance.

87 If the best translation of Luke II: 49 is "Did you not know that I must be about my father's business?", and if we accept these words as an allusion to the eschatological manifestation of God's glory in the Temple of Jerusalem, then we see that Luke is consistent in attributing to Jesus the language of Wisdom. Cf. R. Laurentin, *Structure et Théologie de Luc I-II*, Paris, 1957, pp. 141-146.

88 *Das mandaische Buch des Herrn der Grösse*, pp. 42-43. Cf. also BULTMANN, *Der religionsgeschichtliche Hintergrund des Prologs zum Johannesevangelium*, in *Eucharistērion Hermann Gunkel dargebracht*, 2 Teil, Göttingen, 1923, pp. 6-7. Even without agreeing with Bultmann on the formation of St. John's prologue, one might see, as he does, in Matthew XXIII: 37 and Luke XIII: 34, a sort of outlined reference to the prologue.

In any case, this exclamation is surprising, if we consider the point of view of the Synoptics, who record only one "journey" of Jesus to Jerusalem.

However, we are not prepared to say that this is the only acceptable exegesis of the passage.[89] It is not necessary, for one thing, to suppose a citation from a lost work. We can see the scene set in Wisdom, either explicitly (Luke) or implicitly (Matthew). Thus Jesus alludes to texts such as Wis. VII: 27, in which divine Wisdom is presented as transforming men into prophets, and, above all, Prov. IX: 1-6, where Wisdom is shown sending her servants, who can be none other than the prophets.

That Jesus may have accorded some attention to this last passage is evident from at least one of His parables (Mt. XIII: 1-24; Lk. XIV: 15-24), which uses the theme of the Messianic Banquet; the master sends his servants to invite the guests, saying that all is prepared for the feast. Such is exactly the case in Prov. IX: 1-6; we might add that, according to H. Renand[90] in each case it is the least desirable who come to enjoy the banquet. In Prov. they are the simple, those who lack understanding; in the Gospel they are the sinners, rejected by the Pharisees.

As for the Acts of Thomas, which mention a wedding banquet at which the soul becomes united to Wisdom, we consider it arbitrary to hold, as does Arvedson,[91] that this idea of Wisdom's marriage is at the base of Prov. IX, and that in Matthew's parable (which is the only one to speak of a wedding banquet; Luke mentions simply a great supper), Jesus takes the place of Wisdom. We might say only that the Savior probably had this Old Testament passage in mind, and that Wisdom's banquet becomes in the Synoptics the messianic wedding banquet of the Son of God.

Need we mention that the banquet parable, recalling Wisdom's Banquet in the Old Testament, announces in its turn the

---

89 According to many exegetes, these passages indicate that even the Synoptics saw Jesus as coming to Jerusalem a number of times during the course of His ministry.

90 *Sainte Bible* (Pirot), Paris, 1943, Tome VI, p. 81. Whereas Luke speaks of a single servant being sent, Matthew writes "He sent his servants to call in those invited." Some suggest that Matthew's text was influenced by Prov. IX: 3: "She has sent out her maidens," Cf. McNEILE, *St. Matthew*, p. 314.

91 *Das Mysterium Christi*, pp. 214 sq.

eucharistic banquet? Jesus, in sending His apostles as servants to prepare for the Last Supper (Mk. XIV: 12-16 and parallel texts), performs a gesture of messianic implication (cf. the messianic triumph of the palm procession, and the preparation for it, Mt. XI: 1-6 and parallel texts). Thus both Prov. IX and the gospel parables of the banquet begin to be fulfilled, and we see once again the basic harmony existing between John and the Synoptics.

THE JOHANNINE LOGION

We would cite still more texts,[92] but we prefer to go directly to the passage which is, beyond a doubt, the most interesting, usually referred to as the Johannine Logion because of its relationship to the Christology of the fourth Gospel. However, we have presented elsewhere [93] a lengthy study of this text, and so we will limit ourselves here to presenting some conclusions.

Both Matthew (XI: 25-28) and Luke (X: 21-22) render this hymn of jubilation in almost the same terms, but with this difference, that Matthew has it in three verses, 25-26; 27; 28), whereas Luke has it in only two. Matthew's text adds, "Come to me, all you who labor," which seems to be a logical consequence of the intimate relationship existing between Christ and the Father ("No one knows the Father except the Son and him to whom the Son wishes to reveal him," XI: 27). Otherwise, as Dom Butler notes well,[94] both the first and last verses have this in common, that they are each an implicit criticism of the attitude of the pharisees. In effect, the wise and prudent to whom the Father refuses His light, are the scribes, who are full of contempt for the little ones, who burden down men's souls, "And they bind together heavy and oppressive burdens, and lay them on men's shoulders; but not with one finger of their own do they choose to move them" (Mt. XXIII: 4), whereas, on the contrary, Christ's yoke is sweet, and His burden light (Mt. XI: 30).

---

92 Cfr. Th. PREISS, *Jésus et la Sagesse,* in *Études Théologiques et Religieuses,* Montpellier, 1953, no. 1, pp. 67-75.

93 *Jésus et la Sagesse divine d'après les évangiles synoptiques, Le logion johannique et l'Ancien Testament,* in R. B., 1955, pp. 161-186.

94 *The Originality of St. Matthew,* Cambridge, 1951, p. 52.

This is to say that we agree with the many exegetes (Lagrange; Klostermann; Bacon; Dibelius; Creed; Schniewind; Dom Butler),[95] who consider the appeal to souls as proper to Matthew, as an integral part of the hymn of jubilation. If Luke has suppressed this verse, it is perhaps because of its Jewish tone, since the burdened and weary, to whom Jesus issues His invitation, are burdened and weary precisely because of the intolerable burden of the Law and the pharisaic observance of it. It may be also, Dibelius says,[96] because in Luke the hymn of jubilation serves as a conclusion to the mission of the seventy-two (or the sixty-six) disciples, in which context the last verse would be out of place.

Msgr. Cerfaux has rightly emphasized the apocalyptic coloring of this hymn,[97] which has several close relationships with Daniel. It is also worth emphasizing [98] that it is not merely a johannine text which found its way accidentally into the Synoptics. For one thing, the vocabulary is not typically johannine; furthermore, the ideas expressed in this passage have some partial parallels in the Synoptics (cf. especially Mt. XIII: II; XVI: 17; Lk. XXII: 29).

All this can be conceded, except that some aspects of the terminology (the reciprocal formula; the absolute use of *ho hyios* and *panta*, cf. John I: 3; III: 35; V: 20; XIII: 3; XV: 15; XVII: 7) recall the fourth Gospel.[99] Above all, we maintain, along with

---

95 Cf. E. NORDEN, *Agnostos Theos, Untersuchungen zur Formgeschichte religiöser Rede*, Leipzig - Berlin, 1913, pp. 277-308; Lagrange, *Évangile selon Saint Mattheiu*, Paris, 1941, p. 228; KLOSTERMANN, *Das Matthäusevangelium*, Tubingen, 1938, pp. 101-102; BACON, *The Gospel of Mark*, Its Composition and Date, New Haven, 1925, p. 250, note 1; DIBELIUS, *Die Formgeschichte des Evangeliums*, Tubingen, 1933, p. 280; CREED, *St. Luke*, Londres, 1953, p. 143; SCHNIEWIND, *Das Evangelium nach Matthäus*, p. 149; DOM BUTLER, *The Originality of St. Matthew*, p. 52.

96 *Die Formgeschichte des Evangeliums*, p. 280, note 1.

97 *Les sources scripturaires de Mt. XI: 25-30* in *Éph. Théol. Lov.*, 30 (1954), pp. 704-746; 31 (1955), pp. 331-342. Cfr. also H. MERTENS, *L'Hymne de jubilation chez les Synoptiques*, Gembloux, 1947; A. M. DENIS, *L'investiture apostolique par "apocalypse,"* in R. B., 1957, pp. 498-502.

98 *L'Evangile de Jean et le Logion Johannique des Synoptiques*, in *L'Evangile de Jean* (ouvrage collectif), 1958, pp. 147-159.

99 Cfr. B. NOACK, *Zur Johanneischen Tradition*, Copenhagen, 1954, pp. 60-61.

Norden, Lagrange, and many others, that the hymn of jubilation is related especially to the great Old Testament texts on divine Wisdom, which are the chief Old Testament source of John's Christology. This should hardly surprise us, since we have seen how in the Synoptics, and much more in John, Jesus refers to Himself as Wisdom. Also, Daniel's Son of Man speaks [100] but he is also divine Wisdom incarnate.

Clearly the Savior's call, "Come to me," which has a phraseology very like that of Sirach (VI: 24-28; XXIV: 19-28; LI: 23-27), recalls Wisdom's invitations to men. However, already in the first verse, the contrast between the wise (*sophoi*) and the little ones (*nēpioi*) is characteristic of the wisdom literature. It is true that these writings give this contrast a different meaning, but there are other cases in which Christ's message continues, and at the same time corrects, that of the Old Testament. We gather from these divergences, only that the words in question are not a mere application to Christ of an Old Testament reference, and that Jesus' message still preserves all of its originality.[101]

---

100 We think that *panta moi paredothē* is related primarily to Dan. VII: 14; and the universal royal power given to the Son of man (*edothē autō exousia*): compare the wording with Matthew XXVIII: 28; Luke IV: 6; John XVII: 2; 7. There is question here with the giving of a power, not of the passing on of a revelation. Cf. J. DUPONT, *Gnosis*, Louvain, 1949, p. 60; F. BUCHSEL, *T.W.N.T.*, II, art. *paradidōmi* p. 173; VAN SWIGGHEM, *De terugkeer van de 72*, in *Geref. Theolog. Tijdschrift*, 50 (1950), p. 155. However, we must keep the idea of knowledge which the text requires. We might see an explanation of *panta moi paredothē* in terms of John XVII: 2-3, in which, as BOISMARD remarks well, "It seems that the power which Christ exercises over all creatures is precisely that of giving the knowledge of God, the source of life." (R. B., 1958, p. 302). On the Sapiential nature of the last verse of Matthew, cf. G. LAMBERT "Mon joug est doux et mon fardeau léger," in *N. R. Th.* 1955, pp. 963-969.

101 The word *nēpios* (simple) belongs to the vocabulary of the sapiential literature (cf. Prov. I: 4; 22; 32; VII: 7; VIII: 5; IX: 4; 6; 16; XIV: 15; 18; XIX: 25; XXI: 11; XXII: 3; XXVII: 12; cf. also the sapiential psalms, especially XIX: 9 and CXIX: 30. This fact alone is sufficient to show that the apocalyptic literature cannot of itself explain this passage. In the sapiential writings the simple are the ignorant, the indelicate, and all those who have not learned true wisdom. Sometimes, however, the word has no pejorative connotation at all, as in Ps. CXVI: 6: "The Lord keeps the little ones; I was brought low and he saved me." In later Judaism the term takes on a religious meaning, that the simple are identified with the poor and humble, as in this passage from the *Habacuc Pesher*:

As for the second verse of the passage, which treats the mutual relationship of the Father and the Son, and in which the Father and the Son share the one divine mystery, it seems to us that this verse acts as a synthesis of the themes which they have in common with the wisdom texts: no one knows Wisdom except God; no one knows God except Wisdom. (For the first statement, cf. Job XXVIII: 24-26; Sir. I: 1-10; Prov. XXX: 2-6; Bar. III: 27-28; for the second, cf. Prov. VIII: 28-30; Wis. VIII: 3-4; IX: 9-18. Only this last, however, can rightly be called a parallel text.)

It seems evident that the case of Daniel, the only person initiated by God into the secrets (*mystēria*) which are unknown to the Chaldean wise men, (Dan. II: 20 ff.) is infinitely removed from that of Jesus, Son of God, who alone knows the Father and enjoys the power of revealing Him. The same can be said for Sirach, brought to receive the wisdom which he proposes to teach. Christ's relation to the Father is of a much higher order, recalling the divine Wisdom itself. One might compare also Mt. XI: 27 and the following texts from John, which have their prototypes in Old Testament affirmation referring to Wisdom: "No one has at any time seen God. The only begotten Son, who is in the bosom of the Father, he has revealed Him" (I: 18); "He who comes down from heaven is over all. And he bears witness to that which he has seen and heard.... For he whom God has sent speaks the words of God, for not by measure does God give the spirit. The Father loves the Son, and has given all things into his hand" (III: 31; 32; 34; 35); "Not that anyone has seen the Father except him who is from God, he has seen the Father" (VI: 46).

Certain conclusions seem inescapable; in the Synoptic hymn of jubilation, at least according to Matthew's rendering of it,

---

The statement refers to the wicked priests and means that God will mete out to him the treatment that he meted out to the needy. "Lebanon" stands here for the Communal Council, and "wild beasts" for the simple-minded Jews who carry out the Law (Torah) (1Qp Hab XII: 4).

Cf. E. Sjöberg, *Der verborgene Menschensohn in den Evangelien*, Lund. 1955, pp. 185-187. We might be inclined to agree with S. LÉGASSE, *La revelation aux nēpioi* in *R. B.*, 1960, pp. 321-348, that Jesus extends the realm of knowledge to the traditional poverty which is praised in the Scripture. Thus it is quite an original element in the polemic against the Jewish doctors, who are infatuated with their own knowledge of the Lord.

we see clearly the pattern which is characteristic of the discourses of Wisdom in the Old Testament and of Jesus in the fourth Gospel. There is the claim to titles of nobility, applied to a divine being (Wisdom–Christ), wishing to be heard by men; an urgent invitation to men to come and to be taught and fed. If it were necessary (as some critics maintain it is) to consider the last verse ("Come to me, all you who labor") to have been originally separate from the preceding context, it would still suffice by itself to show that Christ's invitations in the johannine Discourse on the Bread of Life are basically much closer to the Synoptics than we probably would have originally supposed.

(4) The Disciples of Christ According to the Synoptics and the Fourth Gospel

We have already had occasion frequently to compare the disciples of John's Christ with those of divine Wisdom. In both cases, the disciple is placed in such a state of dependence upon his master, that he must recur to him for his food. Such, of course, is precisely the essence of the mystery of the Eucharist, prepared in the Old Testament by the image of Wisdom's banquet.

We would like to dwell for awhile on this most original idea of Christ's disciples, found in both John and the Synoptics. To clarify the point, we shall study again the preparatory stages in the old Covenant, taking also into consideration the data of Judaism of Christ's time.[102]

THE OLD TESTAMENT AND JUDAISM

The disciple is one who follows the teaching of a master, or

---

102 In Vigoroux's *Dictionnaire de la Bible* there is hardly a column for the word *disciple,* in which the author does little more than list the occurrences of the word in the Scripture. Hastings' *Dictionary of the Bible* and Cheyne's *Encyclopaedia Biblica* do no more. However, in Kittel's T.W.N.T. the word *mathētēs* is treated (by H. Rengstorf) for over 50 pp. (vol. IV: pp. 417-465), in addition to the treatment of *manthanō* in the same work. This fact shows what great progress has occurred in recent years in biblical studies and how much greater interest is paid nowadays to the theological aspect of the biblical problems, by both Catholic and Protestant commentators. Cf. also R. SCHÜTZ, *Apostel und Junger,*

more precisely,[103] one who voluntarily belongs to the master's school and shares his views. Originally *mathētēs* meant "learner" [104] but "disciple" is the usual equivalent, and this is almost always the corresponding term given in the biblical versions.

Whereas in the New Testament the word *mathētēs* in the sense of "disciple," is very frequently used, in the Old Testament the Hebrew word which best corresponds, *talmid,* appears only in I Chr. XXV: 8, to mean, not disciples properly so called, but the sons of the levites, who "the elder equally with the younger, the learned and the unlearned (*talmid*)," were charged with performing the chants in the Temple. The word *mathētēs* appears not at all in the LXX, and its appearance in Jer. XIII: 21 and XXVI: 9 in some witnesses of the *Codex Alexandrinus* is erroneous.

There must be some reason for the all but complete absence of the word "disciple" in the Old Testament. Even if the concept were to be found hidden in some other terms, the fact remains that it had no more than a minimal importance in Old Testament religion. This religion is presented as revealed, coming directly from God. It is Jahweh who speaks; He is the cause and source of teaching and of salvation; His word, not Moses, is the basis of the history and progress of the chosen people.[105] Thus Moses could not have disciples. Josue is Moses' servant, not his disciple (cf. Ex. XXIV: 13; XXXIII: 11; Num. XI: 28; Dt. I: 38). The "sons of the prophets" (2 Kgs. II: 3; 5; 7; 15), and the relationship of Eliseus to Elias, are exceptions, because the charism of prophecy is directly from God alone.[106]

Giessen, 1921 (cfr. R. B., 1922, pp. 304-306); J. WACH, *Meister und Junger,* 1925.

103 In French there is a distinction between *"élève"* and *"disciple."*

104 In French, again, *"élève"* or *"apprenti."*

105 It is important to note that Moses, considered as mediator of the covenant, or as the first of the prophets, acts and speaks in the name of Jahweh. Thus it is that the Old Testament authors allude more to the mosaic era than to the person of Moses; cf. Amos V: 25; Osee II: 27; X: 10; XI: 1 ff; Is. XXX: 29; Jer. II: 2 ff; VII: 21-23, etc. Later Judaism on the other hand (Sirach) tends to exalt the great heroes of the past, often for the purpose of putting them up against the heroes and sages of the Greeks.

106 The sons of the prophets are prophets associated in some sort of society or confraternity. If in the difficult text of 2 Sam. XIX: 20 (cf. L. DESNOYERS, *Histoire du peuple Hébreu dès Juges à la captivite,* Paris, 1930, t. III, p. 177, note 3), Samuel appears to the leader of these sons

Isaia transmits a rich doctrine on God's plan, to a circle of chosen hearers, called once his disciples (VIII: 16; *limudim;* Vg., *discipuli.*)[107] His teaching, however, is presented not as the personal reflections of a human mind, but as divine Wisdom.

The same applies to the sages; where they have disciples, whom they call "children" (Ps. I: 8; 10; Ps. II: 1; cf. above), they merely teach them the traditions of Jahwism, founded in the fear of the Lord (Prov. I: 7; 29; II: 5; VIII: 13; IX: 10; X: 27). Commenting on Sir. XXIV: 30-34, Fr. Spicq says: "Sirach gives not his original teaching, as would a Greek philosopher; rather, he seeks to bring to all, the divine instructions of the Torah., of which he is happy to have enjoyed the blessing".[108] Eschatological hope is rooted in history; to the historical event of the Sinai revelation corresponds the expectation of a teaching to be given directly by God, no longer to one people, alone, but to all men, placed in their hearts by grace instead of being written only on tablets of stone. This is one of the highest forms of messianic hope, and the one which best prepares for the New Testament concept of the disciple of Christ.

The idea seems to come originally from Isaia in II: 2-4, which treats of "the days to come" (the messianic era.[109] "Come, let us climb the Lord's mountain, to the house of the God of Jacob,

---

of the prophets, there is no indication that these ecstatics had any sort of personal relationship with him. The same applies to the case of Eliseus living with Elias; Eliseus follows Elias as a "servant" (I Kgs. XIX: 21; 2 Kgs. III: 11). As Elias is about to leave earth, Eliseus asks for a double portion of his prophetic spirit; however, it is Jahweh who will give this double portion (2 Kgs. II: 9; 10) and it is in the name of Jahweh that Eliseus is to act (2 Kgs. II: 14; 24; III: 14 ff.). R. DE VAUX, *Les Livres des Rois,* (*Bible de Jérusalem*), Paris, 1949, pp. 127-128, note c.

107 The only other occurrence of *discipulus* in the Old Testament is in Mal. II: 12, but this is an error in translation.

108 *La Sainte Bible,* (Pirot), t. VI, Paris, p. 691.

109 On the question of whether or not this oracle is truly Isaian, (cf. Duhm, Procksch, Kissane, Steinmann, ea al.). These authors hold the affirmative, but the question is still disputed. Perhaps we should add Is. XXX: 20-21, if the meaning is that in the messianic era Jahweh will be the teacher of His people. Cf. the commentaries of Procksch and Fischer *ad loc., and* our article *"Isaie"* in *SDB.,* col. 670. In favor of the authenticity of Is. II: 2-5, cf. H. WILDBERGER, *Die Volkerwallfahrt zum Zion,* in *Vet. Test.,* 1957, pp. 62-81. R. MARTIN - ACHARD, *Israel et les nations.* Neuchâtel-Paris, 1959, pp. 55-67.

that he may instruct us in his ways, and we may walk in his paths." But it is above all Jeremia who leads the way in presenting this concept (XXXI: 31-34): "I will place my law within them, and write it upon their hearts. . . . No longer will they have to teach their friends and kinsmen how to know the Lord. All, from the greatest to the least, shall know me." Born itself of the painful realization of a law written only on tablets of stone, this oracle recalls that of Jer. XXIV: 7: "I will give them a heart with which to understand that I ˙am the Lord." Exechiel (XXXVI: 25-28) continues this powerful image.

These predictions are the source of several others, especially of this one, which Jesus Himself cites in the Discourse on the Bread of Life: "All your sons shall be taught (*limudim*) by the Lord" (Is. LIV: 13). The free manner in which John quotes this text (*kai esontai pantes didaktoi Theou*) is probably based on the LXX. (Cf. also Is. XLVIII: 17; LV: 1-3).

The cry of the bride in the Canticle of Canticles, "Oh, that you were my brother . . . you would teach me" (VIII: 1), probably is inspired by the same tradition.[110] In the same line of thought, we might mention the function performed by the Servant of Jahweh (Is. XLII: 1; 4). If he teaches, he merely presents the things which he himself, a faithful disciple of Jahweh, has learned; which fact assures us that his teaching is in itself divine. "The Lord has given me a well-trained tongue, that I may know how to speak; every morning he opens my ear that I may hear" (Is. L: 4).

In general the Psalms repeat individually the eschatological aspirations of the prophets. Often we see in the Psalms the desire for a teaching to be given directly by God, e. gr., the author of the *Miserere*, who begs God to place wisdom in the depths of his heart (v. 8). Cf. also the repeated invocations of Ps. CXIX: "Teach me; open my eyes; make me understand; give me understanding; bend my heart" (vv. 12; 18; 26; 27; 33; 34; 35; 36; 64; 66; 68; 73; 108; 124; 125; 133; 144). Cf. also Ps. XXV: 4; 5; 8; 9; Ps. XCIV: 12-13; CXLIII: 8-10. On Ps. CXIX A. Robert writes:

> Seeing the great intensity of the psalmist's prayer, his whole being turned toward God, the frequency and the sincerity of his prayer, the boldness with which he prays,

---

110 Cf. A. ROBERT, *Le Cantique des Cantiques*, Paris, 1951, pp. 56-57, note g. Unfortunately, too many authors simply presume to correct the text.

we understand that in his eyes human masters have little
to offer... he is not concerned with bending his efforts
to appreciate the delicacy of a *mashal*, or even with clutter-
ing his memory with principles of common sense... he
writes only to pray, to open his soul to God's action; he
knows that the heavenly teacher acts inwardly upon his
powers, bringing them into harmony with the external
teaching.[111]

Another tradition which we could place on the plane of fulfilled eschatology, and which is of considerable importance for
the understanding of the New Testament, is that represented by
the developments in the sapiential books on the theme of divine
Wisdom personified (Prov. I: 20-33; VIII - IX; Sir. XXIV; Wis.
VI - IX). Wisdom calls men to herself, to make them her disciples.
However, we have said enough on these texts, so that now it
should suffice merely to mention them.

Later Judaism introduces a new development: the Law becomes an object of instruction properly so called, to be interpreted
by human teachers. Alongside the priests, who have been the
traditional guardians of the Law (Jer. XVIII: 18; Osee IV: 6;
Mich. III: 11; Dt. XVII: 8-12; XXXI: 26), now arises a new
class of teachers, whose power and influence will continue to
grow.

The text of Sir. XXVIII: 19-26, which begins to distinguish
between one kind of wise man and another, sees "different
representatives of this class, born in Israel, of well-meaning
teachers, whose prestige grows at a rapid pace. They imitate the
Egyptian scribes and the Greek philosophers, claiming before
the masses to be teachers (cf. *paideia*, v. 23). Without claiming
to hold the place of the prophets, who by now have disappeared,
they take over more and more the priest's function of guidance
and moral instruction" (cf. Mt. XXIII: 2, ff.).[112]

In the Gospels and the Acts of the Apostles there is often
mention of the Doctors of the Law (*didaskaloi, nomodidaskaloi*
cf. the scene of the boy Jesus in the midst of the *doctors*), and
of scribes (*grammateis*), who are usually associated with the
pharisees, and recruited principally from their ranks, although
they are not to be equated with them. About the beginning of

---

111 *Le Psaume CXIX et les Sapientiaux*, in R. B., 1939, pp. 14-15.
112 C. SPICQ, in *La Sainte Bible* (Pirot), t. VI. p. 754.

the Christian era, the rabbis begin to appear; St. Paul recalls that he was a disciple of Rabbi Gamaliel (Acts XXII: 3). Rabbinism must have developed especially after the destruction of the Temple.

This development is quite normal in itself. Every law, however perfect, needs to be explained and adapted to circumstances, and the Mosaic Law is no exception. This latter was adapted at first by the addition of new prescriptions. Once the canon of sacred books was definitively fixed, since no one could add anything to the Pentateuch, the prescriptions which it contained had to be interpreted and made observable. Thus the work of the doctors was not only useful; it was indispensable.

However, the doctors did not stop at this. Led on at the beginning only by the burning desire to defend and propagate the Law, they came little by little to add to it their own personal notions, to which they would credit, if not the same importance, at least the same binding force as that of the Mosaic code itself. They became thereby a source of doctrine, arrogating to themselves real authority, which is the very basis of the relationship between teacher and disciple. Their pupils, growing ever more numerous, because of the strict duty enjoined upon every Jew to study the Law, became, in effect their disciples, depending on them intellectually and morally, just as the disciples of the Greek philosophers depended upon their masters.[113]

---

113 In an article in R. B. (*La Chaine de la tradition pharisiene, R. B.*, 1952, pp. 44-54), E. BIKERMANN discusses the great innovation which the Pharisees brought about by their way of justifying the unwritten laws and traditions. In the Old Testament the high priests were charged with guarding the law, and great effort is made to justify the teaching of the priests by the recording of genealogies which show the unbroken tradition from fathers to sons. Thus also "The Chronicler lists fourteen high priests from Aaron to Azarias, who was the first High Priest in Soloman's Temple, and the fourteen again between Azarias and Juddua" (I Chapter V: 29-41 and Neh. XII: 10 (p. 49). The Pharisees replaced the familial line (from ancestors to descendants) with the magisterial line (from master to student). The Fathers (Aboth) of whom we read in the pharisaic texts are the professors and teachers. "The Pharisees, after the death of Hillel and Shammai, toward the beginning of our era, drew up a sort of spiritual genealogy of their teaching" (p. 51). By so doing, the Pharisees resemble the Greeks, who had schools for passing on the teachings of the great masters. For more than 800 years, until 529 A.D., the *Academia* taught the works of Plato; the *Lyceum* propagated Aristotle; the stoic

The use of the word *talmid* is thus quite correct, in relation to rabbinic Judaism, designating those who study the Scripture and the rabbinic tradition contained in the Mishna, the Talmud and the Midrashim.

THE NEW TESTAMENT

The word *mathētēs*, which occurs quite frequently in the New Testament,[114] is found there only in the Gospels and in the Acts; it invariably refers to those who have recognized Jesus as teacher.

The only exceptions to this general rule are as follows: a few references to the discourse of John the Baptist (Mk. II: 18 and parallel texts; Jo. I: 35; III: 25; IV: 1; Acts XIX: 2-4) and the disciples of the pharisees (Mk. II: 18 and Lk. V: 33; Mt. XXII: 16); one reference in John IX: 26 to the disciples of Moses (in the Alexandrian text of Acts IX: 25 there is mention of the disciples of St. Paul, "his disciples"; however, the better reading seems to be that of Antiochian texts, which have "the disciples," (i.e., the Christians).[115]

Frequently in the Gospels, although not always with the explicit mention of the number twelve, the word "disciples" refers to the Apostles (Mt. IX: 1; XII: 1; Mk. VIII: 27; Lk. IX: 8; Jo. III: 22). However, it would be an exaggeration to say that this is always the case in St. Matthew (cf. VI: I; VIII: 21), although it is true that he shows special interest in the Apostles. As a matter of fact, his Gospel (like that of Mark) has been called the Gospel of the Twelve Apostles. Luke is the only one who mentions the seventy-two (or seventy-six) disciples. In general, Luke has an outlook extending far beyond the twelve Apostles; his Gospel, therefore, can be said to be the Gospel of the Disciples!

---

school of the *Portico* was allied to the teachings of Zenon. "Already about 200 B.C. Zotion published lists of school-masters. After this the series of "successors" (*diadochoi*) forms the outline of the whole history of Greek philosophy. We read, e. gr., in the works of a contemporary of Hillel and Shammai, that the Epicurean school lasted (after the death of Epicurus) until the first Caesar, i.e., 227 years, during which time there were fourteen successors" (p. 49.)

114 The word *mathētēs* occurs approximately 250 times in the New Testament, and once in the feminine form *mathētria*.

115 This latter reading is found in the *Bible de Jérusalem*.

No disciple of Christ undertakes to recruit any disciples. Even Peter, James and John, the "pillars of the Church," (Gal. II: 9), have no disciples. The word does not occur at all in St. Paul's epistles. In the two cases in which the Apostles are directed to "make disciples" (Mt. XXVIII: 19, *matheteusate panta ta ethne* and Paul and Barnabas at Derbe, Acts XIV: 21, *matheteusantes hikanous* the disciples whom they attract or are to attract, are disciples of Christ Himself (cf. 1 Th. IV: "You yourselves have learned from God" [*theodidaktoi este*], which is probably an allusion to Jer. XXXI: 34).

In the Gospels the word "disciple" refers to those who have entered into personal contact with Jesus, and have attached themselves to Him as His followers.[116] In Acts the same word, with no explanation, (cf. IX: I: "the disciples of the Lord"), is used often (only beginning with ch. VI), to refer to the Christians (VI: 1; 2; 7; IX: 1; 10; 19; 25; 26; 38; XI: 26; 29). Here the word does not imply (as it does in the Gospels) that Jesus may have been known personally; the disciples who appear are frequently the fruit of someone's missionary endeavors (those of Paul, of Barnabas, etc.). By placing the accent on the need for faith, and by bringing forward the personal contacts of everyday life (cf. II: 11; VIII: 31; XX: 29, etc.), the fourth Gospel intimates how the widening of the sense of the word has been possible. Cf., for example, Jo. VIII: 31: "If you abide in my word, you shall be my disciples indeed." Here, "disciples" means "believers." Cf. Jo. I: 2 and Acts II: 44.

There are, on the outside, quite a few similarities between the disciples of the Jewish doctors, and those of Jesus, so much so, that Jesus would give the impression of being a rabbi among rabbis.[117] In reality, Jesus, who is called *rabbi; didaskalos;*

---

116 Expressions such as "many followed Him" (Matthew XII: 15); "a crowd of his disciples" (Luke XIX: 37); "many of his disciples" (John VI: 60), suggest that at least during part of His public ministry Jesus had a large following. In contrast, the fourth Gospel says that, after the discourse on the Bread of life many left Him and "no longer went about with Him" (VI: 67).

117 For example: In the Gospels, Jesus imposes austere discipline upon His disciples; He shares His own way of life intimately with them; He accepts their services and in return introduces them to His innermost secrets. The disciples of the Jewish doctor was also subjected to considerable mortification; he was attached to his master, and held it a great

epistatēs (This last term only in Luke), has a manner all His own, of gathering and forming His disciples.

Whoever aspired to follow the lessons of a Jewish doctor had to undergo both intellectual and spiritual preparation for this honor.[118] Neither type of preparation, strictly speaking, was imposed on those who were to become Jesus' disciples. Even if the call is not forcible or spectacular, or even visible, it is clearly Jesus or the heavenly Father who have taken the initiative (Mk. I: 17; 20 and parallel texts; X: 21 and parallels; Mk. IX: 9; Lk. V: 27-28; John I: 29; 42; 44; XV: 16). Where Jesus alone knows the Father and is able to reveal Him (Mt. XI: 27 and many texts in John), only the Father knows Jesus and can reveal the mystery which surrounds Him (Mt. XI: 27; XVI: 27). These texts can be compared with the johannine phrase, "those whom the Father has given to Jesus," (VI: 39; X: 29; XVIII: 11) and the formula used in the Discourse on the Bread of Life: "No one can come to me unless the Father, who sent me, draw him" (VI: 44).

We are here face to face with a divine mystery, the one which had been announced to Jeremia, Ezechiel and Second Isaia (cf. above). As Fr. Biard [119] says well, "The presence of God in Christ, which is attested to by His works, can be known only by one who has received a new power from above." We might note in passing, that like the Gospel texts, I Jo. will consider as already realized in the Christian dispensation the oracles of Jeremia

---

honor to be able to serve him. He would carry his sandals, minister to his needs, help him when he travelled, accompanying him, caring for his animal, etc. Usually the disciple would enter into such a close relationship with his master that he would sometimes come to imitate his gestures and mannerisms. At times the disciple would show such deference as never even to speak in the presence of Him "whose water he drank," much less contradict Him. The rabbis, for their part, were usually considerate of these disciples, careful to defend them, and to show the greatest care for them. Cf. J. BONSIRVEN, *Le Judaisme Palestinien*, Paris, 1935, pp. 275-282; *T.W.N.T.* V., art. (Lhose), col. 962-966; TOWA PERLOW, *L'éducation et l'enseignement chez les Juifs a l'époque talmudique*, Paris, 1931, especially pp. 50-72; D. DAUBE, *The New Testament and Rabbinic Judaism*, London, 1956, pp. 266-267; R. TRAVERS HERFORD, *Les Pharisiens*, Paris, 1928.

118 The rabbis usually required that the candidates have at least a certain minimum knowledge of the *halakah*.

119 *La Puissance de Dieu*, Paris, 1959, p. 133.

and Ezechiel on the new Covenant, and the Law written in men's hearts, as an interior principle of action. This explains some of John's passages, as, e. gr., I Jo. II: 27: "Let the anointing which you have received from him dwell in you, and you have no need that anyone teach you" (cf. Jer. XXXI: 34; IV: 13: "He has given us of this spirit." cf. Ez. XXXVI: 27); and, especially, V: 20: "We know that the Son of God has come and has given us understanding, that we may know the true God...." (cf. Jer. XXIV: 7).

The relationship which unites Jesus to His disciples is not exclusively, or even primarily, intellectual.[120] He says, "Follow me." In all four Gospels, the verb "follow" (*akolouthein*) is frequent. When it is used in a religious sense, it always expresses attachment to the person of Jesus, cf. Mk. I: 18; II: 4; VIII: 34; X: 21; 28; Mt. VIII: 19; X: 38; Lk. IX: 59; 61 XVIII: 22; Jo. I: 44; VIII: 12; X: 4-5; 27; XII: 26; XIII: 36-37. (Outside the Gospels, cf. the only occurrence in this sense, Apoc. XIV: 14, alluding to Mt. X: 38).[121]

Faith, which is the fundamental theme of the fourth Gospel, is not a mere adherence to abstract truths. Opposed to the love of the darkness, human glory, and to the egoistic love of one's own life or works, in so far as they are evil, faith is a man's personal

---

120 Since the word *mathētēs* comes from *manthano*, we might expect to see this latter verb frequently in the Gospels. However, such is not the case. Matthew uses it three times, Mark once, and Luke not at all. Jesus was not concerned primarily in giving His disciples an intellectual heritage. Cf. O. GLOMBITZA, *Die Titel didaskalos und epistates für Jesus bei Lukas*, in Z.N.W., 1958, pp. 275-278. According to Luke, Jesus is not a *didaskalos* in the eyes of others; when Jesus is invited to exercise His *exousia*, Luke uses the word *epistatēs*. Apparently Luke is concerned to show that the Church is not a school of philosophy with Jesus as its head.

121 The Old Testament often uses the phrase *halach aharei*...which the LXX always translates literally, *poreuesthai opisō*.... However, this phrase is used ordinarily to refer to idolatry; by following (going after) false gods, the people separate themselves from Jahweh. (Jdg. II: 12; Dt. IV: 3; I Kgs. XXI: 20; Jer. VII: 6-9; IX: 13; XI: 10; Osee I: 2. It is used only rarely to refer to the service of Jahweh, Dt. I: 30; I Kgs. XIV: 8; XVIII: 21; 2 Kgs. XXIII: 3; Jer. II: 2. Probably the authors were hesitant to apply to the service of Jahweh such a concrete and material phrase, especially since it was already profaned by the constant reference to pagan practices (Cf. *T.W.N.T.* I Art. *akoloutheō* (Kittel), pp. 210-216.

response to the unspeakable love of God, who has given His Son to the world (cf. especially III: 14-21; VIII: 42-47; XII: 25; 43). To believe, to love the truth, the light, or the glory of God, or to love Christ, who is all these things, or to follow the Good Shepherd in all one's moral conduct, is all the same thing.[122]

The fact of following Jesus implies right away a break with the past. In the case of privileged disciples, such as were the Apostles, the break with the past must be total. However, this is only the negative side of being a disciple. On the positive side, the disciples must model their conduct on that of Jesus, hearing His teaching and conforming their life to that of the Savior (Mk. VIII: 34-35 and parallel texts; X: 21 and parallels; X: 42-45 and parallels; Jo. XII: 26). Above all, they must love one another as He has loved them; this is the sign by which men will recognize that they are His disciples (Jo. XIII: 34-35). After He has gone, they must be one as He and the Father are one; this will be for men the motive of credibility.

The disciple who attaches himself to a doctor because of the doctor's knowledge of the Law, tends to reclaim his freedom and to become a doctor in his own right (cf. Lk. VI: 40: "When perfect, everyone will be like his teacher"). Jesus' disciples attach themselves to Him not in view of what He knows or says, but in view of what He is; they are drawn to remain close to Him, because of the supereminent excellence of His person, revealed in His miracles and in all of His bearing. Further, there is no question of their reclaiming their freedom. When they run away at the time of the Passion, Luke no longer calls them "disciples" (cf. especially XXII: 49: *hoi peri auton* XXIII: 49: *hoi gnostoi autou* or *autō*). They are more attached to their Master than they are to their father or mother. Jesus demands that they surrender even the most cherished family ties, if these threaten to be an obstacle to their being disciples (Lk. XIV: 25; 26; Mt. X: 37).

Jesus also teaches in various ways that the fate of His disciples, and especially that of the twelve Apostles, is linked to His own. First of all, he associates them closely with His work of inaugurating the Kingdom of God. Furthermore, the solemn prediction of His Passion which follows Peter's confession of faith at

---

122 Cfr. T. BARROSSE, *The Relationship of Love to Faith in St. John*, in *Theological Studies*, 18, 1957, pp. 538-559.

Caesarea Philippi, are joined invariably to instructions on the necessity of the disciples' carrying their cross in turn. Cf. Mk. VIII: 34-38; IX: 35-37; X: 35-45, and the johannine parallels, especially XII: 23-25; XIII: 13-16; XV: 18-20; XXI: 15-19. Following such a Master, therefore, is not without risk; and Jesus makes no attempt to hide this from His hearers.

However, there is also an emphasis placed on the sharing in Jesus' privileges. Jesus is Lord of the world to come; His own people, and especially the Twelve Apostles, will share in His Lordship; the sacrifice of temporal goods and family ties brings promise of a spiritual hundred fold on earth, and a glorification and eternal life afterward (Mt. XIX: 28-29; XXVI: 29; Lk. XXII: 28-30; Jo. XII: 26; XIV: 3; XVII: 2; 11; 13; 19; 22; 24; 26).

The dignity of the disciples comes from the intimacy of their relationship with Christ. Even a glass of water given to the least will have its reward (Mt. X: 42; Mk. IX: 41). Even the smallest of them are so dear to the heavenly Father, that He has placed them under the care of the angels who are before His face. (Mt. XXIII: 10). Also, to scandalize one of them is the gravest of sins.

It is in just this context that we should place the institution of the Eucharist, which is destined to establish the most profound and intimate link imaginable, between Jesus, who is about to leave the earth, and the disciples whom He will leave behind. By reason of what has rightly been called the personal structure of the faith,[123] whereby the disciple attaches himself first and foremost to the person of his Master, the eucharistic mystery appears as the mystery of faith *par excellence*. In a manner of speaking, we might say that it is in the logic of the disciples' faith in Christ, because faith is the act whereby the whole human person (not merely the intellect) works to accept the God who invites him. Faith and sacrament are closely linked; "The sacraments are essentially sacraments of faith, *sacramenta fidei*, as St. Thomas usually calls them; faith and the sacraments have divine power, whereby man receives access to the treasures of Christ's redemption".[124]

---

123 J. MOUROUX, *Je crois en Toi*, Paris, 1948. DOM VONIER, *La Clef de la doctrine eucharistique*, Lyon, 1943, places the closest connection between faith and sacrament, according to the teaching of St. Thomas.

124 DOM VONIER, *Le Clef de la doctrine eucharistique*, p. 14.

According to John VI: 43-44, discipleship is a grace which comes from the interior teaching given by God, and from being drawn by the Father. There is a most intimate relationship between the specific food of the eucharistic mystery and the Word placed by God in the hearts of men, instead of being merely engraved on tablets of stone. The Last Supper narrative of Mk. XIV: 24 and parallel texts refers to Jer. XXXI: 34. A. Robert, in his explanation of Cant. VIII: 1-2 in the *Bible de Jérusalem,* shows a relationship between the Law written in men's souls in Jer. XXXI: 33-34, and Wisdom's Banquet in Prov. IX. Similar ideas are at the base of Jo. VI. The interior enlightenment which transforms men into disciples of Christ really gives Christ to men and men to Christ; it feeds them already on Christ, the Bread of Life, which will be received in the sacrament. "No one can *come to me* unless the Father who sent me draw him ... he who *comes to me* shall never hunger; he who believes in me shall never thirst." Still, the distinction remains between faith and the sacrament. Even if the faith is basically a gift of God, it is no less a coming of man toward Christ, whereas the sacrament is a coming of Christ to men.

In the light of this explanation, we can understand better in what way the two developments of the Discourse on the Bread of Life (35-47; 48-58) can draw men to the Christ of the Eucharist, even though the first requires only that one believe in Jesus, the Bread of Life, but not yet that one eat of His flesh. Faith is a first communion, preceding the sacramental rite, and oriented intrinsically to it. This is precisely the justification for limiting to adults capable of making an act of faith, the obligation imposed by Christ of having recourse to the Eucharist in order to be admitted to the life of God. Christ's words in v. 53 are absolute; "The Greek Church concluded from this teaching that the Eucharist should be given to children; Augustine agrees. The Latin Church waits until the age of reason, basing its view on the solid reason that Jesus requires that the first step toward Him be the act of faith" (vv. 35; 45; 47) (Lagrange, ad loc.).

Thus it is difficult to see how we could over-emphasize the gospel concept of discipleship, or that of Jesus as doctor (teacher) of men. Does this mean that these concepts are absent from the Old Testament revelation, in which the word "disciple" hardly occurs? On the contrary, there is a close connection between them, as we have indicated above. Again, judging only from the face of things, one might be inclined to take Jesus as one rabbi among

many. In reality, however, Jesus, severe critic not only of the
"hypocrisy" of the scribes and pharisees (Mt. XXIII: 2-4) and
their endless casuistry (Mt. V: 33-36), but also of the purely
human manner of their traditions and teachings (Mt. XV: 1-20),
"refuses to recognize in the 'holachot' of the rabbis the authority
of the Torah".[125] and seeks to return to the great Old Testament
tradition, in which God Himself is the teacher, and men only His
representatives. Better still, (cf. Mt. XXIII: 8-10,[126] Jo. VI: 45,
and implicitly the antitheses of the Sermon on the Mount),
Jesus applies to Himself one of the most startling eschatological
aspirations of the old Covenant, that of God making Himself
directly and immediately the teacher of men. *Here is the unspeakable wonder of the New Testament, that Christ, fully
conscious that He is divine Wisdom come to earth, fulfills*

---

125 H. J. SCHOEPS, *Jésus et la Loi juive,* in *Revue d'Histoire et de
Philosophie religieuses,* 1953, p. 4.

126 We should look carefully at the text of Matthew XXIII: 8-10, in
which Jesus insists that no man can set up himself as teacher of other
men, and at the same time declares that He alone is the teacher of mankind; "But do not you be called 'Rabbi'; for one is your master (*didaskalos*)
and all you are brothers. And call no one on earth your father, for one is
your father, who is in heaven. Neither be called masters, for one only is
your master, the Christ." As P. SPICQ, O.P., observes (*Une allusion au
Docteur de justice dans Mt. XXIII:10?* in *R. B.,* 1959, pp. 387-396),
this triple injunction should be separated from the preceding context and
attached to v. 2, "The Scribes and the Pharisees have sat on the chair
of Moses." Jesus therefore criticizes not so much the privileges of the
Scribes, Pharisees and Doctors, as their pretentions to be the infallible
teachers and guides of the mass of the people. No one on earth has a right
to present himself as Father (in the sense of teacher of righteousness) in
place of God. The third of these phrases, which defines the role of Christ,
is held by many critics to be an addition made either by the evangelist
or by the primitive Christian community. P. SPICQ considers it authentic,
insofar as Jesus declares Himself the sole qualified interpreter of God's
will, in opposition to the Scribes and Pharisees. It could also be a reaction
against the unique position attributed to the *Teacher of Righteousness*
by the sectaries of the New Covenant. Apparently the *Kathēgētēs* (*hapax
legomenon* in the Scripture) is equivalent to *Moses* (teacher, instructor)
which occurs with a messianic overtone in Is. XXX: 20 and Joel II: 23.
Cf. L. SAGGIN, *Magister vester unus est. Christus* (Matthew XXIII: 10)
in *Verbum Domini,* 1952, pp. 211-213. Even if the mention of His own
name should be considered impossible on Christ's lips, the rest of the
passage is certainly authentic. As SCHNIEWIND has seen (*Das Evangelium*

personally this ancient expectation.[127] This is also how, through the mystery of the Eucharist, He is able to establish between Himself and His disciples a relationship so deep that men would never have been able to wish, or even to imagine, the like.

Blondel has said, "Men have no disciples, because they are incapable of addressing themselves to the mysterious depths of the soul".[128] In the New Testament, Jesus has His disciples. He is almost the only one to have them, because He is Son of God, and divine Wisdom incarnate. Although strictly speaking the Old Testament does not present the mystery of the Eucharist (which presupposes the redemptive Incarnation), still, because of the personal character of the act of faith in Jesus, the divine Wisdom, the Old Testament texts which treat of the eating of divine Wisdom by her own disciples is surely a most profound and fitting preparation for it.

The wisdom literature of the Old Testament comes to the fore once again, placing in relief the essential characteristic of the disciples of Christ. According to these texts, it is the benefits which Wisdom offers which should draw men to her, and lead them to become her disciples. These benefits, however, are unique;

Nach Matthaeus, Goettingen, 1950, p. 228), it is a reference to Jer. XXXI: 21 (the new covenant will be characterized by a teaching given directly by God, without any human intermediary). This prophetic text is of fundamental importance for understanding the New Testament: Christ will recall it at the Last supper (Mark XIV: 24 and parallels).

127 Even if the disciple of Jesus is not primarily one who is taught, still the work of teaching which Jesus does is primary in the gospels (hence the verb *didaskō*). Even more, in the New Testament it is principally Jesus who is the Teacher. Not even Paul is a teacher the way Jesus is. The Pauline Corpus has only ten of the ninety-five occurrences of *didaskō* in the New Testament.

128 M. BLONDEL, *L'Action,* Paris, 1893, p. 141. This reflection might be considered similar to the attitude of Socrates, who, unlike the Sophists, denied that he had disciples or that he was a *didaskalos.* Cf., e. gr., Plato, *Apologia,* 33A: *Egō de didaskalos men oudenos pōpot' egenomēn.* Cf. E. ZELLER, *La Philosophie des Grecs considerée dans son développement historique,* tr. by E. Boutroux, 2nd part, tome III, Paris, 1884, p. 65. However, Socrates is an exception. Generally among the Greeks there were disciples of the philosophers, such as those of Protagoras, Aristotle, Pythagoras, Epicurus, Apollonius, etc. They usually had the greatest reverence for their masters, accepting their guidance, or at least following their systems. Occasionally, as in the case of the Pythagoreans, their attachment to their master's teaching was religious in tone.

they are not extrinsic to Wisdom, but ultimately identified with her; it is her own substance by which she promises to feed those who belong to her; to accept her teaching is, in a way, to "eat" her (Prov. IX; Sir. XXIV: 18-21). One must, therefore, love Wisdom more than all else, more than gold or silver, more than jewels, crowns, or scepters (Prov. III: 14-15; IV: 14-15; IV: 7; VIII: 10; 11; 19; XVI: 16; Wis. VII: 8-10). "Those who love me I will also love (*ego tous eme philountas agapō*) and those who seek me find me" (Prov. VIII: 7). "Her I loved and sought after from my youth" (*tautēn ephilēsa kai exezētēsa ek neotētos mou*), declares the Pseudo-Solomon, in Wis. VIII: 2.

The verb *philein*, which occurs here, means properly "to love, to cherish." It often has the same meaning as *stergein*, to designate the affection which unites friends or members of the same family, the closeness of neighbors, or a mistress and her maid. In its widest sense, *phileō* means affection pure and simple, without any restriction.[129] Aristotle asked whether friendship toward God were possible (*philia pros theon*), and replied in the negative, explaining that friendship can exist only between two equal or similar persons.[130] Whatever be the case in the Greek world, the fact remains that the word *philein* never occurs, either in the LXX or in the New Testament, to indicate the love of man for God.[131] And still, as we have seen, the sacred authors use this word freely to indicate the love of men for divine Wisdom personified.

Both in John (XVI: 25; XXI: 15-17) and in the Synoptics (Mt. X: 37), Jesus uses this same word to describe the exclusive attachment to His own person. He, like Wisdom, wishes to be loved more than all else, "He who loves (*ho philōn*) father and mother more than me is not worthy of me," he says. The coincidence is all the more strikng with the use of the rare phrase, "worthy of me," because the adjective *axios*, which ordinarily is not used in profane Greek with the genitive of the person,[132]

---

129 C. SPICQ, *Agapè, Prolégomènes à une étude de théologie néotestamentaire*, Louvain-Leiden, 1955, pp. 12-13.

130 Magn. Mor., II, II, 120b.

131 Cfr. LAGRANGE, *Évangile selon saint Matthieu*, p. 213; McNEILE, *The Gospel According to St. Matthew*, p. 148.

132 In pagan texts and inscriptions, the adverb *axios* often refers to moral conduct, such as in Rom. XVI: 2: *axios tōn hagiōn*, "as becomes saints." In the *Manual* of Epictetus (XV) there is the following phrase:

has a corresponding formula in Wisdom: "She makes her own rounds, seeking those worthy of her" (*tous axious autēs* VI: 16; cf. III: 5).

General Conclusions: UNITY OF THE DISCOURSE; JOHN'S EUCHARISTIC DOCTRINE

A number of conclusions are evident from our study, some of them literary, referring to the composition and interpretation of the Discourse on the Bread of Life, others of a theological nature, relative to the fourth Gospel's eucharistic doctrine.

At the beginning of this study we alluded to the many discussions which the exegesis of John VI has occasioned. Our study and the results of it enable us now to state our own position. First of all, the Discourse is one; the last part (51b-58) cannot be taken as an insert, because all the preceding material prepares the way for it; the Old Testament sources of the Discourse, as well as the Synoptic parallels, show that the theme of eating the Eucharist is inseparable from that of faith in Jesus, considered as the spiritual manna of the messianic era and as divine Wisdom incarnate.

A difficulty remains, however, which we must frankly acknowledge. With their absolute exclusion of "the flesh" as a principle of salvation, and their insistence on Christ's return to heaven (which must prove that He came from heaven), vv. 60-66 seems to be more intelligible as Jesus' reply to the objections raised by the Jews in vv. 41 ff. The johannine origin of vv. 51-58 is beyond question, as E. Ruckstuhl has shown.[133] But it seems possible that the entire Discourse on the Bread of Life is a synthesis of various johannine texts which were originally distinct.

In any case, we doubt that it is possible to distinguish two completely separate parts; a discourse treating faith separately beforehand, and then treating the Eucharist. These two themes, although distinct, are inseparably intertwined. It also seems evident to us that the eucharistic theme, already prepared by the

---

"Thou shalt be fit to dine with the gods *esē axios tōn theōn sympotēs*. However, it does not seem as if profane Greek ever used the adjective *axios* governing a personal genitive. Cf. LAGRANGE *L'Evangile selon St. Matthieu*, pp. 212-213 and *T.W.N.T.* I. Art. (Foerster), pp. 378-380.

133 *Die literarische Einheit des Johannesevangeliums*, pp. 220-271.

word *eucharistesas* in vv. 11 and 23 (deliberately repeated), is announced from the beginning (v. 27 with *brosis; dosei,* used in this verse, recurs in v. 55). The close relationship which the eucharistic eating establishes between Jesus and His disciples, is connected to the very original conception which He makes of these disciples, like the "children" of Wisdom in the Old Testament. Otherwise the old Covenant, which does not know the Eucharist, is far surpassed, as much as the manna is surpassed by the mystery of the Eucharist. In the one case, God limits Himself to giving different kinds of benefits to men; in the other, He gives Himself.

An objection arises, as to whether or not such a Discourse, inculcating so forcefully the mystery of the Eucharist, is likely to have come from the lips of the historical Christ, addressing the Galilean multitudes. Leon-Dufour answers [134] by distinguishing two perspectives: that of the Savior's immediate hearers, for whom the whole Discourse is directed toward faith in the person of Jesus, who is the true heavenly bread; even vv. 48-55 must be understood in this way; the flesh and blood refer thus to the concrete person of the Son of God, destined to die, while the couplet, flesh-blood, as the couplet *come to me-believe in me* of v. 35, describes not two distinct acts, but simply adherence to the whole person of Christ. On the other hand, in the perspective of those who were contemporary to the redaction of the Gospel account, vv. 48-58 undoubtedly have a sacramental meaning. The Christian cannot help seeing in these verses the body and blood of the Christ of the Eucharist. Even the first part of the Discourse, which speaks of bread and drink, takes on a new meaning, or, rather, a more exact one, for it is principally by the sacrament of the Eucharist that Christians receive this heavenly bread, which is the Logos incarnate.

Fr. Leon-Dufour's study seems to us to have two particular merits. First of all, he emphasizes, as we have also tried to do, the point suggested by the wisdom texts which are at the base of the Discourse on the Bread of Life; because the disciples' faith in Jesus is essentially personal, there is a sort of logical continuity between adhering to Christ by faith and participating in the mystery of the Eucharist. Secondly, the Discourse on the Bread of Life has a decidedly Semitic flavor, which is too often

---

134 *Le Mystere du Pain de vie,* in R. S. R., 1958, pp. 481-523.

ignored.[135] Thus the phrases, "eat flesh" and "drink blood," which mean to take the whole human person. Therefore the terms "flesh" and "blood" should not be considered separately, as we do when we speak of the body and the blood. This is proven in the context; "He who eats *me* will live by me" (cf. v. 51); "He who eats *this bread* will· live forever" (cf. v. 58).

This solution, however, does not remove all difficulty. In interpreting some deeds and sayings of Christ, it is, of course, helpful to invoke this distinction of the two stages of understanding, that of the Christians of the late first century, and that of Christ's immediate hearers. However, the application of this distinction seems more difficult in the case of an account as long as the Discourse on the Bread of Life. We are more inclined to see the substance of the Discourse as coming certainly from Jesus, although the thoughts of the Master come to us transmitted and explained by the evangelist, who makes his own additions, in keeping with the practice of the Church.[136] We cannot forget that this Gospel, like the others, was preached before it was written!

There are many reasons why we prefer this opinion. First of all, there is the impossibility of understanding the last part of the passage except as applied to the eating of the Eucharist. These verses presuppose Calvary; in order to be drunk the blood must first be spilled. Even granted the Semitic character of the terms "flesh and "blood, the phrases "eat flesh" and "drink blood,"

---

135 In the same sense, cf. J. Bonsirven, *Le Temoin du Verbe, le disciple bien-aimé,* Toulouse, 1956, pp. 197-198.

136 The case is like that of the interview between Jesus and Nicodemus (III: 1-21) in which the necessity of Christ's baptism is presented very clearly. The basic ideas of this dialogue are surely from Jesus, but the passage, taken in its entirety, "contains all the elements of a baptismal catechesis, like that of Eph. V: 8-14" (D. MOLLAT, *L'Évangile de S. Jean,* (Bible de Jérusalem), Paris, 1953, p. 15). There is an especially interesting similarity of phraseology between John III: 19-21 and Eph. V: 8-14. In these short fragments there are as many as seven words or phrases in common: *en Theō; en Kyriō; alētheia; skotos, phōs; erga; phaneroō; elengchō.* The similarity of the ideas is all the more striking if the verb in either case has the sense of "expose." John surely has presented Jesus' original teaching, with regard to the Church's baptismal practice. Léon-Dufour sees in the word "water" (v. 5) ("unless a man be born again of water and the Spirit") a sacramental allusion made by the evangelist himself (*L'Actualité du quatrieme Évangile*) in *N. R. Th.,* 1954, pp. 450-451.

which correspond to Christ's words at the Last Supper, seem to presuppose the institution of the sacrament, and to come from a eucharistic liturgy. This would also explain, partly, the evident similarity existing between these phrases and the eucharistic texts of Saint Ignatius of Antioch (cf. especially Eph. XX: 2: *pharmakon athanasias, antidotos tou me apothanein, alla zen en Iesou Christo dia pantos*. In any case, it seems improbable that Jesus would have been able, during His public life, to impose such careful and precise terminology on His hearers.

Already in the New Testament (2 Cor. V: 6-8; Acts XX. ff.), we have some evidence of a Christian Paschal feast based on the Jewish Pasch. Recent studies have suggested that John VI is influenced not only by the Christian liturgy, but also, at least through the Christian liturgy, by the Paschal liturgy of the Jews. The question placed in the Discourse (vv. 28-30 ff.; 42; 52) recalls the question which the Jews asked during the course of their Paschal meal. Christ's response, on the other hand, can be compared to the replies which the one presiding at the Paschal meal was supposed to make.[137] We can recall also I Cor. X: 1-5, although the thinking is slightly different; whereas John VI, as well as the Synoptics (cf. the temptation account) deprecate the manna, Paul here calls it spiritual food.

There is a second reason for our preferring this point of view; and this second argument convinces us that the Discourse of John VI cannot be read without a eucharistic meaning. Christ had to prepare His disciples for the great event of the Last Supper. We follow V. Taylor in this regard.[138] First of all, it is unlikely that the Synoptics record every word that Jesus said to His disciples at the Last Supper; Mt. XIV: 22-24 would be most difficult to understand without some sort of explanation. As for the Discourse on the Bread of Life in John, there are two possibilities: either the evangelist has added to Jesus' Discourse following the multiplication of the loaves, some of the tidings

---

137 Cfr. especially B. GÄRTNER, *John 6 and the Jewish Passover* in *Coniectanea neotestamentica*, XVII, Lund, 1959; G. ZIENER, *Johannes-evangelium und urchristliche Passafeier*, in *Biblische Zeitschrift*, 1958, pp. 267-274; E. J. KILMARTIN, *Liturgical Influence on John 6*, in *Cath. Bibl. Quart.*, 1960, pp. 183-191; D. DAUBE, *The New Testament and Rabbinic Judaism*, London, 1956.

138 *Jesus and His Sacrifice*, London, 1951, pp. 243-244.

which He said at the Last Supper,[139] or else the miracle of the
loaves was already the preparation for the institution of the
Eucharist. Taylor dismisses the third possibility of a fictitious
discourse which John VI would have placed on the lips of Jesus.

Although it is no more than a hypothesis, we have thought
it worthwhile at least to mention the possibility of an influence
upon John VI, of the Jewish Paschal *Haggadah*, by way of the
Christian Paschal ritual. B. Gaertner offers another, and rather
plausible, conjecture. St. John's chapter VI is placed in the setting
of the season of the Pasch; furthermore, v. 60 tells us that the
Discourse was pronounced in the synagogue of Capharnaum.
In such a time and place, the synagogue instruction must naturally
have been based on the approaching Passover observance. It
seems possible, therefore, that Jesus might have made use of
the occasion to show for the first time the connection between
the Jewish Pasch and the Messianic Banquet. Gaertner surmises
that in John VI we have not the evangelist's free theological
construction, but an original grouping of materials, in which
we can find traces of the Synoptic tradition, although the original
order has been subjected in some respects to the addition of
other elements (cf. especially Mk. VIII: 34, the multiplication
of the loaves linked to an instruction by Jesus; VI: 11, a request
for a sign from heaven, connected to an account of the miracle
of the loaves). J. Jeremias and W. Grundman as well as some
other exegetes, think that Jesus Himself is meant in VIII: 14, the
"one loaf" which the disciples have in the boat with them. We
do not intend, however, to enter here into a detailed discussion
of this hypothesis. Nonetheless, this idea, as well as many others
presently current, reflect the general tendency of modern critics
to re-evaluate the fourth Gospel.

Be this situation what it may, we still are of the opinion that
because of the close connection which we have discovered between John's Discourse on the Bread of Life on the one hand,
and the Old Testament and the Synoptics on the other, given
John's explications, this is the way in which the Savior had to

---

139 We should bear in mind the many relationships between the discourse on the bread of life and the events and discourses of the Last
Supper. We have already mentioned the eucharistic reference in the
allegory of the vine; by faith and by the sacrament of the Eucharist
(cf. VI: 56) the disciple is able to follow the command of XV: 4:
"Abide in me and I in you."

dispose souls to accept the mystery of the Eucharist. The Old Testament parallels which we have indicated suggest more than faith in Christ. Word and Wisdom of God; they lead further to a liturgical and sacrificial communion. Thus, whatever part may eventually be credited either to the Christian or to the Jewish liturgy, we certainly cannot reduce John VI to a mere Christian homily.

We now feel prepared to offer a synthesis of the doctrinal richness of the fourth Gospel with regard to the Eucharist; the relationship of the mystery of the Eucharist to the Incarnation, to Calvary, to the Ascension, and to the founding of the Church; its relationship to the Old Testament anticipation; its universalist orientation, and its simultaneously personal and communal (ecclesial) meaning (the precept of mutual love).

Whereas the Synoptics and St. Paul make of the Last Supper a memorial of the Savior's Passion and the announcement of the Parousia, John places the eucharistic mystery in connection with that of the Incarnation. The true Bread of Life is the Son of God, descended from heaven. During His public ministry (cf. "The hour is coming and is now here," IV: 23; V: 25), Jesus is the Bread of Life for those who believe in Him. The word *sarx*, which John prefers to *soma* ("to eat the flesh of Christ," instead of "to eat His body," which we find in the Synoptics and in St. Paul), recalls the phrase of the Prologue, "The Word was made flesh" (1: 14; cf. also I Jo. IV: 2; 2 Jo. VII: 7, "Jesus Christ has come in the flesh."

By the doctrine of the Incarnation, Jesus teaches a truth which neither the Synoptics nor St. Paul emphasized, that he who believes in Christ and in His doctrine is nourished by Christ, the Word come forth from the mouth of God, and Wisdom of God. The intimate relationship existing between the Word of God and the Eucharist have their most solid foundation here in John VI.

In emphasizing the primary role of the Incarnation as the source of men's divinization, the evangelist remains faithful to the primitive tradition which places the Eucharist in direct dependence upon Calvary. This is to say that the gift of the Eucharist food, properly speaking, is reserved to the future. It will be nothing else than the flesh of Christ, previously given for the life of the world (v. 51). Christ's salvific work already inaugurated by the Incarnation (the Hour is, in a certain way, already here) will be fully realized only when He returns to the

Father ("The hour is coming"). The Eucharist supposes, therefore, besides Calvary, the heavenly exaltation of the Savior. This
is why the eating must be something entirely special ("Does
this scandalize you? What then if you should see the Son of
Man ascending where He was before?" v. 62).[140] Faith is the
act whereby man goes to Christ. The Eucharist, the act whereby
Christ comes to every man and gives Himself to him, presupposes
the previous giving by Christ of His entire self to all of humanity.

Finally the sacrament of the Eucharist supposes the Church.
It has its *raison d'etre* only in the Church, which is the earthly
continuation of Christ's mission. Christ, returning to His heavenly
Father, keeps the closest imaginable contact with His disciples
here below, whose life and words are all for Him and through
Him. In general, in the fourth Gospel, Christology and eschatology are inseparable, yet they are distinct. As long as the Son
of Man, living sacrament of the new Covenant, dwells on earth,
the Church and the sacramental system are not needed. There
is need only for signs, such as Cana and the multiplication of the
loaves, both symbols of the Eucharist. In recent times the sacramental significance of the fourth Gospel (Christological, then
ecclesial) has been falsified and exaggerated by those who did
not have this perspective. Only after Jesus has returned to the
side of His Father, does the Church come forward with its sacraments, as an earthly substitute for the visible presence and action
of the incarnate *Logos*.

The question is often asked, why John omitted the account
of the Last Supper. One of the most probable reasons is that he
saw the institution of the Church and of the sacrament situated,
properly speaking, on Calvary (cf. the blood and water flowing
from Christ's pierced side).[141] St. Thomas writes: *Sacramenta
Ecclesiae specialiter habent virtutem ex passione Christi, cujus*

---

140 This phrase, which still is uncertain, has been taken in two ways:
the surprise will be even greater when Jesus returns to His Father, or
the opposite: it will be less, or even there will be none at all. No doubt
both interpretations should be kept together. The way of return to the
Father is through Calvary, (which is the supreme scandal), in order to
reach the Ascension, which will clarify finally the entirely spiritual nature
of this eating. Verse 62 would make much more sense if it were taken
as a response to the objections raised in vv. 41-42.

141 Cfr. A. B. HIGGINS, *The Lord's Supper in the New Testament*,
London, 1954, pp. 74-78.

*virtus quodammodo nobis copulatur per susceptionem sacra-
mentorum; in cujus signum de latere Christi pendentis in cruce
fluxerunt aqua et sanguis, quorum unum pertinet ad baptismum,
aliud ad Eucharistiam, quae sunt potissima sacramenta* (IIIa
Pars, q. 62, art. 5). There is no reason, therefore, for holding with
A. Schweitzer [142] that John sees the Synoptic account of the Last
Supper as erroneous and unacceptable. They are rather complementary, not contradictory; the Last Supper of the Synoptics is
in itself oriented toward the Cross.

Throughout the Office of the Blessed Sacrament, and especially
in the Antiphon at Lauds, the Church celebrated the feast of the
Eucharist in terms of the Old Testament preparations, which
themselves recall the Discourse of John VI, principally (as it
should be) Wisdom's Banquet, as well as the manna in the desert
and the sacrificial liturgy of the Old Testament: *Sapientia
aedificavit sibi domum, miscuit vinum et posuit mensam; Ange-
lorum esca nutrivisti populum tuum et panem de caelo praesti-
tisti eis; Sacerdotes sancti incensum et panes offerunt Deo.*

Still, St. John does not present his teaching on the Eucharist
exclusively as the fulfillment of the eschatological waiting of the
Old Testament, but (cf. the double reference of *alethinos* to the
types of the Old Testament and to perishable realities) still
more as *a response to the deepest aspirations of humanity as a
whole.* The great johannine symbols, light, water, bread, the
vine, correspond to a universalist intention, expressing in effect
the basic needs of every man's physical life. But, precisely because they are symbols, they tell us that men should not limit
their aspirations to their physical life. Created by God, made for
God, he suffers a hunger and thirst after God Himself; nothing
short of God can fully satisfy him; every perishable earthly food
(John VI: 27) leaves man unsatisfied. In speaking to Galilean
peasants, who earn their daily bread at the cost of hard toil and
labor, Jesus takes as His point of departure the material bread
which they know, in order to stimulate their desire for heavenly
blessings; likewise, at Jacob's well, He begins with material
water. The water which quenches, the bread which satisfies,
are of another order!

Some Old Testament writers seem to have suspected this
great truth; this is especially true of Is. LV: 1-3: "Why spend

---

142 *Die Mystik des Apostels Paulus,* Tubingen, 1930, p. 365.

your money for what is not bread, your wages for what fails to satisfy?" Also, ch. I-IX of Proverbs teach that every man may have communion with divine Wisdom, provided only that he observe her commands. John VI prolongs and emphasizes surprisingly this wonderful insight: "As the living Father has sent me, and as I live because of the Father, so he who eats me, he shall also live because of me" (v. 57). The incarnate Son of God is depositary of all the riches of the divine life, which He receives from His Father. By the eucharistic mystery he passes this life on to His disciples, who share in Jesus the very life of God. Physical death cannot of itself lead to this life (vv. 49; 50; 59); what is more, it must lead to the glorious resurrection, showing, as the fourth Gospel does (and as do the Synoptics and St. Paul as well), the essentially eschatological orientation of the Eucharistic rite.

Some hesitate in v. 58 between the translations *through* and *for* the Father; *through* and *for* Him (Jesus).[143] The former seems preferable (one lives *by* food), although the second also has merit. Just as Jesus is the envoy of the Father, so too the communicant is consecrated to the service of Jesus, as His ambassador in the world, designed to work *for* Him. The powerful formula, "He who eats my flesh and drinks my blood abides in me and I in him" (v. 57), profoundly resuming, as we have said, the covenant formula, opens the way to the most intimate union with Jesus and to the highest mystical aspirations, without compromising the necessary distinction between Christ and His disciples.

At the end of v. 56, D and some texts of the *Vetus Latina* compare the mutual indwelling of Christ and the Christian to that of the Father and the Son, and call for receiving the body

---

143 The meaning "Through" usually goes with the genitive after *dia*, while with the accusative it means rather "for." Still it could have the sense of "because of" or "through" ("by"), as in the stoic text; *Dia* (*Zeus*) *epeidēper di'auton panta ginetai*, and other stoic texts in NORDEN, *Agnostos Theos*, p. 347. Most modern authors translate, "by the Father" or "by me," because man lives by food. Thus the mention of Christ's mission becomes secondary. But, if we are to keep His role as primary, then we should translate, with Lagrange and Abel, "for the Father, for him"; all the more so because of the future form (shall live), which indicates a future end to be realized by communion. Man "learns to consecrate his life to Jesus" (Lagrange).

of the Son of man as bread of life. These words could be authentic, omitted by homoioteleuton; more probably they are a western addition.

The fourth Gospel also emphasizes the communal or ecclesial point of view, which is so wonderfully expressed in St. Paul's eucharistic doctrine: "Because this bread is one, we, though many, are one body" (I. Cor. X: 17). This idea is not clear in the Discourse on the Bread of Life, but the allegory of the vine, which complements it, teaches as well as could be desired, that the disciple must "bear fruit," i.e., to make up the "whole Christ." Intimately united to the vine, which is Jesus, the faithful are because of Him, one vine, all the branches of which carry the same supernatural life-fluid. Thus they are the true vine, the new Israel, the Church. John's allegory of the vine corresponds to St. Paul's concept of the (mystical) body of Christ. In either case it is proper to see a reference to the Eucharist, principle of Christian unity.

The vine allegory is closely united to the precept of mutual love, which must mark the disciples of Christ: "This is my commandment, that you love one another as I have loved you" (XV: 12). This command had been formulated after the washing of the feet, symbol of the redemptive humiliations which are to lead to the sacraments (cf. XIII: 33-34). Unlike the Synoptics, (cf. e. gr., Mt. V: 43-48) John accentuates not love for all men, including enemies, but the mutual affection which should unite the new people of God to one another. This restriction is not at all, as has been said,[144] a change in the Christian notion of *agapé;* it has none of the sectarian exclusivism found in such communities as that of Qumran.[145] The truth is rather, as Dibelius notes,[146] that John is the only New Testament author

---

144 Cf. especially A. NYGREN, *Eros et Agapè, La notion chrétienne de l'amour et ses transformations,* Paris, 1953.

145 Cf. our paper: *La litterature de Qumran et les écrits johanniques in Bulletin du Comite Des Etudes,* (Compagnie de Saint Eulpice), janvier-mars 1959, pp. 440-456.

146 *Joh.* 15, 18; *Eine Studie zum Traditionsproblem des Johannes-Evangeliums,* in *Festgabe für A. Deissmann,* Tubingen, 1927, pp. 166-186.

147 On the relationship between Agape and Eucharist in the fourth Gospel, cf. C. SPICQ, *Agapè,* III, Paris, 1949, pp. 143-145; 149-150; 179. Some authors, as BARRETT (pp. 370-371) think, as did a number of the Fathers, that John XIII: 18 is a reference to the Eucharist which Judas had shared.

who gives a metaphysical basis for Christian *agapé*, making of it the link of love which unites the Father and the Son, "in order that the love with which thou hast loved me may be in them, and I in them" (XVII: 26), and thus a fruit of the communion existing between the Father and the Son, hence of the eucharistic communion. Such charity, obviously, can be found only in those who, being born of God (in 1 Jo. Christian charity is closely related to supernatural regeneration, IV: 7; V: 1), are fed on faith and on the Eucharist, on Christ, the Bread of Life.

Thus is clarified the deep connection relating the eucharistic rite with the great commandment of mutual love, formulated right in the context of the Last Supper. Each is a memorial to His unspeakable love, which was pushed to the limit (*eis telos*, XIII: I); each is a substitute for the visible presence of Christ on earth among His own. But the practice of the commandments, especially that of fraternal charity, one remains united to the eucharistic vine, which is Jesus, or (which amounts to the same thing) "Remain in love," that love which led to the Incarnation, to Calvary, and to the Eucharist. "Abide in me and I in you . . . as the Father has loved me, I also have loved you. Abide in my love. If you keep my commandments, you will abide in my love. . . . This is my commandment, that you love one another as I have loved you" (XV: 4; 9; 10; 12).[147] Fraternal charity is man's response to God's love, which is manifested by the redemptive Incarnation, and by the Eucharist.

NOTE: Two works have appeared relative to the structure of John VI, which offer a new insight. P. Borgen, *The Unity of the Discourse in Jn. VI*, ZNW, 1950, pp. 277-278; E. J. Kilmartin, *The Formation of the Bread of Life Discourse*, Scripture, XII, 1960, pp. 75-78. According to their outlook, John VI: 32-58 is an explanation of VI: 31: "Bread from heaven he gave them to eat." Jesus first makes a fundamental revelation (vv. 32-40): the bread from heaven comes down from Him and from the Father, not from Moses; Jesus Himself is the bread from heaven. Christ replies immediately to the Jews' objection (vv. 41-51): How can He say He is *come down from heaven?* The last part of the Discourse, which concerns the eating (vv. 52-58), explains the words: "He gave them to eat." Considering the structure of the passage to be thus, one could hardly regard this last element as an interpolation! (A point well made!)

CHAPTER IV

THE COMPOSITION OF CHAPTERS IX - XII [1]

Both the language and the style of the fourth Gospel give a clear impression of unity. Still, one who undertakes a serious study of this text comes upon any number of defects in composition, repetitions, lacunae, apparent inconsistencies or transpositions, unexpected changes of situation, etc. Many exegetes, following Schwartz and Wellhausen, have attempted to resolve these problems by dissecting the fourth Gospel, in order to identify its various sources. As in the case of the Pentateuch, they have invoked everything from simple additions to a primitive text, to a compilation of various documents. However, not all critics have adopted this method; many, even among the foremost, have been more reserved.[2]

This study envisages the possibility of another solution, i.e., that of a displacement of the text. This hypothesis can be presented mainly in two ways: the former, and more popular, suspects that the primitive order of the gospel was disarranged, either accidentally (as if the pages had been dropped on a floor and then picked up again in disarray), or by a redactor. The second form of this hypothesis, that followed by Bultmann,[3] suspects that the fourth Gospel, originally composed from various sources, (revelation discourses [Offenbarungsreden]; signs (Semeia-Quellen); and separate accounts like that of the Passion), came in a state of complete disorder, to the redactor, whose task

---

1 First published in *Mélanges Bibliques redigés en l'honneur dé Andre Robert*.

2 On this question cf. J. LAGRANGE, *Où en est la dissection littéraire du quatrième évangile?* R. B., 1924, p. 320-342; Ph. MENOUD, *L'évangile de Jean d'après les recherches recentes*, Delachaux et Niestle, Neuchâtel-Paris, 1947, pp. 12-14.

3 *Das Evangelium des Johannes*, II durchgegebene Auflage, Göttingen, Vandenhoeck und Rupprecht, 1950. Since the Book has no synthetic introduction, Bultmann's views on the composition of the fourth Gospel are dispersed throughout the commentary.

was to establish, or re-establish, the original plan of the evangelist, although his work was never finished; thus modern exegetes
are seeking to pick up the work at precisely this juncture. Surely
it would be out of place here to examine thoroughly all the rami-
fications of this dislocation theory. Rather, we intend to test it,
in a few concrete cases, in chapters IX-XII, which present problems of composition familiar to all exegetes. In the first part
of the chapter we shall present some of the more typical examples
of this displacement, and the ways in which the projected
hypothesis would seek to solve them. In the course of our treatment it will become obvious that we are less than fully convinced
by this hypothesis. In the second part we will try to show that
the present order of the gospel can be justified in itself, thus
allowing (at least with regard to the chapters in question)
that the text be preserved as it stands.

(1) Defects of Composition; Displacements Suggested

Many exegetes are sure they have uncovered unnatural trans-
itions in chapters IX-XII of John's Gospel, and have had recourse to the hypothesis of displacement of the text to explain
them. Since we cannot study all the forms of this hypothesis in
detail, we shall present three of them here, those of Bernard,
Bultmann, and Hoare.

Bernard seems to us to have presented the most solid and
reasonable hypothesis of textual dislocations.[4] He sees two of
them in the section under consideration (chh. IX-XII); he suggests that in Chapter X, vv. 19-29 originally preceded v. 18, and
that the last verses of Chapter XII (vv. 44-50) originally followed
v. 36b, so that vv. 36b-43 followed 43. Bernard offers the following
reasons: Ch. X opens with the words, "Amen, amen I say to
you," which appear nowhere else in the fourth Gospel at the
beginning of a discourse. The theme treated in ch. X, that of
the shepherd and the flock, has no connection with the healing
of the man born blind of ch. IX. On the other hand, vv. 19-21
of ch. X appear to have no connection with their immediate context, and would be a good natural conclusion for the miracle
account. These three verses, therefore, should be transposed to
the end of ch. IX. Furthermore, the controversy with the phari-

---

4 *The Gospel according to St. John*, Edinburgh, Clark, 1942, vol. I,
pp. XXIV: XXVI, et vol. II, commentary *in loc.*

sees, which is begun by the healing of the man born blind,
at the Feast of Tabernacles (end of September, beginning of
October), could have lasted several weeks. However, when the
author mentions (X: 22) the Feast of the Dedication (end of
December), the controversy is long since over, and a new para-
graph begins. The hostile Jews have decided to ask Jesus directly,
"Art thou the Christ?" (X: 24). Jesus replies that if they do not
believe, it is because they are not of His flock. As is His custom,
He attributes their lack of faith to their evil dispositions; if they
were of His flock they would hear His voice, and He would
protect them. The allegory of the shepherd and of the flock
(X: 1-18) is introduced quite naturally, developing the theme
already suggested by vv. 27-29 of chapter X. Thus, the pericope
X: 1-18 is out of place; the sequence should be X: 27-29; 1-18.
The scribe who placed vv. 27-29 after vv. 1-18 thought, perhaps,
that v. 29 ("What my Father has given me is greater than all;
and no one is able to snatch anything from the hand of my
Father") should be next to v. 30 ("I and the Father are one").
But this same verse fits better after vv. 17-18

> For this reason the Father loves me, because I lay down
> my life that I may take it up again. No one takes it from
> me, but I lay it down of myself. I have the power to lay
> it down, and I have the power to take it up again. Such
> is the command I have received from my Father. I and
> the Father are one.

Only this assertion ("I and the Father are one") explains the
apparent contradiction of v. 19. ("The Son can do nothing of
Himself") and X:18 ("I have the power to lay it down and
I have the power to take it up again").

Verses 44-50 of chapter XII are out of harmony with the preceding context. In 36b the evangelist says that Jesus hid himself
from the Jews, emphasizing the unbelief of the Jews, in which
he sees the fulfillment of the oracles of Isaia LIII: 1; VI: 9-10.
He adds that several notables among the Jews believed in Him
nevertheless, although in secret, not daring to profess their belief
openly, lest they be put out of the synagogue. Following these
indications, which obviously are the conclusion of the public
ministry, suddenly (and surprisingly) appears another discourse!
Furthermore, the discourse is introduced by the word *ekraxe*,
which appears to contradict the *ekrybē* of v. 36b. The theme
presented in vv. 35-36 on light and darkness seems to be con-

tinued in vv. 44 ff. But vv. 35-36 do not say what or who is the light; VIII: 12 is too far away. Verse 46 offers an explanation: "I am come a light into the world." In other words, vv. 44 ff. are a continuation of vv. 35-36a, which would make no sense without them. Besides, vv. 36b-43 are a normal conclusion for the whole discourse.

Tatian's Diatesseron seems to confirm this opinion, modifying the order of John XII as follows: John 19-36a plus some verses taken from Matthew and Luke, plus John 36-41. This order differs from Bernard's only with regard to vv. 42-43.

Bultmann's proposed restoration of the text is partly in conformity with that of Bernard, but more complicated. We cannot give more than the general lines of it here.[5] The Master of Marburg sees the source of the disorder in chapter X to be the present position of vv. 19-21. These verses are evidently the conclusion of the healing of the man born blind and of the discussion which follows it; this discussion should not coincide with the good shepherd allegory of X: 1-18, which has no connection with the miracle narrative. Furthermore, this allegory seems to be introduced by the pericope X: 22 ff.; these two passages should not be separated by a long interval of several weeks, as is supposed by the present order of the text. Thus, X: 1-18, which follows normally the scene begun in X: 22, must have been originally after X: 26.

Bultmann, however, does not limit himself to these remarks, as Bernard does. He proceeds to rearrange the entire order of the text. First of all, like the miracles of chapters V and VI, that of chapter IX must be a preparation for a discourse, the conclusion of which is X: 19-21. Originally this discourse, centered on the theme of light (cf. IX: 4 ff), contained more than IX: 39-41. Thus Bultmann reconstructs this discourse by lining up the sections as follows: VIII: 12 plus XII: 44-50 plus VIII: 21-29 plus XII: 34-36. Likewise, instead of placing the good shepherd allegory (chapter X) after Christ's reply to the Jews at the Dedication Feast, i.e., between vv. 26-27, he changes the order of the allegory as follows: 11-13 plus 1-10 plus 14-18 plus 27 ff. Thus we have first the parable, made up of two parts, the good shepherd and the hireling (X: 11-13); the good shepherd and the robbers (X: 1-6). Finally comes the interpolation (X: 7-10; 14-18; 27-30).

---

5 Cf. *Das Evangelium des Johannes,* pp. 236, 272-274.

Verses 40-42 of chapter X are considered to be an introduction to the raising of Lazarus (XI: 1-44), which is followed by the meeting of the Sanhedrin (XI: 45-54), by the ·anointing at Bethany, and by the solemn entry into Jerusalem (XI: 55 - XII: 19). Bultmann shortens the discourse following the death of Jesus, having already joined to the discourse on the light which follows the healing of the man born blind, the two pericopes 34-36 and 44-50. He sees the present discourse (XII: 20-33) as followed by VIII: 20-40 and V: 60-71. These two sections fit badly in their present context, indicating the dénouement of the discussions with the Jews and preparing for chapters XIII ff., where Jesus limits His attention to His disciples. Thus these sections are concluded normally by the passage on the Jews' disbelief XII: 37-43.

Bernard's emendations of the text are based first of all on arguments of internal criticism, as well as on an appeal to the ancient MSS.[6] Hoare, a Catholic, seems to have gone furthest along this line. His system follows:[7] The present text of the fourth Gospel is obviously in disorder. Still, neither the versions nor the ancient MSS offer any order different from the present one. Since there are solid reasons for suspecting the presence of textual displacements, they must be supposed to have occurred prior to the publication of the work. They may have come about in this way: In his old age, the Apostle John is obliged to dictate his gospel to a secretary, who transcribes it first of all in the form of a rough draft, then copies it onto papyrus sheets. The papyrus sheets are written on one side only, and are intended to be placed side by side so as to form two scrolls (chapters I-XII and XIII-XXI). The final copy is read to John, who approves it; the rough copy is destroyed. Then, an accident occurs, whereby the loose papyrus sheets fall from the table to the floor and are disarranged. The secretary attempts to replace the sheets in order, but can count on no help from John, who now is in his death agony. His efforts at rearranging the pages meet with only partial success, and the fourth Gospel is published, complete but defective, with all subsequent copies reproducing the defective order of the chapters.[8]

---

6 *The Gospel according to St. John,* vol. I, pp. XXVIII-XXX.

7 *Original Order and Chapters of St. John's Gospel,* London, Burns Oates and Washbourne, 1944.

8 *Original Order,* pp. 103-105.

The task now is to discover the manner in which the secretary rearranged the pericopes. Hoare begins this project on the supposition that the pages of ancient MSS, as well as those of scrolls and codices, were usually of more or less the same length. Given what we might call the unit of measure of a page, each section displaced should correspond to this unit of measure, or a multiple of it. Now, on the basis of internal criteria, or of arithmetical calculations, the author divides the Gospel into twenty-one sections, which, in the present work, have no logical or natural connection. Each of these sections has from two to forty-two pages. Each page has twenty-one lines of eighteen to nineteen letters (397 letters). The entire work would have 71,579 letters on 185 pages (not counting the narrative of the woman in adultery).

On the basis of all this data, Hoare attempts to reestablish the original order. For the first part of the Gospel (II-XII) in which narratives predominate and serve as settings for discourse, the reconstruction of the order consists above all in attaching the discourses to those events which occasioned them. For chapters IX-XII, Hoare arrives at the following results: IX: 1-41 plus X: 19-42, plus XI: 1-33, plus XII: 23b-33, plus XI: 34-57, plus XII: 1-23a plus X: 1-18). The pericope XII: 34-50 goes between VIII: 28a ("When you have lifted up the Son of Man, then you will know that I am he"), and VIII: 28b ("Of myself I do nothing; but that I preach only what the Father has taught me").[9]

Not all critics accept the transposition theory. It is certainly subject to suspicion when it is presented in as mechanical a way as that of Hoare. One merely starts with a pericope which, for reasons of internal criticism, seems out of context; then proceeds to measure it, using this same unit of measure in order to find other passages which also seem dislocated. However, as Uricchio says,[10] if such arguments and measurements were valid, one would have to arrive at the same unit of measure, which the critics do not do. Spitta has 789 letters;[11] Bernard has 375, or

---

9 Among those who prefer to effect transpositions within the section Jo. IX-XII, are also F. W. LEWIS, *Disarrangements in the Fourth Gospel* (1910); G. H. C. MAC GREGOR, *The Gospel of John*, London, Hodder and Stoughton, 1949.

10 *La Teoria delle transposizioni nel Vangelo di S. Giovanni, Biblica,* 1950, p. 147.

11 *Zur Geschichte und Literatur des Urchristentums,* I (1893), p. 189.

750, counting both *recto* and *verso* sides of the page; Hoare has 379. Some authors have several units of measure. Thompson has three; 160-165; 220; and 370.[12] Brinckmann proposes four: 450; 468; 486; and 560.[13] We might mention that in the MSS of the Christian era which have come down to us, the unit of measure varies from 120 to 770! Given therefore, the absence of the original text of the fourth Gospel, and since we do not know whether it was a scroll or a codex (codices were, apparently, in use in the first century, especially among Christians), it is quite impossible for us to determine the unit of measure for the original pages.

Not even those critics who appeal to arguments based on internal criticism, as Bernard and Bultmann, are inclined to form their conclusions hastily. Some adduce geographical arguments in favor of one or other transposition, e. gr., some place III: 22-30 between II: 12 and II: 13, in order to render more plausible Jesus' journey from Capharnaum to Jerusalem (across Judea); some place VI between IV and V, to obtain a better geographical cohesiveness. However, even without going so far as to say, as does Strachan,[14] that John attaches no importance at all to Jesus' journeyings, it does seem necessary to maintain that Jesus' journeys are no more than secondary in the mind of John, who is first and foremost a theologian. There is a way of accepting the shifts of thought and the interruptions of them, says Strachan, in so far as such sudden movements of thought are habitual with John. As a matter of fact, interruptions of this kind are so commonplace in John that the simplest solution seems to be to see this as a habit of the author. This answer also invites comparison with I Jo., which may well have come from the same hand as did the fourth Gospel, and in which we see an entirely similar phenomenon. In the prologue to I Jo., v. 2 obviously fits better between vv. 1 and 3. E. Lohmeyer notes that in this verse the rythm is much weaker than in the rest of the pericope, which leads him to speak of a prose interpretation (*prosaische Interpretation*) of the expression *peri tou logou tes*

---

12 *Expositor, IX, Accidental Disarrangements in the Fourth Gospel,* pp. 430-433.

13 *Gregorianum, 1939, Qualis fuerit ordo originarius in quarto evangelio,* p. 568.

14 *The Fourth Gospel, its Significance and Environment,* London, Student Christian Movement Press, 1947, p. 81.

zoes at the end of v. 1; however, he adds, it is impossible to separate the hymn and its interpretation, which affect each other mutually.[15] Likewise, it seems to us gratuitous to maintain that the two passages of the Prologue on the Baptist (I: 6-8; 16) were not part of the original passage, on the grounds that they interrupt the chain of thought. In I Jo. there are two themes which alternate back and forth; that of the purity of faith and that of charity. For the first of these, cf. I: 5 to II: 2; II: 12 to III: 10; IV: 1-6; V: 1-21; for the second, cf. II: 3-11; III: 11-24; IV: 7-21. Undoubtedly, these two themes could be isolated from one another in this order, but such an order would then not be that of the author!

The same kind of phenomenon would be discernible throughout the fourth Gospel, if this were the place to undertake a deep study of its literary structure. One must concede at least that the better thing is to make every effort to account for the present order of the text, rather than to disrupt the whole thing. This we shall now try to do with regard to chapters IX-XII.

(2) *Justification of the Present Order of the Text*

It seems necessary, in studying the literary structure of John IX-XII, to distinguish IX-X from XI-XII. These are two distinct units in the author's thought, joined together, beginning with facts, especially the miracle accounts, and then passing directly to discourses, which, more or less clearly, serve as a commentary on the facts. This same division was quite evident in chapters V-VI, leading us to believe that the discourses of X and XII: 20-50 are related to the facts presented immediately before them, i.e., to IX and to XI-XII: 1-19.

Some have questioned the connection between chapters IX and X, even from patristic times. Clement of Alexandria [16] could see no logical connection between them. The good shepherd allegory does not follow the words of Christ in chapter X, but is a reply to the secret thoughts of the pharisees. St. Thomas Aquinas says that, after treating the theme of Christ's *virtus illuminativa*, John proceeds to discuss His *virtus vivificativa*.[17]

---

15 *Ueber Aufbau und Gliederung des ersten Johannesbriefes,* in *Zeitschrift f.d. neutestamentl. Wissenschaft,* 1928, p. 227.

16 *In Johannis Evangelium,* lib. 12, P. G., 73, in h. 1.

17 *Expositio in Evangelium Johannis, in* H. 1.

Lagrange [18] also thinks that if it is inserted into the narrative of chapter IX, then the subject treated now is partly new.

On the contrary, some commentators find a very close connection between the miracle of the man born blind and the good shepherd parable, and see in this parable a strongly polemic intent. Godet, for example, sees X: 1-21 as "in close relationship with the facts narrated in the preceding chapter. It is really a repetition in parable form, of these same facts".[19] Plummer is of about the same mind, insisting also that the picture presented is authentic.[20]

Dodd observes,[21] more profoundly, that chapter IX ends in a condemnation of the Jewish authorities, the spiritually blind, who have come to expel the man born blind, and cured, from the synagogue. In the Old Testament, especially in Ezechiel, the allegory of the shepherd has a distinctively polemic significance, being directed against the evil shepherds who have led the nation to disaster and exile. The messianic good shepherd (Ez. XXXIV) is opposed precisely to them. This is to say that basically the end of John IX, in which Jesus opposes the pharisees, and the beginning of chapter X, in which He denounces the false shepherds, are both centered on the same theme.

We must distinguish, it seems to us, between the real historical background of the good shepherd allegory, which we think is a substantial reproduction of Jesus' teaching, and the relationship which the author of the fourth Gospel wished to establish between these words and the preceding scene. It is quite likely that the good shepherd parable was not spoken immediately after the healing of the man born blind. It certainly does not continue the theme which chapter IX develops. The evangelist's intention, however, is to link them together, as is evident from X: 1: "Amen, amen I say to you," which otherwise occurs within

---

18 *Évangile selon saint Jean,* Paris, Gabalda, 1927, p. 73.

19 *Commentaire sur l'evangile de saint Jean,* Neuchâtel, Attinger, 1902, 2e partie, p. 74.

20 *The Gospel according to St. John,* Cambridge, University Press, 1923, p. 211. Cf. also P. SCHANZ, *Commentar über das Evangelium des hl. Johannes* Tübingen, Franz Fues, 1885, pp. 377-378.

21 *The Interpretation of the Fourth Gospel,* Cambridge, University Press, 1953, p. 359s.

a discourse, but never at the beginning of one. X: 19-21 refers
to the healing of the man born blind, from which we are invited
to understand that Jesus, the good shepherd, opposes the spiritual
leaders of the Jews, who are evil shepherds, as they show by
their attitude toward the man cured of blindness. We might say
that here, as elsewhere, the development of thought is required
by a certain parallelism. X: 19-21 recalls IX: 1-41; the *schisma*
produced in X: 19 recalls that mentioned in IX: 16. Furthermore, it is also evident that the statements made by Jesus on
the Feast of the Dedication (X: 22-39) refer partly to the parable.
Lagrange says that, if this parable were not read at the beginning
of chapter X, "one could not understand vv. 26 ff., but in the
present context it is undeniably an allusion to a previous discourse."

There is, therefore, good reason for leaving the text as it
stands, with the parable of X: 1-18, the short narrative of X:
19-21, and the statement of X: 26-29, even though it may be
surprising to see Jesus continuing on the Dedication Feast a
discourse which He began some months before. We can also come
to detect John's method; like the Synoptics, he has been able to
establish literary and theological relationships between facts and
discourses which were originally separate, thereby emphasizing
one or other point which he wishes to make, either by way of
teaching or by way of observation. This is not at all an attack
on the historicity of the work; rather, it shows all the more clearly
that it is at base not history, but a theological interpretation of
history. In the same vein Calmer writes of the difficulties raised
by the present order of John X:

> We must recognize that there is no really acceptable
> basis for the transpositions which some propose. The diffi-
> culty arising from the comparison of the two parts of the
> tenth chapter come only from the point of view which
> one adopts toward the text. Those who insist on taking
> into account all the little details arising from Jesus' actions
> and discourses in the fourth Gospel, find themselves sur-
> rounded by countless difficulties. The true point of view
> is that of the evangelist himself, as he reports Jesus'
> words and deeds. For the sacred author, it is a question
> of the same teaching being presented in various historical

circumstances. He does take pains to indicate the circumstances, somewhat precisely, but the time gaps between them are not intended to break the chain of his thought.[22]

Schneider,[23] a German exegete, has given the decisive proof why there should be no transpositions within chapter X. The chapter opens with an enigmatic discourse (cc. 1-6), which must be interpreted. This interpretation is given in vv. 7-18 and 27-30, which explain respectively the three key-words of the *paroimia*: the door (*thyra*) of v. 1; the shepherd (*poimēn*) of v. 2; and the flock (*idia probata*) of v. 3. First of all, vv. 7-10, which twice repeat the phrase, "I am the door," show that Jesus is the only door, through whom the shepherds must pass in order to come to their flocks (v. 7). (Those who do not pass through this door are the thieves and robbers already mentioned in v. 1), and through which the sheep also pass, in quest of pasture (v. 9). Secondly, vv. 11-18, which also contain a formula twice repeated ("I am the good shepherd"), contrast Jesus the good shepherd, and the hirelings (vv. 11-13); they then go on to show the characteristics of Jesus, the good shepherd (vv. 14-18), who loves His sheep and willingly gives His life for them. The last verses (27-30) state who truly are Jesus' sheep (*ta idia probata*); they are those who hear His voice and who follow Him; He knows them, gives them eternal life, and cares for them, together with the Father.[24]

Msgr. Cerfaux makes some observations [25] which confirm this outlook; the Synoptic parables (cf. Mt. XIII; Mk. LV; Lk. VIII: 4-18; also Mt. XV: 15-20; Mk. VII: 14-23) seem linked to a literary context which stresses the following themes: that of the Jewish apocalyptic tradition (cf. Ez. XVII; Daniel;

---

22 *L'Évangile selon saint Jean*, Paris, Lecoffre, 1904, pp. 320-321.

23 *Die Komposition von Jo. 10, Conjectanea Neotestamentica XI, in honorem Antonii Fridrichsen*, Lund, 1947, pp. 220-225.

24 We agree with DODD that the controversy in X: 22-32 centers around the dominant theme of Christ's "works" (cf. vv. 25; 32; 33; 37; 38), and that the mention of the sheep in vv. 26-28 is related to the first appearance of this theme, so that it would hardly be acceptable to separate this mention from the present controversy in order to put it somewhere else. (*Interpretation of the Fourth Gospel*, p. 356).

25 *Le theme littéraire parabolique dans l'évangile de saint Jean, Conjectanea Neotestamentica XI, in Honorem Antonii Fridrichsen*, Lund, 1947, pp. 15-25.

Parables of Henoch; 4th Esdras; Apocalypse of Baruch), according to which God reveals the secrets of the future kingdom by way of parables (*meshalim*) and puzzling visions; the theme of the intelligence of the hearers, deriving from the concrete circumstances of Christ's preaching, and that of the explanation of the riddle, which Christ gave to His disciples. Now, given come modifications, which are evident enough, all these elements recur in John X, where the *paroimia* is equivalent to the Synoptic *parabole*, stressing only the meaning of the riddle. The riddle is presented in vv. 1-5; the intelligence of the hearers is indicated in v. 6 (cf. also IX: 39-41); the explanation is in the following verses. The flow of ideas in John X is, therefore, quite traditional.

We may now pass on to the second literary unit, chapters XI-XII. These chapters have the same composition; first a series of facts or deeds (XI-XII: 19); then a parallel series of discourses, which, in the mind of the evangelist, are to serve as a commentary on the deeds. To see how the two elements (deeds-discourses) correspond, and how it is consequently incorrect to change the present order of Jesus' words, we must first try to understand what, in John's mind, is the essential significance of the deeds. These deeds are three: the raising of Lazarus (XI); the anointing at Bethany (XII: 1-11); Christ's triumphant entry into Jerusalem (XII: 12-19).

The raising of Lazarus is surely the most outstanding of the miracles adduced to show Jesus as source of life and resurrection. However, it is by His death that Jesus will give His life to the world; Caiphas unintentionally indicates this in XI: 50-51. The raising of Lazarus seems to us to be precisely the announcement, the definitive acceptance, we might say the foretaste, of this life-giving death. This, we think, is evident from the various circumstances of the narrative. When Jesus proposes to return to Judea to recall Lazarus to life, His disciples fear that He is taking a terrible risk; "Rabbi, just now the Jews were seeking to stone thee; and dost thou go there again?" (XI: 8). Jesus is determined to go; Thomas cries out, "Let us also go, that we may die with Him!" (v. 16). Before performing the miracle of raising Lazarus, Jesus groans in spirit (*enebrimesato tō pneuma*ti, v. 33; *palin embrimōmenos en heautō*, v. 38), and is troubled (*etaraxen heauton*, v. 33). Lagrange sees this groaning as a gesture of sympathy and a sharing of the general sorrow.

This opinion, however, is difficult to accept, since, as Hoskyns says,[26] Jesus willed the death of Lazarus, delaying His journey to Bethany in order that Lazarus might die; when He approaches the tomb, He is fully aware of His control over life and death. Thus, regardless of the meaning of *embrimaomai* in some profane writings, in biblical Greek the word always expresses indignation and anguish; cf. Dan. XI: 3; Lam. II: 6 (LXX); Mt. IX: 30; Mk. I: 43; XIV: 5; Is. XVII: 13 (Symm.); Ps. VII: 12 (Aquila). We disagree with Loisy's contention that "Jesus is saddened at the sight of so many weeping over a dead man in the presence of the Master of life and death"; [27] this would mean that Mary and the Jews are blameworthy; besides, Jesus Himself weeps (v. 35). We are sure that the emotions of Jesus at this moment are related to the trouble which He will feel (*etarachthē tō pneumati* XII: 21), when He announces to the disciples the treason of Judas. Furthermore, they are related to the exclamation (XII: 27) which reflects Jesus' awareness of His impending Passion, "Now my soul is troubled. And what shall I say? Father, save me from this hour! No, this is why I came to this hour." Like this exclamation, the groaning of XI: 33-38 serves as a prelude to the agony of Gethsemane and Golgotha. Jesus realizes that to raise Lazarus will be to sign His own death warrant (Calmer). Still he does it, giving His life, as it were, in advance, for His friend, and offering at the same time a sign to the unbelieving Jews.[28]

If the raising of Lazarus is a foretelling of the death of Jesus, source of life, then the anointing at Bethany must also have a symbolic meaning; as the Synoptics, although more deliberately than they, John gives this as a foretelling of Christ's burial. Aside from the context, we might translate v. 7 as follows: "Leave her alone, so that she may save it (the ointment) for the day of my burial (to come)." However, according to Mark, Mary breaks the jar with the intention of letting the ointment flow out, and as John says himself, the house was filled with the fragrance of the ointment. There is no indication that only a part of it was poured out; furthermore, the rest of it could hardly be called *auto!* This also renders Judas' objection less

---

26 *The Fourth Gospel*, London, Faber and Faber, 1947, p. 404.

27 *Le quatrieme évangile*, Paris, Nourry, 1921, p. 350; cf. W. BAUER, *Das Johannes Evangelium*, Tübingen, Mohr. 1933, p. 152.

28 Cf. DODD, *The Interpretation of the Fourth Gospel*, p. 367; GODET, *Commentaire sur l'évangile de saint Jean*, t. III, p. 140-141.

plausible. The better thing seems, therefore, to agree with La-grange, Hoskyns, and others, that there must be some thing implied in v. 7; if the ointment was not sold (cf. v. 5), it was in order "that she might save it for the day of my burial." Thus the sense is the same as that of the Synoptics.

The *textus receptus* has *tetēreken,* instead of *hina tērēsē,* a correction made for the sake of clarity, and which inter-prets the text perfectly.

Still, there are some significant differences between John and the Synoptics. Matthew and Mark speak only of an anointing of Jesus' head; John ignores this gesture, and mentions another, more unusual one, the washing of His feet. If John has a point to make in this last gesture, it must be, as Mollat says, "that it was altogether extraordinary (Lk. VII: 46), and thus better adapted to the burial rite".[29] In Mark (XIV: 8) Jesus says "she has anointed my body in preparation for burial" (*eis ton enta-phiasmon*). In Matthew the phrase is turned in such a way that, as Lagrange says, there are no longer two acts, one a symbol of the other; we might say that the woman has already gone on to perform the burial (XXVI: 12). This is even clearer in John, because for John the phrase *eis tēn hēmeran tou entaphiasmon* means the same day on which the woman performs the anointing. The day of the anointing at Bethany is symbolically the day of Christ's burial.

After the anointing at Bethany, John presents the triumphant entry of Christ into Jerusalem, as an anticipation of Jesus' final glorification, which will come after His death (XII: 9-19). The Synoptics also make this point, seeing in the event perhaps also a recollection of the pomp of royal processions of entry into the various cities, and of the shouts of popular acclaim which marked them. Undoubtedly, this triumphal entry, which Jesus wanted and planned, is a symbol of His future messianic victories. All of the four Gospels have this point, but John has some aspects of it which are peculiar to his Gospel alone. First of all, he emphasizes more than the others the hellenistic *parousia* aspect of the entry; he also refers more definitely to the final *parousia* of Christ. The crowd comes to meet Jesus (*eis hypantēsin*) as the people of Pergamum were directed to receive Attalus III

---

29 *L'Évangile selon saint Jean* (Bible de Jérusalem), Paris, Éditions du Cerf, 1953, p. 141.

(138-133 B.C.),[30] and, as Josephus tells us, they came out to meet Titus at Antioch.[31] Thus, at the end of time, the elect will come to meet the Lord (*eis apantēsin*) I Thess. IV: 17. The reference to the palms is also peculiar to John. Mark (XI: 8, *stibades*) and Matthew (XXI: 8, *kladoi*) speak only of tree branches. Since there were no palm trees in Jerusalem itself (Lagrange thinks, however, that they might have been nearby, in the warm eastern valley), Schlatter and Eissler think that they may have been palms used previously, at the Feast of Tabernacles, which the pilgrims had taken to their homes.[32] If this is so, then the detail of the palms, joined to the expression *eis hypantesin*, lends emphasis to the messianic character of the entry. In any case, palms are a normal part of a royal triumph (1 Macc. XIII: 51; 2 Macc. X: 7; Apoc. VII: 9). Besides, it is interesting to note here that John is the only one who narrates the greeting "King of Israel," attributed to Jesus on this occasion.

Still, John notes, the disciples had at this moment, no idea of the full meaning of this apparently modest triumph. Only when Jesus was glorified did they realize that this occasion, a literal fulfillment of Zach. IX: 9, was in itself a prelude to that glorification (v. 16), and that they themselves had had a part in the realization of the messianic prophecies.

Lagrange thinks that the account of the Greeks asking to see Jesus, is part of His triumph of the moment, and a foretelling of the triumph to come, which will include the conversion of the pagan world. It is related, in effect to the reflection of the pharisees in v. 19: "Do you see that we avail nothing? Behold, the whole world has gone after him!"

We have uncovered, therefore, a deliberate, logical connection linking together the events narrated in chapters XI: XII; the raising of Lazarus announces Jesus' life-giving death; the anointing at Bethany foretells His burial, and the entry into Jerusalem indicates His final triumph. We think that there is a parallel linking of the various parts of the discourse which follows the

---

30 *Orientis Graeci Inscr.* no. 332, I, 26, 39, quoted by L. CERFAUX, *Le Christ dans la théologie de saint Paul*, Paris, Éditions du Cerf, 1951, p. 30.

31 *Bellum Judaicum*, VII, 100-103.

32 Cf. BULTMANN, *Das Evangelium des Johannes*, p. 319, note 7; A. SCHLATTER, *Der Evangelist Johannes*, Stuttgart, Calwer, 1948, p. 265.

narrative of these events, and which the evangelist has here as a commentary on them (vv. 23-33; 34-36; 47-50).

The first section (XII: 23-33) corresponds to the raising of Lazarus. Jesus, who has saved Lazarus at the implied price of His own life, says here that His work of salvation is to be the fruit of His own death. He is troubled as the Hour approaches, just as He was troubled at Lazarus' tomb; also, these two refer- ences to Jesus as being troubled, are both a prelude to the agony in Gethsemane, which John does not narrate.

The second section (XII: 34-36) seems to correspond to the anointing at Bethany. Jesus sees in this anointing a prelude to His burial and announces to His disciples that they will not have Him always with them (XII: 7). Now He speaks formally of His departure from their midst: "Yet a little while the light is among you. Walk while you have the light, that darkness may not overtake you" (v. 35). Then, as if these words were not enough, Jesus adds a gesture full of meaning, a sort of foretaste of His departure: "These things Jesus spoke, and he went away and hid Himself from them" (v. 36). Godet comments: "This was more than a cloud hiding the sun; the sun was setting: the night had come".[33]

The final section (XII: 37-50) is worthy of special notice. As we have said above, many exegetes would like to change the order of this text. However, the present order seems to us to be required, given the statement that this last pericope corre- sponds to the triumphant entry into Jerusalem. The death of Jesus will be calamitous, but it really will be the work either of the unbelief of the Jews, which John seeks to relate to the divine plan (vv. 37-41), or of the weakness of men, who, because of human frailty, are afraid to declare themselves as disciples of Christ (vv. 42-43). The unbelief of the Jews is not a frustration for Jesus, any more than it was for Isaia, contemplating in the Temple the vision of the glory of Jahweh, King of the universe (VI: 1-6), a vision with an obviously eschatological significance,[34] and which the evangelist interprets as a contemplation of the glory of Christ the King.

There seems to be another allusion to this triumph in the

---

33 *Commentaire sur l'evangile de saint Jean*, t. III, p. 208.

34 This Eschatological meaning is stressed by V. HERNTRICH, *Der Prophet Jesaja* (chap. 1-12), *Göttingen, Vandenhoeck und Ruprecht*, 1950, p. 99.

words of Jesus which follow. As we have said, it seems strange at first (Jesus has gone away and hidden Himself from the Jews), that John does not terminate the public ministry account here, but brings Jesus back again, and has Him speaking once more. Nevertheless, we are of the opinion that we should keep the present order of the text. The author, who has shown the triumphal entry into Jerusalem following the anointing at Bethany (the symbolic prelude to His burial), does now wish not to end Jesus' discourse to the Jews with a statement of His coming disappearance, such as that presented in vv. 35-36. Jesus' earthly ministry should not end on such a somber note. Such is the impression suggested by XII: 44-50:

> He who believes in me, believes not in me but in him who sent me.... And if anyone hears my words, and does not keep them, it is not I who judge him.... He who rejects me, and does not accept my words, has one to condemn him. The word which I have spoken will condemn him on the last day. For I have not spoken on my own authority, but he who sent me, the Father, has commanded me, what I should say, and what I should declare.

In other words, Jesus, who must die, still cannot fail, because He is one with the Father, who sent Him, and whom He represents. He has come upon earth not to judge but to save; these are the same words which He will address to the damned, the unbelievers; He will have the last word. This final victory is the ultimate symbolic meaning of Christ's solemn entry into the Holy City.

Modern exegetes, including Knabenbauer, agree that the pericope John XII: 44-50 (about which we know neither where nor to whom it was spoken), is not historically a discourse of Jesus. On the other hand, it should be more than an invention of the author pure and simple. Some suggest, as does Dodd,[35] who refuses for this reason to accept any transposition, that John wishes to present here a summary of the discourses which Jesus pronounced before. We disagree, however, and maintain that as a synthesis, it is obviously incomplete, lacking even some essential details. We are inclined rather to the opinion that, just as the raising of Lazarus and the anointing at Bethany have their re-

---

35 *The Interpretation of the Fourth Gospel*, pp. 380-381.

spective commentaries in the words of Jesus which follow, likewise the triumphant entry into Jerusalem has a commentary in
these words, which, as does the triumphant entry itself, recall
the judgment to be held at the time of the Parousia.[36]

We do not wish to imply that all the ideas we have presented
are certain, or that any hypothesis calling for a transposition of
the text must be rejected *a priori*. The fourth Gospel is in itself
no more immune to the possibility of transpositions, than is the
rest of Scripture. We do wish, however, to maintain that before
presuming to undertake any changes in the present order of the
text, we should be sure that we have exhausted every reasonable
attempt to explain it as it stands.[37] The examples which we
have indicated should show clearly the correctness of this position.

Our general impression of the fourth Gospel is as follows:
Apparently this Gospel, before being subjected to final redaction,
had a primitive form (as did the Synoptics), possibly the form
in which the Apostle John preached it. The miracles and discourses of Jesus which John brought into his preaching, without
neglecting to present the thoughts of his Master, were sometimes
described in terms of chronological or geographical circumstances,
sometimes not. Once decided to assemble these various accounts
into a single work (of which there may well have been numerous
others), the author sought to maintain the general outline of the
life of Jesus, bringing in incidental details of time and place in
connection with some of the episodes. However, he gave to the
entire account a more fundamental theological framework, in
conformity with his purpose, and which is expressed most eloquently in the Prologue. This explains at least partially the un-
easiness of the transition from some passages to those which
follow. It is also possible, although we cannot prove it, that the
Apostle himself may have been unable to put the finishing touches
personally on the work.

NOTE: Critics have often considered the narrative of the raising
of Lazarus as a piece of didactic fiction, made up of two episodes
from St. Luke's Gospel, that of Martha and Mary (Lk. X: 38-42)
and that of Lazarus and Dives (Lk. XVI: 19-39). R. Dunkerley

36 Cf. the reflections of LOISY *Le Quatrième Évangile*, Paris, Picard,
1903, pp. 700-701.

37 DODD insists several times in his excellent book, on this elementary
critical necessity (*Interpretation*, pp. 289-290; 308-309; 340; 399-400.)

suggests that these two passages should be reversed; this re-arrangement would result in an indication very much in favor of the historicity of the johannine account (*Lazarus*, in New Testament Studies 5 (1959), pp. 321-327. Luke's parable seems related to the Perean section of Jesus' public ministry; Jesus was in Perea when He learned of Lazarus' illness (John X: 40). The disciples try to dissuade Him from returning to Judea (John XI: 7-8). Finding the Master adamant, however, they begin to hope that He will bring the crowds to favor Him again, by raising Lazarus. Jesus then tells them the parable: the Jews would follow neither Moses nor the prophets; how then, could even Lazarus, risen from the dead, (Lk. XVI: 31), convince them? This hypothesis follows the direction which we indicated above. The really poignant element in the raising of Lazarus, is the fact that Jesus works this miracle with the conviction that it will not be useless, but that it will lead eventually to His own condemnation and death.

CHAPTER V

THE TIME OF THE CHURCH IN ST. JOHN [1]

The Judeo-Christian religion is inseparably linked to a history of salvation gradually developed over a long period, which in itself comprises definite periods, each marked by its own distinctive characteristics. These periods are the preparatory stage of the Old Testament, the time of Christ's earthly sojourn, and the present era, extending from Christ's heavenly exaltation to His Parousia. The Christian of the present time lives in an era distinct from both that of the Jews of the Old Covenant, and from that of the disciples who followed the Master along the roadways of Galilee and Judea. Yet, he belongs to the Church, which the Old Testament era pre-figured only imperfectly, and which was born of the redemption on Good Friday as well as of the victory of Easter morning. This *time of the Church* and the distinctive characteristics of this period in the history of salvation will be the subject of this chapter.

We shall begin our study with a consideration of the Fourth Gospel, because, although the Synoptics speak quite a bit about the Church, the Messianic community based on the conviction that Jesus is the promised Messiah, the eschatological Shepherd, still He cannot be the Messiah without a messianic community, a Shepherd with a flock.[2]

One might object that St. Matthew speaks of the Church more than does St. John. This is only apparently true, however. John's gospel has its basic theme the person of the incarnate Son of God, through whom the mysterious riches of divine life are revealed and communicated to men. *But in so far as it is Christological, it is also ecclesial*, since it is principally in the Church that these riches are offered. John alone of the four

---

1 Published in *La Maison-Dieu*, no. 65, 1961.

2 Cf. *Introduction à la Bible*, t. II, *Nouveau Testament*, Paris, 1960, pp. 800-818: *L'Église, actualisation du Regne de Dieu d'après les Évangiles synoptiques*.

evangelists stresses this truth. It is the basis of his gospel story, directly oriented toward Jesus' Hour, which is also that of the Church and the sacraments.[3] The Savior's public ministry, His preaching, His miracles announce this great work, and this era, as we see in the statement, "The hour is coming and is now here" (IV: 23; V: 25).[4]

Nothing shows, better than the Discourse on the Bread of Life (John VI), this relation between the time of Jesus living on earth and that of the Church; at the very moment in which Jesus speaks, a sort of communion with Him is already possible by faith, "I am the bread of life; he who comes to Me shall not hunger, and he who believes in Me shall never thirst" (John VI: 35). It matters not that the eucharistic communion will not take place as long as Christ's flesh has not yet been given up for the life of the world (VI: 51), and that the Son of Man has not yet ascended where He was before (cf. VI: 62).[5]

After these considerations of the Fourth Gospel, we shall study the Apocalypse, which is inseparable from it, and which completes it. This book, admittedly difficult to interpret, need not bring us any entirely new lights, but, since it was composed in response to a particular concrete situation (which we shall recall) it presents some aspects of the life of the Church, which appear only vaguely in the Gospel. Furthermore, whereas the other New Testament writings treat of the Christian community in itself, the Apocalypse has the unique characteristic of describing this Christian community in relation to the history of the entire world. Thus it is often ranked with the prophetic books of the Old Testament, especially with that of a Second Isaia, a sort of Christian book of Daniel.

Our conclusion will consider the beautiful symbol of the

---

3 Cf. our study *L'Heure de Jésus et le signe de Cana,* in *Ephemerides Theologicae Lovanienses,* 1960, pp. 5-22.

4 Cf. A. CORELL, *Consummatum est, Eschatology and Church in the Gospel of St. John,* London, 1958, pp. 107 ff. St. John constantly looks beyond Jesus' earthly life, death and resurrection; he always had in mind the Church, for which Christ primarily came. This explains the difficult phrase, "The hour is coming, and is now here"; i.e., Christ's earthly life is but an anticipation (now is) of His action in the Church (the hour is coming).

5 Cf. our work, *Les themes bibliques majeurs du discours sur le pain de vie* (*Jo. VI*) in *Nouvelle Revue Théologique,* decembre 1960, pp. 1058-1059, as well as Chapter III above.

woman as the people of God, which is common to both the Apocalypse and the Fourth Gospel, and which summarizes magnificently the teaching of these two books on the *time of the Church*.

(1) *The Fourth Gospel*

It would be a complete study in itself to collect and analyze al the teachings of St. John's Gospel relative to the time of the Church. Since this is not the place for so exhaustive a work, we shall limit ourselves here to the discourses after the Last Supper, in which Christ instructs His Apostles as to how they are to conduct themselves after His departure.[6] We shall allude to some illustrations in chapters XIX, XX, and XXI, in which the dying and risen Savior shows us the beginning of the fulfillment of all His promises.

The greatness of man in the Scripture comes from the fact that he is allowed to speak to God.[7] In the discourse after the Last Supper, Chapters XIV and XVI describe exactly how Christians in the Church are to carry on this sacred dialogue. We might reduce these instructions to the three following points: (a) Jesus is going to go away, but He will come again and will be closer than ever to His disciples; (b) The Father will care in a special way for the disciples during the era from Christ's departure until His Parousia; (c) The Father and the Son will send the Holy Spirit, the Paraclete, to the disciples, to enlighten and fortify them. We shall now review each of these parts briefly, to see what is the time of the Church *from the point of view of men's relations with God*. From the other elements of the discourse after the Last Supper, we shall see what is the time of the Church, *from the point of view of the disciples' relations with each other*.

---

6 Cf., besides the various commentaries on St. John, the following monographs: C. HAURET, *Les adieux du Seigneur* (Jn. 13-17), Paris, 1951; H. VAN DEN BUSSCHE, *Les discours d'adieu de Jésus*, Editions de Maredsous, 1959; G. M. BEHLER, *Les paroles d'adieux du Seigneur* (Lectio Divina), Paris, 1960.

7 In the Greek world, on the contrary, man's greatness is defined by an abstract reflection on what he is in himself. The two points of view are not opposed, but complementary.

THE TIME OF THE CHURCH AND MEN'S RELATIONS WITH GOD

(1) Christ

The effective presence of the risen Christ should be the primary characteristic of the time of the Church, according to John XIV-XVI. The disciples who have left all to follow Christ, and who have been privileged to be close to His person, are disturbed to hear of His imminent departure, and feel an anguish like that of a child about to be separated from his parents. They are to take courage (XIV: 1). For those who do not believe, Jesus will go and be no more than a person of the past. The disciples, however, will see Him differently. He will not leave them orphans (XIV: 18). He will return to take them to Himself, to make them sharers of His glory (XIV: 3), not only at the time of their death of this Parousia; but immediately after the sorrow of His departure will come the joy of His return, just as the pains of childbirth give way to the joy which celebrates the birth of a new man into the world (XIV: 18 ff.; XVI: 19 ff.), "I go away and I am coming to you" (XIV: 28). After He has become invisible to the world, Jesus will make Himself visible to His own: "Yet a little while and the world no longer sees me. But you see me, for I live and you shall live" (XIV: 19).

These promises certainly are related to the bodily appearance of the risen Christ, which will be granted to a privileged few, especially to the Twelve. Their real meaning however, is much deeper and more general. They refer to the spiritual vision of Christ, which shall be granted to the believers of all time according to the measure of their faith. The presence of Christ at their side will fill them with a joy which no one shall take from them (XVI: 22 because it will come from His heavenly triumph, and will be His joy also (cf. XVII: 13).[8]

Yet, it will be more than a presence of Christ among them. As a friend, He will come with the Father to make His abode

---

8 D. MOLLAT, L'Évangile de Saint Jean (Bible de Jérusalem), Paris, 1953, p. 171, note 7. From this element, and from some others of the same kind, comes the following conclusion: If Christ's earthly life is an anticipation of His action in the Church, then the life of the Church is in its turn (in the Johannine corpus) an anticipation of the blessedness of the after-life. (We can do no more here than merely allude to this).

among them (XIV: 23), until the time comes to bring them to
the many heavenly dwellings which He has prepared for them
(XIV: 2-3). The same Greek word occurs in each of the two
sections, indicating that there is a connection between these two
presences of Christ of His own. The only condition which Jesus
lays down for those who wish to enjoy these blessings, is complete faith in the word which Jesus has spoken and which is the
Father's own word. The Church must live on the conviction
that its *Founder is always present. Resurrexi et adhuc tecum sum*
(Easter Mass Introit).

Two incidents in chapters XX and XXI confirm these observations. On the evening of Easter day, as Mary Magdalene tries
to touch Him, the risen Savior says, "Do not touch me, for I
have not yet ascended to my Father!" (XX: 17).[9] This means
that the deepest relationship with Christ is not physical touch,
as the crowds of Galilee and Judea thought during His public
ministry, (beneficial as such a touch might be, cf. the Synoptics,
who record healings resulting from it). Paradoxically, it is only
after Christ shall have ascended to his Father that His disciples
will be able to "touch" Him in the most effective way, which
will be the way of faith and the sacraments.[10]

Jesus will be at the side of His disciples, aiding them, particularly in their apostolate, making it fruitful. This is the symbolic
meaning of the miraculous catch of fish. (XXI: 1-13). In the
mind of the Evangelist this is not a new miracle of Christ, but
an act of the Church, performed through the all-powerful assistance of its Founder. The drama of the Passion, which appeared
to be the triumph of the darkness over the light, was really the
defeat of the darkness. No Evangelist saw as clearly as did John,
that Calvary was a sort of epiphany of Christ the King and

---

9 Greek has a present imperative which forbids the object to continue
doing an action which he has already begun. On the mysterious meaning
of these words cf. the excellent observations of W. Thusing, *Die Erhöhung
und Verherrlichung Jesu im Johannesevangelium*, Münster i. W., 1960,
pp. 275-276.

10 Cf. C. K. BARRETT, *The Gospel according to St. John*, London,
1955, p. 470: "The resurrection has made possible a new and more intimate spiritual union between Jesus and his disciples; the old physical
contacts are no longer appropriate." Cf. also H. VAN DEN BUSSCHE,
Les discours d'adieu, p. 74.

signified to the inauguration of His kingdom,[11] a kingdom which is not of this world, but which rules the world none the less (cf. below on Christ the King in the Apocalypse).

In general, in the Fourth Gospel the Christophanies of the Easter Period are much more than an attestation of the fact of the Resurrection (even though they are primarily this, with Christ being seen and touched by those who are to be the official witnesses of His return to life). They are the tangible and visible proof of the abiding presence and action of the incarnate and risen Son of God among men, especially in the intimate circle of His disciples. They are the announcement and representation of His invisible presence and action, which charaterizes the whole era between the Ascension and the Parousia. Although this miracle is with a kind different from those of His public life, these latter are also signs of the work accomplished in the Church by the risen Savior (cf. the use of *semeion* in XX: 30). The joy and the peace of those who enjoy these apparitions are but a foretaste of the joy and a peace which Jesus mentioned in His Discourse after the Last Supper and to which all Christians will have access in the Church.[12]

(2) *The Father*

The Son's actions show that He is inseparable from the Father

Just as He will help His own close to Himself, even after His departure, the Father too will help them This does not entitle them to look forward to some extraordinary spectacle, as Philip seems to have been expecting when he said, "Lord show us the Father and it is enough for us. (XIV: 8). Those who come to know the Son, know the Father also. To see the Son with the eyes of faith, is to see the Father (XIV: 9-11); those who keep Jesus' word can be sure of receiving the Father's love as well as that of the Son (XIV: 23). Since Jesus came forth from the Father, and is one with Him, the disciples' love

---

11 Cf. J. BLANK, *Die Verhandlung vor Pilatus* (*John.*, XVIII, 28 XIX, 16) *im Lichte Johanneischer Theologie*, in *Biblische Zeitschrift*, 1959, pp. 60-81; I. DE LA POTTERIE, *Jésus, Roi et Juge* d'apres Jo. 19, 13, in *Biblica*, 1960, pp. 217-247.

12 Cf. H. VAN DEN BUSSCHE, *Les discours d'adieu*, p. 63, and especially W. THUSING, *Die Erhöhung und Verherrlichung, Jesu,* pp. 263 sq.

for Jesus will earn for them the protection of the Father, who will come to them as a continuation of the presence of His glorified Son (XVI: 26-28). It follows, therefore, that their prayers to the Father addressed to Him in the name of His Son (not only by the invocation of His name, but by those who are *disciples*, appointed to continue the Son's work on earth) will surely be heard (XIV: 13-14)[13] as are the prayers of the Son Himself (cf. XI: 42); what is more, they will have the same power as one glorified Savior, and do works greater than that done by the Son Himself during His stay on earth (XIV: 12), this will enable them to work effectively to plant the kingdom of God in the world.

This new intimacy between the disciples and the Father is implied in the message which the risen Savior addresses to Mary Magdalene, "Go to my brethren and tell them that I ascend to my Father and your Father, to my God and your God" (XX: 17). This is the only passage in all four gospels in which Jesus not only calls His disciples friends, but also declares that His Father is their Father as well. (In the Synoptics Jesus often says "your Father" or "Your heavenly Father"). This passage has often been misunderstood,[14] as if its purpose were to show that the God and Father of Jesus is not God and Father of the disciples in the same way. There may be some indication along this line, but the sense is rather that Jesus wishes to say that Calvary and the Resurrection have brought a new Covenant, extending the privilege of sonship to all believers. Christ has become our brother; His Father has become our Father.[15]

The word "brethren" ("Go and find my brethren") is probably an allusion to Ps. XXII (v. 13: "Nuntiabo nomen tuum fratribus meis"), which the four passion accounts present as messianic. Heb. II: 9-12 provides a parallel: "Made a little lower

---

13 Cf. H. VAN DEN BUSSCHE, *Les Discours d'adieu*, pp. 76-77.

14 Cf. e. gr. LAGRANGE, *Évangile selon saint Jean*, Paris, 1927, p. 513: "Note in the phrase at the end that God is not the God of Jesus in the same way that He is the God of those whom He nevertheless calls His brethren; neither is He their Father in the same way."

15 Cf. Mgr. CATHERINET, *Note sur un verset de l'Évangile selon saint Jean*, (xx, 17), in *Memorial Chaine, Facultes Catholiques*, Lyon, 1950, pp. 51-59; R. BULTMANN, *Das Evangelium Johannes*, Cottingen, 1950, pp. 333-334; T.W.N.T., V, p. 1001 (Schrenck); W. THUSING, *Die Erhöhung und Verherrlichung Jesu*, p. 213; R. H. LIGHTFOOT, *St. John's Gospel*, Oxford, 1956, p. 335.

than the angels, but crowned with glory and honor, because of
His having suffered death, that by the grace of God He might
have death for us all. . . . He is not ashamed to call them brethren,'
saying, 'I will declare thy name to my brethren, in the midst
of the Church I will praise thee'." And, to Msgr. Catherinet,[16]
John XX: 17 recalls the words of Ruth to Noemi when she proposed to return to Moab, "Wherever you go I will go, wherever
you lodge I will lodge, your people shall be my people, and
your God my God" (I: 10).

This interpretation of the *Ascendo ad Patrem* text confirms
our explanation of *noli me tangere*, of the same verse (XX: 17).
In each case a new relationship is established by the covenant
of grace, with both the Son and the Father, who will be, each
of them, closer than before to the disciples.

(3) *The Holy Spirit*

It is said often in the Fourth Gospel that Jesus' departure
and glorification is to coincide with the gift of the Spirit (VII:
39; XVI: 7). In the discourses after the Last Supper the Spirit
is called the paraclete (intercessor, advocate). According to
chapters XIV-XVI, as well as according to the entire structure
of the Fourth Gospel, we can see the Spirit's future role in the
Church. He alone will give to earthly, carnal men, the possibility
of coming to supernatural reality, the contact of man with God
which is through new birth (III: 3). But the Spirit does more;
He will continue to lead the Disciples to a deeper understanding
of the teachings of God's incarnate Son, making them know better
their heavenly Father and Christ their Brother, the heads of the
divine family of which they have been made members. Besides,
in the midst of any unbelieving and hostile world, He will bear
witness to Christ, showing that His apparent defeat (continued
in the many apparent defeats which beset the Church), is really
His triumph (XIV: 16-17; 26; XV: 26; XVI: 7-15).

These promises contained in His farewell discourses apply to
all Christians for all time, even though the apostles are to be
the first to benefit from this. Thus there is no need to look for
a parallel in XX: 19-20, which describes in effect the giving of
the Spirit to the apostles by Christ before His return to the
Father (just as the farewell discourse presupposes the Ascension).

---

16 *Note sur un verset de l'évangile de saint Jean*, p. 55.

Furthermore this gift is obviously reserved to the hierarchy, and is designed to make of the Church's heads the bearers of pardon for sin and of the giving of the Spirit. We can also recall the end of the Passion account (XVIII: 30) where the words *tradidit spiritum* (*paredoken to pneuma*) probably have a double meaning;[17] at the moment in which Jesus *gives up* His Spirit, He *gives* the Spirit to the world (virtually), just as He found the Church with its sacraments (the blood and water flowing from His side). Thus His death is His victory. I John also has a parallel text: "There are three that bear witness,... The Spirit and the water and the blood, and these three are one" (V: 8).

THE TIME OF THE CHURCH AND MEN'S RELATIONS AMONG THEMSELVES

United to the Holy Trinity by Faith and Love (determined simply by the keeping of the commandments), Christians will be also united to each other by the keeping of the new commandment, that of brotherly love. Just as Jesus' various works (pl. *erga* V: 20-36; VI: 28; VII: 3; IX: 3 ff.; X: 25; 32; 37; XIV: 10 ff.; XV: 24 ff.) all are directed toward the great work (*ergon* IV: 34; XVII: 4), which summarizes all His previous works, the work of redemption, with its immediate effect, the founding with the Church; so too the various commandments (pl., *entolai*, XIV: 15; 21; XV: 10) are all summarized in the one commandment of brotherly love (sing. *entolē* XIII: 34; XV: 12). This one commandment corresponds to the one commandment which the Father gave to the Son, to give His life for the life of the world, and which is always before Jesus' eyes (X: 18; XII: 49; XIV: 31). This is, of course, the sacrifice of Calvary, the great proof of Jesus' love for the Father and also of Jesus' love for His own, the act *par excellence* which gives meaning to the commandment of brotherly love, the commandment whereby we are to give our life for our brethren.[18]

There are also some sections of the Synoptics,[19] especially

17 LOISY admits this double meaning in *Le quatrième évangile*, Paris, 1903, p. 882; C. HOSKYNS, *The Fourth Gospel*, London, 1947, p. 532; R. H. LIGHTFOOT, *St. John's Gospel*, pp. 319-320.

18 Cf. W. THUSING, *Die Erhöhung und Verherrlichung Jesu*, pp. 58 ff., 123 ff.

19 Cf. L. CERFAUX, *La charite fraternelle et le retour du Christ* (Jo XIII, 33-38), in *Recueil L. Cerfaux*, Gembloux, 1954, t. II, pp. 27-40.

the parable of the wicked servant (Mt. XXIV: 45-51; Lk. XII: 41-46), which suggest that the exercise of brotherly love should be the principal concern of Christians throughout this era between Jesus' departure and His Parousia. The great tribunal of the Parousia (Mt. XXV: 31-40) also gives the impression that the last judgment will be exclusively based on this one point, whether we have recognized in the poor and needy whom we meet, the mysterious presence of God's Son, Who has taken human misery to Himself. The Fourth Gospel implies this too, when the commandment of brotherly love is called new, because, being founded and based on the divine love which led to Calvary, it is the characteristic commandment of the new era.

According to John's gospel, the practice of mutual love, corresponding to Jesus' work *par excellence* (*ergon*, Sing., cf. above), is the chief characteristic of this time of separation, which is essentially the *Time of the Church*. Add to this the beautiful idea of I John, that in awaiting the direct sign of God, which is above all, the keeping of this commandment—the great commandment which brings souls to God and God to souls,: "Little children, yet a little while I am with you. Where I go you cannot come; a new commandment I give you:—that you love one another; that as I have loved you, you also love one another" (John XIII: 33-34); "God abides in us and His love is perfected in us" (John IV: 12).

Unlike the Synoptics (e. gr., Mt. V: 43-48), the Fourth Gospel places the accent not so much on the love which we must have for all men, including our enemies, as on the mutual affection which must bind together the new people of God. This is by no means an exclusivism, or a sectarian separation.[20] Rather it is a metaphysical basis which only John gives to *agape*, making it the bond of love which unites the Father and the Son, "In order that the love with which thou hast loved me may be in them, and I in them" (XVII: 20). Obviously, this union of

---

20 Likewise at Qumran the members of the community are united to each other by bonds of real brotherly affection; the *Rule of the Community* returns continually to this point (I: 10; II: 24; V: 4; 25-26; VIII: 2; 4-8; X: 26). However, the Qumran texts identify the children of light with the members of the sect (those who share the same interpretation of the Torah) and recommend hatred of others. Cf. our study *La Litterature de Qumran et les écrits johanniques*, in *Buletin du Comite des Etudes* (Compagnie de Saint Sulpice), no. 24, janvier-mars, 1959, pp. 440-456.

charity can exist only among disciples. One might feel inclined to suspect that it is related to Eucharistic communion.[21]

Far from making the disciples a group apart, this love should be the source of their going out to others. Strengthened by *agape*, and having as source and model the unity of the Father and the Son, the unity of the disciples will be the chief sign of credibility presented to men, bringing men of good will to believe that Jesus is really the Envoy, the Son of God (XVII: 21). Love, manifested by Christ on Calvary, founded the Church. Resting on an ontological communion with the Father and with the Son, ("And the glory that thou hast given me I have given them, that they may be one, even as we are one" XVII: 22), the disciples' brotherly love and unity will build up the Church and assure its growth.

(2) THE APOCALYPSE [22]

The religious message of the Apocalypse is understandable only to those who place themselves in the situation in which it was written, and appreciate the pressing difficulties which beset the Church of that time, and to which the author proposed to react. These problems were of two kinds; the one was the question of the relationship of the Church to the Jewish world after the destruction of Jerusalem in 70 had cut the two apart; [23] the other problem of the time was that of the relationship of the Church to its pagan milieu, especially to the Roman empire, in which the members of this new community had to live. This second point will be the object of this study.

Although the Roman rulers had not opposed Christianity at first, the situation changed radically after the Christians had

---

21 On Agape and the Eucharist in the fourth Gospel cf. SPICQ, Agape, III, Paris, 1949, pp. 143-145; 149-150; 179.

22 Besides the well-known and accepted commentaries on the Apocalypse, we have relied especially on the following studies: H. M. FÉRET, *L'Apocalypse de saint Jean, vision chrétienne de l'Histoire*, Paris, 1943; E. F. SCOTT, *The Book of Revelation*, London, 5e edit., 1959; M. RISSI, *Zeit und Geschichte in der Offenbarung des Johannes*, Zurich, 1952.

23 Cf. our two studies *Le chapitre 10 de l'Apocalypse, son apport dans la solution du problème eschatologique*, in *Sacra Pagina, Miscellanea Biblica Congressus Internationalis de Re Biblica*, Paris-Gembloux, 1959, vol. II, pp. 414-429; *Essai d'interprétation du chapitre XI de l'Apocalypse*, in *New Testament Studies*, vol. IV, 1957-1958, pp. 183-200.

been blamed for the burning of Rome in 64. Nero's persecution started at this time, but was not to be in itself the beginning of a permanent conflict; this was to come under Domitian, whose demand that he be honored as a god brought about in effect a state religion, without at the same time suppressing the other cults. Hence it was mainly a political thing, designed to unite the disparate elements of the empire.[24]

The emperor's decree caused little trouble for most, since one god more or less was no problem for polytheists. The Christians, however, took just the opposite attitude; seeing the cult of Caesar as an open declaration of hostility, a satanic attempt to bring heaven to earth by exalting the emperor, together with all his material wealth and all his military power. They saw it also as a mockery of Christianity, a mere mortal claiming to be incarnate divinity, as did Christ, arrogating to himself, the title of God and demanding the adoration of every race and class of men! Such a disposition was intolerable to the Christians, as it was also for the Jews; Jews, however, could easily find ways of being dispensed from cultic obligations contrary to their beliefs. The Christian Church, however, presented itself as a supra-national religion, destined to spread and expand. This set it apart publicly from Judaism, and was the cause of the persecution which was to perdure for a painfully long time.

The Apocalypse was published just when this persecution was about to be unleashed, toward the end of Domitian's reign (Irenaeus, *Adv. Haer.*, V: 30). It set down the course of action to be followed in this time of crisis, which was testing the very existence of the new religion. The author leaves no doubt about the Christian's obligation; they are to remain unshaken in their fidelity, even to the point of martyrdom, to Christ, the only King of the world. Their spiritual forces, represented by a handful of Christians, will resist all the material power of a totalitarian state which proposes to set itself up in place of God. Even though the description of the fall of Babylon (pagan Rome), which is poetic and symbolic rather than a proximate expectation of an event to come, was not fulfilled to the letter, still, with regard to the general sense of the book, history has justified the Seer of Patmos;

---

24 Cf. E. STAUFFER, *Christus und die Caesaren, Historische Skizzen,* Hamburg, 1952, pp. 160-209; Domitian und Johannes; L. CERFAUX and J. TONDRIAU, *Le Culte des Souvérains dans la civilisation gréco-romaine,* Paris-Tournai, 1957, pp. 355-356; 390-392.

the handful of Christians did prevail against invincible Rome. The Apocalypse has a particular significance for our modern time, in which totalitarian states, possessing formidable weapons of material destruction, again threaten the weak and unarmed Church of Christ.[25]

It is precisely in this context of real crisis and tragedy that we must see the Apocalypse author's idea of the Time of the Church. We can only summarize here the author's rich and powerful thought.

THE PRESENCE OF CHRIST IN HISTORY

The time of the Church is first and foremost *the presence of the Risen Christ in history*. John's Apocalypse is specifically Christian, differing from the Jewish apocalypses, which are directed entirely to the future, in so far as it sees Christ's Parousia only in relation to His first coming, in which, he says, the peak of human religious history has already been attained; this is to say that, in principle, salvation and victory over evil are already a fact. The persecuted Church is victorious, because its Head, Christ, has triumphed through His Blood over all hostile forces.

We need to dwell on this idea of the risen Christ as the only real King of the world. It is one thing to accept the abstract concept of the existence of Christ in glory, and another to see Him, after the first Easter morning, as the sovereign Lord of history. This is the idea which the Apocalypse author seeks to present, since it is the only one capable of sustaining the beleaguered Christians. Totalitarian despots will not decide the fate of humanity; Christ will, as He holds in His hand the divine book of destiny, and He alone has the power to open it.

In John's Passion account (which, as we said above, is a sort of epiphany of Christ the King), Jesus tells Pilate that political power is subject to the higher power of God, to which all, including the heads of the State, must render homage (XIX: 33-38).[26] Political power which refuses to submit to this higher

---

25 Cf. on this point the excellent work of E. F. SCOTT, *The Book of Revelation*, pp. 175-178.

26 Here we are happy to follow H. SCHLIER, *L'État selon le Nouveau Testament*, in *Lumière et Vie*, nº 49, 1960 (Autorité et Pouvoir), pp. 99-108.

authority, or even remains neutral to it, as did Pilate, heads for its own ruin. The author of the Apocalypse says the same thing, but more aggressively in accordance with the circumstances.

It has been said,[27] that the style of the letters in the first part of the Apocalypse have the same format as the edicts of Domitian: the heavenly Imperator, who alone fully deserves the title, also has ambassadors charged to carry His message to the Churches, which do His work on earth. This explains the titles given to Christ, which are pointedly anti-imperial: ruler of the kingdoms of the earth (I: 5); king of kings and lord of lords (XIX: 16); lord of lords and king of kings (XVII: 14). It also explains the solemn manner of the enthronement of the lamb, and the general insistence on Christ's royal prerogatives. R. Schutz [28] has detected some almost verbal similarities between the titles attributed to Christ in the Apocalypse and those given to Domitian while he was still alive: *holy, sacred* (*hagios, hosios* VI: 10; XV: 4) and *sacer* in Martial (V: 1: 190; V: 2: 177); *glory* (*doxa* I: 6; IV: 2; XIX: I) and *terrarum gloria* in Martial (II: 91: 1); *salvation* (*soteria* XIII: 10; XIX: 1) and in Martial *salus* (II: 91: I; V: I: 7); *power* (*exousia;* XII: 10) and *potestas, potens* in Martial (IX: 79); worthy to receive power (V: 12) and *quo non dignior has subit habenas* (Stace, Silv. IV: 3; 128); *thou has created all things* (IV: II) and in Martial (*parens orbis* (VIII: 7; 5; IX: 6; 1).

The presence of Christ in His Church is inseparable from that of the Holy Spirit. This is why in the letters, when the Son speaks at the beginning ("Thus says he who holds the seven stars in his right hand; the first and the last; he who was dead and is living forevermore" etc.), the Spirit appears at the end of each letter to endorse the directions which Christ has given

27 E. STAUFFER, *Christus und die Caesaren,* p. 198.

28 *Die Offenbarung des Johannes und Kaisar Domitian,* Göttingen, 1933, pp. 34 sq. Cf. also P. TOUILLEUX, *L'Apocalypse et les cultes de Domitien et de Cybele,* Paris, 1935, p. 102.

29 Many exegetes have seen in the seven spirits of Apoc. I: 4 the seven higher spirits which later Jewish tradition has before the face of God. In this regard cf. J. MICHL, *Die Engelvorstellungen in der Apokalypse des Johannes,* I Teil, *Die Engel um Gott,* München, 1937, pp. 112-210.

("He who has an ear, let him hear what the Spirit says to the
Churches"; II: 7; 11; 17; 29; III: 6; 13; 22).

The author of the Apocalypse is less interested in the person
of the Holy Spirit than in His action in the world. Thus he
speaks of seven spirits (I: 4; III: I; IV: 5; V: 6), denoting
thereby the one Holy Spirit under the figure of His many operations, or under that of the seven churches in which He works
and which represent the entire Christian community.[29] The "seven
eyes which are the seven spirits of God sent forth into all the
earth" (V: 6), suggest the seven eyes of Jahweh in Zach. III:
9-10 and IV: 10. Nothing happens on earth unknown to Christ
and His Spirit.

THE BATTLE BETWEEN CHRIST AND ANTI-CHRIST

No other book of the New Testament is as dedicated to combat as the Apocalypse, which presents the Time of the Church
as a time of open warfare between Christ and Anti-Christ. The
great attack against the Church is pictured in the time immediately preceding the Parousia (XX: 7-10), but wages even now.
The dragon (the ancient serpent) is mortally wounded; Christ
is victorious over him (ch. XII). He is no longer able to carry
on his evil works, which are presented under the two symbols
of the beast coming up out of the sea and the beast coming
up out of the earth (ch. XIII).

The emperor is partly the incarnation of the beast coming
up out of the sea (the West); in XIII: 3 the wounding and
healing of the beast (an allusion to the legend of *Nero redivivus*),
are a caricature of the Passion and Resurrection of Christ (cf.
V: 6); its enthronement by the dragon is a mockery of the
enthronement of the Lamb (XIII: 4; 5; 8 ff.); the adorers of
the beast are marked on their forehead, as were those of the
Lamb (cf. XIII: 16; 17; VII: 2; XIV: I).

The second beast, coming out of the earth (Asia), acts like
a prophet, and places its religious strength at the service of the
first beast. No doubt John took this new symbol as an incarnation
of the pagan philosophical and religious trends of the time, and
of all time, which freely favored the cult of the divinized rulers.
This second beast gives the State its ideology and its spirit.
M. Rissi [30] says that there are good reasons for seeing in it a

---

30 *Zeit und Geschichte in der Offenbarung des Johannes*, pp. 81 sq.

caricature of the Holy Spirit; while the Holy Spirit teaches the doctrine and the Person of Christ the King, Son of God, this pseudo-spirit makes men adore their sovereigns, who are determined to rule in place of Christ.

In chapters XVII-XVIII of the Apocalypse, the divinization and degeneration [31] of the State is symbolized by Babylon, described (as in the prophetic texts of the Old Testament) as an excessively rich and powerful, seductive courtesan, who supplies every kind of benefit to the world, deceiving all by her witchcraft, while promising them endless happiness ("I sit a queen; I am no widow, and I shall not see mourning," XVIII: 7). She does not realize, however, that she courts her own end by her opposition to God and to His Christ.

Scott observes [32] that in these powerful, vivid texts, John sees the pagan Rome of his own day, but that he is not at all guided by any blind fanaticism; he recognizes, even respects, the greatness of Rome; the workers, the merchants, the artists, who work for the great city are sad at its fall, because for them, life has lost its charm. Besides, when John wrote these lines, Rome was in a period of splendor; there was no sign of a coming decline. Still, he foretells it to the Christians, saying that they must keep this in mind during their trial.

However, we should not think that the author of the Apocalypse wants to lull the disciples of Christ into a comfortable illusion.[33] He stresses the trials which beset and are to beset the Church, thereby stopping any false notion of effortless progress. He explains that the beast may kill some Christians, but that their sacrifice, not their arms (cf. XIII: 9-10), will make them followers of Christ's example, thereby making them victorious over the devil and his forces.

The historian who is interested in the philosophy of history, studies the present in the light of the past, seeking in ancient events, wars, disasters, etc. a pattern of laws and guiding principles, valid for all times, including the present. Like the prophets of ancient Israel, the author of the Apocalypse explains his own contemporary segment of the history of salvation in the light of the future, because contemporary events have a true

---

31 Cf. H. SCHLIER, *L'État selon le Nouveau Testament,* in *Lumière et Vie,* nº 49, pp. 120-121.

32 E. F. SCOTT, *The Book of Revelation,* pp. 86-89.

33 Cf. E. F. SCOTT, *The Book of Revelation,* pp. 152-154.

meaning only in relation to their final outcome. Since its in-auguration, the Church has developed well; now, however, John sees its very existence endangered. The Seer of Patmos shows how the Church's sufferings at the hands of an all-powerful totalitarian state, are part of God's plan; he then predicts the outcome. As we said above, the Roman emperor is not lord of history; the risen Christ is. The awful attacks against the Church are the last attempts of the dragon, already mortally wounded, to prevail.

There is still another aspect of the Apocalypse message that we should note here. Even more than the fourth Gospel, which modern commentators see as closely related to the Church's sacramental life,[34] the Apocalypse has a most striking liturgical character. Many recent studies [35] show its relationship with both the liturgy of the old covenant and with that of the Church. We have already explained [36] how the twenty four elders (*presbyteroi*) round the throne (IV: 4; 10; V: 5; 6; 7; 11; 14; VII: 11; 13; XI: 16; XIV: 3; XIX: 4) are a heavenly prototype of of the Church's hierarchy, suggesting the elders of the churches assembled for the eucharistic liturgy along with their bishop, whom Ignatius of Antioch (Magn. III:1) compares to "The Father of Jesus Christ, the bishop of all."

The doxologies, hymns and acclamations scattered through-out the Apocalypse (I: 5-6; IV: 8-11; V: 8-14; XV: 5-6; XIX: 1-8) echo the liturgical songs of the Christians. It is first of all in the liturgy that the Christian experiences and celebrates his own being a son of God, as well as the presence and action of the risen Christ and of the Holy Spirit, receiving thus the assurance that he can overcome all the forces of the evil one. The liturgical element is evident in the beautiful promise contained in the letters at the beginning of the book. "To him who overcomes I will give the hidden manna" (II: 17; cf. John VI, where the

---

34 Cf. *Introduction à la Bible*, t. II, pp. 673-674.

35 Among the most recent of these works are G. DELLING, *Zum Gottesdienstlichen Stil der Johannes - Apokalypse*, in *Novum Testamentum*, 3 (1959), 107-137; S. LAUCHLI, *Eine Gottesdienststrukur in der Johannes-Offenbarung*, in *Theologische Zeitschrift*, 16 (1960), 359-378; M. H. Jr. SHEPHERD, *The Paschal Liturgy and the Apocalypse*, London, 1960.

36 *Les vingt-quatre vieillards de l'Apocalypse*, in *Revue Biblique*, 1958, pp. 5-32, and below, part II, Chapter I.

eucharistic bread is compared to the manna); "Him who overcomes I will permit to eat of the tree of life" (II: 7; cf. John VI:
51-58, where, as we said above,[37] the eucharistic food is compared to the fruit of the tree of life); "Behold, I stand the door
to me, I will come in to him and will sup with him, and he
with me" (III: 20). Cerfaux and Cambier say of this text, "The
eschatological banquet is anticipated in the mystical joy which
Christians can experience now in their relationship to Christ
in the liturgy." [38]

Conclusion

We would like to end this short study with a few words
on the symbol of the woman, which in both the fourth Gospel
and the Apocalypse, represents the Church, and characterizes
its situation. We shall begin with the text of the Apocalypse,
since it is the clearer of the two in this regard.

Many of the authors who have written recently on the
woman of Apoc. XII [39] see her principally—or even exclusively—
as the Blessed Virgin Mary. However, in the Old Testament
texts (cf. Is. LXVI: 7; XXVI: 17 ff.; cf. also Cant. VI: 10) the
woman of the vision is the ideal Sion of the prophets, who, after
giving Christ to the world, becomes the Christian Church.[40]
While waiting for the Parousia, she lives in the desert, protected
and fed by God (XII: 6; 14), as the Jews of the old Covenant

---

37 *Les themes bibliques majeurs du discours sur le pain de vie,* in
Nouvelle Revue Theol., 1960, pp. 815-816 and above, p. 63.

38 *L'Apocalypse de saint Jean lue aux chretiens,* Paris, 1955, p. 39.

39 For a composite view of the very many works produced on this
subject, cf. J. MICHL, *Die Deutung der apokalyptischen Frau in der
Gegenwart,* in *Biblische Zeitschrift,* 1959, pp. 301-310; P. PRIGENT,
Apocalypse 12, Histoire de l'exégèse, Tübingen, 1959; *Pour une exégèse a la
fois ecclésiale et mariale d'Apoc. 12;* cf. especially F. M. BRAUN, *La Mère
des Fideles,* 2d edition, Tournai-Paris, 1954, pp. 133-176.

40 Cf. our study, *Le Messie et sa Mère d'après le chapitre 12 de
l'Apocalypse,* in *Revue Biblique,* 1959. pp. 55-86. On the relationship
between Apoc. XII: 1 and Cant. VI: 10, cf. especially A. M. DUBARLE,
La Femme couronée d'étoiles, in *Mélanges Bibliques, redigés en l'honneur
dé A. Robert,* Paris, 1957, pp. 512-518. United as it is to other scriptural
references which look to the ideal Sion of the prophets, the Apocalypse
author's allusion to Cant. VI: 10 presupposes on his part a prophetic-
allegorical reading of this mysterious love-poem.

lived in the desert of Sinai. If the Blessed Virgin Mary is in the
vision secondarily, (as we think she is, at least in the first verses
of the chapter), it must be as an incarnation of the people of
God, who has given the Messiah to the world through her. She
is the incarnation of Israel, the mother of the Messiah, who has
brothers (XII: 17, the rest of her offspring); at the same time
she is the figure of the Christian Church, which gives Christ to
men every day in the sacraments and in her preaching. In the
vision the woman is both triumphant and embattled; through
Mary the Church is already triumphant in heaven.

There is a certain limit, however, to the marian interpretation of this text. There is a possibility, which we should avoid,
of replacing the essentially *heilsgeschichtlich* point of view of
the Apocalypse author with some modern and anachronistic
elements of modern individualistic marian piety.[41]

We shall reexplain this with regard to the farewell of Christ
to His mother in John XIX: 25-27. This text must be understood
in relation to its context, which is entirely ecclesial. In the various
accounts of the Passion and of the Easter-time Christophanies,
the evangelist's basic concern is for the Church, the principal
fruit of Christ's messianic work, and the privileged area in
which He will perform His salvific activity. How could XIX:
25-27 be an exception to this pattern? Even Hoskyns, [42] a
Protestant, admits that here Mary (the Woman) is a figure of
the Church, which concords with what we have said of Apoc.
XII.

In the Book of Consolation (Is. XL - LXVI), Jahweh often
tells the woman Sion that she is to undergo a miraculous childbirth; He tells the children of Sion, who think themselves aban-
doned, that His care for them will be more tender than that of
a mother for her offspring (Is. XLIX: 14-15; XVI: 12-15). Like
the Sion of the prophets, Mary, figure of the Church, receives
on Calvary offspring which she has not really borne (the disciples
of Jesus, represented by the beloved disciple). In foretelling
Sion's miraculous childbirth, Jahweh has said, "As nurslings
you shall be carried in her arms, and fondled in her lap; as a
mother comforts her son, so will I comfort you ... when you

---

41 In this regard, the warnings of J. MICHL (note 36 of his article
mentioned above) are most fitting.

42 *The Fourth Gospel,* pp. 529-530; cf. also LIGHTFOOT, *St. John's
Gospel,* p. 317.

see this, your heart shall rejoice" (Is. LXVI: 12-14; cf. John XVI: 21-22). When they shall be deprived of Jesus' visible presence, the Christians will be loved by God, as by the tenderest of mothers, thanks to the Church, which Mary represents, and which will continue on earth the salvific action which Christ has performed.

Basically, John VI: 17 and XIX: 25-27 are complementary, being both related to this stage of salvation history, the Time of the Church. In the one we learn that after Jesus' departure, His disciples will have the heavenly Father Himself for their father; in the other we learn that they are to have a Mother on earth (cf. Gal. IV: 26: "But that Jerusalem which is above is free, which is our mother"). Such is the privileged condition of Christians on earth, from the Ascension to the Parousia. And this privileged condition finds its expression, first of all, in the liturgy, as the Apocalypse clearly implies.

CHAPTER VI

PARTICIPATION IN THE LIFE OF GOD ACCORDING TO THE FOURTH GOSPEL [1]

Origin and Meaning of the Concept

We need hardly emphasize here our conviction that the author of the fourth Gospel teaches that Christians enjoy a share in the very life of God. Some exegetes, however, have refused to acknowledge any mystical meaning whatever in johannine thought. Bultmann, for example, would have in John no more than a "radicalizing" of traditional eschatology, whereby the fourth Gospel gives a "radical value" to the truth that the coming of Christ as Revealer is the decisive eschatological event, the *Krisis*.[2] However, the text itself belies such impoverishment of johannine theology. As a matter of fact, the text is so clear that most authors see it as distinctively mystical.[3]

The problems which we propose to treat here, however briefly, is how we should understand this lofty teaching, and what is

---

1 Published in *Texte und Untersuchungen zur Geschichte der altchristlichen Literatur*, Band 73, (Studia Evangelica) Berlin, 1959.

2 This thesis of Bultmann, which is scattered throughout the pages of his commentary on the fourth Gospel (*Das Evangelium des Johannes*, Göttingen, first ed. 1911; eleventh ed., revised, 1950), is found in an important monograph, *Die Eschatologie des Johannesevangeliums*, (Glauben und Verstehen, Gesammelte Aufsätze, Tübingen, 2nd ed., 1st vol., 1954, pp. 134-152); cf. also the article zaō in Kittel's *Theologisches Wörterbuch*, Band II, pp. 871-874.

3 Although there are many varying definitions of mysticism, we prefer the following: the believer's present enjoyment of blessings which are properly divine, and which are to be the lot of the elect in the happiness of heaven.

its source. Both questions, that of the source and that of interpretation, are, obviously, inseparable.

(1) *Johannine Mysticism and Hellenistic Mysticism*

Some authors see in this johannine idea of the sharing by
Christians of the very life of God, a more or less exact reflection
of hellenistic mysticism. Fewer, however, would accept completely the views developed 'by A. Schweitzer in his famous
book on the mysticism of St. Paul;[4] more popular is the idea
that John's doctrine has been influenced by the Greek world.
We will propose two examples. The first is the already long-
established thesis of J. Lindblom on eternal life,[5] which holds
that life, which in the Synoptics, the Acts and the Apocalypse,
is essentially eschatological, is in John's Gospel rather close to
the physico-metaphysical concepts of the Greeks, without, however, sacrificing the essence of Jesus' message. The second example is in C. H. Dodd's excellent work of a few years ago,
on the interpretation of the fourth Gospel.[6] Dodd's erudition
and prudence, as well as his deep religious sense, have won the
admiration of many. The eminent professor of Cambridge recognizes that johannine thought owes much to the Bible itself,
and to the rabbinical tradition. He sees in it, furthermore, no
little influence of the hellenistic milieu in which it was produced.
Unlike Bultmann, he discounts any influence of the Mandean
texts upon John's Gospel, but he does recognize traces of a
relationship to Philo and to the hermetic literature.

When Jesus says, "He who believes in me, even if he die,
shall live" (XI: 25), he treats of an atemporal concept, eternal
life, having neither past nor future, lived in the endless present,
apart from the action of death, an idea which recalls the thoughts
of Plato and of Philo. John unites closely eternal life and knowledge (cf., e. gr., "Now this is everlasting life, that they may
know thee" (XVII: 3). The mysticism of such hellenists as
Philo or the hermetics also holds that knowledge deifies man,
making him a child of God, and God himself. Dodd concludes
that John's thought combines elements of both the Hebrew and

---

4 *Die Mystik des Apostels Paulus*, Tübingen, 1930, pp. 324-364.

5 Das ewige Leben. *Eine Studie über die Entstehung der religiösen
Lebensidee im Neuen Testament*, Uppsala-Leipzig, 1914.

6 *The Interpretation of the Fourth Gospel*, Cambridge, 1953.

hellenistic traditions, making of them an entirely new and original synthesis.[7]

We are of the opinion that there is merit in the idea that the author of the fourth Gospel tried to adapt the Christian message somehow to the Greeks, showing them in this message the fulfillment of their own legitimate religious aspirations. For example, John stresses forcefully that Jesus is the only Revealer, because He alone has seen the Father. One might be inclined to think that he says this thinking of hellenism, in which mysteries, gnosis, and also philosophy, pretend to lead men to the knowledge and even the vision of God. Bultmann says that John deliberately uses these terms, which he knows to be current among the Greeks, and gives them an entirely new meaning.[8]

Still, the deeply Semitic and biblical foundations of johannine thought recommend caution in making such an affirmation. Furthermore, as P. Mollat says,[9] even within Judaism itself there was a school of thought, recently brought to light by the Dead Sea scrolls, which attributed great importance to knowledge (gnōsis), and which used a gnostic vocabulary. It is not impossible that this may be the only way, however indirect, in which John was subject to Greek influence. Further research may lead to considerable enlightenment on these questions.

In any case, we must maintain that John's mysticism, like that of Paul, cannot at all be reduced to that of the hellenists, and that in speaking of hellenistic mysticism, we have in mind the contemplation of God in ecstasy, as in the hermetic texts, or the vision of God which comes from the celebration of the mysteries. In either case the result is a substantial union with God, the deification of man, and all this without any need of moral effort! The salvation thus given and obtained is merely a liberation from matter, and sometimes from fate.[10]

---

7 *The Interpretation*, pp. 144-150.

8 Art. *zaō*, *Th. W.Z.N.T.* KITTEL, t. II, pp. 873-874, cf. also R. H. LIGHTFOOT, *St. John's Gospel, A Commentary*, Oxford, 1956, pp. 49-56.

9 *L'Évangile selon saint Jean*, in *la Bible de Jérusalem*, Paris, 1953, pp. 11-12.

10 We recommend on this point the excellent study of Ph. H. MENOUD, *L'originalité de la pensée johannique*, in *Revue de Théologie et de Philosophie* 116, Lausanne, 1940, 233-261. In the work of J. LINDBLOM, *Das ewige Leben*, pp. 78-148, is a long presentation of ideas on life found in the Greek mysteries and in their religious speculations.

John's mysticism is obviously different from this outlook—even opposite to it. It is not man who decides to go to God, by the practice of certain rites or intellectual exercises; but it is God, whom no man has seen, who, at a determined time of human history, introduces Himself to the Greek world, through Jesus, His incarnate Son. Everything comes back to God's free love for men. A. Nygren [11] has shown that the Greeks had no knowledge of such a love.

Furthermore, the great obstacle to man's union with God, which Jesus wishes to remove, is not matter, or fate, but sin. Nor is this union with God a divinization. John's mysticism differs from the hellenistic concept of man's being identified with God ("Thou art I· I am thou"); John is always most careful to maintain the measureless abyss which separates man from God, even in the passages which teach the mutual indwelling of Christ and Christians. The same Christ who says, "He who eats my flesh and drinks my blood abides in me and I in him," distinguishes Himself clearly from his own disciples, saying, "I will raise him up on the last day" (John VI: 55-56). Although man may have some experience of the divine, he can never enjoy on earth the perfect vision of God; he is always oriented toward the Parousia, which the coming of the Paraclete to men's souls can prepare, but never replace. It is interesting that the words *athanasia* and *aphtharsia*, which are rather common in St. Paul, are entirely absent from the johannine writings. John never substitutes the Greek notion of immortality for the radically biblical notion of eschatology.

Bultmann himself admits that John has not suppressed Christian eschatology, but he holds that John had "radicalized" it, making of its various manifestations (death, judgment, resurrection, entry into eternal life) so many actual events, occuring at the moment in which Jesus speaks, or at the moment in which men take a position by faith or unbelief, for or against Jesus.

It seems that, in a way, there may be some merit in this interpretation of John's Gospel; the writer is fully aware of the drama which unfolds continually in the history of men's hearts. However, to recognize what has been called the "actuality" of

---

11 *Erôs et Agapè, La notion chrétienne de l'amour et ses transformations*, translated by P. Jundt, Paris, 1943, especially pp. 201-222. We do not agree with Nygren that John prepared the way for an alteration of the idea of *agapé* by the Greek idea of *eros*.

the fourth Gospel [12] is not at all to suppress its properly eschatological dimension, as Bultmann does. The Master of Marburg can sustain his thesis only by eliminating a number of texts from the fourth Gospel and from I John on the second coming of Christ and on the resurrection of the last day,[13] a dissection hardly justified.

As Dom Dupont has emphasized, John maintains the traditional eschatological perspective, which can be harmonized with the mystical perspective. The Christian now shares really, although imperfectly, in the life of God, but he will share it fully only at the Parousia. In another study [14] we have attempted to show how already in the Old Testament, especially in the psalms, there is a real mysticism united to some eschatological and apocalyptic aspirations. Those who keep such Old Testament texts in mind will find little difficulty in reconciling these two tendencies of the fourth Gospel. They would it is true, be contradictory, if johannine mysticism were essentially Greek, but, as we have seen, it is fundamentally biblical, notwithstanding some possible borrowings from hellenism.

(2) Johannine Mysticism and the Synoptic Gospels

We have yet to face what seems to us to be the most important question, i.e., if it is true that the Christ of the fourth Gospel teaches that His disciples share (now) in the life of God (which we consider beyond question), how do we explain the apparent absence of such a lofty doctrine from the Synoptics? Is it really a teaching of the historical Jesus? Or would it not be better to admit rather that the doctrine thus attributed to Jesus in the fourth Gospel is pure fiction, unrelated to the real doctrine which Jesus gave to men? The answers to these questions are obviously beyond the scope of this limited treatment. We shall limit ourselves therefore to the essential points.

Certainly the idea of life has a greater place in John than

---

12 Cf. X. LÉON - DUFOUR, *Actualité du quatrième évangile,* in *Nouevlle Revue Théologique,* 76, (1954), 449-468.

13 These texts are: V: 28-29; VI: 51b-56; VI: 39; 40; 44; XII: 48; and I John II: 28; III: 2; IV: 17. Cf. *T.W.N.T.*, article *zaō,* pp. 371-373.

14 In a work entitled, *Mysticisme et Eschatologie dans quelques écrits bibliques,* to appear shortly.

in the Synoptics. Also, in the Synoptics it is almost always eschatological, referring to the new manner of being which will come about either at the Parousia and general judgment, or, in some texts, at the death of the individual. These are only a few rare passages (e. gr., Luke XV: 32; perhaps also Matthew IV: 4; Luke IV: 4) in which the words "life" and "live" might be said to refer to a spiritual life on earth. Yet, how different it is in John! Whereas in the Synoptics the proclamation of the Kingdom is the basic theme of Jesus' preaching, in John it occurs only once or twice, (III: 3-5 and perhaps XVIII: 36), being replaced by that of life. We think that the first element of a solution to this problem is to be found precisely in the relationship which exists between these two themes.

In the Synoptics the Kingdom is a purely eschatological thing; Jesus' thought, however, is not as simple as some partisans of consequent eschatology would have it. Although in some passages, the Kingdom is a thing of the future, still, many of these texts, especially the parables of the Kingdom, presuppose that Jesus has already laid the foundation of this Kingdom. If this Kingdom is to be first of all a dynamic reality, the decisive intervention of God in human history, of which the prophets spoke,[15] then, thanks to the coming of Jesus to earth, to His teaching, His healings and to His driving out of devils, this supreme intervention has already begun. When Jesus forgives sins, heals the sick, raises the dead, sin is conquered as are death and sickness, which entered the world together. Jesus establishes a close link between His miracles and the establishment of the kingdom. Still more profoundly, Jesus brings us the Kingdom of God; because He is uniquely the Son of God, perfectly subject to the Father. He is Himself the Kingdom of God (*autobasileia*), according to the beautiful expression of Origen. This explains why the choice which Jesus offers for or against the kingdom is a choice for or against His person; those who become His followers, enter the kingdom thereby.

Thus, the idea of (present) access to divine life is not as removed from the Synoptics as may seem at first glance. The Synoptics themselves equate "enter into the Kingdom" and "enter

---

15 On this point cf. H. D. WENDLAND, *Die Eschatologie des Reiches Gottes bei Jesus*, Gütersloh, 1931, p. 15 sq.; Cf. also our own work *Les Psaumes eschatologiques du Règne de Yahweh*, in *Nouvelle Revue Théologique*, 73 (1951), 361-362.

into eternal life" (Mark IX: 43; X: 17; Matthew XVIII: 3; XIX: 17; Luke XVIII: 29-30). Doubtless they mean here only the final kingdom, but since there is a certain anticipation of the entry into the kingdom, beginning with the moment in which one makes himself a follower of Jesus, a parallel anticipation of entry into life can be presumed to be part of the logic of the Christ of the Synoptics.

We think we could go further and say that, in fact, the Christ of the Synoptics promises, as does the Christ of John, access to the eschatological blessings from the moment in which one consents to follow Him. After all, the Kingdom of God is linked to the salvific blessings (pardon of sin, divine worship) which men enjoy on earth. The chief reason for our affirmative opinion here is the so-called johannine logion, as it appears in Matthew XI: 25-30 and Luke X: 21-22.[16] Although some have arbitrarily thrown doubt on the authenticity of this passage, because of its apparent relationship to hellenistic mysticism,[17] Jesus presents Himself as the great Messiah of Daniel, possessed of sovereignty over the future.[18] Far from expressing a secret teaching such as a manifestation of divine blessings in a *gnōsis*, the phrase *panta moi paredothē* has the same meaning as the *edothē autō exousia* of Daniel, that the Son of Man is given power over all the nations of the earth. However, as we have said in an article on this subject in *Revue Biblique*, this dependence on Daniel is not the most essential characteristic of this declaration. The more important thing, and which has not been sufficiently emphasized, is that the structure of Matthew XI: 25-30 is based on that of the great sapiential texts of the Old Testament, in which the invitation to join the ranks of the followers of divine Wisdom ("Come to me"; "Listen to me") appears as the direct result of her prerogatives. Just as divine Wisdom foregoes, in a way, titles of nobility, in order to draw more to follow her teachings, so too Jesus emphasizes His special ineffable intimacy with the Father in order to draw His hearers to become disciples.

---

16 Cf. our study, *Jesus et la Saggesse divine d'après les Évangiles synoptiques*, in *Revue Biblique*, 62 (1955).

17 E. Norden exemplifies this denial and presents the objections commonly raised, in *Agnostos Theos, Untersuchungen zur Formgesschichte religiöser Rede*, Leipzig-Berlin, 1913, pp. 277-308.

18 Cf. on this point L. CERFAUX, *Les sources scripturaires de Mt. XI*, 25-30, in *Ephemerides Theologicae Lovanienses*, 31 (1955), 331-342.

This is no mere servile literary imitation devised by Christian writers, placing in Jesus' mouth words taken from the Old Testament. Rather, we are well within the realm of inspiration; Jesus knows that He is the Son, and to express His relationship with the Father, and His mission of teaching humanity, He invokes quite naturally the Old Testament passages which describe Wisdom's intimate relationship to God and her role among men.

Thus, when Jesus invites those who labor and are heavily burdened to come to Him and find their rest, the rest of which He speaks is that of the eschatological oracles of the Old Testament.[19] Still, He promises it to them as a good to be enjoyed now, provided only that they attach themselves to His person. He can give rest and He can give life, as can Wisdom; He uses the same phraseology as Wisdom; He is the supreme source of these blessings. In the Old Testament, divine Wisdom, which is not the Messiah but which has the role of the Messiah (cf. the explanation given [20] by A. Robert), has as an essential characteristic the actualizing of the eschatological blessings, because these blessings, and especially life, come forth in some way from its very being. By the same token, Jesus, by the simple fact of His presence among men, actualizes the blessings inherent in the final Kingdom of God.

Although the johannine logion does not mention the gift of life explicitly, the rest which it promises would be illusory without it. This logion is related to many passages of the fourth Gospel in which Jesus gives to those who cling to His Word a hope of finding in Him light and life. Against Norden, K. Kundsin [21] has shown that the revelation discourses of John's Christ are structurally distinct from all the suggested parallels found in the oriental religions. Rather than seeking only the glory of the Revealer by heaping Him with titles of honor, the phrases, and

---

19 The phrase "you will find rest for your souls" is taken from Jer. VI: 16. Cf. K. STENDAHL, *The School of St. Matthew*, Lund, 1954, pp. 141-142.

20 Cf. *Les attaches littéraires de Prov. I-IX*, in *Revue Biblique*, 43 (1934), 42-68; 172-204; 374-384; 44 (1935), 344-365; 502-535. Wisdom is not the Messiah, but fulfills his function, as one continually present in world history, rather than appearing only at the end of time.

21 *Charakter und Ursprung der johanneischen Reden*, in *Acta Universitatis Lativiensis*, Theologijas Fakultates, Serija, I, 4, Riga, 1939, pp. 185-303.

other similar texts of the fourth gospel, are essentially designed to serve as a basis for the promises of salvation. This is why they are usually followed by a secondary proposition indicating the condition on which the believer may have access to salvation, light and life (cf. VI: 35; 51; VIII: 12; X: 9; XI: 25; XV: 5; XVIII: 37 . . .). This is precisely the structure, not only of the great Old Testament texts on Wisdom, but also of many declarations by the Christ of the Synoptics relative to His person (Mark VI: 50; XIV: 62 and parallel texts), especially of the famous johannine logion, particularly as it is reproduced in Matthew XI: 25-30). These are all so many reasons why the language which John attributes to Jesus, and the mysticism which He expresses, are more than a pure creation of the evangelist.

All in all, the Synoptics make a different arrangement of Jesus' teachings from that of the fourth Gospel. John has much from the eschatological point of view; he has none of the apocalyptic genre found in the Synoptics, none of the coming of the Son of Man on the clouds of heaven, no scene of the tribunal of the last judgment. We might speak of a partial actualization of eternal life, as of the manifestation of Jesus' glory, of salvation and of judgment.

Some explain this difference in doctrine between John and the Synoptics by saying that in the Synoptics Jesus speaks to the mass of the people, whereas in John He moves among the more cultured element of the Sanhedrin, and the Doctors. This is partly true. At the end of his fine discourse on "The gospel tradition and its beginnings",[22] H. Riesenfeld shows in John's Gospel a tradition which, like that of the Synoptics, begins in the life and activity of Jesus; but here, he adds, (in John) is a treatment especially of discourses and meditations which Jesus made within the limited circle of His disciples. Some have said also that the Synoptics and John present two different aspects of the teaching which the Christian community offered about Jesus, E. Levesque [23] speaks of a basic catechesis, showing that Jesus is the

---

22 The complete title of this conference, given Sept. 16, 1957 at the Oxford International Congress on the Study of the Gospels, is as follows: *The Gospel Tradition and its Beginnings: A study in the Limits of Formgeschichte.* The text was published separately (London, 1957, A. R. MOWBRAY). In the Congress vol. it is on pp. 43 ff.

23 *Nos quatre évangiles,* Paris, 1917, pp. 206-212.

Envoy of God, without insisting on His divine nature, and which the Synoptics follow. The fourth Gospel, on the other hand, reflects a loftier teaching about Christ, concerned principally with His person, a teaching which has some traces in the Synoptics (cf., e. gr., Mark XII: 35-37 and parallels; Matthew XI: 25 ff. and parallels; Matthew XVI: 13-20 and parallels). The actualization of divine life is thus linked, as we have seen, to this placing in relief of the real divinity of Jesus.

We feel that this comparison is deceiving. The fourth Gospel also has long discourses addressed to simple people: the conversation with the Samaritan woman (IV: 7-26), the Discourse on the Bread of Life (VI), or on Christ's saving death (XII: 23-36). These teachings are just as profound as those addressed to the more polished audiences. What is more, the Baptist speaks like Jesus (cf. I: 29-31; III: 27-30); so does the evangelist in the prologue and in those passages which seem to be his own personal reflections (III: 14-21; 31-36). It is significant that there is a direct transition here from the words of Jesus to those of the Evangelist. The first Epistle of St. John has the same literary and theological characteristics as Jesus' discourses in the fourth Gospel. From these observations we conclude that, at least with regard to the teaching on the gift of eternal life, John has given to Jesus his own manner of expression, whereas the Synoptics have preserved Jesus' words more literally, in their original form.

This does not mean, however, that John became so absorbed in metaphysics as to be indifferent to the facts of His account, or to attribute to Jesus his own personal speculations. Rather, he attached such great importance to the historical period of the activity of the Son of God on earth that he meditated continually on His words and deeds, coming thereby to understand their real meaning even better than the Synoptics who had written before him. Knowing that he was a privileged witness, and being an inspired interpreter·of these divine deeds and words, he proposed to present not so much the material form of Jesus' words as their profound meaning. Profiting from the light which he received from pauline doctrine, as well as from the life of the Church over a period of several decades, and from his own mystical experience, he determined to be a faithful translator of the most intimate thoughts of Jesus, inaugurator on earth of the Kingdom of God by the sole fact of His presence among men, Who, precisely because He is the Son, is also for His disciples the source of divine blessings.

St. Paul had shown the Christians the importance of their being associated with the risen Christ, thus being themselves sons of God, dependent upon the Son, *filii in Filio*. He had taught them their right to address God as Jesus did, as *Abba, Father* (Gal. IV: 6; Rom. VIII: 15; cf. Mark XIV: 36, and parallel texts; Matthew XI: 25-26 and parallels; Luke XXIII: 34; 46; John XI: 11; XII: 27-28; XVII: 1; 5; 11; 21; 24; 25). Such a formula had been unknown to the Jews as prayer, as J. Jeremias has shown,[24] being used only by children referring to their earthly father. The fourth Gospel presents a similar phenomenon, equally moving and even more significant as regards the sharing of God's life. The statements of John's Christ, about His relationship to the Father, are far distant from the deductions of theologians on the mutual relations of the Persons of the Trinity. Given always the historical fact of the Incarnation, they are full of deep humility, which Lagrange emphasizes in his commentary. For example, when Jesus says, "The son can do nothing of himself, but only what he sees the Father doing" (verse 19), and "of myself I can do nothing. As I hear, I judge" (verse 30), this impossibility is obviously on the human moral level. Jesus is constantly aware of what the Father has done; His whole human intelligence and will serve only to render the most perfect homage to the Father. But, as the context shows, this moral limitation, whereby Jesus cannot act without the Father is merely a continuation of the Son's absolute inability to act outside the Father in the Trinity.[25]

We see this dependence in equality of the Son upon the Father, shown in a human way in Jesus, so that His disciples may take Him as their model, receiving divine life from Him and living themselves as true Sons of God. "He gave them the power to become Sons of God" (I: 12).

Thus the fourth Gospel does more than affirm that Christians now share in God's own life. Following St. Paul, and in an even better manner than he, John shows us in Jesus dwelling on earth, a sort of existential definition of the condition of those who

---

24 We refer here to the study of J. JEREMIAS, *Kennzeichen der ipsissima vox Jesu*, in *Synoptische Studien . . . A. Wikenhauser dargebracht*, München, 1953, pp. 86-89.

25 The formulas which Jesus adopts to express His relations with the Father are of varying kinds; at times they stress primarily His humility; at others, the emphasis is on His transcendence.

are Sons of God. Living the life of God, they must also have their eyes always on the Father, with concern for the glory that comes from men (V: 44; XII: 43), thinking only of the Father's glory, as Jesus did (cf. V: 41; VII: 18; VIII: 50). The ideal would be nexer to do anything of themselves which would be outside the limit of this filial dependence.

Exegetes always find in the fourth Gospel problems which are both exciting and difficult. It seems more oriented toward the Greek world than any other New Testament writing, yet its doctrine is authentically biblical. The author marks out his own path, different from that of the Synoptics, with no apparent desire to make his account match theirs. What is more, he attributes to Christ a new kind of language. Yet, the basic trends of the fourth Gospel are closely allied to those of the Synoptics, as we have tried to show, using the idea of life as an example.

We have by no means exhausted the possibilities of this important question. As a matter of fact, we are convinced that deeper studies would lead to a fuller appreciation of the harmony between John and his Synoptic colleagues, a harmony which is as more significant as it is less evident, and which seems never to have been sought.

Part II
The Apocalypse

CHAPTER I

THE TWENTY-FOUR ELDERS OF THE APOCALYPSE [1]

Twelve times in his descriptions of the heavenly world, John's Apocalypse mentions the twenty-four elders, or ancients (Presbyteroi; IV: 4; 10; V: 5; 6; 7; 11; 14; VII: 11; 13; XI: 16; XIV: 3; XIX: 4). The identity of these elders has been discussed at great lengths, most exegetes seeing in them either angels or a group of rulers. Each of these interpretations has any number of varieties in itself as well. We cannot discuss them all here, of course, since our purpose is not to present a history of this exegesis, but merely to propose our own personal thoughts on the matter.[2]

We are of the opinion that elders are not angels, but men [3] gathered together, particularly the saints of the Old Testament, the ancestors, in the faith, of the Christians. This interpretation is not new, although until now only a few have held it in exactly

1 Published in *Revue Biblique*, vol. LXV (1958).

2 Bibliography: E. B. ALLO, *L'Apocalypse*, Paris, 1933; G. BALDENS-PRERGER, *L'Apocalypse*, Paris, 1938; J. BEHM, *Die Offenbarung des Johannes*, Göttingen, 1949; M. E. BOISMARD, *L'Apocalypse*, Paris, 1950; J. BONSIRVEN, *L'Apocalypse de saint Jean*, Paris, 1951; W. BOUSSET, *Die Offenbarung des Johannes*, Göttingen, Paris, 1955; R. H. CHARLES, *A Critical and Exegetical Commentary on the Revelation of St. John*, Edinburgh, 1920; A. GELIN, *L'Apocalypse*, Paris, 1938; W. HADORN, *Die Offenbarung des Johannes*, Leipzig, 1928; M. KIDDLE, *The Revelation of St. John*, London, 1940; H. J. HOLTZMANN, *Evangelium, Briefe und Offenbarung Johannes*, Frieburg i. B., 1891; LOHMEYER, *Die Offenbarung des Johannes*, Tübingen, 1953; A. LOISY, *L'Apocalypse de saint Jean*, Paris, 1923; I. ROHR, *Der Hebraerbrief und die Geheimne Offenbarung des hl. Johannes*, Bonn, 1932; H. B. SWETE, *The Apocalypse of St. John*, London, 1907; A. WIKENHAUSER, *Offenbarung des Johannes*, Regensburg, 1949; Th. ZAHN, *Die Offenbarung des Johannes*, Leipzig, 1924-1926.

3 There would need be little discussion of this exegesis, if we could read *hēmas* after *to Theō* in the song of the elders in V. 9: "thou hast redeemed *us* for God." However, although this reading is attested to by all the principal MSS except A, still most critics reject it on the grounds

this way.[4] The excellent monograph of J. Michl on this problem leaves little to be said.[5] We wish to pursue the question, however, because the arguments which Michl presents, somewhat obscured amid the wealth of detail which he puts forward, have not been discussed, and, furthermore, because they can in some ways be completed and somewhat modified. Also, the solution of their problem depends, we think, on the meaning of the first prophetic part of the Apocalypse (Chapters IV-XI), as we shall indicate in our conclusion.

We shall examine briefly the twenty-four elders, their characteristics, their title of elders, and their place and function in heaven. We shall collect references which will show clearly that they are not angels, but glorified men. Then in the second part of the chapter we shall see whether these elders are to be sought in the Christian Church or among the people of God of the Old Testament.

---

that it is difficult to reconcile with the *autous* which most MSS have in the following verse. Some would defend the *hēmas* of v. 9 on the grounds that otherwise there would be no direct object given for *ēgorasas*. This problem could be solved, however, especially in the light of the johannine style as a whole. On this textual question cf. J. MICHL, *Die 24 Ältesten in der Apokalypse des heiligen Johannes*, München, 1938, pp. 68-71. It is worth noting that H. C. Hoskier's well known studies of the Apocalypse text (*Concerning the Text of the Apocalypse*, London, 1929, 2 vols.) retains the reading, "Thou hast redeemed us."

4 Ancient writers almost unanimously saw the elders as men. Many considered them to be Old Testament figures, but few thought them to be primarily such, e. gr., Oecumenius, who undertook to determine the identity of each of the twenty-four, and concluded that twenty-two of them were Old Testament saints and the remaining two were saints of the Christian Church. Cf. H. C. HOSKIER, *The Complete Commentary of Oecumenius on the Apocalypse*, in *University of Michigan Studies*, 1938, p. 70.

5 Cf. above note. In his very favorable review of Michl's work (*R.B.*, 1940, pp. 282-284), P. Benoit considers his opinion "very probable." The all too brief treatment of the problem of the twenty four elders in WIKENHAUSER'S *Commentary* (pp. 46-47) show that he too follows MICHL. We might mention here another study, much briefer than Michl's, but one which is equally worthy and which concludes partly in the same way: A. SKRINJAR, *Vigintiquattuor Seniores*, in *Verbum Domini*, 1936, pp. 333-338; 361-368.

(1) *The Twenty-Four Elders are Glorified Men*

The twenty-four elders have three characteristics; thrones, white robes and golden crowns. The elders place their crowns before the throne of God (IV: 10), showing thereby that their dignity is less than His and comes from Him. Such a gesture of vassalage was well known in ancient times (cf. Cicero, *Pro Sestio*, 27; Plutarch, *Lucullus*, 522; Tacitus, *Annals*, XV: 29). We shall examine each of these characteristics carefully.

The Scripture often mentions the presence of the throne of God and of Christ in heaven, a royal seat for the tribunal of the Parousia. In Mt. XIX: 28 and Luke XXI: 30 (texts subject to considerable controversy) Jesus says that, in the "regeneration," the Apostles shall sit upon twelve thrones. These could be judgment seats in the strict sense, or simply royal thrones, although in antiquity the royal and judiciary powers were one. In Eph. II: 4-6 the Christians are to share Christ's throne in heaven. Apocalypse III: 21 makes a similar promise to the victorious members of the Church of Laodicea. Still in all, apart from the twelve Apostles and the confessors of the faith and martyrs in Apocalypse XX: 4, the Scripture does not usually speak of separate personal thrones in heaven for glorified Christians. However, neither does it ever present a clear picture of angels seated on thrones. Not only in the Bible (I Kgs. XXII: 19; 2 Chr. XVIII: 18; Tob. XII: 15; Job I: 6; II: 1; Lk. I: 19; Apoc. I: 11; VIII: 2) but also in the later Jewish writings (Hen. XIV: 22; XXXIX: 12; XL: 1; XLVI: 3; XLVIII: 10; 4th Esdras VIII: 21; etc.), the angels stand around the throne of God (we shall speak further on about Dan. VII: 9). If we recall that the Apocalypse speaks in royal terms of the faithful members of the people of God, (I: 6; V: 10), we can see how the image of the throne fits such a description extremely well, and applies better to men than to angels. In the Apocalypse of John IX: 12, thrones are promised to the Old Testament saints.

In St. Paul, late Judaism and in early Christianity (Col. I: 46; Testament of Levi III: 8; Testament of Adam IV: 19; 22; Slavic Henoch XX: 1; Apocalypse of Elias: XXI: 1 ff.; Const. Apost. VII: 35: 3; VIII: 12; 8; 27; Pseudo Dionysius. P. G. III: 205), thrones are a class of angels, called such no doubt because they are considered close to the throne of God. They have nothing in common wtih the elders of the Apocalypse, so that Allo's statement identifying them is unfounded. The same applies to the thrones mentioned in the Ascension of Isaia, (VII: 14; 21; 27; VIII: 8; XI: 25) if we see them as angels, notwithstanding the fact that the Latin and Slavic versions have the word in a material sense.[6]

The color white and white robes have many meanings in the Bible.[7] They can be simply the sign of joy and prosperity, Qoh. IX: 8, Epistle of St. James II: 3. Mostly they refer to the heavenly order. Because of its brightness, white is the color of God and of the beings close to Him, the angels and the blessed (cf. Dan. VII: 9; 2 Mac. XI: 8; Mt. XXVIII: 3; Mark IX: 3; John XX: 12; Acts I: 10; X: 30; Apocalypse I: 14; XIV: 14; XIX: 11). Applied to men, white robes are closely associated with their moral conduct. In the Apocalypse the faithful Christians wear them beginning with their earthly existence (III: 4, 18; V: 11; VII: 14; XIX: 8; cf. Is. I: 18; Ps. LI: 9). Add to this the fact that in the Jewish and pagan liturgies (at least in Asia Minor), white robes (white linen) were, if not required, at least usual, and we can understand still better why the blessed wear them in the Apocalypse, which describes eschatological happiness in terms of a liturgy. White is furthermore a sign of triumph and victory; it is quite normal, then, to find this image in a book such as the Apocalypse, which is designed to describe the eschatological triumph of Christ and His Christians.

The variety of meanings assigned to white robes and to white in general, make it necessary to look further for the real meaning of the figure of the twenty-four elders, which in itself could apply to angels as well as to glorified men. It is worth noting that John's Apocalypse refers six or seven times to the white robes of the saints, and that only once does the text refer to angels (XIX: 14). The other apocalypses also refer more often to the heavenly robes of the saints (I Hen. XLII: 16; 2 Hen. XXII: 8; 4 Esd. II: 39; 45; Asc. of Isaia IV: 16; VII: 22; VIII: 14; Apoc. of Abr. XIII: 15; Apoc. of Elias XXXIX: 4; Apoc. of Sophonia XIII: 2), than to those of angels, (I Hen. LXXI: 1; Test. of Levi VIII: 2; 2 Hen. I: 5; VI: 1; XIX: 1; Apoc. of Abr. XI: 2). The indication, therefore, although not conclusive, cer-

---

6 Cf. E. TISSERANT, *L'Ascension d'Isaïe*, Paris, 1909, pp. 149-150 note on VII, 14.

7 Cf. ALLO, *Excursus XIII, La couleur blanche dans l'Apocalypse* pp. 59-61.

tainly favors the possibility that the reference is to men, not to angels.

The golden crowns are less difficult to understand. In the Bible the crown, either of leaves or of metal, can be a sign of joy of happiness and well being (Job XIX: 9; Jer. XIII: 18; Lam. V: 10; Ps. XXIV: 4; Prov. IV: 9); it can be a sign of moral or religious victory (Cant. III: 11; Ez. XVI: 12; Wis. IV: 2; Tob. III: 21; Sir., Vulgate, VI: 31); finally it can symbolize the special dignity of a king (2 Sam. XII: 30; Esth. XIII: 15; Sir. XL: 4) or of a priest (Sir. XLV: 12; 2 Ach. VI: 11; 14; 2 Macc. X: 20). In the New Testament, aside from this passage in the Apocalypse which we are attempting to understand, and discounting also the crown of mockery placed on the head of Jesus during His Passion, the crown otherwise is always an image of man's victory over his troubles (Phil. IV: 1), and especially of the final triumph of the elect. (I Th. II: 19; I Cor. IX: 25; 2 Tim. IV: 8; James I: 12; I Peter V: 4). Such a crown could hardly apply to angels, who do not have to gain such a moral miracle. There is no reference to crowned angels in Scripture, and only rarely does the figure appear in the Apocrypha (Joseph and Aseneth XIV: 9; Apoc. of Abr. XI: 2). John's Apocalypse assigns a crown twice to the faithful Christians (II: 2; III: II); once to the rider of the white horse (VI: 2); once to the women (XII: 1); once to the victorious Christ (XIV: 14), but never to angels. Once there is reference (IX: 7) to the locusts ready for battle, having on their heads crowns, as it were, like gold; also, the angel coming down from heaven (X: 1), clothed in a cloud, has a rainbow over his head.

Taking these three characteristic marks together now (the thrones, white robes, crowns) we see them already associated in the letters at the beginning of the Apocalypse, to refer to the eschatological blessings promised to faithful Christians. We have the throne in III: 21; the white robes in III: 5, the crown in II: 10 and III: 11. It seems correct to presume that these three symbols should have the same meaning which applied to the twenty-four elders, and that these elders are men and not angels. In an important text (IX: 6-12) which we shall see later, the Asc. of Isaia applies these three characteristics to the saints of the old covenant who are admitted to heavenly happiness. This parallelism becomes particularly striking when we see here that the just of the Old Testament receive individual thrones, as do

the twenty-four elders of the Apocalypse, and as do the twelve
apostles in Matt. XIX: 28.

The personages of the Apocalypse are called elders, (*presbyteroi*). In ancient times, the aged and experienced members
of the community enjoyed a specially privileged status in public
affairs, they often sat together in a council, the council of elders
(*presbyterion*). They were accorded special privileges, not so
much because of their age as because they were members of the
council. Israel was no exception to this practice. In the LXX
(116 times, according to Michl) the *presbyteroi* are the ancients,
or elders, of the tribe, of the city, the priesthood, the army, or
of the people in general.

The New Testament speaks once (Luke VII: 3) of the elders
of Capharnaum; twenty-five times of the elders of the Jews or
of the leading heads of families, who together with the Scribes,
made up the august assembly of the Sanhedrin; and fifteen times
of the elders of the Christian Church, placed in charge of the
various Christian communities. The letters of St. Ignatius of
Antioch tell us that in Asia Minor at the end of the first century
(the milieu in which the Apocalypse was composed), the churches
were governed by bishops assigned by a council of elders or
ancients. "Your *venerabile presbyterium*, truly worthy of God, is
united to the bishop as are the cords of a lyre" (Eph. IV: 1); [8]
"Your hearts are united in submission to the bishop and to the
presbyterium, breaking all of you the same bread" (Eph. XX: 2).
The bishop and the presbyters together represent the whole
Church, "I have had the honor of seeing you in the presence of
Damas your holy Bishop, and of the worthy presbyters Bassus
and Apollonius, and of the deacon Zotion, my companion. I hope
to have the pleasure of his presence, for he is submissive to the
bishop as to the grace of God, and to the presbyterium as to the
law of Christ" (Magn. II: 1). The presbyters are to obey the
bishop as they would the Father of Our Lord Christ, who is
bishop of all: "Your bishop's youth must not lead you to too

---

8 The author's French translations of the patristic texts cited here
are from "*Textes et Documents*," published under direction of H. HEMMER
and P. LEJAY, *Les Pères Apostoliques; Ignace d'Antioche et Polycarpe de
Smyrne*, Paris, 1927. The English versions given above are from the
ANCIENT CHRISTIAN WRITERS series, *The Epistles of St. Clement of
Rome and St. Ignatius of Antioch*, translated by James A. Kleist, S. J.,
Westminster, Maryland, 1949. (Tr.)

great a familiarity with him; you are to see in him the powers
of God Himself, and reverence it fully in him. This your holy
presbyters do, as I know well: they have not abused his apparent
youth, but they have been inspired by the Wisdom of God Himself and have been submissive to him, or rather, not to Him
but to the Father of Our Lord Christ, the bishop of all" (Magn.
III: 1). And again, "Do everything in a spirit of harmony (which
is pleasing to God) under the leadership of your bishop, who
takes the place of God, of the presbyters, who represent the
Senate of the Bishops and of the deacons, to whom goes my
special affection, since they are charged to do service in the
name of Christ, who was with the Father before all ages, and
who revealed Himself at the proper time" (Magn. VI: 1; cf.
also Magn. VII: 1; Trall. II: 2; VII: 12; XII: 2; XIII: 2; Phila-
delph. IV: 1; V: 1; VII: 1; Smyrn. VIII: 1; XII: 2). Such an
abundance of texts leaves no doubt of the point at issue (at
least in the mind of St. Ignatius).

In the synagogue services of the Jews, the elders or ancients
had a place of honor.[9] It is possible that as soon as the end of
the first century the presbyters of the Christian communities
may have been seated this way at the liturgical services. We
know that at least a little later they were accorded this privilege,
while the deacons had to remain standing (cf. *Didascalia Apost.*
II: 57: 3 ff.; *Const. Apost.* II: 57: 4; VIII: 12: 3).[10] The fact
that the twenty-four elders are seated about the throne of God
may well be a reflection of their practice.

Be this last part what it may, when Christian readers of the
Apocalypse heard mention of the *presbyteroi*, they surely had
no reason to think of angels, who never have this title in Scripture
(except in Is. XXIV: 23, an obscure passage which we shall
see later). Rather, it would be quite natural for them to think
of men in heaven grouped as a sort of privileged elite, very
much like the presbyters of the church gathered around their
bishop, whom Ignatius compares so beautifully to "the Father
of Our Lord Christ, the bishop of all." The twenty-four elders
seem to be a heavenly presbyterium, grouped around God Himself. The Apocalypse thus appears to show the heavenly orders

9 Cf. STRACK - BILLERBECK, *Kommentar zum Neuen Testament
aus Talmud und Midrasch*, IV, Erster Teil, *Das altjüdische Synagogeinstitut*,
Munchen, 1928, p. 120.

10 Cf. J. MICHL, p. 4, note 2.

as a sort of prototype of the earthly hierarchy. Lohmeyer notes that in IV: 11, the chant of the elders, with the characteristic phrase "worthy art thou," suggests the formula used later at the enthronement of bishops. The historian Socrates (*Hist. Eccl.* IV: 30) says this formula was used in reference to Ambrose as Bishop of Milan.[11]

There is also in the Scripture an angelic court, which in some cases seems to have the role of a deliberative council. The question arises, therefore, whether the twenty-four elders of the Apocalypse are to be placed in relationship with these angels. We should examine the passages in question.

The principal texts which could possibly come under consideration here are the following: in I Kgs. XXII: 9, Yahweh asks the heavenly army, i.e. the angels, "Who shall deceive Achab, King of Israel"? In Job I: 6-12 and II: 1-6, among the sons of God, i.e. the angels who present themselves before Yahweh, Satan appears, and dares to advise God and obtains from Him the leave he seeks to torment Job. The same book (Job. XV: 8) seems to show a council deliberating with Jahweh.[12] A similar figure appears in John XXIII: 18 and also in Ps. LXXXIX: 8: "God is terrible in the council of the holy ones; he is great and awesome above all round about him." The ever-increasing insistence of later Judaism upon God's transcendence may explain why in Dan. VII the heavenly court seems to include only angels. Their role there is to pass on the divine decree, for the "decree" and the "judgment" follow the "decree of the Most High" (V: 22). However, even in these cases, Yahweh does not consult with the angels; they merely serve him; there is none of the "extravagant and blasphemous" deliberation spoken

---

11 Cf. E. LOHMEYER, *Die Offenbarung des Johannes*, p. 50. For a more detailed study of this canticle cf. E. PETERSON, *HEIS THEOS, Epigraphische, formgeschichtliche und religionsgeschichtliche Untersuchungen*, Göttingen, 1926, pp. 176-180. Note that in Apoc. V: 9 the four living creatures and the twenty-four elders all sing the same "worthy art thou, etc." to Christ. In I Peter Christ is called "guardian" (*episkopos* II: 25) and "prince of shepherds" (*archipoimēn*, V: 4); this last title occurs within the context of an exhortation which Peter addresses to the "elders" (*presbyteroi*), charged to "feed the flock of God" (V: 1-2) in his name.

12 This interpretation is not certain. Cf. DHORME, *Le Livre de Job*, Paris, 1926, p. 191.

of in later Judaism [13] (cf. Sanh. 38b, "The Holy One does nothing without consulting His heavenly family".[14] The more Jahweh's solitary greatness stands out, the less and less place remains for the idea of a creature really able to advise Him on the governing of the world:

Who has directed the spirit of the Lord,
or who has instructed him as his counselor?
Whom did he consult to gain knowledge?
Who taught him the path of judgment, or
showed him the way of understanding?
Is. XL: 13-14

In any case, the twenty-four elders of the Apocalypse certainly have not even the least direct share in the governing of the universe, although, as we shall say below, they are associated with it in a way. They are not even consulted by Jahweh, as are the angels of some Old Testament texts. Their function, as we see in these passages, is altogether different from that of the angels.

We have yet to consider two texts that merit special attention, because they have been used more than any others, to explain the figure of the elders of the Apocalypse. These are Dan. VII: 9 and (especially) Is. XXIV: 23.

We do not think we can get much from the passage in Dan. VII: 9. It is clear from the phrase "Thrones were set up," that the Ancient of Days, who takes his throne to judge the Beast, is not the only one to have a throne. He has a council, but what they are is not clear. Some have referred here to the Son of Man, who comes upon the scene a little further on; others have mentioned the ancients of Israel, or the Angels,[15] the angels being the most commonly accepted.[16] Even if this is the correct inter-

---

13 Thus R. H. CHARLES, *Commentary on the Book of Daniel*, Oxford, 1929, p. 93.

14 On this question Cf. J. BONSIRVEN, *Le Judaisme palestinien au Temps de Jésus-Christ*, Paris, 1934, t. I, p. 231, note 5; F. WEBER, *Jüdische Theologie auf Grund des Talmud und verwandter Schriften*, Leipzig, 1897, p. 715.

15 Cf. J. A. MONTGOMERY, *Commentary on the Book of Daniel*, Edinburgh, 1937, pp. 296-297.

16 Cf. CHARLES, *The Book of Daniel*, p. 184.

pretation, it has no direct bearing on our Apocalypse text, because the twenty-four elders have no judging function whatever. Yet, they are always round about God's throne.

The passage in Isaia XXIV: 23 is much more interesting. It belongs to the Apocalypse of Isaias, and follows a passage describing divine judgment which will affect all the inhabitants of the universe. The gates of heaven shall be opened, as for a new flood (V. 18). Not only the kings of earth, but also the "heavenly army" will be visited. This last reference undoubtedly refers to the pagan divinities associated with the stars (cf. Dt. IV: 19; XVII: 3; Jer. VIII: 2; XIX: 13; Soph. I: 5; Job XXXI: 26 ff.). This judgment will signal the inauguration in Sion of the Kingdom of God, which will manifest God's glory in the sight of His elders (*Basileusei Kyrios ek Seiōn kai eis Ierousalēm kai enōpion tōn presbyterōn doxasthēsetai*, v. 23).

J. Steinmann seeks to identify these "elders" who witness God's glory, as the stars, "signifying the constellations and the angelic forces".[17] They seem to refer rather, as most commentators say, to men, as representing the eschatological Israel. This scene, they say, is a recall to Ex. XXIV: 9 ff., in which, at the rite concluding the alliance, God shows Himself on Sinai to Moses, Aaron, Nadab, Abiu, and sixty-six of the elders of Israel as representatives with the entire chosen people.

Although we cannot prove beyond doubt that the author of the Apocalypse wrote of the twenty-four elders with this verse in mind, still in all, the conjecture is at least plausible; most commentators hold it. In each case there is an eschatological scene, a group in the presence of God, who witness His victory. In each case the group are called *presbyteroi*, and both passages refer to the apparition of Jahweh to the "elders" of Israel on Sinai. In the Isaia text the allusion is more clear, whereas in the Apocalypse passage it is less obvious. However, as Swete and Allo say, v. 6 refers to the vision granted to Moses and the elders in Ex. XXIV: 10, while the preceding verse recalls Ex. XIX: 5.

For all the reasons which we have indicated, it seems that the twenty-four elders of the Apocalypse must be taken as men, acting as representatives of the entire people of God, like those of Ex. XXIV: 9 and Is. XXIV: 23. This interpretation, which, rather than being forced, is quite natural, was the most favored

---

17 *Le Prophète Isaie*, Paris, 1950, p. 352.

among the Fathers and the ancient commentators of the Apocalypse (cf. Clem. Alex., *Strom.* VI: 13 P.G. IX: 325-329). Cf. also the commentaries of Victorinus; Andreas of Caesarea; Oecumenius; Primasius; Bede; Albert the Great; Alcazar; Cornelius a Lapide; Bossuet. There are a few exceptions, such as Maximus the Confessor (P.G. IV: 225-228). However, it is mostly modern exegetes who have tried to make a case in favor of angels in this text, but the reasons which they adduce do not seem to us to be convincing or strong enough to counter all the arguments which we have presented above.

Charles [18] gives three reasons why he favors the interpretation favoring angels. First of all, in VII: 14, the speaker addresses one of the elders as "My Lord" (*kyrie*). However, even the angels are occasionally addressed this way in the Scripture (Zach. I: 9; IV: 5; 13; VI: 4; Gen. XIX: 2) and especially in the apocalyptic texts (Dan. X: 16; 19; XII: 8; Jubilees XXXII: 25; Test. of Levi V: 5; 2 Hen. XXI: 4; 4 Eso. II: 3-5). The same can be said of men, especially when they are the object of some special reverence (Gen. XXIII: 6; XXXI: 35; John XXII: 21; XX: 15). If, as Lohmeyer holds,[19] the title in Apocalypse VII: 14 were to refer to an attribute of God, then it would no longer fit either an angel or a man (an angel actually declines this title in Asc. of Isaia VIII: 4-5).

Charles adds another reason, namely that in Apocalypse VII: 14 the elder fulfills the role of an interpreting angel. This is true enough, but such a function is by no means limited in the Scripture to angels; in the books of Jeremia and Ezechiel, God Himself often offers to explain visions (Jer. I: 12, 14 ff.; Ez. II; VII: 6-9); in 2 Macc. XV: 12-16, the high priest Onias, not an angel, comes upon the scene to identify the prophet Jeremia. As for the consoler of Apocalypse V: 5 and the mediator of V: 8; both parts fulfilled by elders, there seems to be no compelling reason why they should have to be angels. In the text of 2 Macc. XV: 12-16, to which we referred just above, Juda tells how Jeremia appeared to him to comfort him. It was he who appeared in the guise of an elder, of a man, "admirable for age and glory and environed with beauty and majesty." Skrinjar [20] observes

---

18 *The Revelation of St. John*, vol. I, p. 130.

19 *Die Offenbarung des Johannes*, p. 46.

20 Art. cit., pp. 337-338, Cf. also our article, *Isaïe*, in *Suppl. au Dictionnaire de la Bible*, t. IV, Col. 711-712.

well, that in the Bible it is more often men (Abraham, Moses, the prophets) than angels who fulfill this function of mediator, including the just who have died, such as Jesus, presented as "A lover of his brethren and of the people of Israel; this is he that prayeth much for the people and for all the Holy City" (2 Mac. XV: 14).

THE TWENTY-FOUR ELDERS ARE THE SAINTS OF THE OLD TESTAMENT

Once given that the twenty-four elders are glorified men and not angels, the question arises whether they are to be identified with the members of the Christian Church, and with the members of the chosen people of God in the Old Testament. True enough, in a Christian work such as this is, one would naturally be inclined first of all to see these elders as representing Christians. Such a hypothesis, however, labors under some serious difficulties.

Sure enough, in the after-life which we see depicted in this scene of the Apocalypse, presenting as it were an uninterrupted liturgy in honor of God and Christ, the twenty-four elders appear to fulfill a role somewhat like that of the presbyters assembled about the bishop in the liturgy of the earliest Christian churches. Like them, they praise God in the name of the human family (IV: 10-11; V: 14), offering to God the reverent homage of his servants of earth, and holding in their hands, as it were the golden vials full of perfume, which is said to be the prayers of the saints. (V: 8). We see them thanking God "for giving the reward to thy servants—the prophets, and the saints and those who fear thy name, the small and the great" (XI: 18). They join in the "Alleluia" of the assembled throng (XIX: 1-5). Dr. Michl has stressed quite correctly that, despite some details borrowed from the Old Testament liturgy (harps, incense, etc.), the homage of the twenty-four elders recalls rather that of the presbyters in the Christian cult. Given this, it seems that they are supposed to represent the idealized Church. This interpretation was held in ancient times (Tyconius; Pseudo-Augustine; Primasius; Bede), and has recently found new defenders, such as Swete; Skrinjar; Cerfaux; Cambier.

Attractive though this explanation is, we do not consider it acceptable at all. The twenty-four elders cannot be taken as a sort of symbolic heavenly counterpart of the Christian Church in its totality, because in V: 9-17 and XV: 2-4 (cf. XIV: 3) these elders are clearly distinguished from the thrones of the

Christian faithful, and again in XIX: 5-9 they are distinguished
from the spouse of the Lamb. Some have suggested that they
may be a special group of saints charged with the care of the
Church. Thus the elders have been compared with the angels
of the Christian communities mentioned in the letters at the
beginning of the Apocalypse. This comparison is not valid, because whereas the angels are charged with responsibility for
these churches to such a point that they actually share the reproaches directed to them, the elders on the other hand always
act in their own name.

Because they are dressed in white robes, like the Jewish
priests in the liturgical services, and because of the number
twenty-four, recalling the twenty-four classes of priests in the
Book of Chronicles (see below), some have suggested that these
elders are priests (Alcazar). Charles, who sees them as angels,
would nevertheless see all the faithful as exercising a sort of
heavenly priesthood. However, besides the fact that their func-
tions are quite far removed from those of the priests of the old
covenant, (they play harps whereas in the Old Testament the
Levites, not the priests, are in charge of sacred music), they
are furthermore called not *hiereis* but *presbyteroi*, although the
author does occasionally use the word *hiereis* I: 6; VI: 10; XX: 6.
The word *presbyteroi* occurs also in the fourth Gospel (VIII: 9)
and in the johannine epistles (II: 1; III: 1), but never in the
sense of "priest." Therefore, if the elders are priests, it is in the
same broad sense in which the term is applied to all Christians,
("kings and priests," I: 6; V: 10; XX: 6) and in which all Christians appear as chanting unceasingly the praises of God, rendering
Him worship both day and night in His Temple (cf. VIII: 9-13)
and the scene of the four living creatures praising God day and
night (IV: 8-11); (this scene is related to that of the twenty-four
elders).

At the time of the composition of the Apocalypse the best
known group among the members of the Christian community
is that of the twelve Apostles. Be this as it may, the elders
certainly are not the twelve apostles. The apostles are explicitly
mentioned in XXI: 24, with their proper title of Apostle and
with the proper number of twelve, whereas these elders are
distinctly numbered at twenty-four. Furthermore, presuming that
John wrote the Apocalypse, it is inconceivable that he would
have had such an idea of himself, represented as acting in heaven.
Furthermore, the song of vv. 9-10 hardly fits on the lips of

the Apostles (we have already said that the *hēmas* of v. 9 is probably not authentic). When they mention the fact of the Redemption, they are not content to celebrate it objectively, as it were, but they number themselves among the elect. This view excludes also all the hypotheses which identify the twenty-four elders as the twelve apostles plus twelve others (to explain the number twenty-four), as, e. gr., the patriarchs and the apostles. It would be equally arbitrary to split the group to twenty-four elders into two units of twelve.

There are various indications which seem to lead to the conviction that the twenty-four elders of the Apocalypse are a figure of the great heroes or saints of the Old Testament. It is a fact that in the New Testament, as also in later Jewish texts, the outstanding personages of the old covenant had a special place in the after-life, praying for men and caring for their lot and interesting themselves in their trials.

In the parable of Lazarus and Dives, (Lk. XVI: 19-31), Lazarus the poor man is taken by angels after his death to the "Bosom of Abraham" (v: 22). Michl says that Abraham here is a figure of the prince and leader of the other world (*"Fürst und Verwalter des Jensseits"*).[21] Interestingly enough, the rich man, instead of addressing God indirectly, calls upon Father Abraham to relieve his suffering (vv. 24-27). This is an eschatological concept that is typically biblical: the saints in heaven do more than enjoy passively the reward which they have received; they share actively with God the function of governing the world, as in Dan. VII the saints of the Most High are intimately associated with the destiny of the mysterious "son of man" who appears on the clouds (vv. 18, 27; cf. v. 14; also Wis. III: 8).

We have already had occasion, especially in speaking of the parables of the servant (Mt. XXIV: 45-51; Luke XII: 41-48),[22] of the talents and the minae (Mt. XXV: 14-34; Luke XIX: 17-27)[23] and of the unjust steward (Luke XVI: 1-12)[24] to show this teaching of the Gospel, which seems to us to be little understood as yet. We should note well that, in the thought of Jesus, all glorified Christians are constituted "stewards of the other

---

21 *Die 24 Ältesten*, p. 109.

22 *La Synthèse eschatologique de saint Matthieu*, in R. B., 1950, pp. 68-69.

23 *La Synthèse eschatologique de saint Matthieu*, *ibid.*, pp. 83-86.

24 *Les riches intendants du Christ*, in Rech. Sc. Rel., 1947, pp. 30-54.

world," as Michl phrases it. If the leaders of the various communities have been found vigilant at the time of reckoning, and are placed over all their divine Maker's goods, (Mt. XXIV: 47), then the simple Christians will hear in their turn, "Well done, good and faithful servant; because thou hast been faithful over a few things, I will set thee over many" (Mt. XXV: 21; 23; cf. Luke XIX: 17; 19). In return for their generosity, the rich will see themselves at the moment of death, being received into the everlasting dwellings (Luke XVI: 9).

However, if this lordship over eschatological blessings is to be accorded thus to all the blessed, then, *a fortiori*, this must be true of the great persons of the Old Testament, the fathers in the faith, of Christ's disciples. The promise was made to Abraham (Gen. XI: 3; XVIII: 18; XXII: 18), to Isaac (XXVI: 4) and to Jacob (XXVIII: 14), that all the nations of the earth would be blessed (or would bless themselves) through them. The New Testament recalls these promises frequently: Jesus is the first to pay particular attention to them. In Jesus' eyes, the only God to be God of the whole world is the God of Abraham, Isaac, and Jacob. In a prophecy recorded by both Matthew and Luke, and which J. Jeremias shows to be typically Semitic in character, and hence reliably authentic as well as profoundly important,[25] Jesus states that "many will come from the east and from the west, and will feast with Abraham and Isaac and Jacob in the kingdom of heaven but the children of the kingdom (the Jews, natural heirs of the promises made to the patriarchs), will be put forth into the darkness outside" (Mt. VIII: 11; 12). In the corresponding passage in his gospel, Luke adds to the names of Abraham, Isaac and Jacob a reference to all the prophets of the Old Testament. It is important to understand the high place which Jesus assigns in the final Kingdom of God to these leading characters of the old Covenant. They are already in the kingdom, and are considered to be receiving the disciples of Christ as they enter.

It is clear that in speaking this way, Jesus is referring to ideas and conceptions which are current in His own time, and which He corrects by injecting the idea of unlimited universalism, a notion far removed from the minds of His Jewish contemporaries. Worth noticing here are the formulas of 4 Macc., which is

---

25 *Jésus et les païens,* Neuchâtel-Paris, 1956, pp. 49-65. J. Jeremias' explanation of the text is not, however, above criticism.

generally dated in the first century of the Christian era.[26] In XIII: 17 the Maccabee brothers encourage each other: — "After our sufferings, we shall be received by Abraham, Isaac, and Jacob; all the people shall praise us." In XVI: 25, the author says of them and of their mother, "They were sure that when one dies for God, one lives on in God, as do Abraham, Isaac, and Jacob and all the patriarchs." The work ends thus: "The sons of Abraham, and their victorious mother are now together with the fathers, who received pure and immortal souls from God, to whom be glory through all ages. Amen." (XVIII: 23-24).

This same tradition persisted among the Christians as it had among the Jews. St. Ignatius of Antioch speaks in his letter to the Philadelphians, of "Jesus Christ, the door which leads to the Father, and through which pass Abraham, Isaac, Jacob, the Apostles, the prophets and all the Church" (IX: 1). The Epistle of Barnabas (VIII: 4) also speaks of "Abraham, Isaac and Jacob, the three who are great before God . . ." According to the Apocalypse of Paul, which dates from the end of the fourth century, the saints are united in heaven with the prophets (XXV). Paul is allowed to contemplate these, as well as the great patriarchs and leaders of the Old Testament, especially Abraham, Isaac, and Jacob (XLVII-LI). The ending of this section is worth quoting here:

> I saw three men coming from afar, beautiful with a beauty like that of Christ, they were radiant: their angels were with them. I asked the angel, 'My lord, who are these?' and he replied 'Do you not know?' I told him, 'No, my Lord, I know them not.' He told me then, 'These are the fathers of the people, Abraham, Isaac and Jacob.' They came to me and greeted me, saying, 'Hail, Paul, beloved of God and men. Blessed are thou who suffer violence for the sake of the Lord.' Then Abraham said to me, 'These are my sons, Isaac and my beloved Jacob . . . We too were loyal to the same Lord whom you preach; we worked to help all those souls who believe in Him, and to serve them, as fathers serve their children".[27]

---

26 Cf. J. B. FREY, *Apocryphes de l'ancien Testament,* in *Supplément au Dictionnaire de la Bible,* t. 1, Col. 445-447. A. DUPONT - SOMMER, *Le Quatrième Livre des Macchabées,* Paris, 1939.

27 Cf. the Greek text of this work in TISCHENDORF, *Apocalypses*

In the Apocryphal letter of Titus, edited by Dom de Bruyne, which is really a sermon extolling the chastity of a Priscillianist heretic,[28] the saints of the Old Testament are presented as the heroes, the fathers and judges of the Christians:

> Virgo desponsata Christo, cum alio inventa viro, adducantur utrique ad ultimam sententiam in conspectu veteranorum, id est Abraham, Isaac et Jacob, quorum cura est cognoscere causam filiorum. Tunc patres abnegabunt liberos sibi operarios iniquitatis.

Recall also the mention of Abraham, Isaac, and Jacob in the canon of the Roman Mass, the invocation of the patriarchs and prophets before that of the prophets in the Litany of the Saints, and the prayer in the Office of the dead, "*Suscipiat te Christus qui vocavit te, et in sinum Abrahae Angeli deducant te.*"

In the Qumran texts there are ideas which, if they are not the same, are at least related. In the *Hodayoth,* or *Psalms of Thanksgiving,* the Qumran community is described as the "ante-chamber of heaven"; its members are colleagues of the heavenly choirs and of the heavenly armies."[29] In the *Rule of War,* the sons of the light, who are to engage in eschatological combat against the sons of darkness, have allies and helpers in heaven, who are, of course, primarily the angels, but we believe they are also the saints of the chosen people. This seems to be the meaning especially of XII: 1-8:

> For (with thee) in heaven are a multitude of holy beings, and armies of angels are in Thy holy abode, to (serve as) Thy (legionaries); and down on earth Thou hast (likewise) placed at Thy service the elect of a holy people. The roster of all their host is with Thee in Thy holy habitation, and the (   ) in Thy glorious abode. And

---

apoccryphae Moisis, Esdrae, Pauli, Johannis, item Mariae Dormitio ... Lipsiae (Leipzig), 1866; the Latin text is in James, *Apocrypha Anecdota,* Cambridge, 1893 and 1897. The author's French text is taken from the Latin version found in F. Amiot, *La Bible Apocryphe; Évangiles Apocryphes,* Paris, 1952, p. 326. (Tr.)

28 *Epistola Titi discipuli Pauli de dispositione sanctimonii;* cf. *Revue Benedictine,* 1925, p. 51.

29 G. VERMÉS, *Quelques traditions de la communauté de Qumrân,* in *Cahiers Sioniens, mars* 1955, p. 55.

the benefits of Thy blessings and Thy covenant of peace hast thou inscribed for them in a charter of (Eternal) Life—an assurance that through all the epochs of time Thou wilt be their king, and that when Thou contendest in judgment against the upstarts of the earth Thou wilt muster an army of (these) Thine elect, in their thousands and tens of thousands, side by side with Thine holy beings and Thine angels, and that they shall prevail in battle and along with the heavenly elect (be triumphant).

O God, Thou, resplendent in Thy sovereign glory, and the congregation of Thy holy beings are indeed in our midst as a perpetual help. We have poured contempt upon kings, scorn and contumely upon mighty men. For the Lord (Adonai) is holy, and the King of Glory is with us, along with the holy beings. Warrior angels are in our muster, and He that is Mighty in War is in our throng.[30]

The question which is of special interest here is whether the holy beings (qodeshim) who dwell in heaven are the same as the angels, or distinct from them. The word is used in the Bible to refer both to holy men (Ps. XVI: 3; XXXIV: 10; Dan. VII: 18; 21; 22; 25; VIII: 24), and to angels (Job V: 1; XV: 15; Dan. VIII: 13). It seems to us that in this context the holy beings are a group apart, distinct from both men and angels. This seems to be required by the phrase, "side by side with Thine holy beings and Thine angels," which, of course, would make no sense at all if holy beings and angels were one and the same. (The "and with" which Dupont-Sommer proposes as a textual correction (w'm), is not acceptable to van der Ploeg;[31] however, it does seem plausible in itself). Furthermore, line one itself

---

30 The author cites the translation of Dupont-Sommer, which he approves with some reservations (*Règlement de la guerre des fils de lumière; traduction et notes,* dans *R.H.R.,* 1955, t. XCLVIII, pp. 162-163.) I have replaced this French translation with the English version of T. Gaster, (*The Scriptures of the Dead Sea Sect in English Translation,* London, 1957, p. 275). (Tr.)

31 Van der Ploeg (*Vetus Testamentum,* 1956, pp. 386 and 412) proposes to restore *sh m t h;* thus he is inclined to place the word "angels" in a new sentence parallel to the preceding one. However, this verb seems to be too long. T. GASTER, *The Dead Sea Scriptures in English Translation,* New York, 1956, p. 296, has the same text as Dupont-Sommer.

shows us three groups whose names are with God, "in His holy abode"; the holy beings, the armies of angels and the elect of the holy people. If this last group is distinct from the former two, then they must also be distinct from each other.

The most interesting passage in the *Rule of War* for our purpose is *Col.* 1, *line* 13, where there is a reference to three successes (*goraloth*) of the sons of the light against three successes of the army of Belial. Dupont-Sommer explains this as follows:— "The author wishes to say, no doubt, that on three occasions the sons of the light will win, and that on three others they will lose—as is likely to happen in a battle in which the sides are equal—but that on a seventh occasion God will step in to secure the victory of His own".[32] One hesitates to limit this interpretation by using the word "occasion," since the word so often used in the *Rule of War* otherwise always has in it the meaning of "part," or "side," at least in those passages in which it is certainly present (I: 1; 5; 11; IV: 2; XIII: 2; 4; 5; 9; 17; XV: 1; XVII: 6; 7; 16). In the *Rule of the Community,* or *Manual of Discipline,* the same word occurs with equal frequency and almost always in the sense of "part" a "lot" or "destiny" (I: 10; II: 2; 5; 11; 23; III: 24; IV: 24; 26; V: 3; VI: 16; 18; 22; IX: 7; XI: 7).

J. Carmignac suggests that the meaning of I: 13-14 of the *Rule of War* seems to be that the cause of the sons of the light will be defended by three groups, the angels, the glorified just, and an earthly army, against whom will be ranged the three groups of the sons of Belial. The final victory, however, will come at the intervention of a seventh party, which will be none other than the all-powerful hand of God.[33] If this is the meaning, then

---

32 *R.H.R.*, 1955, t. CXLVIII, p. 33, note 2.

33 In our view, I: 13-14 and XII: 1-8 seem to explain each other. Through the gracious permission of the author, we are happy to reproduce here the following passage from J. Carmignac's translation and commentary on the (Qumrân) Rule of War: "Who are these groups, which the author (of I: 13-14) considers so evident that he fails to name them? From the whole structure of the book we can gather quite surely that the first are the earthly warriors; the second group are the souls of the dead; the third are the angels, both good and evil; at the head of the entire assembly is God, who guarantees the final victory of Light over Darkness (line 14). The second and third groups are sometimes described as *'l w m* ("Heavenly beings") I: 10, 11; XIV: 16; XV: 14; XVII: 7 or as *ruhoth* ("spirits") X: 12 (?); XII: 9; XIII: 10. However, they are distinguished more clearly with regard to the Sons of Light, the souls of the dead are called *qdwshim*

the whole image is strikingly parallel to the one described in the Apocalypse, which is also a book of war, showing the struggle which the Christians must wage against the forces of evil, watched and aided by the angels and saints of heaven.

We do not propose to decide finally here whether or not these ideas which we have discussed are genuine elements of Qumran thought. However, there seems to be no doubt at all that such ideas occur within the New Testament itself. In the stirring eleventh chapter of the Epistle to the Hebrews, which Père Spicq has described [34] as one of the most eloquent and moving texts of the Bible and of all literature, the author describes faith as an indispensable condition for being allowed a share in the blessings promised by God. He renders his exhortation all the more vivid by recalling the great heroes of Israel: Abel; Henoch; Noe; Abraham and Sara; Isaac; Jacob; Joseph; Moses; Josue; Rahab; Gideon; Barac; Samson; Jephthe; Samuel; the prophets,—proposing their faith as something which Christians should seek to imitate.

Such listings of heroes of the faith should not surprise us. Later Judaism makes a regular practice of recalling the past and of praising the fathers in a didactic way (cf., e. gr., Sir. XLIV-L; Wis. X-XII; I Macc. II: 51-60).[35] The special thing about this passage in Hebrews is that in it the fathers are called *presbyteroi,* the same term used in the Apocalypse. What is more, they are clearly distinct from the Christians, for whom they are, as it were, models and spectators. At the same time their chief interest is the struggle waged by Christ's disciples, who fight the

("saints"), I: 16; X: 12; XII: 1; 4; 7; 8; XV: 14; XVIII: 2; (?); angels are also called *m l' ch i m* (L: 15; VII: 6; XII; XIII: 1; 4; 8). These groups dedicated to the triumph of good are presented (XII: 1; 4; 8) as clearly as possible. The same distinction occurs in the *Sayings of Moses* (IV: 1) and doubtless also in the *Formulary of Blessings* (IV: 26); for the Sons of Darkness, the author gives very little detail, but nevertheless he does make use of the terminology of angels (XIII: 11; 12), and of spirits (XIII: 2; 4; 12; XIV: 10; XV: 14).

34 *Épître aux Hébreux, II, Commentaire,* Paris, 1953, p. 334.

35 The author of Hebrews certainly was influenced by Philo, who narrates the lives of the patriarchs, showing in them the "living laws," for the purpose of leading his readers to practice the same virtues as the patriarchs practiced (*de Abrah. 4*). Cf. E. BREHIER, *Les idées philosophiques et réligieuses de Philon d'Alexandrie,* 3rd édit., Paris, 1950, p. 26; C. SPICQ, *L'Épître aux Hébreux,* I, *Introduction,* Paris, 1952, p. 77.

good fight before the eyes of these ancestors in the faith. These saints of the old covenant are "as it were the veterans who have won many battles, and who now encourage the young whom they see engaged in battles like their own".[36] Thus we read the admonition in XII: 1: "Therefore, let us also, having such a cloud of witnesses over us, put away every encumbrance and the sin entangling us, and run with patience to the fight set before us."

A little further on in the same Epistle, we find another text containing an idea similar to this figure of the Apocalypse. The author proposes to stimulate his audience to keep up the fight against sin; to do this he contrasts the awesome events which marked the promulgation of the old law at Sinai, with the infinitely more moving vision of the Christian Church, as both an earthly and a heavenly reality, so that its members already belong, in a certain way, to the other world of the after-life. Such an idea, as we can see, is clearly johannine. Yet it is but one of the many similarities which link the Epistle to the Hebrews to the writings attributed to the Apostle John.[37] The Epistle describes the new economy by an enumeration, of which we should observe the various members:

> For you have not approached a mountain that may be touched and a burning fire, and whirlwind and darkness and storm, and sound of trumpet and sound of words; which sound was such that those who heard entreated that the word should not be spoken to them. . . .
>
> But you have come
> 1) to Mount Sion, and to the city of the living God, the heavenly Jerusalem;
> 2) and to the company of many thousands of angels;
> 3) and to the Church of the firstborn, who are enrolled in the heavens;
> 4) and to God, the judge of all;
> 5) and to the spirits of the just made perfect;
> 6) and to Jesus, mediator of a new Covenant;

36 C. SPICQ, *Commentaire*, p. 384.

37 Cf. C. SPICQ, *L'Épître aux Hébreux, Introduction*, c. IV, pp. 109-138.

7) and to a sprinkling of blood which speaks better than Abel.

(Hebrews XII: 18-20; 22-24) [38]

Thus punctuated, the text suggests that the "Church of the firstborn" is a new group, distinct from the countless myriads of angels who already are a sort of cultic assembly in heaven (*panēgyrei*). It seems correct, following the most ancient versions, the fathers, and most modern exegetes, to attach *panēgyrei* to the preceding, regarding it as in opposition to *myriasin*. Thus the word *angelōn* can be a complement of either of these words. [39]

What are we to understand from the phrase, "Church of the first-born"? Along with most commentators (Calvin; Bengel; Reuss; Michl; Windisch; Bonsirven; Medebielle), we think these are not angels but men. As Windisch observes, [40] the writing of the names of the first-born in heaven would have no meaning if they were angels, since the heavenly books contain only the names of men predestined to eternal life (cf. Ex. XXXII: 32; Dan. XII: 1; Ps. LXIX: 29; Henoch XLVII: 3; CIV: 1; CVIII: 3; Phil. IV: 3; Apoc. III: 5; XIII: 8; XVII: 8; XXI: 27. [41]

We can note furthermore that, in the Old Testament, Israel is called the first-born of God (Ex. IV: 2; Jer. XXXI: 9), and that the audience to whom Hebrews is addressed are not members of this "Chuch of the first-born," because they are presented as going out to meet it. There is also merit in the observation of Calvin, Bengel and Hering, that the *prototokoi* are only the elect of the old Covenant, [42] who are joined by a certain number of Christians, "the spirits of the just who have come to per-

---

38 This text raises a number of problems, which we are not prepared to treat here: cf. the standard commentaries, especially on points of textual criticism and of translation. It seems credible that there are here two deliberate septets, by which the author contrasts the characteristics of the old economy with those of the new.

39 Although the punctuation of the passage is subject to considerable dispute, we follow that which most commentators accept (Médebielle, Lemonnyer, Bonsirven, Spicq, Moffatt, Michel, Héring...); Windisch and Osty attach *panēgyrei* to what follows. However, Windisch still considers the first-born to be men, not angels.

40 *Der Hebraerbrief*, Tübingen, 1931, p. 114.

41 Cf. SCHRENK, art. *biblion*, T.W.N.T. I, pp. 618-619.

42 Cf. J. HÉRING, *L'Épître aux Hébreux*, Neuchâtel-Paris, 1954, p. 119.

fection." Perhaps it was to distinguish the saints of the old
Covenant from those of the new that the author inserts the
name of God between them ("first-born" and "spirits of the
just") instead of before both, which would have been normal.
Still, Dr. Michl, who is not concerned with the first-born, is
inclined to see in the "spirits of the just" the men of the old
Covenant,[43] which seems to us to be rather improbable.

Be this last part what it may, we have in Hebrews XII an
image of the heavenly Jerusalem, altogether like the one described for us by the seer of the Apocalypse; each is composed
of God, of Jesus, the angels, the saints of the Old Testament and
finally of Christians. Is it not curious to note that the "thousands
and thousands" of angels of V: 11, who are round about the
throne, correspond to the "many thousands" of angels of Hebrews
XI: 10, in which the mention of the city built on a solid foundation (*ten tous themelious echousan polin*), with God as Archi-
tect and Builder, recalls directly the description of the foundation
of the eschatological Jerusalem in Apocalypse XXI: 14; 19?
These are unmistakeable signs of the close relationship which
links in a general way the heavenly sanctuary and liturgy of
the Apocalypse, to those of Hebrews.

We have considered it preferable to study the identity of
the elders in relation to their number of twenty-four, the meaning of which is not clear. Gunkel,[44] followed by Allo and
Bousset, see in the number a reference to the twenty-four stellar
divinities of the North and South of the Zodiac in the Babylonian
religion, or to the twenty-four *Yazatas* or lesser gods of the
Iranian cult. Reitzenstein, Hadorn, de Saussure[45] and others

---

43 Die 24 *Aeltesten,* p. 109.

44 *Schöpfung und Chaos in Urzeit und Endzeit,* Göttingen, 1921, p. 307.

45 Cf. REITZENSTEIN, *Poimandres,* Leipzig, 1904, 301, Anm. 2;
HADORN, *Die Offenbarung,* p. 71; L. DE SAUSSURE, *Le cadre astrono-
mique des visions de l'Apocalypse,* in *Actes du Congrès international
d'Histoire des Religions,* held in Paris, Oct. 1923, t. I, Paris, 1925, p. 488;
cf. the same author, *Journal asiatique,* 1924, *La Série septenaire, cosmolo-
gique et planetaire,* p. 353. Cf. VICTORINUS DE PETTAU (*Traité de
Fabrica Mundi,* 10; cf. *CSEL.,* vol. 49, J. HAUSSLEITER, Vindobonae,
1916, p. 9): *Constituti sunt itaque sine dubietate diei angeli duodecim,
noctis angeli duodecim, pro numero scilicet horarum. Hi sunt namque
XXIV testes dierum et noctium, qui sedent ante thronum Dei, coronas*

see in it an image related to astronomy, with the twenty-four elders being the twenty-four spirits charged with guarding the twenty-four hours of the day. Lohmeyer [46] cites a passage in Aristotle's Metaphysics (1093 B; cf. W. Christ, Leipzig, 1886, p. 314), and recalls the teaching of the Pythagoreans on the relationship of the twenty-four letters of the alphabet to the twenty-four tones of the flute, which number is used to describe also the fullness of heaven. (*arithmos isos te oulomeleia tou ouranou*).

We prefer to follow our method of seeking parallels in the Bible itself. Beyond a doubt, the number twenty-four is not mentioned nearly as often as are, for instance, seven or twelve, nor does it have as much importance as these numbers. This fact, however, should serve to draw all the more attention to the unusual care of I Chronicles, in which the number twenty-four has an unusual importance. There it refers to the organization of the liturgy which, according to the Chronicler, David set up for the chosen people. The prophet-king divided the priests into twenty-four classes (cf. Josephus, *Antiq. Jud.*, VII: 14: 7) also the singers (XXIV: 6-31) and the doorkeepers (XXVI: 17-19). The twenty-four classes of priests lived apart, headed by twenty-four chiefs or princes, who later were called "ancients" or "elders" (cf. *Mishna: Joma* I: 5; *Taanit* IV:2; *Sukka* V: 6-8).[47] If the *Rule of War* of Qumran (Col. II. line 2) speaks not of twenty-four but of twenty-six classes of priests, this is due no doubt to their sectarian calendar, which has fifty-two weeks.[48] The Chronicler is so intent on relating the number twenty-four to the work of David, that in I Chr. XXVII the soldiers subject to David are divided into twelve divisions, each having twenty-four thousand men.

It seems sufficient to hold to these general lines of com-

---

aureas in capitibus suis habentes, quos Apocalypsis Johannis apostoli et evangelistae seniores vocat, idcirco quia seniores sunt et aliis angelis et hominibus.

46 *Die Offenbarung*, p. 47.

47 Cf. E. SCHÜRER, *Geschichte des Jüdischen Volkes im Zeitalter Jesu Christi*, Leipzig, 1898, t. II, pp. 234-237.

48 Cf. D. BARTHÉLEMY, *Notes en marge des manuscrits de Qumrân*, in *R.B.*, 1952, pp. 199-202; A. JAUBERT, *Le calendrier des Jubilés et la secte de Qumrân*, Vetus Testamentum, 1953, pp. 250-264; A. DUPONT-SOMMER, *R.H.R.*, 1955, tome CXLVIII, p. 34, notes 1 and 4.

parison without seeking to determine whether the twenty-four elders correspond to the twenty-four classes of priests (Alcazar, Renan), or to the twenty-four classes of singers (Zahn). As a matter of fact, the twenty-four classes of priests and chanters are never described as being all together in the temple, whereas the twenty-four elders are grouped together around God's throne. We believe rather that the author of the Apocalypse, desiring to place in relief the close relationship of the Christian. Church to the elements which prefigure it in the Old Testament, and to show in the twenty-four the elite and the heavenly representatives of the chosen people, recalled the number twenty-four from Chronicles, in which it characterizes the organization, especially the cultic organization, of God's people. This interpretation seems to gather strength from the fact that, like the Levites and singers who are divided into twenty-four classes, the elders are pictured as playing on harps (V: 8, cf. I Chr. XXV: 1). The number twelve would have been less fitting, because for Christians it would immediately suggest the twelve apostles, the representatives *par excellence* of the Christian community (cf. Jerusalem with its twelve gates guarded by twelve angels, XXI: 12). The author, recalling the *Presbyterium* of the Churches in the description of the elders, wished to make of them a symbol of the people of the Old Testament. They are thus associated with the twelve apostles who also have their own thrones (Mt. XIX: 28 and Luke XXII: 30),[49] and with the martyrs and confessors of the faith, who later in the Apocalypse (XX: 1-4; cf. III: 21) are to have thrones for the entire duration of the symbolic millenium. Furthermore they are to preside over the Government of the world, and especially over the destinies of the Christian world.

The only serious objection which has been raised (and rather often) against the identification of the twenty-four elders with the glorified men, especially with the saints or "fathers" of the Old Testament is that it seems strange to see them present in heaven before the coming of Christ the Savior upon the scene, which does not occur until V: 6 ff. The objection, however, does not stand up in the face of the evidence. Michl offers a solution in the literary order, which is in itself quite satisfactory. Answering Allo's assertion that the logical order of the vision suffers if the men take their seats in heaven before

---

49 On this text cf. *Nouvelle Revue Théologique*, 1949, pp. 715-722.

the Lamb has opened it to them, Michl replies well that any reader of the Apocalypse is sure to have the impression that John speaks and writes from the point of view of eschatological hope, which was strong in his own time. True enough, the Lamb comes upon the scene only in V: 6, but his appearance coincides with the time of the Ascension; there is no reason why in Ch. IV the seer must be considered to be abstracting completely from the fact of Christ's Resurrection and glorification.

Still, we must admit that these elders are not newcomers to heaven; on the contrary, they appear to have been there for some time. We think we can explain this part sufficiently by appealing to the complexity of the eschatological expectations of later Judaism and of primitive Christianity.

According to Hebrews VI: 20, Christ entered first into the heavenly sanctuary, as precursor, at the time of the Ascension; further, in Heb. XI: 40, "God had something better in view for us, i. e. something better in view for the Christian than for the saints of the Old Testament so that they should not be perfected without us" (*hina mē chōris hēmōn teleiōthōsin*).

Exegetes disagree widely on the meaning of these texts, especially of this last one.[50] In any case we should also consider another tradition according to which the great personalities of the Old Testament, Abraham, Isaac, Jacob and others, are admitted after a time to the after life of intimate association with God, and seem to enjoy a status of privileged elders with regard to Christians, in belonging to the ultimate Kingdom. As we have seen, Jesus Himself often alludes to this tradition, especially in the parable of Lazarus and Dives, or when, in discussing the resurrection with the Saducees, as reported by all

---

50 Some commentators (St. Thomas, Cajetan, Médebielle, Spicq) understand *teleiōsis* in terms of that heavenly blessedness which Christians enjoy immediately at death, while the believers of the old covenant remain in Limbo. Others (Augustine, Chrysostom, Estius, Westcott) refer the word to the final consummation and to the resurrection of the dead, which the faithful of the Old Testament will enjoy only after their Christian brethren have joined them. Many authors (Erasmus, Bengel, Dom Calmet, Riggenbach, Moffatt, Strathmann) thinking, as did the others, of the "end" of history, understand the *teleiōsis* much more vaguely. They relate the "better lot" of Christians of the "better Covenant" of VII: 22 and VIII: 6; thus the former generations must wait for the Christians in order to enjoy with them the fulfillment of the promise. Cf. C. SPICQ, *Commentaire*, pp. 367-369.

three Synoptics (Mark XII: 18-27; Matthew XXII: 23-33; Luke XX: 27-40), He recalls the apparition of Horeb in which Jahweh reveals Himself to Moses as the God of Abraham, Isaac and Jacob. As has been said recently on this point, all of Jesus' line of argument is designed to show that Jahweh, in speaking to Moses, "cannot call Himself the God of persons who no longer exist, or have any intimacy with Him. If God speaks in this way to Moses, it means that at this moment, Abraham, Isaac and Jacob are living still, as His friends".[51]

We could never emphasize enough that, according to the Scripture, there is no heavenly beatitude without Jesus or without the victory which He has obtained over the forces of evil. It follows from this that there can be no vision of God in the other world apart from Him. But, as for the sanctification of souls, has His action not been anticipated, *at least to some degree?* We do not propose to solve this problem, but, if we hold too strictly to these rigid notions, then how will we ever be able to explain Jesus' promise to the good thief: *"Hodie mecum eris in paradiso"* (Luke XXIII: 43) before His heavenly exaltation? In the Ascension of Isaia (IX: 6-12) all the just who preceded Isaia enjoy beatitude already in his time, and are closely associated with the angels, which recalls the Epistle to the Hebrews, and also the *Rule of War* of Qumran. Still, they have neither thrones nor crowns, and the context (cf. IX: 18) seems to suggest that they will receive them only when Christ comes to enter heaven.[52]

---

51 Y. B. TREMEL, in *Lumière et Vie*, Cahier 24, *De L'immortalité de l'homme entre la mort et la resurrection d'après le Nouveau Testament*, pp. 744-745.

52 "And he took me up to the seventh heaven, and I saw there a wonderful brightness, and angels beyond counting. And I saw there all the just who lived since Adam; I saw the holy Abel there, together with all the just; and Henoch and all who were with him; they had taken off their robes of flesh, and I saw them dressed in their heavenly robes; they were like angels living in great glory. But they were not sitting on their thrones, and their crowns were not on their heads. And I asked the angel who was with me, 'How is it that they have been dressed in their robes, but are not sitting on their thrones or wearing their crowns?' And he told me, 'They have not yet received either their crowns or their thrones of glory, but they see, and they know which of them will have the Crowns and the thrones, when the Beloved comes down in the form in which you shall see him coming down." (Translated from the French version of E.

As for the canonical Scriptures, we must admit that they develop eschatological notions which are extremely complex. Besides the tradition which seems to delay entry into glory until the glorification with Christ Himself at the Parousia, together with the resurrection of the dead, there is another, supported by the examples of Henoch and Elias, which holds, or at least suggests that there is a life of friendship with God upon which death can have no effect. If in later Judaism the simple faithful could nourish such aspirations for their own future, then how could they have imagined that the great saints for whom they cherished such veneration should be definitely separated from God? There must be a way to reconcile these two notions, which seem at first glance to be very different, not to say contradictory, since the Epistle to the Hebrews itself, which affirms (VI: 20 and XI: 40) the fundamental subordination of the old Covenant to Jesus, seems to speak nevertheless (XII: 23) of the presence in heaven of an assemblage of the first-born, whom we consider to be the saints of the Old Covenant. Some have opposed this exegesis on the basis of XI: 40, seeing the first-born as angels; but such harmonization of texts seems to be bought only at the price of sacrificing the natural meaning of the words.

In drawing this study to a conclusion, we would like to present the great advantages which derive from this hypothesis of identifying the twenty-four elders of the Apocalypse with the Fathers of ancient Israel. Those who see them as angels introduce thereby a category of angels which occurs nowhere else, and which does not correspond naturally to the title, especially in the light of the traditional meaning always given to the term

---

TISSÉRANT, which the author cites. (Tr.) We have here the three characteristics of the elders of the Apocalypse: robes of glory (which certainly are not their glorified bodies, as Charles holds they are. Cf. E. Tisserant, p. 174 and note); thrones and crowns. However, only the robes have been given to them. In the Apocalypse, however, the elders already have all three of these objects. The difference seems to us to be due to the respective dates of composition of these two works. Although the Apocalypse is pre-dated by a fiction (as we think it is, although we are not prepared to explain here all the reasons for our position on this point), it is only by some few decades, so that the author places himself at the beginning of the Christian era, following the coming and exaltation of Christ, which have opened the last era; the author of the Ascension of Isaias, on the other hand, takes his readers back (fictitiously) to the time of the prophet.

(Antiquity recognized no distinction of degree among angels). Those who wish to consider them as glorified Christians are embarrassed to explain why they are called thus, and why they should be a class apart from the martyrs and from the assembled throng of the faithful, from whom they are clearly distinguished. What is more, it seems that neither of these explanations helps at all to explain the fundamental meaning of the Apocalypse.

The reference to the great saints of the Old Testament opens up a fuller and more satisfying explanation of the scene. Because of the pre-eminent positions held by the outstanding personages of the old Covenant in both Jewish and Christian traditions, it is quite normal that the author of the Apocalypse should see fit to mention this. On the contrary, the Apocalypse's picture of the Church as triumphant would be lacking an essential element if the saints of the Old Testament were to be left out.[53]

The idea that the Old Testament saints are present throughout the unfolding of history, and that they take a lively interest in the destiny of Christians, is nothing short of magnificent. One could hardly be more eloquent in expressing the internal unity governing the whole history of salvation and the essential link uniting both testaments. The fact that throughout the Apocalypse the choir of the elders is united to both the choirs of angels and the songs of the Christians, invests the visions of this inspired book with a breadth and a majesty which have no equal.

It seems to go without saying that this interpretation is fully in harmony with the context. It fits well, first of all, into the immediate context, for thus, given that the elders are the saints of Israel, we can see how in IV: 11 they sing the praise of God the Creator in "terms which are not specifically Christian",[54] and recall the object of faith suggested in Hebrews XI: 3, which follows immediately upon the mention that "the men of old had testimony borne to them" in XI: 2. We can understand also how in V: 5 one of the elders refers to Jesus as "the Lion of the Tribe of Juda, the root of David." The plainly objective manner in which the elders praise Christ the Savior in V: 9-10, which is difficult to understand of Christ's disciples, is much more

---

53 In the *monitum* which precedes the ordination of a priest, the *Pontificale Romanum,* cites as precursors and models both the ancients whom Moses selected to be his helpers, and the seventy-two disciples whom Christ selected to be helpers of His Apostles.

54 ALLO, *L'Apocalypse,* p. 73.

natural and acceptable on the lips of the saints of the Old Testament. Of course, they are also related to Christ, as are the Christians, but since it is rather by way of anticipation, with their lot being definitively settled, it is not too surprising to see that they express themselves in a way different from that of Christians who are still engaged in the struggle against evil.

However, the principal value of this exegesis is in the fact that thus the entire section, chapters IV-XI, given this interpretation, can be oriented in a new direction, which solves many difficulties. For our part, we are convinced that the system *of recapitulation*, such as that held by Allo, is difficult to justify, since the Apocalypse does not, in our view, presume to ignore the quesion of chronology, or to repeat the same facts in different ways. There must also be an explanation of the clear division of the prophetic part of the Apocalypse into two sections, followed by the surprising return in Chapter XII, which takes us back to the birth of Christ. There are a number of distinctly Jewish characteristics to be accounted for in Ch. IV-XI, as well as some allusions made there to the Jewish war.[55] Furthermore, can it be a mere accident that the elders come upon the scene in Chapters IV-VII? Chapter VII must be patient of a non-violent interpre-

---

55 Cf. S. GIET, in *Revue des Sciences Religieuses*: Janvier, *l'Apocalypse*, pp. 1-29; Octobre, 1952, *Les épisodes de la Guerre des Juifs et l'Apocalypse*, pp. 325-362. However, we are by no means fully in accord with all that is said in these articles, especially with regard to the identity of the seven kings or emperors of XVII: 10-11. The more normal explanation seems to be the one held by Holtzmann, Bousset, Swete, Charles, Gélin, Kiddle, Cerfaux-Cambier. According to this explanation one is led logically to suppose that the Apocalypse, *fictitiously predated*, is presented as written under Vespasian, before the catastrophe of 70, "the greatest crisis yet faced by the primitive Christian community" (J. SCHMITT, *La reflexion sur le salut des premiers Christians*, in *Compte rendu des XXXes Journées Universitaires*, Nancy, 1953, p. 70), and a crisis to which the Apocalypse rightly pays the greatest attention. The first four emperors are Augustus, Tiberius, Caligula, and Claudius; the fifth is Nero; the sixth, presently reigning, is Vespasian; the seventh, whose reign is to be brief, is Titus (79-81), *imperii felix brevitate*, (Ausone, quoted by Swete, p. 221); the eighth, a sort of *Nero redivivus* because of his cruelty, is Domitian (the real time of composition of the Apocalypse). It seems arbitrary to us to list Julius Caesar among the emperors. Allo counts the emperors not from Augustus, but from Nero; he also insists on including among them two of the three rulers of the Interregnum (Galba and Otho or Vitellius), the last two of whom, as he admits, had no authority in the provinces. This

tation; but such is surely not the case if we hold that, on the one hand, the 144,000 signed members of the flock, belonging to the twelve tribes of Israel, and exactly signed, and on the other hand the great number that no one can count, coming from every nation and from every tribe, are but one and the same Christian Church, seen under the double guise of its heavenly and earthly aspects. Such an interpretation is hardly acceptable. Contrary to the opinion of many commentators, we think that rather than two distinct visions of the one Christian community, there is rather one vision of two groups, not only different, but completely separate.[56]

We have no more to add for the present on this point, except to say that in studying the difficult problems of New Testament eschatology, it has not been sufficiently emphasized that in spite of Christian universalism, the greatest attention is always paid to Israel's privileges, and that the religious history of the world is considered successively in relation to the Jews and to the Gentiles. Jesus' point of view was certainly no different; He was conscious of His mission of preaching and bringing salvation to the world, yet He chose to limit His ministry to Israel. The same perspective is present in varying degrees throughout the New Testament, and should be borne in mind by exegetes who undertake to sound the depths of the message of the Apocalypse author.

Remarks: Our explanation of the twenty-four elders poses the problem of the liturgical nature of the Apocalypse, which is under considerable discussion today. Obviously, the Apocalypse is not a liturgical writing, but a prophecy and an account of the author's visions. Still, we can hardly fail to take notice of its strongly accented liturgical character. This is due ultimately to the essentially eschatological orientations of the Christian liturgy,

---

position, obviously, is too arbitrary. We are inclined to the same identification as that proposed by M. ALBERTZ, *Botschaft des Neuen Testaments*, I Band, II Halbband, Zürich, 1952, p. 352, R. SCHÜTZ, *Die Offenbarung des Johannes und Kaiser Domitian*, Göttingen, 1933, pp. 48-49.

56 Similar observations are in order regarding Chapter XI: the Jewish tone of the Chapter is so pronounced, that several critics have maintained that there must be a Jewish document here. In any case, the chapter cannot be interpreted without some explanation of the Jewish elements in it. In general, we dare say that so far no one has produced a completely satisfactory exegesis of Apocalypse VI-XI. We shall treat these points again in another work which we are preparing, to be entitled, *Le Problème eschatologique du Nouveau Testament*.

particularly of the Eucharistic rite, in which we "announce the death of the Lord until He come" (I Cor. XI: 26; cf. *Didache*, IX-X). As a memorial of Christ's Passion and Resurrection, the cult of the Eucharist assures the real presence of Christ in His Church, but only as an indication of the ultimate union of the Bride and Bridegroom in the celebration of their eternal marriage. It follows from this that John, wishing to translate into words the great eschatological aspiration of the Church, describes it under the guise of a heavenly liturgy, expressing himself by means of formulas and images borrowed from the liturgical practices of both the old and new Covenants, such as, for example, the figure of the twenty-four elders.

CHAPTER II

THE VALUE OF APOCALYPSE FOR THE SOLUTION OF THE ESCHATOLOGICAL PROBLEM [1]

John's Apocalypse is an almost exclusively eschatological work. Some say that it does no more than take up the great themes of primitive Christian eschatology, orchestrating and adapting them to the contemporary situation. Even if this were true, it would be of great interest because of its continual reference to the oracles of the Old Testament, of which it is a sort of Christian résumé.

We think, however, that the Apocalypse is much more than this, and that it makes an at least partly new and original contribution to the eschatological problem, the most serious of all the problems which faced the primitive Church. Of course, only a detailed study of the entire book could suffice to show this, but we shall have to content ourselves here with a careful examination of the tenth chapter, which offers in itself a precious insight into this question.

We shall offer first of all a cursory exegesis of this short chapter, seeking primarily to show the anomalies in it, which seem to be quite intentional. We shall then attempt to determine its eschatological significance and to assign its place in the over-all plan of the Apocalypse.

(1) Exegesis

As is evident, the tenth chapter of the Apocalypse, placed as it is between the sixth and seventh trumpets, serves as an interlude in the unfolding drama. But we can determine the real meaning of the passage only after a detailed examination of the text. For the sake of convenience we shall divide the chapter

---

1 First published in *Sacra Pagina, Bibliotheca Ephemeridum Theologicarum Lovaniensium*, vol. XII-XIII, 1959.

into three episodes: the seer's vision of the angel; the angel's cry and oath; and finally the investiture of the prophet.

FIRST EPISODE: *The Seer's Vision of the Angels* (vv. 1-2)

An angel comes down from heaven, clothed in a cloud with a rainbow over his head. He holds a little open scroll in his hand, his right foot on the sea and his left on the earth. Each of these details is full of meaning.

Already in v. 2 a "strong" angel invited the Lamb to open the sealed scroll. The other "strong angel" appearing here, corresponds to the first one. Also, the little open scroll which the latter angel holds is related to the scroll of the seven seals (v: I). This undeniable parallelism between the two chapters invites us to compare the two scenes.

The angel of Chapter X is more majestic than the one of Chapter V; he is clothed in a cloud, like Jahweh in his theophanies, or like the Son of Man of Dan. VII: 13 (the Masoretic Text has *"with* the clouds, as a son of man"). True enough, some of these traits recall so clearly those attributed to the Son of Man in Apocalypse I: 15-16, that some commentators have mistaken him for Christ.[2] His gigantic dimensions correspond to the magnitude of his ecumenical mission. The placing of his right foot on the sea and his left foot on the earth signify that he is to announce the content of the book to the entire world. The phrase "sea and land" is commonly used in the Old Testament to refer to the entire world (Ex. XX: 4; 11; Ps. LXIX: 35, etc.). The rainbow above the angel's head does not have the same function here as in IV: 3, where it is an allusion to Ez. I: 28, describing the splendor of a real theophany. Here it could be used to recall Genesis IX: 12-17, i.e., the covenant established after the flood, between God and all mankind. In any case, since the scene of V: 1-12, with the titles attributed to Christ (Lion of the tribe of Juda; Root of David, V: 5) and the role of the twenty-four elders (who, as we have explained, we think are the saints of the old Covenant [3]), appears to look to the chosen people (without

---

2 E. B. Allo says that this is true of Pettau, Primatius, Haymon of Alberstadt, and Albert the Great.

3 Cf. our study, *Les vingt-quatre viellards de L'Apocalypse*, in *Revue Biblique*, t. 65, 1958, p. 5-32; cf. also the preceding chapter of this present work.

forgetting the other men, e. gr., of V: 9), the present passage must be oriented directly toward the entire human race.

The little scroll seems less important than the scroll with the seals. It is called *biblaridion*, a *hapax legomenon* of the New Testament containing a double diminutive,[4] indicating that it contains materially less. Further, it is given, not to Christ, but to an angel, unlike the scroll with the seven seals—all of which factors tend to indicate that it is of a lesser dignity.

Naturally, exegetes differ in their explanations of these factors. E. B. Allo[5] considers the word scroll to be a fragment of the large scroll, as a parallel to the relationship of the Roman Empire to the Christian Church. J. Behm[6] also sees it in a restricted sense. H. Schlier[7] sees it as containing in the form of a prophetic vision that which has already taken place in the history of Israel. At first glance these different explanations seem to agree in so far as Chapter X clearly has a much more universalistic direction than Chapter V. The first paradox which the commentator must bear in mind is that *the smaller the scroll, the wider the perspective!*

As a working hypothesis, we propose that this paradox corresponds to the relationship which exists between the Old Testament and the Gospel. It is significant that, unlike the scroll with the seven seals, this new scroll is presented to the seer already opened. The large sealed scroll of Chapter V, which a detailed exegesis of the succeding Chapters shows to be linked to a definitely Jewish context, must have to do primarily with the destiny of the chosen people, without, however, losing sight of the entirety of mankind, who have a religious dependence on Israel. This scroll represents the Old Testament writings, especially the oracles of the prophets, enigmatic writings especially about Israel, to which only Christ can give the key (cf. Mark XIII: 14; Mt. XXIV: 15: Jesus interprets Daniel: "Let him who reads understand"; Luke XXIV: 27; 32; 45; Christ explains, or "opens" the Scriptures: 2 Cor. III: 14: in Christ alone is the veil drawn back from the Scriptures).

---

4 Here, as well as in vv. 8, 9, 10, the word varies in the MSS as *biblion, biblarion, biblidion, biblidarion.*

5 *L'Apocalypse*, Paris, 1933, p. 139.

6 *Die Offenbarung des Johannes*, Göttingen, 1935, p. 56.

7 *Vom Antichrist. Zum 13. Kapitel der Offenbarung Johannis*, München, 1936, p. 112.

The little scroll, on the contrary, with its essentially universalistic content, seems to represent Jesus' message, which is less extensive than that of the Old Testament but much clearer, and which St. Paul describes as preaching unveiled (cf. 2 Cor. III: 12 - IV: 6). If the angel who bears it is shown as clothed in a cloud like the Son of Man of Daniel and the Synoptics, a characteristic found nowhere else among the biblical angelophanies, then it seems that it should be designed to indicate that he is a servant of Jesus, the Son of Man *par excellence*.[8] We shall have occasion later on to return to the relationship between these two scrolls.

SECOND EPISODE: *The Seven Thunders and The Angel's Oath*
(vv. 3-7)

The angel from heaven cries out with a loud voice, which is echoed by seven thunders, but the seer is commanded from heaven not to reveal the things that the seven thunders spoke. Then the angel, calling upon the Creator as witness, proclaims solemnly that God's design for the entire world is about to reach its final fulfillment. Here even more clearly than in the preceding episode, the author has juxtaposed two apparently contradictory episodes. We should try to explain the relationship between them.

First of all, what is the object of the angel's cry and of the reply made by the seven thunders? There is reason to believe that they are both related to the destiny of the whole world. The angel sends out his cry while he holds his right foot on the sea and his left on the earth. Furthermore, the Bible describes thunder as "the voice of God"; the seven thunders of the Apocalypse correspond to Ps. XXIX, in which the voice of Jahweh, mentioned seven times, shakes all the compartments of the universe: the waters, the mountains, the forest, the desert—a most eloquent description of Jahweh's rule over the world.[9] There-

---

8 Cf. Ch. BRÜTSCH, *Clarté de l'Apocalypse*, Genève, 1955, p. 114.

9 A. ROBERT (*Initiation Biblique*, 1st ed., Paris - Tournai - Rome, 1939, p. 163), sees in Ps. XXIX rather than a mere description of the storm, an eschatological segment foretelling the final judgment of the wicked, and the era of blessedness which is to follow the judgment. This interpretation, which confirms, or at least favors, the allusion which the

fore, the words of the seven thunders, probably recalling Ps. XXIX,[10] refer to the judgment of the universe (in the Bible God's judgments are usually accompanied by thunder and lightning). We might recall here with H. B. Swete the passage in Isaias XII: 28, in which a voice from heaven, which the bystanders take for a clap of thunder, announces the judgment of the world.

Unlike the fourth Gospel the Apocalypse here sees the universal judgment as a thing still far off. The seer is told to "seal up the things that the seven thunders spoke" (X: 4). A glance at Dan. VIII: 26; XII: 4; 9; Apocalypse XXII: 10, (cf. also Is. VIII: 16) shows us that in the apocalyptic writings the things which are sealed, i.e., secret, are the messages communicated by God, which will be fulfilled only in the distant future. We read, for example, in Dan. VIII: 26: "Keep secret the message and seal the book until the end of time." Apocalypse XXII: 10 has just the opposite: "Do not seal up the words of prophecy with this book, for the time is at hand."

The sense of these two texts is so clear that it should be unnecessary to look any farther for the sense of our passage. The idea of the communication of heavenly messages which must not be revealed until a long time after they are read, and to be kept secret in the meanwhile, is a common feature of the Apocalyptic literature in general.[11] Commentators of this passage have often suggested some sort of divine revelation of a particularly unspeakable nature, such as those which St. Paul describes in 2 Cor. XII: 4. We would not wish to exclude this last explanation, which would serve to indicate *the former one,* given the fact that John, unlike Daniel, is commanded not to seal what has been written, but to seal and not to write. Still, Kiddle objects:

Apocalypse makes to Ps. XXIX, was omitted in the 3rd edition of the work, published in 1954 (*Guide to the Bible,* the English translation of *Initiation Biblique,* by Arbez-McGuire, is based on the 3rd French ed.) (tr.)

10 This recollection has been recognized especially by H. H. HOLTZMANN, *Evangelium, Briefe und Offenbarung des Johannes,* Freiburg i. B., 1891, pp. 298-299; W. BOUSSET, *Die Offenbarung des Johannes,* Göttingen, 1896, p. 362; A. LOISY, L'Apocalypse de Jean, Paris, 1923, pp. 196-197; J. BEHM, *Die Offenbarung,* p. 56. Cf. also H. B. SWETE, E. B. ALLO, *ad loc.*

11 Cf. ROBERT - Tricot, *Guide to the Bible* (Translation of *Initiation Biblique,* 3rd ed., 1954) 2nd ed., Paris, Tournai - Rome - N. Y., 1959 pp. 509-512.

To imagine, as some have done, that the Seer was concealing things too sacred for utterance (like St. Paul's secrets, 2 Cor. XI: 4), is to ignore the extent of the revelation already given; we have looked through "a door standing open in heaven," we have seen the Throne and the Lamb, we have witnessed the opening of the scroll or destiny itself.[12]

The conclusion which seems to us to flow from all this, is that the scroll with the seven seals opened by the Lamb is not meant to include, strictly speaking, all the religious history of the world, especially that which the seven thunders have said, and which is to be kept sealed. The author wished rather to express primarily the idea of new events still in the future, as Boismard has noted well.[13]

In contrast to this suggestion that the end is not yet near, the angel's oath, spoken in the name of the Creator of the three parts of the earth, (land, sea, sky), proclaims rather that there is to be no more delay. The Greek formula (*chronos ouketi estai*) should be understood, not, as some have seen it,[14] with the elimination of time and its replacement with eternity (in which case *chronos* should be modified by the article), but of the elimination of all delay (the classical meaning of the word), and consequently of any intermediate stages in the fulfillment of God's plan. This sense results clearly from the parallelism of this scene with Dan. XII: 7, in which an angel swears that a certain period of time is to elapse between the present time and the ultimate end.[15]

We feel compelled to conclude from this passage of the Apocalypse that the history of salvation is in its last stage, the one immediately preceding the sound of the trumpet, which will indicate, as the author says, that "the mystery of God is accomp-

---

12 *The Revelation of St. John*, London, 1946, p. 170.

13 Cf. *L'Apocalypse ou Les Apocalypses de Jean*, in *Rev. Bibl.*, t. LVI, 1949, p. 511; cf. also *Bible de Jérusalem*, *L'Apocalypse*, Paris, 1950, p. 52, note b.

14 ALLO lists as favoring this exegesis St. Venerable Bede among the older writers, and F. Spitta and W. Weiss among the moderns.

15 In favor of this exegesis are H. B. SWETE, *The Apocalypse of St. John*, London, 1909, p. 129; R. H. CHARLES, *The Revelation of St. John*, Edinburgh, 1920, vol. I, p. 263; E. B. ALLO, etc.

lished." The word *mystērion* occurs four times in the Apocalypse (I: 20; X: 7; XVII: 5; 7). For St. Paul the mystery (of God or of Christ) consists particularly in the inclusion of the Gentiles in the Church (Rom. XVI: 25-26; Col. I: 26-27; II: 2; IV: 3; I Cor. II: 1; Eph. I: 9-10; III: 3; VI: 9). In Mark IV: 11, the mystery is related to the kingdom ("the mystery of the kingdom of God"). The sense does not seem to be much different here, although it is more clearly eschatological (cf. below). The term undoubtedly refers to God's eschatological plan for all of humanity —*Das Walten Gottes in der gesamten Menschheitsgeschichte*, as E. Lohmeyer [16] calls it. Masson says:

> In the apocalypse (cf. Dan. II: 28; 29; 47), mysteries are clearly of an eschatological character. They are the events of the end of time, already laid down in God's plan and kept secret until the moment of their accomplishment, except in so far as God chooses to make them known beforehand, by revealing them to his servants, the apocalyptic writers.[17]

Thus we have in Apocalypse X: 3-7 two little scenes: the former (vv. 3-4) indicating that the universal judgment is still far off; the second, (vv. 5-7) that the end is near nevertheless.

We see the purpose of this deliberate antithesis, from a comparison of our text with Dan. XII: 4-9, which is undoubtedly its chief source.[18] Daniel is commanded to seal up the revelations which he has received: a "man clothed in linen" (an angel) raises his right hand to heaven, swearing by "him who lives

---

16 *Die Offenbarung des Johannes*, Tübingen, 1953, p. 86. Of course we cannot exclude the "mystery of iniquity," of which St. Paul speaks in 2 Th. II: 6-8. However, the Apocalypse author does not seem to have it particularly in mind here.

17 Ch. MASSON, *L'Épître de saint Paul aux Colossiens*, Neuchatel-Paris, 1950, p. 112, note 3.

18 It is important to point out here that the reference of Apocalypse to this precise passage of Daniel is quite certain, especially as regards vv. 5-6 (the oath and the right hand raised to heaven). The Phraseology, however, is not taken either from the LXX or from Theodotion, but, is a rather free adaption of the Hebrew text of Daniel, as Charles shows, adding, "I do not know of the combination 'he lifted up his hand and swore' occurring elsewhere in the canonical literature save in these two passages"; vol. 1, p. 263. The phrase "*ōmosen en tō zōnti eis tous aiōnas*"

forever" that the accomplishment will take place only after a certain delay, "a year, two years, a half-year." "Go, Daniel;— because the words are to be kept secret and sealed until the end of time." The Apocalypse scene is identical; John also seals which he has heard, and an angel raises his right hand to heaven, swearing by the Creator that there shall be delay no longer. The re-working of the text of Daniel is patent. The author, in doing this, does not contradict himself, but wishes rather to express a paradox, which as we shall see later, is of the greatest importance.

THIRD EPISODE: *The Prophet's Investiture* (vv. 8-10)

A voice from heaven, the same as the one which had forbidden John to write down the things said by the seven thunders, now directs him to take the little scroll and eat it, a symbolic expression of a command to transmit the contents once he has managed to take it into himself. This is therefore a clearly evident case of prophetic investiture, obviously imitative of Ez. III: 1-3. Ezechiel had spoken only of the sweetness of the honey (III: 3) whereas here there is mention of both bitterness and sweetness. Many commentators explain this by saying that the Gospel is a blending of both the sweetness of grace and the bitterness of judgment. It may refer also to the sufferings which are to befall the preachers of the Gospel, such as was the lot of the prophets (cf. Jer. XV: 16; 18, which mentions both the joy and the pain of the prophetic ministry).

The prophet's investiture occurs normally at the beginning of his career or at the beginning of the book which contains his utterances (cf. for example, the opening passages of Jeremia and Ezechiel). In the Apocalypse an opening vision of the Son of Man (I: 9-20), which is a recollection of Ezechiel's opening vision (compare Apoc. I: 13 and Ez. I: 26; Apoc. I: 15 and Ez. I: 24), commands John to "Write, therefore, the things that thou hast seen, and the things that are, and the things that are to come hereafter" (v: 19). This refers to the letters to the seven Churches (chapters II-III) and to the visions of the things that

---

of Apocalypse X: 6 is similar to the *"ōmosen en tō zōnti ton aiōna"* of Theodotion. Cf. R. H. Charles, ibid., P. LXXX. The phrase *"ethēken ton poda ... gēs,"* could have been influenced by Dan. XII: 5. Cf. R. H. CHARLES, ibid., p. 260.

are to come (chapters IV-XXII). Furthermore, in Chapter IV, a new vision, related organically to the vision of Chapter I,[19] serves as a special introduction to the whole prophetic part of the book. This vision is also clearly inspired by the imagery of Ez. I and X.

The investiture conferred then on John in Chapter X has some factors which can surprise the commentator, because this episode of the swallowing of the little scroll marks the beginning of a whole new series of visions, and hence of earthly happenings. This seems to contradict vv. 5-7, which announce the approaching consummation of the Kingdom of God. There is no parallel to this phenomenon in all the prophetic literature.

The significance of this new paradox seems to be indicated in the words which the heavenly voice addresses to the seer while he eats the book: "Thou must prophesy again to many nations and peoples, and tongues and kings" (v. 11). This command can be carried out in either of two ways; either John is to continue doing what he has done up until now, or else he is to undertake a prophetic ministry different from what he has done in the past.

A detailed exegesis of the preceding chapters and a comparison of these visions with those beginning in chapter XII. will show that John's new mission is to be different from his former work. The predictions made and contained in the sealed scroll were directed not to "many nations and peoples and tongues and kings," but to the chosen people, whose tribes are enumerated clearly in Chapter VII. The new prophecies regarding the Gentile world will begin not in Chapter XI, which still deals with Jerusalem, and is part of the seven trumpets, but in Chapter XII, as has been seen by E. B. Allo, H. B. Swete, and many others.[20] Beginning with Chapter XII, there is a new start, with emphasis on the "many nations and peoples and tongues and kings" (cf. XII: 5; XIII: 7; XIV: 6; 8; XV: 4; XVII: 15). Whereas the first prophetic part of the Apocalypse opened with a vision of the "Lion of the tribe of Juda, the root of David" (V: 5), the second prophetic part (XII-XIII) opens with the birth of a

19 Cf. E. B. ALLO, L'Apocalypse, p. 67.

20 Cf., e. gr., M. E. BOISMARD, L'Apocalypse ou "les apocalypses" de Saint Jean, in Revue Biblique, t. LVI, 1949, p. 511: "Most agree that v. II prepares for the visions of ch. XII ff.; cf. also CALMES, Épîtres catholiques, Apocalypse, Paris, 1907, p. 166.

messianic child who "is to rule all nations with a rod of iron" (XII: 5). This reminds us of the division of the prophetic books into oracles against the chosen people and against the nations, except that here the message to the nations is regarded as a new and decisive stage in the history of salvation, preceded by a new prophetic investiture. A. Gelin thinks (correctly, we might add) that the kings envisioned in X: II are related to the kings of chapter XVII (vv. 9; 10; 12).[21]

It may be worthwhile to glance briefly at the Old Testament sources used in X: II. Certainly, the eating of the book recalls Ezechiel. However, up to now, the seer has been inspired all along by the utterances of the son of Buzi, in order to draw out their meaning (as is also the case at the beginning of Chapter XI, in the scene of the measuring of the Temple), whereas the universal mission which he now receives is altogether the opposite of the mission which was confided to Ezechiel, who was sent "to a people with difficult speech and barbarous language" (Ez. III: 5), but exclusively to the house of Israel (III: 4-5). The words addressed to John in this scene recall those which Jeremia heard at the moment of his call: "A prophet to the nations I appointed you.... See.... This day I set you over nations and over kingdoms, to root up and to tear down, to destroy and to demolish, to build and to plant" (I: 5, 10).[22]

We might say in brief that the new prophetic mission confided to John in Chapter X is an echo of the investiture of Jeremia as "prophet to the nations." By contrast, the preparatory vision at the opening of the book of the seven seals (Chapters IV-V) recalls very closely the inaugural vision of Ezechiel, Jewish prophet *par excellence*. This confirms what we said before, that the Apocalypse is concerned first with the chosen people (Chapters IV-XI) and then with the nations (Chapters XII ff.).

(2) *Eschatological Significance of the Passage*:
Its Place in the General Plan of the Apocalypse

Not all commentators have noticed the apparent anomalies and incoherences which characterize the text and the context of

---

21 Cf. A. GELIN, L'Apocalypse, in *La Sainte Bible* de Pirot, t. XII, Paris, 1928, pp. 624-625.

22 Cf. L. CERFAUX - J. CAMBIER, *L'Apocalypse de saint Jean lue aux chrétiens*, Paris, 1957, p. 78, in h. 1.; cf. also H. B. SWETE, in H. 1.

Apocalypse X. M. E. Boismard,[23] however, has uncovered them with great grace, although he has arrived at the conclusion that the passage is composite, a hypothesis which we consider unwarranted. He sees here one more proof for his view that there were originally two independent apocalypses, which eventually were joined together to form one continuous work. Following this line of thought, he separates one set of verses from another as follows: vv. I: 2b; 5-7 belong to text A, while vv. 2a; 3-4; 8-11 are parts of text B.

We prefer to see here not a contradiction, but an eschatological concept which is at once complete and powerful, and hence difficult to perceive, but nonetheless important to understand. The end is near; the Lion of Juda, the scion of David, is about to come into the midst of his chosen people; hence, all the divine judgments which are to be the immediate consequence of this coming, especially the punishment of the unbelieving Jews (described, we think, by the septets of seals and trumpets), have brought all of humanity close to the final stage of its evolution. The "mystery of God" which is His plan for the world, announced by His servants the prophets (of both testaments),[24] is on the point of reaching its complete fulfillment. The Christian dispensation, which has replaced Judaism, is the final dispensation; after this there is to be only the seventh and last trumpet. This is the forceful and solemn message of X: 5-7.

---

23 *L'Apocalypse ou les Apocalypses,* in *Rev. Bibl.,* t. LVI, 1949, pp. 511-512.

24 Many exegetes, such as R. H. CHARLES (vol. 1, ad. loc., p. 266) and W. BOUSSET (ad loc., p. 366) see here only the prophets of the new covenant, who are the Apocalypse seer's contemporaries. However, H. B. SWETE (p. 131) rightly refuses to accept the distinction between Jewish prophets and Christian prophets. Also E. Lohmeyer remarks not only that the phrase "the servants of God, the prophets," occurs in the Old Testament (2 kgs. XVII: 13; 23; XXI: 10; Jer. VII: 25; XXV: 4), but also that our verse is a recollection of Amos III: 7. Lohmeyer adds that the seer of the Apocalypse considers himself the last in a long series of prophets, (Die Offenbarung Des Johannes, p. 86). In XI: 8, the prophets are those of both covenants, but primarily those of the Old Testament (cf. *New Testament Studies,* vol. IV, 1958 p. 197). While in Eph. III: 5 and IV: 11 the prophets whom St. Paul mentions are certainly Christian prophets, there is less agreement on II: 20, "you are built on the foundation of the Apostles and prophets." Most exegetes think this refers

The appearance of Christ upon the stage of history marks a major step forward in the history of salvation. The only great event still to come will be the seventh angel's sounding the trumpet, the consummation of the mystery of God by the resurrection of the dead and the judgment of the nations (XI: 15-19).

In this sense, then, we have come almost to the end of world history. The author of the Apocalypse, quite conscious that he is following Daniel XII: 7-9, introduces an element of counterbalance to it, replacing the delay which is to occur before the end ("a year, two years, a half year") with the absence of all delay. This is the basic difference between the two dispensations with regard to time. We live in a time which is no longer a period of waiting pure and simple; the end is about to come. Still, it is to be a time in coming. This is the message not only of the command given to John to seal up the words of the seven thunders, but also of the scene of the eating of the book, which necessarily implies a new series of divine decrees to be accomplished, as were those of the sealed scroll.

Here we must return to the second scroll which John mentions, to seek its meaning. It is called small because basically it does no more than develop one of the elements of the scroll with the seven seals, and hence it is much more limited than the latter one. In God's plan the vocation of the Jews was directed ultimately toward the vocation of the Gentiles, as towards the establishment of a universal religion, which already contained the Gentiles germinally (cf. Gen. XII: 3 ff., in which the destiny of Israel is always linked to that of other nations). Likewise, the conclusion of the "time of the Jews" which, (we think) is the object of the scroll with seven seals, *following the synoptic apocalypse*,[25] includes germinally the "time of the nations," which is the object of the little scroll, as seems to follow from X: II (we shall explain later why it is correct to use Lucan terminology here). We might recall here Rom. XI: 11; 15; in which the mis-

---

to the prophets of the primitive Church, although some see it as an allusion to those of the Old Testament (F. Prat, K. L. SCHMIDT, *R.H.P.R.*, 1937, p. 318, note 5; RENGSTORF, *T.W.N.T.* I, p. 442 ff.) We are inclined, here as well as in the Apocalypse, not to separate the two groups, and even to admit that St. Paul's thought is here primarily on the prophets of the Old Testament.

25 R. H. CHARLES explains well the obvious parallelism between the two texts.

take of the Jews has brought salvation to the world; their rejection thus brings about the reconciliation of the world.

According to X: 7, the contents of the little scroll are to be accomplished before the sound of the seventh trumpet and before the consummation of the "mystery of God." Furthermore, Chapter XII shows Christ, especially Christ glorified (cf. the powerful image of XII: 5) and the decisive battle raging between the kingdom of God and Satan, begun by the coming of Christ to the world.

The verb *evangelizo* of X: 7 is characteristic. The only other occurrence of it in the Apocalypse is in XIV: 6, in which the reference is to an "everlasting gospel," which E. B. Allo thinks is "the Gospel itself, called eternal because it never changes" [26] We are quite sure that these two scenes correspond to each other. It is difficult to understand the beginning of XIV: 6: "And I saw another angel," because this angel is the first of a series. This could be explained better if this "other angel, having an everlasting gospel" were to be considered identical with the "other angel" who carries the open scroll in X: 1-2. It would follow then with even more probability that the little open scroll contains the good news (*evangelion*) of the mystery of God (X: 7), which is the same as the "everlasting gospel" to be announced to "those who dwell upon the earth, and to every nation and tribe and tongue and people" (XIV: 6).

We should speak here of another characteristic, which we mentioned above. The two "strong angels" which we saw carrying the scrolls in V: 2 and X: 1 are, as we have said, parallel. Now, whereas the angel who presides at the opening of the sealed scroll is merely a "strong angel," the one who carries the little scroll is "clothed in a cloud, and the rainbow was over his head, and his face was like the sun, and his feet like pillars of fire." (X: 1). This distinction means that the smaller of the two scrolls contains something more lofty than the larger, sealed one, even though the smaller may be already contained virtually in the larger, with a much wider field of vision. We see thus the weakness of Loisy's statement that, "Our Church, with its little scroll, is as it were a double of the vision of the scroll with the seven seals, a sort of preliminary to it".[27]

In summary, then, the basic purpose of Apocalypse X is, we

---

26 *L'Apocalypse,* p. 238.
27 *L'Apocalypse,* p. 203.

think, to introduce the period of the preaching of the gospel, and to emphasize particularly the paradox which is to characterize it, namely that, although the end is near, still it must be preceded by an indeterminate period of waiting. Such a paradox thus shows that there is much more involved than the mere question of the date, with regard to the nearness of the end which early Christianity mentions so frequently.

In presenting this doctrine, the author of the Apocalypse is not really introducing any new doctrine, strictly speaking; rather, he is throwing a clear light on the most obscure part of the New Testament message. It seems correct to conclude, as does John II: 18, "Dear children, it is the last hour." Does it seem likely that John, writing toward the end of the first century is really concerned with trying to show the *temporal* nearness of the Parousia, especially with the use of so strong an expression as "the last hour"? Or does he really know anything about the date of this last coming? Rather, the coming of the Savior, whenever it is to be, should be considered as near. We would say nowadays that it is the eleventh hour; the decisive and final period of the world's history has begun.

It is not too difficult to determine the historical situation which led John to formulate this marvelous doctrine. In XVII: 10-11, seven emperors are mentioned: the most normal way to identify them seems to be to begin with Augustus, discounting those of the interregnum between Nero and Domitian, whose authority was never formally recognized by the provinces. The fifth emperor is thus Nero; the sixth, who is described as the one presently in power, is thus Vespasian. The seventh, who is to remain only a short time (V: II), is Titus (79-81 A.D.); the eighth, a sort of *Nero Redivivus* because of his cruelty, must be Domitian. Supposing that the Apocalypse was almost certainly composed under Domitian (Irenaeus, Adv. Haer. V: 30: 9, says, "toward the end of Domitian's reign"; cf. Eusebius, *Hist. Eccl.* III: 18: 3), we are led logically to suppose that the attribution of its writings to the time of Vespasian is a mere fiction; this hypothesis seems to be corroborated by the precedent of the Book of Daniel and by the habitual practice of the Apocalyptic writers.[28]

---

28 We have studied this problem before in the *Revue Biblique* article on the twenty-four elders mentioned earlier, and also in *Essai d'interpré-*

Why should this fiction obtain also for John's Apocalypse? There is no indication of any plan to deceive, or to lead the reader to take these oracles as prophecies *ex eventu*. It seems simply that John wishes to return fictitiously to the era of Vespasian, before both the terrible persecution begun under Domitian, and the destruction of Jerusalem and of the temple, thereby placing himself in a position to evaluate the theological significance of these events. We think that this explanation clarifies sufficiently the development of the visions, the mention of the two scrolls, and the place of the tenth chapter in relation to the general structure of the Apocalypse.

The first prophetic section of the Apocalypse (Chapters IV-XI), with the two septets of the seals and the trumpets, is basically, we think, an explicit reference to the elements contained in the Apocalypse of the Synoptics, particularly under the form in which we read it in St. Luke's Gospel. The theological explanation is based on historical events; the Jewish war and the destruction of Jerusalem are past happenings at the time of the author's writing, and they are of tremendous importance because they mark the definitive independence of the Christian religion from that of Israel, thereby preparing the way for the advance of the Church among the pagans of the Gentile world.

The Christian community might have thought that, in predicting the destruction of the Jerusalem temple, Jesus had proclaimed the imminence of the end of the world and of His own Parousia. However, the author of the Apocalypse, enlightened both by the grace of the Holy Spirit and by the example of the life of the Church, understood even better than the Old Testament authors, that he should guard against this mistake. Thus, for instance, when Jesus proclaims that the coming of the Son of Man is near, He is not fixing a date as much as He is announcing a truth of faith. Christ has come, and by His Resurrection He has brought to human history the new epoch of the glorious Resurrection of the dead; for this reason alone He is near, even though the Parousia itself may be afar off.

The destruction of Jerusalem and of its temple marked not the end of *the* world, but the end of *a* world. It indicated the final separation of Judaism from Christianity, of the synagogue

tation du Chapitre XI de l'Apocalypse, in *New Testament Studies*, vol. IV, 1958, pp. 183-200. Cf. also the following chapter.

from the Church (cf. the beginning of Ch. XI), which thereby opens up principally to the Gentiles.

As far as we can see, this is the reason for the two investitures of the prophet, the two apocalyptic scrolls, and especially for the two clearly distinct sections of the prophetic part of the Apocalypse. The first section (IV-XI) treats of the transition from the people of God of the old Covenant to the people of God of the new Covenant; the second (XII-XXII) concerns the destiny of the Church, especially with regard to its relationship with hostile political forces, which represent the Roman empire. Chapter X, which the author ably inserts just before the end of the septet of the trumpets, is a preparation for this second part, which begins with the calling of the glorious risen Christ, absolute king of nations, which He shall rule with a rod of iron, as the psalmist predicts (Ps. II: 9).

Conclusion

J. Levie makes the following observation on J. Bonsirven's interpretation of the Apocalypse: "the great problem facing the interpreter of the Apocalypse is to unite as rigorous as possible an *historical exegesis* ... with a *spiritual interpretation* of the prophecy, making it useful and instructive for a Christian of the present day. I dare say that so far the perfect accomplishment of this task is yet to come".[29] We agree. Surely we have not said enough to show completely how this historic-theological method is the only one which can open the secrets of the Apocalypse. But we dare to hope that this excursus may at least indicate the direction which further study should take.

Basically, the idea of salvation history which is in the mind of the Apocalypse authors is related to that of St. Luke, as it is presented by H. Conzelmann.[30] We do not, of course, agree completely with Conzelmann's views (we have, for example, serious objections against his hypothesis that Christ's public ministry up to the Passion was free from temptations, being, as it were, a sort of anticipation of heaven). However, we do agree with him that Luke has distinguished better than Matthew or Mark the various stages of salvation history (time of Israel, time of Christ, and

---

29 Nouvelle Revue Théologique, t. LXXX, 1958, p. 60.

30 *Die Mitte der Zeit. Studien zur Theologie des Lukas,* Tübingen, 1957.

time of the Church). The author of the Apocalypse, who is not writing a gospel, does not feel compelled to emphasize the time of Christ; still he is most careful to distinguish the time of Israel from the time of the Church, placing a divine judgment at the end of each of them. We could add to these similarities the many other interesting affinities existing between the texts of the Lucan and Johannine traditions.

CHAPTER III

INTERPRETATION OF CHAPTER XI OF THE APOCALYPSE[1]

The strictly prophetic section of John's Apocalypse (Chapters IV-XXII) is neatly divided into two parts. The second of these (Chapters XII-XXII) arises from a concrete historical situation which is not too difficult to reconstruct. It takes as its point of departure the rabid persecution unleashed by the imperial Roman forces against the members of the Christian Church.

But what is the historical background of Chapters IV-XI; what is their purpose? The majority of commentators are disappointing on this aspect, because they fail to apply to these chapters the same method of exegesis which they use for Chapters XII ff., thus remaining limited to a number of vague generalities. It is true, of course, that some of them, like Renan, try to find in the septets of the seals and of the trumpets some reference to definite contemporary events. However, we are of the opinion that John's Apocalypse, which is intended to be, as is Daniel, a religious interpretation of history, cannot be explained by these historical references alone.[2]

We hope to propose here a rather novel exegesis of Chapter XI of the Apocalypse, corresponding to the different needs which we have mentioned and which will avoid the shortcomings which we have noted in other interpretations. We shall explain in the conclusion how, in our opinion, the preceding chapters (IV-X) might contribute to our study in the same kind of historic-theological perspective.

1 First published in *New Testament Studies* vol. IV, 1957-1958.

2 Bibliography: E. B. ALLO, L'Apocalypse (Paris, 1933); G. BALDENSPERGER, L'Apocalypse (Paris, 1938); J. BEHM, *Die Offenbarung des Johannes* (Göttingen, 1949); M. E. BOISMARD, *L'Apocalypse* (Paris, 1950); J. BONSIRVEN, *L'Apocalypse de saint Jean* (Paris, 1951; W. BOUSSET, *Die Offenbarung des Johannes* (Göttingen, 1896); CERFAUX-CAMBIER, *L'Apocalypse de saint Jean lue aux chrétiens* (Paris, 1955); R. H. CHARLES, *A critical and exegetical Commentary on the Revelation of St. John* (Edinburgh, 1920); A. GELIN, *L'Apocalypse* (Paris, 1938);

The eleventh chapter of the Apocalypse is one of the most discussed parts of the book, especially because of its well-known obscurity. The most promising kind of exegesis will, naturally, be the one which respects all the elements of the text, without proposing to discard any of them. Now, there are two fundamental elements here, both of them quite evident and also quite contradictory, which must be harmonized if we are to come to understand the author's real thought.

The first of these facts is that this is definitely a Christian text (cf. esp. vv. 8, 15). Secondly, it contains a good number of Jewish characteristics. In fact, the Jewish tone of the text is so pronounced, that a number of critics have said it is a separate document, added later to the body of the Apocalypse text.[3]

Naturally, it would not be correct to exclude this hypothesis of a Jewish origin *a priori*. Still, we agree with Zahn, Swete, Allo, and others, that it has not been sufficiently demonstrated to compel assent. Besides, even if it would be true, then the document has certainly been very largely recast, because, as our study will seek to show, the significance of the whole passage is profoundly Christian. In particular, the partial preservation of Jerusalem, which Jesus had said would be totally destroyed, must be interpreted not in a Jewish sense, as some have done, but in a Christian way, as is required by the symbolic nature of its

---

W. HADORN, *Die Offenbarung des Johannes* (Leipzig, 1928); M. KIDDLE, *The Revelation of St. John* (London, 1940); H. J. HOLTZMANN, *Evangelium, Briefe und Offenbarung Johannes* (Freiburg i. B., 1891); E. LOHMEYER, *Die Offenbarung des Johannes* (Tübingen, 1953), A. LOISY, *L'Apocalypse de saint Jean* (Paris, 1923); I. ROHR, *Der Hebraerbrief und die Geheime Offenbarung des hl. Johannes* (Bonn, 1932); H. B. SWETE, *The Apocalypse of St. John* (London, 1907); A. WIKENHAUSER, *Offenbarung des Johannes* (Regensburg, 1949); Th. ZAHN, *Die Offenbarung des Johannes* (Leipzig, 1924-6).

3 Favorable to this hypothesis are VISCHER (*Die Offenbarung Johannes*, 1886), SABATIER (*Revue de Théologie et de Philosophie,* 1887), SPITTA (*Offenbarung des Johannes,* 1889), WELLHAUSEN (*Skizzen und Vorarbeiten,* VI, 221-3), J. WEISS (*Die Offenbarung des Johannes,* 1904), as well as Bousset and Charles. Several of these critics (Bousset, J. Weiss, Wellhausen, Charles) have seen what others missed, i.e., that the historical background of this section, (at least the first verses of it) could be nothing else than the destruction of Jerusalem and of the Temple in 70. However, we question whether this is sufficient reason for postulating a pre-existing Jewish document.

language. Still, there are, on the other hand, too many authors who start out from this premise but fail to account sufficiently for the presence of specifically Jewish or Palestinian elements in the text, and thus never come to see in the passage any more than a vague and generally undefined meaning.

This said, we can proceed to examine the details of the text. There are three scenes to be interpreted: the measuring of the temple (vv. 1-2), the two witnesses (vv. 3-13); the last woe and the seventh trumpet (vv. 14-19).

(1) *The Measuring of the Temple* (vv. 1-2)

John receives a reed like to a rod with which to measure the Temple of God, and the altar, and those who worship therein. But he is told explicitly to reject the court outside the temple, for it has been given to the nations, who are to trample the holy city underfoot for forty-two months.

Most authors recognize that the measuring of the temple refers to a heavenly temple of Jerusalem, and that the symbolism of the measuring signifies the continuation of the curse, as in 2 Sam. VIII: 2b; Ez. XL: 1-6; XLII: 20; Zach. II: 5; and not destruction, as in 2 Sam. VIII: 2a; 2 Kgs. XXI: 13; Amos VII: 1-9; Is. XXXIV: 11; Lam. II: 8.

We believe, along with Swete, Allo, Lohmeyer, Charles, Wikenhauser and others, that the Temple of Jerusalem of which the inner part is to be spared along with "those who worship therein," must be a figure, and cannot be taken in the strict sense. It cannot be otherwise, if John's writing of the text is placed after 70 A.D. Besides, even supposing that the passage is from before 70 A.D., how could the Apocalypse author contradict the saying of Jesus that "there will not be left one stone upon another that will not be thrown down" (Mark II: 2 and parallel texts)? Consider also that the author shows little interest in the Jews as such, seeing rather the Christians as the only true Jews, and the unbelieving members of the race as the "synagogue of Satan" (II: 9; III: 9; cf. John VIII: 44). He has the same mind as Jesus, who toward the end of His public life referred to the temple not as "the house of God," (the phrase which we have here), but as "your house" (the house of the Jews, ff. Mt. XXIII: 38; Lk. XIII: 35). Besides, as Brütsch says, "How can one measure worshippers with a reed"? [4] All these linguistic characteristics indicate clearly that *we have here a pure symbol*. The author is interested only in the real worshippers of the true God, and not a material building.

We cannot limit ourselves, therefore, to merely historical explanations. Renan, who thinks that the Apocalypse was written under Galba, and hence before 70 A.D., says that the author is unable to resign himself to the idea of the destruction of the Temple of Jerusalem.[5] A. Gelin (Commentary, p. 625), speaks of a temporary preservation of the Temple, which was destroyed only at the end of the siege. S. Giet [6] says the same. However, it seems unlikely that John would have attributed so much importance to a material preservation, especially to so precarious a one.

Still, it seems undeniable that he is thinking of the great catastrophe of 70 A.D. For this reason we disagree with the interpretation proposed by Allo and followed quite closely by Boismard, Bonsirven, and Cerfaux-Cambier, that it deals with the Church in general, which exteriorly is persecuted by the impious while "in the interior sanctuary of souls it lies prostrate before God in prayer and peace".[7] To us, this purely mystical kind of exegesis, entirely atemporal and devoid of any relationship between the scene in question and the concrete events of history, is hardly tenable. The interior of the sanctuary, which is spared, is contrasted to the exterior court, which "has been given to the nations . . . who will trample it under foot for forty-two months." This passage recalls those of Zach. XII: 3; Is. VIII: 13 (Theodotion); Is. LXIII: 18 (Aquila); Ps. LXXIX: 1. However, the closest to it is undoubtedly Luke XXI: 24, in which Jesus says, "Jerusalem will be trodden down by the Gentiles, until the time of the nations be fulfilled." Just as Jesus wishes to indicate by these words the future punishment of the guilty Jews, so too the part of the temple which "shall be trampled under foot" must represent those Jews marked for punishment. Allo's interpretation would lead logically to the conclusion that

---

4 Ch. BRÜTSCH, *Clarté de l'Apocalypse* (Genève, 1955), p. 120.

5 *L'Antichrist* (Paris, 1873), p. 401.

6 *Revue des Sciences Religieuses* (1952), *Les episodes de la Guerre juive et l'Apocalypse*, p. 359.

7 Allo, *Commentaire*, pp. 148-149; cf. also BOISMARD, p. 53, note e; BONSIRVEN, p. 193; CERFAUX - CAMBIER, p. 91.

the author of the Apocalypse has taken the oracle of punishment of the Jews who are enemies of Christ, and made it into a prediction of the persecution of the Church. Such a transformation seems hardly probable.

Swete seems much more correct, in seeing here the opposition between the synagogue and the Church, referring to II: 9 and III: 9, in which the true Jews are distinguished from those who are but the synagogue of Satan (cf. Rom. II: 17 ff.; IX: 6 ff.; Gal. VI: 15; John I: 47, etc.). The Gospels have a still more striking parallel, which shows clearly the symbolic nature of the phrase, and the meaning of it. Swete says: "The phrase, 'the court which is outside the temple, reject it' (*ekbale exōthen*) recalls Jesus' statement about the sons of the kingdom who are cast forth into the darkness outside *ekblēthēsontai eis to skotos to exōthen*, Mt. VIII: 12), or cast forth outside," *hymas ekballomenous exō*, Luke XIII: 28; cf. also Mt. XXII: 13).

We should note the force of the phrase *ekbale exōthen*. These words make little sense if they are applied to a material building (which, of course, cannot be cast aside). It seems even more difficult when we consider that the court which is to be rejected (*ekbale exōthen*) is already outside (*tēn aulēn tēn exōthen*). Thus many exegetes, refusing to accept the text literally, presume to alter it. Cerfaux-Cambier, for example, offer: "pass by the outside court; do not measure it." Boismard, Crampon and Osty propose similar emendations in their versions and commentaries.

We think, on the contrary, that it is better to keep the uniquely paradoxical character of the Apocalypse's language, which, after all, is supposed to be metaphorical. The phrase occurs a few times in the New Testament, and almost always it has the sense of expelling or excluding. Besides the passages mentioned above, cf. also Lk. IV: 29; XX: 15; Acts VII: 58. This seems particularly true of the literature of the johannine corpus (cf. John IX: 34-35; XII: 31). Because of its close similarity to the ideas contained in our passage, compare especially John XV: 6: "If anyone does not abide in me, he shall be cast aside," and Apocalypse XXII: 14-15, "Outside (*exō*) are the dogs and the sorcerers and the fornicators and the murderers and the idolators, and everyone who loves and practices falsehood."

At first the Apocalypse text seems to be incoherent ("The court outside the temple, reject it"). But the same paradox occurs in Luke XIII: 25-28, which shows clearly that, here too, as for the expression, "trample under foot," this is the real parallel passage.[8] In this last passage, Luke shows the Jews, proud of their privileged status, standing *outside* the closed banquet hall, seeking in vain to enter (*arxēsthe exō hestanai kai krouein tēn thryran*). Three verses later, it is said that they shall be cast forth outside (*ekballomenous exo*). For this reason Lagrange comments: "One might say that the scene changes, and those who found the door closed were able to enter and look around, and then made to leave".[9]

It seems to us that the paradoxical language can be explained in the same way for both the Apocalypse and Luke: although they are outside the kingdom, the Jews can be conceived as being in a certain sense within the Kingdom. They are both in and out, because the religion of Christ, in spite of its newness, is a continuation and fulfillment of the religion of the old Covenant. Israel's religion is, as it were, the outer court of the Temple, which is the Christian Church. But the Jews' refusal to believe in Christ brings about their definite exclusion ("reject it"). From this moment on they are entirely outside the Kingdom.

As for the part of the temple which is to be measured and preserved, it corresponds to the 144,000 Jews who are spared *because* of the great tribulation of chapter VII.[10] At the sixth seal John contrasts the misery of the wicked (VI: 15-17) and the safety of the Church, composed partly of the 144,000 Jews converted from among the twelve tribes of Israel and partly from among the great multitude of all nations, tribes, peoples and tongues.[11] We see the same procedure for the sounding of the

---

8 As does the fourth gospel, John's Apocalypse shows several remarkable literary similarities to Luke's Gospel. Notice in particular that the septet of the seals, which is certainly based on the synoptic apocalypse, is most especially like that of Luke. Cf. Charles, *Commentary*, I: pp. 158-159.

9 *Evangile selon saint Luc* (Paris, 1927), p. 391.

10 The *Naos* and the *thysiastērion*, therefore, represent good Jews who escape the catastrophe. Lohmeyer notes correctly (p. 91) that in Apocalypse III: 12, the Christian community is also presented under the image of a temple: "He who overcomes, I will make him a pillar in the temple of my God." This recalls the columns of the Temple mentioned in I Kgs. VII: 2; 2 Ch. III: 15-17. Cf. the same image in Gal. II: 9.

11 This passage calls for very detailed exegesis. It would certainly be

sixth trumpet. After describing the sixth plague, which marks the high-point of the punishment, but fails to bring about the conversion of the guilty ones (IX: 13-21), the author passes from this devastating scene to the mass entry of the Gentiles into the Church (cf. the little scroll which is eaten in ch. X, and which has for its object the "mystery of God" of X: 7) understood in the Pauline sense, to which a number of faithful Jews will be added (the part of the Temple which is measured).

Unlike Chapters XII and ff. in which the prayers afflicting the pagans leave no "remnant," *the first prophetic part of the Apocalypse is shot through with the idea of the Remnant of Israel.* The author has said already in IX: 4, that "only the men who do not have God's seal on their foreheads" will be struck. In VIII: 7; 8; 9; 10; 11; 12; IX: 15; 18, the plagues always affect a third part (cf. Ez. V: Zach. XIII: 8-9). Here there is a formal expression of the preservation of the Remnant: only a Remnant will enter Christ's Church, the rest of the Jews will be "cast forth outside."

What we have said has far from exhausted the meaning of the scene. It recalls Ez. XL-XLII, in which there is a measuring of the ideal temple of the eschatological kingdom, the measure being an indication of God's final decision (Cerfaux-Cambier). The Apocalypse author must also have thought of the messianic temple willed by God in which the ancient Jerusalem Temple is to survive. Just as the material edifice of the Temple was destroyed in 70 A.D., so too the spiritual reality which is represented stands intact in the religion founded by Christ. Titus' armies then, contrary to appearances, were far from destroying God's real Temple. True enough, Jesus had said of the Temple that "there will not remain a stone upon a stone." But he had also predicted, "Destroy this Temple and in three days I will raise it up" (John II: 13-22), suggesting thereby that there was in the Jerusalem Temple something that could not disappear. Toward the end of the first century a legend circulated according to which the temple of the holy city was to be mysteriously preserved and the sacred objects contained in it would be spared from the pillaging of the raiders. There is an echo of this idea in the Syriac Apocalypse of Baruch, VI: 3-9, in which an angel

---

daring, to pretend that these two groups, which the author clearly distinguishes (then contrasts), are the Christian Church under both its earthly and heavenly aspects.

takes the most sacred of the temple furnishings and hides them in the depths of the earth, where they are to remain until the end of time. Possibly the image of Apocalypse XI: 1-2 is an allusion to this legend, in which case it would be only to correct it and give it an acceptable spiritual meaning. However, the direct source of our passage remains undoubtedly XL-XLII, explained and clarified by the words of Jesus Himself.

If, as seems quite certain, the scene of Apoc. XI: 1-2 is related to Luke XXI: 24, then the forty-two months during which the Gentiles are to trample underfoot the outer court of the temple, correspond to the "time of the nations" during which the Gentiles are to trample Jerusalem underfoot. The symbolic figure of forty-two months as a description of the time of trial appears elsewhere in the Apocalypse, either under this form (XIII: 5) or expressed in days and years (XI: 3 and XII: 6; 1260 days), XII: 14 (a time and times and half a time). This last passage is taken directly from Dan. VII: 25, in which the word "time" means "year" (cf. also Dan. IV: 13), and in which the longer phrase "a time and times and half a time" refers to the three and a half years' duration of the reign of the persecutor Antiochus, Epiphanes, and figuratively to the duration of the Kingdom of God's enemies, after which God's final kingdom will be inaugurated. The same idea occurs in IX: 27 and XII: 7, and in a different form (2300 evenings and mornings), in Dan. VIII: 14.

Some have suggested that, since three and a half is half of seven, a persecution of three and a half months is one which will run only half its course, and then die out. Be this as it may, the forty-two months (1260 days) of the Apocalypse are certainly a symbolic description of the temporary period of trial which separates Christians from the final establishment of God's Kingdom. The sufferings of the unconverted Jews will continue until then, just as in Luke XXI: 24, they will continue "until the times of nations be fulfilled."

(2) The Two Witnesses (vv. 3-13)

Two mysterious witnesses, clothed in sackcloth, prophesy for a thousand two hundred and sixty days, during which no one may harm them. But once their testimony is finished, the Beast that comes up out of the abyss will kill them. These dead bodies will be unburied for three and a half days in the city in which the Lord was crucified; then they rise and go up to heaven in a cloud. The earth quakes; a tenth part of the city is destroyed, and the survivors glorify God.

Naturally, we are anxious to know the meaning of all these events, and above all, the identity of the two witnesses. Because they are lifted up to heaven, some of the ancient authors (Hippolytus, Tertullian, and others) saw them as Henoch and Elias. Many others think they are rather Elias and Moses, Elias because of the opening of heaven and the drought; Moses because of the changing of the water into blood. Post-exilic Judaism, relying on the text of Mal. III: 23-24, looked for the return of Elias at the end of time. Interestingly enough, Malachia speaks of Moses in the same context (III: 22).

Some have identified the witnesses with Peter and Paul, who died under Nero (the Beast).[12] In this hypothesis, the city mentioned in v. 8 would be Rome. In spite of the fact that all the MSS have them, the words, "where their Lord was also crucified" (v. 8) would thus be considered a gloss. Some have calculated that the thousand two-hundred and sixty days is just about equal to the period extending from the burning of Rome in July of 64, to one of the traditional dates given for the martyrdom of the two apostles. We might mention also the interpretation of A. Gelin (p. 627) who sees here two Christian prophets martyred by the troops of Titus; B. W. Bacon[13] suggests James, bishop of Jerusalem, and John the apostle; Zahn and some others think they are two strictly eschatological personages, who will appear only at the end of the world.

Each of these hypotheses runs into grave difficulties. The two witnesses are certainly Christians, notwithstanding allusions to Moses, Elias, and without doubt also to Jeremia (compare v. 5 with Jer. V: 14, in which God puts His word like a flame in the mouth of Jeremia; because of this similarity, Victorin proposes Jeremia and Elias). Besides, it is at least rash to go against the evidence of all the MSS in placing the martyrdom in Rome instead of in Jerusalem.[14] And we cannot fail to account

12 Cf. J. MUNCK, *Petrus und Paulus in der Offenbarung Johannes* (Copenhagen, 1950); J. BOISMARD, *l'Apocalypse*, p. 53, n. 2.

13 *The Gospel of the Hellenists* (New York, 1932).

14 Doubtless the "great city" of XVI: 19; XVII: 18; XVIII: 10; 16; 18; 19; 21; is Rome, but the entire context shows that in Chapter XI it is Jerusalem. Jeremias speaks of "this great city" (Jerusalem), in a passage which refers to its extra-ordinary punishment (XXII: 8-9) as an

for the Christian color of the scene, in its Palestinian Jewish setting, and at least to attempt an explanation of all the elements of the text. For our part, we think it probable, and even likely, that this is really a reference to definite and precise historical events related especially to the great tragedy of 70. Still, there must be more because the ministry of the two witnesses (1260 days) is the same as the time of trial accorded to the Jews and to the trampling underfoot of Jerusalem by the nations (42 months); thus their ministry lasts from the catastrophe of 70 to the final establishment of the Kingdom of God.[15]

Our interpretation of the two witnesses as a symbolic figure follows particularly the study of L. Cerfaux, *"Temoins du Christ dans le Livre des Actes"*.[16] We should try here to summarize the chief points of this fine article, which gives marvelous insights into the characteristics of *witness,* and explains how *witness* and *message* (*kerygma*) were distinguished among primitive Christians.

Witness is primarily the work of the twelve apostles, who lived with Jesus, and especially with Peter, whom Jesus appointed to strengthen the faith of his brethren (Luke XXII: 32). Occasion-

---

example to the nations. The Apocalypse author refers to Jerusalem as "Sodom" and "Egypt." The Old Testament has several precedents for the application of the name of Sodom to the Holy city and to the chosen people, especially in the prophetic writings, (Is. I: 9-10; Ez. XVI: 46; 55; Jer. XXIII: 14; Dt. XXXII: 32). Jesus also compares his countrymen to the people of Sodom (Mt. X: 15; XI: 23-24; Luke X: 12), and the judgment of Jerusalem to that meted out to Sodom (Luke XVII: 28-31). We should not be surprised to find the name of Egypt mentioned in a septet which refers in its first woes to the plagues of Egypt (Chapters VIII-IX; the first, second, fourth, and fifth trumpets). This septet also contains some recollections of Josephus' *Jewish War;* cf. S. Giet, art. cit., pp. 345-362. It should not seem strange to us that the same city is called "holy city" in XI: 2, and "Sodom" or "Egypt" a little farther on, because in this latter passage, the author has in mind the death of Jesus, for which Jerusalem is held responsible.

15 There are some excellent observations and some well balanced criticisms contrary to Allo's position in L. GRY: *Les chapitres XI and XII de l'Apocalypse,* in *R.B.* (1922) pp. 203-214. However, this author is rather difficult to follow when he treats as equal the forty-two months (or 1260 days) and the 3½ days of v. 9, and when he places the death of the witnesses in 70.

16 (*Angelicum,* 1943), pp. 166-183; reproduced in *Recueil Lucien Cerfaux* (Gembloux, 1954), ii, 157-74.

ally in Acts Paul renders his "witness" when his audience consists of Jews (XVIII: 5; XX: 21; XXII: 18; XVIII: 11). Witness is always to Jesus' earthly activity, and above all to His Resurrection. It is given in Jerusalem and is directed to hostile Jewish persecutors. "There was nothing new to teach the Jews of Jerusalem. They had seen and heard Jesus, and were now looking for the Messia. The task, therefore, was to inform them that Jesus had risen from the dead, and that He was the Christ. Thus the apostles presented their message in Jerusalem, not as bearers of a new idea, or as propagandists for a newly founded cult".[17]

In the face of Jewish hostility, the witness of the Apostles receives strength from the Holy Spirit, who helps them and prevents their constant fidelity to Christ from succumbing to resistance of whatever kind (cf. IV: 13; 29; 31; 33, *parresia*). In their captivity the Apostles are likened to the Old Testament prophets. Like them, they are subject to persecution by their unbelieving compatriots, (cf. Lk. IV: 24; XI: 47-50; XIII: 30 ff.; Acts VII: 57 ff.).

Understood in this sense, their witness has a juridical and religious meaning; the persecuted disciples of Christ are dragged before human tribunals, and are condemned for their faith, which is nothing other than their witness to their Master. However, whereas earthly judges condemn them, Christ Himself becomes their advocate before the divine tribunal, and "confesses" His own before His Father, (Lk. XII: 8) thereby admitting them to heaven. All these elements are present in the account of the martyrdom of St. Stephen (Acts VII) except that the Resurrection of Christ, the chief object of other witnesses, is less emphasized than in the case of the witness of the Apostles.

This witness differs from the message, which is no longer directed to the Jews only, but to every class of men by every preacher, especially by Paul, preacher *par excellence*. It spreads far beyond the city of Jerusalem, and speaks of all the events of Christ"s life and works. We see the distinction between witness and message clearly indicated in St. Paul's talk at Antioch of Pisidia: "But God raised him from the dead on the third day, and he was seen during many days by those who had come up with him from Galilee to Jerusalem, and they are now witnesses of Him to the people. So now we bring you

---

17 Art. cit., pp. 171-172.

the good news (*evangelizometha*—the message) that the promise
made to our fathers, God has fulfilled.... (Acts XIII: 30-32).[18]

The data contained in the Book of the Acts of the apostles
regarding witness are helpful for our better understanding of
Apocalypse XI: 1. Cerfaux writes, "All the elements of witness
are present in the allegory of the two witnesses in Apoc. XI:
3-12." Because of their clothing (sackcloth), the references to
conversion and to miracles, the two witnesses recall Moses,
Elias, Jeremia, and in general are the great prophets of the
Old Testament. And this should not strike us as unusual, since,
the early Christians, like Jesus Himself, liked to emphasize the
similarity existing between the great prophet of the old Covenant,
and the Apostles and all those Christians who bravely bore
witness to the Master. The two witnesses of this passage, whose
ministry takes place at Jerusalem, speak to a hostile audience,
as we can tell from the threats of vv. 5-7. A comparison of
the data of Acts regarding witness shows that these indications
are quite normal, even if taken literally. The conclusion resulting from all this is, therefore, that the two witnesses do not
symbolize the preaching of the Gospel in general (as is the
opinion of Allo and of many others), with Jerusalem representing the whole world;[20] *rather they are the incarnation of the
witness which the Church renders to Christ in the face of a
Judaism grown obstinate in its unbelief.*

Still in all, we should be most careful to take proper notice

----

18 The distinction which L. Cerfaux has made should not be exaggerated. A. RETIF contests it in *Témoignage et prédication missionnaire in
les Actes des Apôtres,* in *Nouvelle Revue Théologique* (1951), pp. 152-
165; cf. by the same author, *Foi au Christ et mission d'après les Actes
des Apôtres* (Paris, 1953), pp. 33-55. However, it seems that the criticisms
thus formulated are based more upon the modern notion of witness than
on the data of philology. Cf. A. DESCAMPS, *Ephemerides Theologicae
Lovanienses* (1955), pp. 140-141.

19 Art. cit., p. 181.

20 We approve whole-heartedly of L. Gry's criticism of Allo's commentary: "When they (the readers) come to understand that the two witnesses, Moses and Elias, represent 'all the good preachers of the gospel';
that the great city in which the apostles are put to death, 'Jerusalem
represents the whole world,' (*Domini est terra et plenitudo ejus*); when
they come to accept a symbolism of which they probably will never come
to appreciate the full extent,—then, I fear, they will feel themselves groping
in an immensity as vague as it is vast!" (*Revue Biblique,* (1922), p. 301.)

of the special characteristics of these two witnesses, who are, as many authors hold, allegorical personages in exercising their function all during the time in which Jerusalem is trampled underfoot by the gentiles. If they recall more particularly Moses and Elias, it is because these are the great representatives of the law and of the prophets, who render witness through the Apostles' mouths to Jesus, showing to the Jews that Christianity is the fulfillment of the old Covenant. Indeed, is it not precisely as witnesses that Moses and Elias are present in the gospel story of the Transfiguration? In Zach. IV: 1-11, the two olive trees (*tufts*), Josue the high priest, and Zorobabel, the *Pekah*, or governor, are charged with guarding a golden lamp-stand, which probably is an image of the reconstructed Temple. In the Apocalypse text the witnesses are olive trees and lamp-stands at the same time (v. 4) perhaps because the material Temple of Jerusalem has given way to the living and spiritual temple, which is the Church.

The violent death of the two witnesses, their resurrection after three and a half days, and their going up to heaven are not to be interpreted as real historical facts, occurring at the time of the destruction of Jerusalem, or even in the future, at the end of time in the strict sense. Since the two witnesses are figurative personages, their martyrdom and the glorification which follows it, are likewise symbols drawn especially from Gospel history and designed to show how the fate of the Church rests upon that of her founder.[21] The author wishes to express the truth, so dear to primitive Christianity, that, if Christ's witnesses are subjected to persecution and martyrdom, still the Church wins precisely in her martyrs, and rises again after the trial,[22] just as Ezechiel had foretold of Israel during the period of Babylonian exile. Thus the picture is clearly

---

21 SWETE (p. 138) notes that the phrase, "when their Lord was crucified" of v. 8, recalls John XV: 20: "No servant is greater than his master. If they have persecuted me, they will persecute you also."

22 Recall that in the fourth Gospel the cross is an exaltation and the beginning of glorification. As for the fear which grips the spectators at the resurrection of the witnesses, note not only that the expression (*Kai Phobos megas epepesen*) is Lukan (cf. Luke I: 12; Acts XIX: 17), but also that the author of the Acts of the Apostles takes pains to mention the terror provoked by the supernatural manifestations which occurred in the life of the Church (II: 6; 12; 43; V: 5; 11; XIX: 17).

drawn, showing the Church as the true Israel. There is more than an accidental similarity between the author's terminology in v. 11 ("The breath of life from God entered into them. And they stood up on their feet...") and the vision of the dry bones in Ez. XXXVII (cf. v. 10). The witnesses go up to heaven in a cloud as did Christ at the time of His Ascension (v. 11; cf. Acts 1: 9); here too, the victory of the Church, like that of its founder, is destined to come only after a necessary period of suffering.

This does not mean, of course, that we must reject the possibility of seeing in this vision any allusion to concrete historical events. Although the scene is laid entirely in Jerusalem and not, as some prefer to interpret it symbolically, in Rome, it may possibly be a reference to the two great witnesses, Peter and Paul, who had sealed their witness with martyrdom. Or, it may be, as Giet is inclined to believe, an allusion to the two Jewish high priests Ananos and Jesus, who Josephus says (*Jewish War* IV: 5: 2; 314-318) were murdered by Idumean fanatics before Vespasian's campaign of 68, and whose bodies were left unburied in the streets of Jerusalem, as a grating affront to the Jews. Giet sees this as one of many references to Josephus' *Jewish War*, which he sees as probable in the vision of the trumpets. If this really was the Apocalypse author's purpose, it could have been such only by way of contrast, because otherwise we find total opposition between our two witnesses and the two high priests whom Josephus describes. Giet explains:

The high priests wore sacred vestments: the witnesses wear penitential robes and prophesy in sackcloth; the high priests fall victim to the Jews and their allies: the witnesses fall under the blows of the Beast which comes up and out of the abyss. One might say that the two apocalypses are superimposed, one upon the other, or rather that the one replaces the other, as the history which Josephus records and interprets in a Jewish milieu as the fulfillment of the final events of the world, receives an altogether new interpretation in the Apocalypse. The witnesses, true enough, have no rich robes, and do not fall victim to factious enemies, because they are not the high priests of Judaism, for the day of the Lord is to come rather from the background of the Law; rather, coming in the spirit and powers of Elias, the precursor and prophet, and of Moses, leader and lawgiver, they are like Zorobabel and Josue, the leaders of the return from exile, and restorers of the Temple".[23]

Even granting some validity to these possibilities, we insist that they are only secondary, and that, in any case, the two witnesses of the Apocalypse are an incarnation of the witness which the Church renders to Christ (together with the law and the prophets) in the face of a hostile and unbelieving Judaism.

We still must consider whether, given the exclusion of any probability of identifying the two allegorical witnesses with historical personages of the past, we should see their symbolic martyrdom and glorification as an expression of Christian truths which find their day-to-day application in the existence and life of the Church. Or should we see them rather at some precise moment in the history of salvation?

The former of these two alternatives seems incompatible with the letter of the Apocalypse text. Given the explanation outlined above, the text means that the law and the prophets will continue to give witness to Christ: the Church, as opposed to the unbelieving Jews, during all the time of the nations, as long as Jerusalem is to be trampled underfoot by the nations (XI: 2; compare with Lk. XIX: 24). This means that the death and glorification of the two witnesses is to occur in the future, at the end of the *present epoch.*

A close study of vv. 7-13 seems to require the same conclusion. Cerfaux-Cambier see this passage as an anticipation of what will be said in the second part of the Apocalypse. Thus the similarity between v. 7 ("and when they have finished their testimony, the beast that comes up out of the deep will wage war against them and will conquer them and will kill them.") and XX: 7-8 ("And when the thousand years are finished, Satan will be released from his prison, and will go forth and deceive the nations. . . ."). The manners of thought and expression are strikingly similar in the two passages. Now, Apocalypse XX: 7-8 announces the great rebellion of the nations against the Church, which Satan is to incite before the last judgment, and which is described some verses further (XX: 11-15). Satan, who was "cast into the abyss" (XX: 1-3) is now "released from his prison," to beguile the nations, and to lead them in war against the saints and against the beloved

---

23 S. GIET, art. laud., pp. 359-360.

city (the Church). The beast then who comes up out of the abyss (Apocalypse XI: 7), and Satan who is released from his prison (XX: 7-8), are one and the same. This identification becomes all the more certain when we see that in either case a mention of the last judgment follows directly afterwards. This judgment is, beyond a doubt, the meaning of XI: 18 and of the longer passage in XX: 11-15.

This interpretation of the killing of the two witnesses is the only one which takes sufficient account of a phenomenon long surprising and even embarrassing to many commentators, i.e., while the ministry of the two witnesses takes place in Jerusalem, the perspective "widens out" [24] in vv. 9-10 to take in the whole world. Thus the whole world, declared enemy of Christ, and including the incredulous Jews, rejoices at the murder of the two witnesses. The reason is that we are here, as also in XX: 7 ff., in the presence of the great final revolt of the nations against Christ. However in Chapter XI, unlike the parallel text in XX, this revolt is considered particularly with regard to the Jewish world, in accordance with the perspective of the entire first prophetic part of the Apocalypse; in resisting and persecuting Christ's Church the Jews really insult and reject the Law and the Prophets.[25]

Still, just as in chapter XX, the victory of the nations (Gog and Magog) over the saints is passing, interrupted suddenly by fire from heaven, ("And fire from God came down out of heaven and devoured them," XX: 9), likewise in Chapter XI the victory of Christ's enemies is but passing, followed by intervention from heaven, especially under the figure of an earthquake (XI: 13). If we recall the 1260 days' length of the witnesses' preaching, the three and a half days during which their bodies lie unburied, express well the uncertain nature of the beast's victory. All these numbers are, of course, only symbolic and relative.

---

24 Ch. BRÜTSCH, *Clarté de l'Apocalypse*, p. 119.

25 It hardly seems necessary to insist that this idea is eminently johannine. Cf. especially John V: 39; 45-47: "You search the scriptures, because in them you think you have life everlasting. And it is they that bear witness to me. Yet you are not willing to come to me that you may have life.... Do not think that I shall accuse you to the Father. There is one who accuses you, Moses, in whom you hope. If you believed Moses, you would believe me also, for he wrote of me. But if you do not believe his writings—how will you believe my words?"

After the murder of the two witnesses come their resurrection and heavenly exaltation, i.e., a marvelous resurrection of the Church and at the same time a divine punishment wrought against the guilty citizens of Jerusalem. This punishment is nevertheless mitigated (directed against only one tenth of the city), as we see by comparing it with the plagues which affect quarters, (VI: 8) or thirds (Chapters VIII and IX). This punishment is designed, as we see from the following verses, to convert men of good will, together with the spectacle of the Church's triumph. We agree with Allo, who observes that the number of victims of this punishment (7000), corresponding to the one tenth of the city "shows that the scene is laid in Jerusalem, and not at Rome, which is much larger" (p. 155).

"And the rest were affrighted and gave glory to the God of heaven" (13b). These words are in noteworthy contrast to IX: 21, in which the guilty refuse to repent. Loisy observes correctly,[26] that the formula, "they gave glory to God",[27] should indicate a conversion, given the antithesis between IX: 20-21 and XVI: 9-11. Furthermore, says Loisy, this phrase "is not the same as to be connected to the one God—and does not prove at all that the author is thinking of a pagan city such as Rome (Wellhausen)." Loisy and many others think this is merely a recollection of the preaching of Rom. XI: 25; 26, in which the Jews are to be converted at the end of time, when "the full number of the Gentiles" shall enter the Church.[28] One might also note the parallelism of this verse with Luke XIII: 34-35 (Matthew XXIII:

---

26 *L'Apocalypse,* p. 216.

27 The phrase is Lukan (cf. Luke XVII: 18; Acts IV: 21; XI: 18; XII: 23; XIII: 48; XXI: 20.

28 This is the exegesis of L. GRY (*R.B.* 1922, p. 207): "At the end of the messianic time, when the world itself is to end, the Law and the Prophets will return to life; the frightened people will recognize them as inspired by God; ... the Jewish people will be reborn, but as a people now converted to the true teaching of the Law and the Prophets (cf. Luke XVI: 31), i.e., to faith in God and in His Christ. The seer, who here recalls Osee VI: 2, had in mind to present here the pauline doctrine (cf. Rom. XI: 25) of the conversion of the Jews to Christianity in the last time." CHARLES (p. 292) distinguishes the primitive meaning of this passage in the Jewish document (the repentance of the Jews and their return to the worship of God) and its meaning in the present context of the Apocalypse (Israel's conversion to Christianity at the end of time).

37-39) in which Jesus appears to predict [29] the conversion of the chosen people under the symbol of the holy city acclaiming Him as the Messiah, as they do on the occasion of His triumphant entry into Jerusalem on Palm Sunday: "And I say to you, you shall say, 'Blessed is he who comes in the name of the Lord'."

The Apocalypse never mentions Christ, but refers to "The God of Heaven." Contrary to Wellhausen, Charles and Loisy think that there is nothing surprising in this expression of the Jews being converted to "The God of Heaven." This expression is rather frequent in the later Jewish texts, both canonical and other, (cf., e. gr. Esd. I: 2; V: 11-12; VI: 9-10; VII: 12; 21; 23; Neh. I: 4-5; Daniel II: 18; 19; 37; 44).[30] It may be that the Apocalypse author, in speaking only of the true God and not of Christ, wishes to show in the late conversion of the Jews the final and supreme outcome of the efforts of the Law and the Prophets (the two witnesses) of the Old Testament. For the Jews, to be united to Christ need not be a change of religion, but rather it would be to be docile to the divine power which was the inner life of the religion of Moses and the prophets.

(3) The Third Woe and the Seventh Trumpet (vv. 14-19)

In Rom. XI: 25-26, the corporate conversion of the Jews, coming after that of the Gentiles, seems to indicate the culmination of God's plan for the salvation of mankind. Likewise here, now that Israel is converted, the seventh trumpet sounds (cf. the last trumpet of I Cor. XV: 52), announcing the end of the world with the final inauguration of the kingdom of God and of His anointed by the punishment of the wicked (this should be the third woe of XI: 14, which is not described) and the giving of the reward to the faithful servants (cf. vv. 15-18). The omission from v. 17 of the phrase "who art to come" after "who art and who wast" (cf. I: 8; IV: 8), and in v. 18 the mention of resurrection after judgment, show clearly that the author is placing himself in the perspective of the end of time. It seems clear from this point on that chapters XII ff. are a return to,

---

29 This is Lagrange's exegesis. We have also accepted it in *N.R.Th.* (1949): *"Le Triomphe eschatologique de Jésus dans quelques textes isolés des evangiles,"* pp. 806-812.

30 Cf. also W. BOUSSET, *Die Religion des Judentums* (Tübingen, 1926), pp. 312-315, n. 5.

or, as it were, a repetition (or resumption) of the theme begun in Chapter X.

The second prophetic part of the Apocalypse ends as did the first, in a scene of the last judgment in XX: 11-15 (cf. XIV: 14-20). However, while XI: 15-18 seems to be merely a foretelling of the judgment, the corresponding passage in XX: 11-15 shows the judgment really taking place. There is a still more important difference between these texts: the second clearly presents the idea of a supranational judgment, as an abnormal conclusion to the time of the gentiles. Allo says: "In XX: 12 the terminology is absolutely universal" (p. 331). "And I saw the dead, the great and the small, standing before the throne." Verse 13 presents the same universalism even more expressively: "And the sea gave up the dead that were in it, and death and hell gave up the dead that were in them; and they were judged, each one according to their works." Again, Allo says (p. 331), "As in the Ethiopian version of Henoch (LXI: 5), there is no place so hidden that it will not have to give up its store of human remains; if 'Hades' is hell strictly speaking, it would be a new reference to the resurrection of the damned; however, it probably means the lowest and most derelict members of humanity."

There is quite a different perspective opened up by the song in XI: 17-18, which is placed on the lips of the saints of the Old Testament (the twenty-four elders).[31] This song presents the universal judgment of the end of time in typically Jewish terms: the wicked who are damned are the "nations who rage" (Ps. II: 1) and ruin the earth. The servants of God who receive their reward are divided into three groups: the prophets, the saints, and those who fear the name of God. These are, of course, Jewish terms, which must be seen in a new light because of the Christian sense of the passage. This imposes a sort of double necessity upon the exegete who proposes to interpret this eleventh chapter.

It is quite normal to see situated in first place the "servants

---

31 We think these are not angels but redeemed men, more particularly the saints of the Old Testament, who were the ancestors of the Christians in the faith. Cf. our study, "Les vingt-quatre vieillards de l'Apocalypse," in Revue Biblique (1958) and Chapter I of this section, above. Cf. also in the same sense J. MICHL, Die 24 Aeltesten in der Apokalypse des Hl. Johannes (München, 1938).

of God, the prophets." Jesus and the early Christians, including the author of the Apocalypse, present these Old Testament prophets, victims of the hostility and hatred of their own Jewish neighbors, as models for the Christians, who are victims of cruel persecution in their own day. However, the Christian community has some prophets of its own, so much so that we should see here an undistinguished grouping of those of the old and new Covenants together. We are sure, nonetheless, that those of the Old Testament are intended primarily; we should be careful not to emphasize the latter to the extent of forgetting the former.

It is more difficult to identify the other two groups, saints and those who fear the name of God. We shall consider first the group of those who fear the name of God. J. Dupont [32] writes, "The Acts of the Apostles uses the phrase—"God-Fearing" (X: 2; 22; 35; XIII: 16; 26) and "adoring God" (XIII: 43; 50; XVI: 14; XVII: 4; 17; XVIII: 7), in a special technical sense, referring to those who are sympathetic to Judaism, accepting its beliefs and moral principles, without going so far as to be assimilated to the point of undergoing circumcision. Luke is particularly interested in this category of persons, perhaps because he was one of this group before becoming a Christian." It is difficult to see how this phrase "God-fearing" could have the same meaning in the Apocalypse as it has in the Acts of the Apostles. To see it in the same light in the Apocalypse would imply a distinction between two classes of Christians, i.e., between the saints and the "God-fearing." Bousset proposes that, by suppressing the *kai*, we could see these two phrases as applied to one single group. Thus instead of three groups there would be two, the prophets and the saints who fear God. The proposal, however, is arbitrary. There is no justification for the omission of *kai*.

The only remaining possible explanation is to Christianize the phrase "those who fear God," without losing sight of its Jewish background. Allo and Charles do this; Bousset himself is also inclined in this same direction. The *phoboumenoi* are thus Christians of pagan origin, Gentile Christians. The "saints" then are Christians of Jewish origin. We know that in St. Paul's writings the "saints" refers primarily to the Christians of Jerusa-

---

32 *Les Actes des Apôtres* (*Bible de Jérusalem*, Paris, 1953), pp. 98-99.

lem.[33] "Only St. Paul was bold enough to extend this privileged title to the Gentile world".[34]

Allo does not take the trouble to explain the reason for the use of such terminology on the part of the Apocalypse author. Others try to explain it somewhat arbitrarily, invoking a Jewish document. It seems quite normal to us that in this part of the Apocalypse, which deals with the Jewish race, the author would choose to describe the end of time by a reference to the chosen people, showing the perfect fulfillment of all the promises made to them and to their forefathers.

It is interesting to compare XI: 18 and XIX: 5. The comparison seems to suggest itself, since in both instances there is an invitation, addressed to those who fear God, the servants, great and small, to praise God. The word *phoboumenoi*, furthermore, occurs only in XI: 18 and XIX: 5. Boismard [35] sees this as a proof in support of his thesis that both these verses belonged to the more recent apocalypse, the one edited in the time of Vespasian or at the beginning of Domitian's reign. This similarity however, is only apparent. In fact, in XIX: 5 the three phrases, "servants," "those who fear God" and "the great and the small" are merely placed in juxtaposition, but they all refer to the same person. There should be no *kai* before *phoboumenoi* (there is none in *Aleph, C*, or *P*, against Boismard and according to most critics). On the contrary, in XI: 18, there are three groups, as is evident from the *kai* which separates them. The servants of God, expressly assimilated here to the prophets, are one group by themselves; the "saints" and the "god-fearing" are also distinct from each other. As we saw above, this manner of speaking shows the author's intention to make his presentation with regard to the Jewish point of view.

The same notion is present in the last verse of the chapter, which describes the opening of the heavenly temple and the appearance of the Ark of the Covenant. We disagree entirely with Allo's unusual opinion that, contrary to the almost unanimous agreement of commentators, verse 19 should be taken from chapter XI and made the introduction to the second prophetic part

---

33 Cf. L. CERFAUX, *La Théologie de l'Église suivant saint Paul* (Paris, 1942), pp. 105-114.

34 *Ibid.*, p. 114.

35 *Revue Biblique* (1949), *L'Apocalypse ou les Apocalypses de saint Jean*, pp. 519-520.

of the Apocalypse. We are rather of the opinion that chapter XI could have no more fitting conclusion than this nineteenth verse.

With regard to the opening of the heavenly temple, we agree with Boismard's fine observation that,

> In verse 19 John speaks of the temple and refers it precisely to the one in heaven, clearly differentiating it from the Jerusalem Temple, which he has mentioned in verses 1 and 2. This distinction shows definitely that verses 1, 2, and 19 are parts of the same vision.[36]

In brief, the heavenly temple comes to take the place of the Jerusalem temple, which has finally disappeared.

The appearance here of the Ark of the Covenant is significant. We read in 2 Macc. II: 4-8 that Jeremia took and hid the Ark along with the altar of holocausts to save them from the Chaldean invaders, and that the Ark will return only when God gathers His people together and shows them His mercy. It may be that the Apocalypse author is referring to this account. It appears from this allusion to the Ark in the heavenly temple, that we have come to the final completion of the covenant between Jahweh and Israel, of which the Ark was the witness. Cerfaux and Cambier explain it well (page 98): "The Ark which we see here in the Apocalypse is the true Ark which was symbolized by the Ark of the Old Testament. We have come to the end of both covenants. Only the Parousia remains."

We are sure that the author of the Apocalypse speaks throughout his work of the fulfillment of the plan of which the Old Testament was a preparation. But he speaks of the ark nowhere else than in this verse. Ezechiel also made no provision for it in his vision of the new temple. The reconstructed temple had no ark (cf. Tacitus, Hist. V: 9: *Vacuam sedem et inania arcana*). Furthermore, no New Testament text (except Apoc. XI: 19) sees the ark (even spiritually) as a specifically Christian thing. The exegesis which we have proposed for Chapter XI explains the use of this symbol without making it necessary to postulate any pre-existing Jewish document (such as the text of 2 Macc. cited above).

From all this study it seems evident that the historical background of Apocalypse XI seems to be the catastrophe of 70 A.D.,

---

[36] *Revue Biblique* (1949), p. 511.

which brought about the final separation of the Church from the synagogue. Many critics, especially those favorable to the hypothesis of a pre-existing Jewish document, have recognized this background. Our exegesis, therefore, is somewhat novel. The author is much less interested in the material aspect of the event than in its historical significance. He shows the true spiritual values of the Jewish religion (the part of the temple which is to be measured), which Christianity keeps intact. He sees the Law and the prophets of the Old Testament as having their true continuation, not in the Jewish world which has refused to accept Jesus as Savior, but in the Christian Church, which will continue until the end of time to render witness to Christ before the mass of the chosen people who remain obstinate in their unbelief (the two witnesses).

The fact that this exegesis explains satisfactorily the antedating of the Apocalypse makes it particularly satisfying. Seven emperors are mentioned in XVII: 10-11. The most normal way of identifying them is that proposed by most commentators, (Holtzmann, Bousset, Swete, Charles, Gelin, Kiddle, Cerfaux-Cambier). The first four are Augustus, Tiberius, Caligula and Claudius; the fifth is Nero; the sixth, *presently reigning*, is Vespasian; the seventh, who has not yet come and who must remain only a short time, is Titus (79-81), *imperii felix brevitate*, as *Ancone* says of him (quoted by Swete, p. 221). The eighth, a sort of *Nero redivivus* because of his cruelty, is Domitian. Since the Apocalypse was almost certainly composed under Domitian (St. Irenaeus says "toward the end of the reign of Domitian"; *Adv. Haer.*, V: XXX: 3; cf. Eusebius, Hist. Eccl. XVIII: 3), we are led logically to suppose that it is only by a fiction that it is said to have been written under Vespasian. This hypothesis can claim as precedents the book of Daniel and the habitual usage of the apocalyptic writers in general.[37]

We may ask, "why this fiction in John's Apocalypse? There is of course, no indication that it is designed to deceive the reader or to lead him to see the prophecies *ex eventu* as oracles of the future. As a matter of fact, our study has shown us that John's emphasis is not on political events in themselves, but only on their religious significance for the Church of Christ.

---

37 This hypothesis of pre-dating was proposed by P. TOUILLEUX in *L'Apocalypse et les cultes de Domitien et de Cybele* (Paris, 1935), and also by A. GELIN.

In our opinion, John simply wished to look backward, placing the scene under the reign of Vespasian, before the destruction of the Temple of Jerusalem, in order to stress the theological meaning of that event, the greatest crisis which the Christian community had had to face to date.

If what we have said is correct, then it becomes obvious that the entire section of Chapters IV-XI is no more than an explication of the synoptic apocalypse, beginning with the catastrophe of 70.[38] We can see, furthermore, that the general plan of the Apocalypse corresponds with that of the ancient prophetic writings; one section of visions (chapter IV-XI) has as its object the Church in its relationship to the Jewish world; the second part (chapters XII ff.) concerns the Church and its relationship to the gentile nations. There is a good reason why Chapter V (verse 5) refers to the Lion of Juda, the Scion of David, and why Chapter XII (verse 5) refers to the King of the nations, who is to rule with a rod of iron. There is also a good reason why there are two scrolls (chapters V and X), two prophetic investitures, two series of plagues (the trumpets and the bowls) which seem to serve a double purpose.

For the present, we are satisfied that our study should give sufficient proof of our hypothesis with regard to chapter XI. The reader may judge whether or not it has made the chapter more understandable.

---

[38] We are of the opinion that the synoptic apocalypse and the septet of the seals explain each other, and also that the Apocalypse author is giving an authentic interpretation of Jesus' prophecy, in the light of the events of 70. However, it is not within the scope of this present work to enter into a complete explanation of this thesis.

CHAPTER IV

THE MESSIAH AND HIS MOTHER ACCORDING TO APOCALYPSE XII [1]

As is the case with all the rest of the book, the twelfth chapter of the Apocalypse is replete with difficulties. Every verse brings the commentators face to face with a new problem. In recent years, Catholic exegetes have shown particular interest in this chapter because of its apparently obvious marian character, but they have far from exhausted all its possibilities. In the following paragraphs we will be forced by the very nature of our study to consider this mariological problem but not as the principal object of our concern. We shall center our attention rather on two points: first, the raising of the messianic child up to heaven *immediately* after his birth; and second, the destiny of the Mother of the Messiah. In the conclusion we shall show the place of the Church in the general plan of the Apocalypse.

Before proceeding, we should say a word about our method. The Apocalypse seems to us to be a re-reading of the Old Testament in the light of Christian teaching, which it further enriches by its personal meaning. In this regard, it is beyond a doubt the most interesting and intriguing book of the New Testament. Almost every verse contains one, or usually many, references to the writings of the Old Testament, especially to those of the great prophetic books of Isaia, Ezechiel and Daniel. To come to know the mind of the author, the reader must follow these references, which are some times hidden, some times grouped together, and also the teachings of the primitive Christian Church, recalling always that the Old Testament becomes subject to a re-interpretation with the coming of the very fact of Christianity. The difficulty of the Apocalypse comes not from its literary genre, which abounds in circumlocutions, but from the necessity of having before one's mind the many various elements which

---

1 Published in *Revue Biblique*, LXVI, (1959).

the author draws from many sources, re-thinking and synthesizing them with the facility of a master.

We shall try to follow this principle in our exposition. It
would be a most serious error to seek to discover Christian
ideas easily in the Apocalypse, to the neglect of appreciating the
author's expert use of the Old Testament. These are more than
simple doctrinal illustrations which he presents: they are rather
the very essence of his work. And another grave error to be
avoided, would be to fail to take sufficiently into account the
fact of Christianity, which transforms and renews all.

(1) *Birth and Heavenly Assumption of the Messianic Child*

STATEMENT OF THE PROBLEM; PROPOSED SOLUTIONS

We read in Apocalypse XII: 4-6: "And the dragon stood before
the woman who was about to bring forth, that when she had
brought forth he might devour her son. And she brought forth
a male child, who is to rule all nations with a rod of iron; and the
child was caught up to God and to His throne. And the woman
fled into the wilderness, where she had a place prepared by
God." This can hardly be a description of Christ's birth in Bethlehem! Much less can it be a description of the Virgin Mother
giving birth to Jesus. Commentators have tried to explain the
passage as a telescoped account of Jesus' work, from His birth
to His heavenly glorification. We consider these explanations arti-
ficial; here we shall study them briefly; and then we shall propose our own, and the reasons which make it seem preferable.

Many ancient authors explained this passage as referring
either principally or exclusively to the Church, giving birth to
the Christian Community (cf. Methodius; Hippolytus; Andrew
of Caesarea; Primasius; [2] Menochius.[3] True enough, in this vision,
as in the letters at the beginning of the Apocalypse, the faithful
are closely united to Christ and share His power. But the author's
thought here is centered rather on Christ Himself, as we can

---

2 The texts of these ancient commentaries are in B. J. LeFROIS,
The Woman Clothed with the Sun, Rome, 1954, p. 18 (Methodius);
p. 15 (Hippolytus); p. 31 (Andrew of Caesarea); p. 28 (Primasius).

3 *Commentarius totius Scripturae,* Lyon, 1731, II, p. 438. Cf. J. H.
NEWMAN: *Certain difficulties felt by Anglicans in Catholic Teaching,*
London, 1891, II, p. 58: "Doubtless the Child represents the children
of the Church."

see from both the reference in verse 5 to Ps. II, and in the phrase "the rest of her offspring"[4] in verse 17.

Most exegetes see here a reference to Jesus and to the mystery of Bethlehem. But why should there be no reference to His earthly career, especially to His Passion and Resurrection? And why should the victorious Messiah be represented by a new-born child?

Rather than enter here into a detailed examination of those interpretations which see here some reference to the various systems of astrology or mythology, or to Jewish legends, we prefer to make Allo's observation our own.[5] If we do not reject the possibility of such an interpretation completely, then it is at least to be subject to the greatest care and prudence, and only after we have determined first of all the biblical context and the historical background.

Alhertz[6] offers the ingenious proposal that the new-born child taken to heaven is an allusion to the son of the emperor Domitian, who died at the age of six years, and who appears on some coins as climbing up to a heavenly throne and playing with seven stars. C. Brütsch[7] speaks of a peculiarity of the Semitic language patterns discovered by J. Jeremias,[8] and consisting in the practice of mentioning only the beginning and the end of an action without taking into consideration the time in between. S. Lyonnet[9] calls attention to the double meaning which is undeniably characteristic of the word *hypsoun* in the fourth Gospel; to be lifted up on the cross and glorified (III: 14; XII: 32-34); thus the death of Christ is seen as an exaltation which is a prelude to the glorification properly so called, which is His heavenly glorification. Likewise the phrase "Was caught up to God" (*hērpasthē*) of Apocalypse XII: 5 refers to "both a violent death

---

4 Cf. in the same sense R. E. MURPHY, *An Allusion to Mary in the Apocalypse*, Theological Studies, 1949, p. 569.

5 *L'Apocalypse*, Paris, 1933, Excursus XXIX, pp. 187-199.

6 *Botschaft des Neuen Testaments*, I Band, II Halbband, Zürich, 1952, p. 352.

7 Clarté sur l'Apocalypse, Genève, 1955, p. 132, note 10 A.

8 *Die Gleichnisse Jesu*, Zürich, 1947, p. 110.

9 *Biblica*, 1957, p. 207: Review of the work of L. CERFAUX and J. CAMBIER, *L'Apocalypse de Saint Jean lue aux Chrétiens*, Paris, 1955. Cf. in the same sense, but with "perhaps," B. J. LeFROIS, op. cit., pp. 166-167.

and at the same time to a beatific ecstasy." This would explain the apparent anomaly of an allusion to the Ascension not preceded by a mention of Calvary.

Allo proposes some fine theological insights, which are well worth considering.[10] "How can the victorious and triumphant Messiah allow Himself to be represented as a new-born child? It can be only insofar as He is identfied with His faithful and His work. Recall that the eschatological point of view dominates this entire vision, the Gospel accounts being no more than a point of departure, or, as it were, the beginning of the *Novissima tempora*, with the days of struggle and glory which are to intervene until the day of the last judgment. Thus the life of Jesus as man can be considered in the historical realization of the messianic work, only as that of the *first-born*, or the *first fruits* of redeemed humanity. This explains why there is no mention of His ministry or of His death, this being implicit in the description of His victory, as the condition required for His being raised up to heaven. Jesus is the author of salvation; His life, death and Resurrection are its cause. However, all the events of His earthly existence are no more than the initial phase, the birth, so to speak, of the life of the mystical and total Christ. Rather than even a phase, these events are but an instant, which is decisive. This is the aspect under which the seer of the Apocalypse envisions these works of Christ. He had no need to turn to a Jewish source to find an image of the Messiah, having Jesus Himself, Who is infinitely superior to any possible symbol.

ARGUMENTS FOR A METAPHORICAL BIRTH OF THE MESSIAH

Allo's remarks are enlightening. However, they seem to us insufficient to justify the omission of a central mystery, the one which primitive Christianity held as inseparable from the Resurrection, i.e., the saving Passion, which serves as a necessary prelude to the Resurrection. Besides, this explanation, as well as many others of the same kind, which could be mentioned, not to mention the special objections which they occasion, all come up against a fundamental difficulty: the Apocalypse author's

---

10 *L'Apocalypse,* p. 193.

description of the birth of the Messiah is not all in conformity with the birth of Christ in Bethlehem.[11]

It seems somewhat surprising that the dragon should stand before the woman, planning to devour her child. Pagan parallels may be interesting, but they fail to convince us of any such extra-biblical source for this image (e. gr., Leto hears Apollo, and is threatened by the serpent Python), or to explain it adequately. Herod's plot to kill the child Jesus [12] can hardly be proposed as a parallel, since the slaughter of the innocents was not accompanied by a lifting of Jesus to heaven. Furthermore, it is an evident fact that the infancy narratives of both Matthew's and Luke's gospels have no apparent part in the johannine tradition.

It is especially inconceivable that the Apocalypse, major part of the johannine tradition as it is, (which is admitted by most, even by those who refuse to accept it as from the same hand as that of the Gospel writer) should depart from this tradition at this crucial point, by bringing the devil upon the scene right from the beginning of the Savior's earthly life.

According to the Synoptics, the devil enters into contact with Jesus at the beginning of His public ministry, shortly after His Baptism in the Jordan river. The fourth Gospel's notion is quite different; it passes by the temptations in the desert and even among Jesus' miracles there is no mention of any case of diabolical possession. John obviously wished to center the reader's attention on Satan only in the Passion stage of his Gospel. It is only at this moment, when "the prince of this world comes" (XIV: 30) that Christ places Himself in opposition to him, and

---

11 By contrast, the going up to heaven can refer only to Christ's Ascension; it surely is not an adaptation of a Jewish image, according to which the Messiah would remain after his birth, hidden in a secret place until the time appointed for his appearance. It is Christ's glorification which established Him as Lord, giving Him dominion over the whole world, as it is said in Ps. II (quoted in this Apocalypse passage). The Ascension, described by a verb in the passive voice and implicitly related to Elias' ascension to heaven, is presented as a taking up (Acts I: 2; II: 22; I. Tm III: 16).

12 Cf. H. J. HOLTZMANN, *Briefe und Offenbarung des Johannes*, (Dritte Auflage besorgt von W. Bauer), Tübingen, 1908, p. 415. A. WIKENHAUSER, *Offenbarung des Johannes*, Regensburg, 1949, p. 84. M. Jugie, who thinks that the Woman of the Apocalypse is primarily the Blessed Virgin Mary, as a figure or type of the Church, sees the painful childbirth as "the interior pangs which Mary underwent because of her Son from

wins the final victory. John sees the Passion as the conflict *par excellence* between Jesus and Satan.[13]

Another surprising element of the description of the woman of Apocalypse XII is the emphasis which the writer places upon her childbirth pains: "And being with child, she cried out in her travail, and was in the anguish of delivery." (verse 2). In the Greek text the verbs are in the present tense, indicating prolonged suffering.[14] Elsewhere in the Apocalypse the words *basanizō, basanizein* (IX: 5; XI: 10; XIV: 10; 11; XVIII: 7; 10; 15; XX: 10) refer to the extraordinary pains or torments which God inflicts upon the evil, the demons or the damned. Such a meaning obviously does not apply here, but it is a fact that in the LXX, the New Testament, the Apocrypha, the papyri and the writings of the Fathers, there is not a single case in which the verb *basanizō* is used to refer to the pains of childbirth.[15] The same applies to the profane Greek writings, with one slight exception of negligible importance.[16] Besides, the participle *basanizomenē* is introduced here as a foreign element, recalling the Old Testament,[17] which indicates all the more that its use is unusual and deliberate.

This deliberate intention of the author to emphasize the

---

the day of the Annunciation to His Resurrection and Ascension" (*La Mort et l'Assomption de la Sainte Vierge, Étude historico-doctrinale*, Città del Vaticano, 1944, p. 26; cf. also P. Jugie's chapter on the Assumption in *Maria, Études sur la Sainte Vierge*, (sous la direction d'Hubert du MANOIR), t. I, Paris, 1949, pp. 625-626). J. F. Bonnefoy would prefer to exclude any ecclesiological interpretation of Apocalypse XII, holding that the Woman is none other than Mary, and that her child is "only the historical Christ, but with that of the Mystical Christ, i.e., of the "rest of the offspring" of Mary (v. 17), who are all Christians, or all the just of all time" (*Les interprétations ecclésiologiques du chapitre XII de l'Apocalypse*, in *Marianum, Ephemerides Mariologiae*, 1947, p. 221).

13 C. K. BARRETT, *The Gospel according to St. John*, London, 1955, p. 392.

14 Cf. F. CEUPPENS, *De Mariologia Biblica*, Romae, 1951, p. 203.

15 Cf. B. J. LeFROIS, p. 143.

16 This exception is a short poem, in which the word *Basanos* is applied to a dog wounded in such a way that help will be very painful and will require considerable assistance; cf. B. J. LeFROIS, p. 143.

17 As we shall have occasion to see below, there is question of the fusion of Is. XXVI: 17 and LXVI: 7. The Apocalypse author's addition is clearly indicated in NESTLE'S Greek New Testament.

pains of childbirth is as much more significant as it is in sharp contrast to the radiant description of the woman, clothed with the sun, the moon under her feet like a pedestal, and her head crowned with twelve stars.

For all these reasons, it seems necessary to conclude that the author, in expressing his thought in this way, has something extraordinary in view, which he presents in the language of imagery (the woman herself is an allegory, cf. below); therefore he must mean something different from the physical sufferings of ordinary childbirth. Still less is it likely that he should be thinking of the historical event of the birth of Jesus. Allo himself recognizes this frankly: "These pains could hardly refer to the joyous virgin birth of Bethlehem." Again he says, "That the woman gives birth amid such pains, is a *characteristic which relates the scene to Christ who is identified with His work, the rebirth of humanity*".[18] These last words (in italics) are an implicit affirmation that the childbirth pains are intelligible only in relation to the mystery of Calvary.

Therefore the fact that in the fourth Gospel the devil (who in Apocalypse XII waits ready to devour the woman's child) sees his function restricted almost exclusively to the Passion, and the Apocalypse author's placing in relief the cruel sufferings of childbirth, lead us naturally to interpret this passage as follows: *The messianic birth of the Apocalypse refers directly not to the birth of Christ at Bethlehem, but to the mystery of Easter morning: the pains of childbirth correspond to Calvary.* This interpretation safeguards and even places singular emphasis upon the traditional inseparable union of the mysteries of the Cross and of the Resurrection, which union is particularly dear in the Apocalypse author; cf. I: 18: "I was dead, and behold me living forevermore"; and II: 8: "Thus says the first and the last, he who was dead and is alive." This also explains how and why Christ going up to heaven is represented as a new-born child.

It seems surprising that so far this exegesis of Apocalypse XII has had few defenders,[19] in spite of the many good arguments in support of it. We might add to these arguments, the following: The text of the Apocalypse which describes the pains of childbirth is an allusion to two passages from Isaia (XXVI: 17 and

---

18 *L'Apocalypse*, p. 178.

19 W. H. Brownlee suggests this briefly in passing, in *New Testament Studies*, November 1956, p. 29, note 2.

LXVI: 7), both of which refer to the metaphorical childbirth which the people of God undergo. The first of these texts (*hōs hē ōdinousa... epi tē ōdini autēs ekraxen*) mentions the crying out which accompanies the pain of childbirth. As Msgr. Cerfaux has noted,[20] the second passage (*prin tēn ōdinousan tekein, prin elthein ton tonon tōn ōdinōn, exephygen kai eteken arsen....*), provides the background of the two elements of the birth of the male child and the flight into the desert, (*eteken hyion arsen... kai hē gynē exephygen*).

These references seem to prove the almost universal conviction of exegetes that the woman is essentially an allegorical figure. Another logical conclusion from these references is that the childbirth itself must be allegorical and thus distinct from that of Bethlehem.

The fourth Gospel supports this exegesis, and even sheds some new light on it. In the Discourse following the Last Supper, Jesus speaks thus to His disciples of the sadness of the coming Passion and the joy to which it will lead:

> A little while (*mikron*) and you shall not see me, and again a little while and you shall see me. Amen, amen, I say to you, that you shall weep and lament, but the world shall rejoice; and you shall be sorrowful, but your sorrow shall be turned into joy. A woman about to give birth has sorrow, because her hour has come. But when she has brought forth the child, she no longer remembers the anguish for her joy that a man is born into the world. And you therefore have sorrow now; but I will see you again, and your heart shall rejoice, and your joy no one shall take from you. (XVI: 19-22)

Curiously enough, the two passages of Isaias (XXVI: LXVI) which the Apocalypse author uses in XII, are also present here in the Discourse account: The phrase, "I will see you again, and your heart shall rejoice," is taken almost verbatim from Isaias LXVI: 14; *opsesthe, kai charēsetai hymōn hē kardia*. The phrase, "Again a little while" recalls the little while (LXX: *mikron hoson hoson*) of Isaias XXVI: 20 that God's anger is to last before giving way to the birth of a new people.

---

20 *La vision de la femme et du dragon de l'Apocalypse en rélation avec le protévangile, Eph. Theol. Lov.*, 1955, p. 29.

But we must explain the exegesis which results from these literary similarities. Jesus' words in the fourth Gospel passage just quoted (XVI: 19-22) mean more than simply the limited idea that the sadness of His disciples will give way to joy, just as the woman's childbirth pains give way to the joy of having brought a man into the world. As Mollat observes,[21] the biblical passages to which Christ refers signify the painful birth of a new world. The fourth Gospel refers to the death of Jesus (cf. John XIII: 1; XIX: 28; 30), the "end" and the childbirth pains which the synoptic Apocalypse mentions in Mark XIII: 7; 8; 13; and parallel passages. The Savior indicates that His Passion will be a sort of childbirth, and that his sufferings will continue to perdure as long as His disciples will continue to reflect them in themselves. Westcott insists that this is the meaning of the particle *oun* (therefore) which introduces the application of this image to the disciples:

> The application of the image (*therefore*) clearly indicates that something more is intended by it than the mere passage of the disciples through suffering to joy. The proper idea of birth-throes is not that of the transition from suffering to joy, but *suffering as the necessary condition and preparation for joy*. Under this aspect, the disciples in some sense occupied *the position of the mother*. It was their office, as the representatives of the Church, to realize the Christ of the Resurrection and present Him to the world (comp. Rev. XII: 2 ff).[22]

W. H. Brownlee [23] quotes Chamberlain, saying that the Apostles taken as a group are compared to a woman in labor, and that her child, called *anthrōpos*, must be the risen Christ Himself, the new man of the messianic era. Recall also that the vocation of the people of God in the old Covenant was to give to the world, by a sort of childbirth, the Savior and the eschatological salvation. Furthermore, in the gospels, the apostles have the role of the Remnant, through which, as the prophets said,

21 *L'Évangile et les Épîtres de saint Jean (Bible de Jérusalem)*, Paris, 1953, p. 171, note b.

22 *The Gospel according to St. John*, London, 1957, p. 233.

23 *Messianic Motifs of Qumran and the New Testament*, in *New Testament Studies*, November 1956, p. 29.

the chosen people was to fulfill its lofty mission.[24] Brownlee suggests further[25] that in the mind of John, the statement "Behold the man" in XIX: 5 could be Pilate's unintentional declaration that a new man has been born into the world (an interesting observation!)

It is undeniable, and universally acknowledged, that primitive Christianity regarded the Resurrection of Christ as a sort of birth. This is why the early Church applied to this mystery the psalm verse, "Thou art my son; this day I have begotten thee" (Ps. II: 7). The application of this text to the Resurrection is affirmed in Acts XV: 33,[26] and perhaps also in Rom. I: 4; Heb. I: 5; V: 5. And immediately after mentioning the birth of the child, our Apocalypse passage repeats a verse from the same psalm, "He is to rule all nations with a rod of iron" (Ps. II: 9). It is tempting to think that the messianic birth of Apocalypse XII is to be interpreted also in the light of Ps. II.

What has been said should suffice to show that it is entirely legitimate to apply to the Passion and Resurrection of Jesus the image of pains and childbirth. We might cite some other texts in relation to this image.

The title "first-born from among the dead" which St. Paul gives to Christ (Col. I: 18) and which the Apocalypse author takes up and modifies slightly (I: 5), might indicate (but not certainly) that Jesus' Resurrection was a birth.[27] The same idea comes forth clearly from the fourth Gospel passage in which Christ, shortly before his death, compares Himself to a grain of wheat (XII: 24), which must die in order to bear fruit (cf. I Cor. XV: 36).

In Acts II: 24 Peter declares that God raised Jesus up from the dead "having loosed the sorrows of hell" (*lysas tas odinas tou thanatou*). The expression is taken from the Greek version

---

24 Cf. on this point, G. GLOEGE, *Reich Gottes und Kirche im Neuen Testament*, Gütersloh, 1929, pp. 244-245.

25 *Ibid.*, p. 29.

26 This is the idea of several exegetes, especially of Dom DUPONT, *Les Actes des Apôtres* (*Bible de Jérusalem*), Paris, 1958, p. 25. Père Spicq prefers to see a relationship between the Incarnation and the two texts of the Epistle to the Hebrews, although he does not exclude the Resurrection.

27 L. B. RADFORD suspects that this is a faint echo of Ps. II: 7, applied here to Christ's Resurrection, *The Epistle to the Colossians and the Epistle to Philemon*, London, 1931, p. 179.

of Ps. XVIII: 6 (cf. also Ps. XCVI: 8; 2 Samuel XXII: 6). The Masoretic text speaks of the bonds of death, but the same Hebrew word, with the vowel points slightly changed, can mean the pains of childbirth; hence the text. In referring to the LXX text, could Peter have thought of Christ's death as a painful childbirth? This is difficult to affirm, especially since Peter probably spoke this in Aramaic. But the idea could have been in the mind of the author of Acts. The phrase *odines tou thanatou* occurs also once in a sepulchral inscription.[28] However, we do not think this line of argument is worth pursuing too much.

A POSSIBLE EXPLANATION; THE METAPHORICAL MESSIANIC BIRTH IN QUMRAN

The interpretation which we have proposed for Apocalypse XII: 4-6 presupposes that an allegorical woman could be regarded as the mother of the personal Messiah. Recently, however, more and more exegetes have tended to deny this possibility. They find support for their Marian interpretation of the Church in the observation of Tobac [29] that, "Although the prophets may speak at times of Sion giving birth to a holy people, (Is. LXVI: 7), they never show her giving the world an individual Messiah." Braun writes, "As a personification of the people of God, the figure of the woman fits well in Apocalypse XII: 17, which refers to a collective posterity, but not in XII: 5, which speaks of her posterity as limited to a single male child".[30]

True enough, no Jewish text speaks clearly of the people of God personified, as the mother of an individual Messiah. The Testament of Joseph (XIX: 11) has the Messiah (the Lamb of God) being born of Levi and of Juda, but it says nothing of his mother: XIX: 8 would be more explicit if the Virgin who gives birth to the spotless lamb were a symbol of Levi or of Juda, but this is not certain in the text. Besides, we cannot eliminate the possibility of a later Christian re-editing of the passage.

---

28 Cf. F. PREISIGKE, *Sammelbuch Griechischer Urkunden aus Aegypten*, no. 4312, *THNESKŌ D'AGNES (I PIKROTATOIS) ŌDINAS PROPHYGOUSA SYNAIMOU'S.*

29 *Les Prophètes d'Israel*, I, Lierre, 1919, p. 267.

30 *La Mère des Fideles*, Tournai, Paris, 1954, p. 139. P. Braun has already said that this affirmation is too strong; (*La Femme vêtue du soleil*, in *Revue Thomiste*, 1955, p. 644.)

The Fourth Book of Esdras (IX: 43 ff.; X: 43 ff.), following
Isaias LXVI: 7, speaks of Sion metaphorically bearing "a male
child" after thirty years of barrenness. However, it is difficult
to identify this child. We are not certain that it is the Messiah;
it could be the people of Israel.[31] If we make much of the angel
in the passage, we might come to say that the child refers to
the temple cult.[32]

The Dead Sea Scrolls have something to offer here. One of
the texts discovered at Qumran seems to draw our attention here,
i.e., lines 6-18 of the third column in the scroll of hymns.[33]
Many exegetes see here a reference to the birth of the Messiah.[34]
The child whose birth is described here, is called, not only,
"man-child," (line 9) (cf. Isaias LXVI: 7), but also *"that marvel
of might and mind,"* a clear reference to the Davidic Messiah
of Isaias IX: 5-6.[35] Furthermore, the phrase "heavy with child"
may be an allusion to Isaias VII: 14.

---

31 Cf. L. GRY, *Les dires prophètiques d'Esdras,* Paris, 1938, II, p. 323.

32 This is the opinion of A. LODS, *Histoire de la litterature hebraique
et juive des origines a la ruine de l'État juif,* Paris, 1950, p. 992.

33 Among the many studies already dedicated to this text, cf. especially
A. DUPONT - SOMMER, *La Mère du Messie et la Mère de l'Aspic in
un hymne de Qumrân,* R.H.R., 1955, pp. 174-188; the same author,
Le Livre des Hymnes découvert près de la Mer Morte, Semitica, VII, Paris,
1957, pp. 39-41; G. VERMES, *Les Manuscrits du Désert de Juda,* 2e édit.,
Paris, 1954, pp. 193-194; M. DELCOR, *Un Psaume messianique de
Qumrân. Mélanges Bibliques redigés en l'honneur de A. ROBERT,* Paris,
1957, pp. 334-340; H. BARDTKE, *Die Loblieder von Qumrân,* T.L.Z.,
1956 (No 10), p. 592; J. V. CHAMBERLAIN, *Another Qumrân Thanksgiving Psalm,* J.N.E.S., 1955, pp. 32-41; cf. also the same author, *Further
Elucidations of a Messianic Thanksgiving Psalm from Qumrân,* J.N.E.S.,
1955, pp. 181-182; J. BAUMGARTEN and M. MANSOOR, *Studies in the
New Hodayot,* J.B.L., 1955, pp. 188-195; J. LIGHT, *Megilloth Hahodayot,*
Jerusalem, 1957; O. BETZ, *Die Geburt der Gemeinde durch den Lehrer,
New Testament Studies,* July 1957, pp. 314-326; cf. also the same author's
article: *Das Volk Seiner Kraft: zur Auslegung der Qumrân-hodajah III,
1-18, New Testament Studies,* October 1958, pp. 67-75.

34 This messianic interpretation is accepted by A. DUPONT -
SOMMER, M. Delcor, J. V. Chamberlain, J. Licht, as well as W. H.
BROWNLEE, *Messianic Motifs of Qumrân and the New Testament,
New Testament Studies,* November 1956, pp. 12-30; Th. G. GASTER,
The Dead Sea Scriptures in English translation, New York, 1956, pp.
135-137.

35 The author cites the annotated French translation of Dupont-

However, the birth described here is a metaphorical one. The woman who bears the Messiah is "amid throes of death ... amid pangs of hell." (lines 8-9). These two expressions, taken from II Samuel XXII: 4-6, symbolize a mortal danger, which seems, according to the beginning of the hymn, to be due to the persecution brought by the wicked.

The woman giving birth is thus an allegorical person. Who is she? The "I" of line 7 causes difficulty, because it leads the reader to believe that the author is describing only his own personal trials. Nevertheless, the reference to the Messiah, which we have mentioned has led to the conclusion that the Mother is Sion or Israel (Brownlee), or, more exactly, "The congregation of the just, exposed to persecution by the wicked" (Dupont-Sommer). The psalmist, in his way, would compare his sufferings with the pain of the allegorical woman, or else he would present the "I" as collective, representing the community (Delcor).

This passage, understood thus, is close to Apoc. XII. The Apocalypse speaks of three persons, the woman, the Messiah and the dragon, which is called "the ancient serpent, he who is called the devil and Satan" (XII: 9). The same three persons are in the Qumran hymn; besides the woman with child and the "*marvel of might and mind*," the text introduces the viper, or asp ('*ph'h*), lines 12; 17; 18. This word occurs three times in the Bible, in Isaias XXX: 6, LIX: 6; Job XX: 16. If this use of the word in the hymn refers to the evil one, then doubtless it is an allusion to Gen. III, and is certainly the same as the ancient serpent of the Apocalypse. Line 18 seems to confirm this by substituting for the "woman pregnant with the asp" of line 12 the "seeds of worthless things".[36]

Thus, one way or the other, the Messiah is born at the price of terrible pain; he is called "male child" in reference to Isaias LXVI: 7, and is contrasted to the diabolical serpent of the Garden of Eden. Since the hymn of Qumran has the woman and her childbirth as metaphorical, it seems to offer support to our exegesis.

Still, we hesitate to insist too much on this similarity, because

---

Sommer. Th. H. Gaster, *The Dead Sea Scriptures in English Translation*, London, 1957, p. 204, note 8, offers this as an approximate translation, proposing more literally, "One who is wonderful in counsel, a hero divine." (Tr.)

36 Cf. GASTER, ibid., note 10.

it is based upon an interpretation that is not entirely certain. O. Betz,[37] for example openly opposes it; and according to him the woman is not a group but an individual, the Teacher of Righteousness, while the child represents the collectivity of the members of the community. There would thereby be an allusion to Num. X: 12; the teacher would be a second Moses, leader of the community. The translation would be, not *"marvel of might and mind"* but *"Wonderful counsellor, people born of divine power."* The passage thus would be related not so much to Apocalypse XII as to some like I Th. II: 7 ff., or Gal. IV: 19, in which St. Paul compares himself to a mother.

A. S. van der Woude is strongly opposed to the messianic interpretation.[38] According to him the phrase of Isaias, "Wonderful Counsellor" should not be applied to the Messiah, because the rabbinic texts never refer to the Messiah in such terms. Thus the author of the Qumran hymn would have changed the text of Isaias IX: 5 deliberately: line ten of the hymn would be "Wonderful, that is, God, counsels with His power, and saves man from the waves." Consequently, the woman who bears the child would be not the mother of the Messiah, but merely a symbol of the community, with the persecutions taken as eschatological trials.

Very probably we have a long ways to go before the last word can be said on this difficult problem. We prefer to leave to specialists on the Qumran material the explanation of the hymn. Whatever may be the eventual outcome of discussion of this question, we should be most circumspect in comparing the Qumran hymn and Apocalypse XII: the resemblances which come to the fore may be due to no more than the using of the same biblical sources or the same traditions, but this in itself is no proof that the meaning is the same in both cases.

(2) The Mother of the Messiah

Given all that we have determined so far, we should like to proceed further and to attempt to explain the whole grouping of the elements contained in chapter XII. However, we prefer to avoid repeating the things which are found in most commen-

---

37 Cf. the articles in *New Testament Studies* cited above (note)

38 *Die Messianischen Vorstellungen der Gemeinde von Qumrân*, Assen, 1957, pp. 144-156.

taries, and to concern ourselves especially with the Woman, the Mother of the Messiah.

The woman, Mother of the Messiah, is described as a "Great sign appearing in heaven." In the LXX the word *sēmeion* is equivalent to the Hebrew *'o th* and means either celestial phenomena (Genesis I: 14; IX: 12), or indications which God gives to men of His presence and His action among them (e. gr., the miracles of the Exodus in Ex. VII: 13 etc.). Particularly the sign proposed by Isaias in Chapter VII, has for its object, as does the sign of Apocalypse XII, a woman bearing the Messiah.

However, given that the sign of the Apocalypse appears "in heaven," we might recall the "sign from heaven" which the Synoptics mention (Matthew XVI: 1; Mark VIII: 11), or the "sign in heaven" (*to sēmeion ... en tō ouranō*) of Matthew XXIV: 30. Should we conclude from these verbal similarities that the seer of the Apocalypse has before his eyes not the interior of heaven, but only a sign, projected, as it were on the vault of heaven? This is possible, although we do not consider it the most natural interpretation.[39] In any case we can already suspect that the sign in question (like that of Matthew XXIV: 30) is an eschatological one, referring to the perfect inauguration of the Kingdom of God.

John presents the woman surrounded by heavenly grandeur; clothed in the sun, the moon under her feet, and a crown of twelve stars on her head. It is at least possible that this description may have been influenced by the heavenly raiment often attributed to some gods and goddesses, especially to Isis and Cybele.[40] However, we should take note of the biblical and Jewish parallels as well. Swete, Charles and others often refer to Joseph's second dream in Genesis XXXVII: 9: "I had another

---

39 Cf. in the same sense J. Coppens, *Eph. Theol. Lov.*, 1947, pp. 18-19; as long as the heavenly temple is open in XI: 19 it seems only normal to place in it the woman of XII: 1. Cf. also B. J. LeFROIS, *The Woman Clothed with the Sun*, pp. 82-91.

40 On the possible relationship of this text with Cybele, cf. P. TOUILLEUX, *L'Apocalypse et les cultes de Domitien et de Cybele*, Paris, 1935; for the opposite opinion cf. E. B. ALLO, in *R.B.*, 1936, pp. 591-592.

dream. . . . The sun, the moon and eleven stars were worshiping me." In this Genesis passage the sun and the moon represent Joseph's father and mother, and the eleven stars are his eleven brothers. It is possible that this may be the Apocalypse author's intended allusion (which would certainly help us to understand the crown of twelve stars).

Many authors (Bousset, Zahn, Lohmeyer, Behm, Wikenhauser) think that the stars probably represent the twelve tribes of the old or the new Israel born of the sons of Jacob. We might recall that in the letters at the beginning of the Apocalypse the "angels" of the various churches are symbolized by stars, and that Jesus, St. James and the Apocalypse author all speak of the twelve tribes of the new Israel (Matthew XIX: 28; Luke XXII: 30; James I: 1; Apocalypse XXI: 12). Boismard holds against J. Le Frois [41] that, "It is certain that in the Apocalypse the number twelve is constantly related to the twelve tribes of Israel or to the twelve apostles (the identical number in either case)." From this data we might surmise that the woman of Apocalypse XII could be the ideal mother of the new people of God. Still, even though the text of Genesis XXXVII: 9 may explain the reference to twelve stars, it says not a word about any radiant woman or of her relationship to the sun and the moon. We need to look elsewhere.

We are not inclined to agree very readily with Charles, Swete, and the many other authors who refer at this juncture to the text of the Testament of Nephthali (V: 3-4). In it Nephthali contemplates the sun and the moon over Jerusalem: "Levi took hold of the sun, and Juda of the moon, and both went up with them. And since Levi was as the sun, a young man gave him twelve palm branches. Juda shone like the moon, with twelve rays of light under his feet.[42] Interesting though it may be, especially if, as Charles holds (Revelation, volume 1, page 316), the twelve rays of light refer to the twelve tribes, still this text says no more about an allegorical radiant woman than the Genesis passage to which we referred above. Hence it can hardly be called a parallel text.

The sixtieth chapter of Isaias has a much closer parallel, than

---

41 Cf. R.B., 1955, pp. 295 (review of the book by B. J. LeFROIS).
42 The author quotes the French translation of J. BONSIRVEN, La Bible apocryphe en marge de l'Ancien Testament, Paris, 1953, p 143 (Tr.).

those so far adduced, although strangely enough it has nonetheless managed to escape the attention of most exegetes. There, Jerusalem, appears suddenly as a woman, the spouse of Jahweh and mother of the eschatological people of God, as a bright sunrise, like the lights of God Himself.

> No longer shall the sun be your light by day, nor the brightness of the moon shine upon you at night; the Lord shall be your light forever, your God shall be your glory. No longer shall your sun go down, or your moon withdraw, for the Lord will be your light forever, and the days of your mourning shall be at an end.
>
> Isaias LX: 19-20

Immediately after, the prophet states that this new Jerusalem shall give birth to a numerous and bold people, the people of the favored era (LX: 21-22), the blessed posterity (*sperma*) of God (LXI: 9; LXV: 23).

There are a number of reasons which compel us to conclude that this passage is the real point of departure for our Apocalypse text. (For that matter, it seems to be the source also of the description given above, in the Testament of Nephthali). If it is true that there are some differences between the woman of Apocalypse XII and the spouse of the Lamb (Jerusalem) of Chapter XXI,[43] the similarities between them are at least equally striking and as numerous; Fr. Boismard has shown this clearly.[44] The Isaian chapters which describe the ideal Jerusalem, especially chapter LX, are literally lifted out bodily by the Apocalypse author in his description of the new Jerusalem. (Compare XXI: 2a with Isaias LII: 1; XXI: 2b with Isaias XLIX: 18 and LXI: 10; XXI: 3 with Isaias XLIII: 18; XXI: 7 with Isaias LV: 1. Compare especially XXI: 11 with Isaias LX: 1; XXI: 12 with Isaias LXII: 6, XXI: 18-21 with Isaias LIV: 12, and this list hardly proposes to be exhaustive).

We might recall here that we have already had recourse to this vision in Isaias to explain the Apocalypse author's mention of the childbirth pains and of the birth of the male child. The Woman—Jerusalem of these oracles is glorified, and still she gives

---

43 On this question cf. A. M. DUBARLE, *Écriture et Tradition à propos de publications récentes*, in *Istina*, 1957, p. 124.

44 Cf. *R.B.*, 1955, p. 295.

birth. The same paradoxical situation occurs in the Apocalypse. The woman is threatened by the dragon or by the serpent; if this dragon (serpent) is a recollection of the serpent of Genesis, (cf. below), the very name of the dragon which he has in Apocalypse XII recalls the dragon-serpent of the Isaian text, in which the destruction of the enemy by Jahweh either at the beginning (Isaias LI: 9) or at the eschatological time (Isaias XXVII: 1) is placed in close relationship with the restoration of the Woman-Sion. We might also recall here the text in Jer. LI (XXVIII): 34, which is placed on the lips of Jerusalem personified: "Nabuchqdonosor, King of Babylon, has swallowed me like a dragon" (cf. Apocalypse XII: 4).[45]

Another text which many commentators (Allo, Swete, P. H. Carrington, Jugie, Dubarle, Weber, and Touilleux [46] invoke, and which even the liturgy associates beautifully with the Apocalypse passage,[47] is Cant. VI: 10: "Who is this that comes forth fair as the dawn, as beautiful as the moon, as resplendent as the sun, as awe-inspiring as bannered troops?" Dubarle observes that these two passages have in common not only the references to actual elements, but also the elements of a struggle with hostile forces.[48] He says further that there are also some other references to the Canticle in the Apocalypse; many exegetes see a similarity between Cant. V: 2 and Apocalypse III: 20; and between Cant. VII: 12 and Apocalypse XXII: 17.

To our eyes the factor which strengthens the value of this

---

45 The image of the dragon's four horns (v. 3) recalls the fourth beast of the vision of the Son of Man in Daniel (VII: 7), which symbolizes an empire about to be destroyed, as a prelude to the establishment of God's people in the era of grace.

46 Cf. ALLO, L'Apocalypse, p. 176; SWETE, The Apocalypse of St. John, p. 147, Ph. CARRINGTON, The Meaning of the Revelation, New York-Toronto-London, 1931, p. 207; JUGIE, La Mort et L'Assomption de la Sainte Vierge, p. 35; DUBARLE, La Femme couronnée d'étoiles, in Mélanges Bibliques redigés en l'honneur de A. Robert, pp. 517-518; J. J. WEBER, La Vierge Marie dans le Nouveau Testament, Paris, 1954, pp. 121-122; P. TOUILLEUX, L'Apocalypse et les cultes de Domitien et de Cybele, pp. 120-121.

47 In the new office and Mass for the feast of the Assumption of the Blessed Virgin Mary, the Canticle text is used as the Benedictus antiphon, and the Apocalypse passage is the Introit text of the Mass. The Canticle text occurs also in the office of the Apparition of Mary at Lourdes (Feb. 11).

48 La Femme couronnée d'étoiles, p. 517.

parallelism, and also which determines its meaning, is the fact that it is basically the same as Isaias LX: 19-20, upon which the Canticle text also depends. Here too, we think, is one of the many reasons favoring the allegorical interpretation of this mysterious love poem.

We might ask why so many commentators who invoke this text, fail to invoke the passage of Isaias which is its source. The Canticle's dependence on the Isaian oracle is rendered all but compelling by the many other similarities which run in the same vein and which lead to the identifying of the people of God and the beloved, who is fair as the moon, bright as the sun. The beloved is "awe-inspiring as bannered troops," a strange description of a beautiful woman! But it has the same meaning as Isaias IX: 18, "You shall call your walls 'salvation,' and your gates 'praise'." Thus the restored people of God will have nothing more to fear from its enemies, who have brought it such disaster, i.e., from the dragon which "swallowed" it at the time of the exile (Isaias LI: 34). A little before this (VI: 4), the beloved of the Canticle is compared to Thersa, which was the capital of the northern kingdom before the time of Omri, and to Jerusalem, capital of the southern kingdom, "you are as beautiful as Thersa, my beloved, as lovely as Jerusalem." If it is improper to speak of cities in comparison to women, then, on the other hand, "women should not be compared to cities," as Cheyne says,[49] and proceeds on this basis to correct the text, although, critically speaking, it is reliable. Budde suggests that it is a gloss.[50] If the woman is Israel, the text becomes quite clear; she will be beautiful as Thersa and Jerusalem, because they will be one, the two kingdoms of the North and South being eventually joined into one, as they were before the schism. This aspiration is frequent in the prophetic writings (cf. Ez. XXXVII: 15-28; Jer. XXIII: 6; Isaias XI: 11-12, XXVII: 13; XXXIII: 5-6; XLIX: 12-23; Zach. II: 10).[51] Isaias LX describes the beauty of the restored Sion which will come especially from the Temple: "The glory of Lebanon shall come to you; the cypress, the plane, and the pine, to bring beauty to my sanctuary, and glory to the place where

---

49 *Encyclopaedia Biblica*, I, 692, art. Canticles, note.

50 *Das Hohelied*, Tübingen, 1888, in h. 1.

51 Cf. A. FEUILLET, *Le Cantique des Cantiques*, Paris, 1953, pp. 52-53.

I set my feet" (Isaias LX: 19).[52] The bridegroom of the Canticle takes this terminology and transposes it into the language of love poetry: "The beams of our house are cedars; our rafters, cypress." (I:17). The coincidence is so striking that Delitzsch, who generally is hostile to allegory, feels compelled to admit it here.[53] Furthermore, in Isaias LX: 17 Jahweh promises to Jerusalem, his bride, "I will appoint peace your governor, and justice your ruler." He says in Isaias LXVI: 12: "I will spread prosperity over her like a river, and the wealth of the nations like an overflowing forest." The bride in the Canticle is called a Sulamite (VII: 1-2), which is a passive participle of an ancient form meaning "peaceful," which means that she has found (or re-found) peace (i.e., eschatological peace); cf. the appendix to the Canticle: "So now in his eyes, I have become one to be welcomed" (VIII: 10).

From all the foregoing we can conclude that the description of the woman in Apocalypse XII, makes very liberal use of some traditional motifs, taken especially from Isaias LX: 19-20 and Cant. VI: 10, in their descriptions of the ideal people of God in the eschatological era. In the first part of our treatment, we said that the childbirth described in these verses cannot be other than metaphorical, and that the mention of the pains which accompany it is based also upon the same Old Testament context, alluding especially to Isaias LXVI: 7-9.

We agree, therefore, with those commentators who see in the woman of Apocalypse XII *first and foremost a personification of the people of God*. We shall speak below of how and to what extent this passage should be seen in a marian perspective. Still, we are sure that it would be plainly incorrect to say that this marian element is principal in the passage. The woman of the Apocalypse appears, at the beginning of Chapter XII, to have the same essential characteristics as the ideal Sion of which the prophets dreamed and sang: glorified, brightened by a divine radiance, giving birth to messianic salvation. St. Paul follows this

---

52 Because of the transposition of prophetic themes into the language of human love, many exegetes do not appreciate the validity of the allegorical interpretation of the canticle. It is over-obvious merely to stress that the canticle speaks the language of human love.

53 "Der Mystischen Deutung bietet hier Jes. 60, 13 einen gunstigen Anhalt," *Hoheslied*, pp. 38-39 (*In Bibl. Kommentar über das Alte Testament*, Leipzig, 1875).

same prophetic tradition, in writing in his Epistle to the Galatians, citing Isaias LIV: 1: "But that Jerusalem which is above is free, which is our mother. For it is written: 'Rejoice, thou barren, that dost not bear; break forth and cry, thou that dost not travail; for many are the children of the desolate, more than of her that has a husband'" (Gal. IV: 26-27).

BASIC MEANING OF APOCALYPSE XII; ITS RELATIONSHIP TO THE WOMAN, MOTHER OF THE MESSIAH

The Apocalypse author shows the allegorical woman of Chapter XII face to face with a great dragon, which lurks waiting to devour her son as soon as he is born (verse 2-4). A few lines further (verse 9) the dragon appears as "The ancient serpent, he who is called the devil and Satan, who leads astray the whole world." This dragon threatens first of all the woman, then her son, the Messiah, and finally, "the rest of her offspring" (XII: 17). P. Braun [54] and Msgr. Cerfaux [55] have shown that this image is a development of the Protoevangelium of Genesis III, 15, which predicts a fight to the death between the woman and her seed on the one side and the serpent and his on the other. We have nothing to add here to this observation.

The scene of Apocalypse XII: 7-13 is indeed awe-inspiring. A battle rages in heaven, between Michael and his angels and the dragon and his. The dragons are conquered and cast down upon the earth. Then a voice from heaven [56] solemnly proclaims the paradox which is characteristic of the earthly existence of Christ's Church: although God and His Christ are ultimately triumphant, "Through the blood of the Lamb and through the word of their witness" (verse 11), still the times have become more difficult; woe to the wicked, for the devil, "knowing that he has but a short time" (verse 12), will renew his attacks against the Church.

Apocalyptic authors usually show earthly events taking place

---

54 *La Mère des Fidéles*, Paris, 1954, pp. 147-153. Alba House, N. Y., 1965.

55 *La vision de la Femme et du Dragon de l'Apocalypse en rélation avec le Protévangile*, in *Eph. Theol. Lov.*, 1955, pp. 21-33.

56 This voice, which is probably that of the twenty-four elders (cf. Allo, p. 184), speaks of "one brethren" (v. 10); this is one more indication that the elders are glorified men. Cf. *R.B.*, 1958, pp. 5-32, and Ch. I, of this part above.

only after they have been prepared in heaven. It seems to us to follow that this scene is paralleled to the preceding one, dealing with the same events, but considering them now under their heavenly aspect. In Daniel X: 13 and XII: 1, Michael is the protector of the people of God; his victory over the dragon corresponds to the victory of the allegorical woman (The people of God), whom the devil's threats cannot prevent from giving the world its Savior, according to the promises of the messianic prophecies, and especially of the Protoevangelium (Genesis III: 15).

The fourth Gospel supports this exegesis; according to John XII: 31, the moment of Christ's death on the Cross, which corresponds (as we have seen above) to the birth pains mentioned by the Apocalypse, is the exact moment in which the final judgment of the wicked takes place, and in which the Prince of this world is cast down (or cast out).[57] Many exegetes before us have remarked at the similarity between the dragon and his angels cast down in Apocalypse XII: 9, and the prince of this world cast down in John XII: 31. The coincidence is all the more remarkable, given the fact that in either case the defeat of the devil is placed opposite the exaltation of Christ (compare John XII: 30 and Apocalypse XII: 6). We think however, that our interpretation of the birth pains makes this similarity more likely still.

At the dragon's threats, the Woman flees to the desert (vv. 6, 13-14). God has prepared this refuge for her, so that she may be nourished there for "a thousand, two hundred and sixty days," or "for a time and times and a half-time." Another sign of God's intervention is that the woman suddenly is given the two wings of the great eagle, to facilitate her flight "into the wilderness unto her peace" (verse 14). These elements are obviously symbols. But of what?

P. Braun [58] is favorable to a delicate line of argument, which leads to his discovering in this passage an allusion to Mary's Assumption into heaven. He sees in XII: 6 as the place prepared

---

57 Although it has less foundation in the witnesses (Koridethi, many MSS of the Vetus Latina; Syr; Sin; Sahidic; several of the Fathers), still the reading "thrown down" (jeté bas) is retained in the Bible de Jerusalem. The present reading "thrown out" (jeté dehors) could be the result of a harmonizing of such passages as VI: 37; IX: 34 ff.; XV: 6.

58 La Mère des Fidéles, pp. 161-167. Trans., Alba House, N. Y. 1965.

by God (*topon hētoimasmenon apo tou Theou*) not the desert strictly speaking, but a definite and determined place in the desert. In the New Testament the word "prepare" (*hetoimazō*) is often used with an eschatological meaning, and applied both to the preparation which men must undergo in order to come to the possession of heavenly blessing (Matthew XXIV: 44; XXV: 10, Luke XII: 40; Apocalypse XXI: 2), and to the preparation or predestination of these same blessings by God Himself (Mark X: 43, Matthew XX: 23; 25; 34; 44; I Peter I: 5; I Cor. II: 9). The most important text is Jesus' promise in John XIV: 2; "I go to prepare a place for you." We might conclude from this that the "place" which is "prepared" for the Woman of Apocalypse XII is the same as that mentioned in these Gospel texts.

Surely, we must admit that this interpretation is at least not the most obvious one. Even supposing that there is a distinction between the "place prepared" and the desert (which is not at all certain), and that these two places are not synonymous, the fact remains that the "place" is located not "in the Father's house," as the place which Jesus has prepared for His disciples in John XIV, but in the desert. In the Bible, when the desert takes on any religious significance at all, as it does in the Apocalypse, it recalls the crossing of the Sinai desert by the Hebrews, before their entry into the promised land. In the Epistle to the Hebrews, which has a number of affinities to John's Apocalypse, the Christians marching toward their place of rest in eschatological beatitude, are compared to the Israelites marching toward the earthly happiness of the land of Chanaan (Chapters III-IV). Thus the crossing of the desert symbolizes their earthly existence; the entry into the promised land prefigures the heavenly blessedness which awaits them. We can see no other correct way of interpreting the data of the Apocalypse, given this identification of the place prepared by God in the desert, with heaven itself.

We must, of course, be most careful to take into account the immediate context and the scriptural allusions in the passage itself. The woman is given the two wings of the great eagle in order to be able to fly to the desert. This image is a borrowing from Ex. XIX: 4 and from Dt. XXXII: 11, in which Jahweh is pictured as carrying his people through the desert toward the promised land in the same manner as an eagle carrying its young. In Isaias XL: 31 the hope for a new Exodus is linked to the symbol of eagle's wings given to the Israelites who are to be brought back home from the exile. There can be no doubt that this Apocalypse text is a reference to the Exodus accounts. The nourishment prepared for the woman in the place prepared for her by God is a recollection of the Manna. In the fourth Gospel (chapter VI) the miracle of the Manna, which is recalled by the working of the miracle of the loaves (also in the desert), which is a type not of the blessedness of heaven, but of the sacrament of the Eucharist. True enough, just as the *living waters* which refer both to grace and to the happiness of the next world, the symbol of the Manna could also have more than one meaning: in Apocalypse II: 17 it could refer to the heavenly reward rather than to the sacrament.[59] However, the same could hardly be said of Apocalypse XII, because of the chronological precision of the thousand, two hundred sixty days (a time and times and half a time). This period, during which the woman is to be nourished, is taken from Daniel (VII: 25; XII: 7), in which it refers to the length of the persecution of the Jews under Antiochus IV Epiphanes. It refers there to the time of trial which is to precede the final inauguration of the kingdom of God. Briefly, this time symbolizes the very opposite of eternity.

It is entirely normal that the woman's stay in the desert should be marked by both trials and favors from God, for this was exactly the situation of the Hebrews during their crossing of the Sinai desert.

Thus the conclusion seems quite obvious; the woman nourished by God in the desert is the Christian Church, which God nourishes and protects during its earthly wandering, as it awaits the Parousia. The eschatological banquet in the New Testament is a prelude to the heavenly banquet of the Parousia (cf. I Cor. XI: 20; Mark XIV: 25 and parallel texts).

Thus, after having given Christ to men, the people of God of the old Covenant has become the Christian Church. The author of the Apocalypse, like all the authors of the New Testament writings, is persuaded that the clear separation of the two economies of the old and new Testaments does not at all prevent the one from being a continuation of the other, since they are both the progressive fulfillment of a simple divine plan.

After attacking in vain the Messiah and His mother, the woman, the dragon goes to wage war with the Christians who

---

59 Cf. F. M. BRAUN, *La Femme vêtue du soleil*, p. 658. For the various meanings of the symbol of living waters, cf. Apoc. VII: 17; XXI: 6.

are "the rest of her offspring" (XII: 17). We should not be surprised at the distinction made here between the group as such (the woman) and the members of the group (the offspring). The same kind of distinction occurs in the prophetic texts between the spouse of Jahweh, or the ideal Jerusalem, and the Israelites, taken as her children; in the New Testament it occurs between the Church and the faithful.[60] The dragon's attack can neither destroy nor harm the Church as such, for it shares in the victory of its Founder (cf., besides the johannine texts, also Matthew XVI: 19-20). The faithful on the other hand, as long as they remain here below, are subject to the devil's threats and attacks, but they are also sure of winning if their faith is firm.

Here we must stop to ask whether we can content ourselves with seeing in the symbols of the Apocalypse no more than a general significance such as we have shown, or whether we should see in these figurative events any definite allusion to the vicissitudes of the primitive Christian Church. We prefer this latter hypothesis, and think that such allusion can be no other than a point of departure, or a partial explanation, given the fact that the sojourn of the woman in the desert is to last all the time of trial until the Parousia itself. This, we think, justifies this second alternative.

Chapter XIII brings the reader face to face with the persecution which the Roman empire directed against the Church. Furthermore, as Allo says,[61] this terrible trial is predicted from the beginning of chapter XII; when the dragon is shown standing on the sand of the sea, the sea (the West) represents the great pagan force of the West, of which the dragon is to avail himself. Likewise, it seems that the preceding could refer to the first persecution which Christ's Church suffered, and which, according to the Acts of the Apostles, was directed against the Church of Jerusalem.

We can observe a certain parallelism between Apocalypse XII and Acts XII. We read in Acts XII of the persecution of Herod

60 In Osee II: 4-7, the children of Israel are called upon to protest against their mother; in Deuteronomy, the emphasis alternates between the personification and the concrete reality, hence the alternation between *thou* and *ye* (singular and plural); the Canticle makes the same kind of distinction between Jerusalem, the spouse of Jahweh, and the daughters of Jerusalem.

61 *L'Apocalypse*, pp. 203-204.

Agrippa, which led to the death of St. James and to the imprison-
ment of St. Peter. Protected by God, and borne on the two wings
of the great eagle, the woman escapes the dragon, just as, long
before, the chosen people had escaped the oppression of their
Egyptian masters. Likewise, "during the days of the unleavened
bread" (Acts XII: 3), Peter is delivered miraculously from prison.
A. Strobel [62] has shown that the terminology used by the author
of Acts to describe this miracle is probably designed to recall
the night of the Passion (compare Acts XII: 6 with Exodus XII:
12; Acts XII: 7 with Exodus XII: 11; Acts XII: 8 with Exodus
XII: 11). Leaving his prison, Peter "departed and went to another
place" (Acts XII: 17), which is not definite (*eis heteron topon*),
but which would be safe from pursuers. Thus this "other place"
corresponds well with the "place" prepared by God as a refuge
for the woman in her flight from the dragon. The dragon pur-
sues her in vain; he "cast out of his mouth after the woman
water like a river," (Apocalypse XII: 15). Herod sends after
Peter; when he is not found, he orders the execution of the guards
who have failed to keep him in prison (Acts XII: 19). The earth
swallows up the river which the dragon sends after the woman
(Apocalypse XII: 16); this is an allusion to the punishment
meted out to Core, Dathan and Abiram in Num. XVI: 32. Dubarle
thinks that the biblical details of the description of the woman [63]
make this also an allusion to the famous passage of the Canticle
of Canticles, "Deep waters cannot quench love, nor floods sweep
it away" (VIII: 7). Herod for his part, is punished too; "An
angel of the Lord struck him down,—and he was eaten by worms
and died" (Acts XII: 23).

---

62 *Passa-Symbolik und Passa-Wunder in Act. XII, 3 fl., New Testament Studies.* April 1958, pp. 210-215.

63 *La Femme couronnée d'étoiles* p. 518. We are not quite convinced
of the certainty of this allusion to the Canticle, although it does become
more probable, and more interesting as well, given the fact that the image
of a river or of rushing waters as a symbol of hostile forces is a rather
traditional element of biblical language. Especially in the prophetic
writings it refers to the dangers threatening the people of God (Is.
VIII: 6-8; XVII: 13; Jer. LI: 55...) In particular, A. ROBERT, has
emphasized the resemblance in vocabulary between Cant. VIII: 6-7, and
Is. XLIII: 2, in which Jahweh promises to protect his people and to save
them from exile: "When you pass through the water, I will be with you;
in the rivers you shall not drown. When you walk through fire, you shall
not be burned, the flames shall not consume you."

We present these historical allusions, of course, with the greatest reserve, fully conscious that they are purely hypothetical. Others could be adduced.[64] In any case, such veiled recollections, which are really clues, are entirely in conformity with the style of the apocalyptic authors. If these similarities which we have indicated are real, they are only so many more indications of the close relationship which we have observed between the Lukan texts and the johannine tradition. Still in all, these allusions are not essential to the Apocalypse, which is intended as a Christian philosophy of history, giving the ultimate meaning of the ancient prophecies.

THE MARIAN INTERPRETATION OF APOCALYPSE XII

So far we have explained Apocalypse XII without applying it to the Blessed Virgin Mary. It may seem at first glance that by resisting any reference to the birth of Jesus in Bethlehem, we have rendered any application of this chapter to Mary at least problematic, if not impossible. If this were the case, there would be no possibility of seeing any value in the argument of B. J. LeFrois,[65] who tries to show that the woman of the Apocalypse can be none other than the Blessed Virgin Mary, because the birth of the child is physical and not merely metaphorical. However, we think that not only is it possible to keep the marian perspective here, but that our exegesis makes it possible to establish it even more firmly.

The marian interpretation of the chapter is virtually unanimous, among ancient as well as among contemporary authors.[66]

---

64 Formerly many commentators used to see in the Woman's flight into the desert an allusion to the departure of the Judeo-Christians from Jerusalem for Pella, before Titus' siege of the holy city (cf. EUSEBIUS, *Hist. Eccl.*, III, V: 3). S. Giet suggests that the river flowing from the dragon's mouth "could symbolize either the nations which come to Jerusalem, or the soldiers who besiege it, or those who pass through Perea." (L'Apocalypse et l'Histoire, Paris, 1957, p. 111).

65 *The Woman Clothed With The Sun*, pp. 145, 217.

66 LeFROIS, *The Woman Clothed with the Sun*, pp. 11-61, undertakes to synthesize the ancient interpretations. Most of the Fathers, both eastern and western, seem to have favored the collective interpretation rather than the marian, of Apoc. XII. As to whether Irenaeus saw the Woman of the Apocalypse as Mary, cf. F. M. BRAUN, *La Femme vêtue du soleil*, p. 642.

There are two principal objections invariably raised against it; first, the pains of childbirth are incompatible with the mystery of Bethlehem; [67] secondly, although Jesus is Mary's only child, the woman of Apocalypse XII has other offspring than the Messiah (verse 17). However, if we keep in mind what we have said of the birth pains being merely metaphorical and referring to Calvary, these objections cease to carry weight, especially if we recall that, in the fourth Gospel, Mary is given at the foot of the Cross to be mother of the beloved disciple.

However, *the mere application of the passage to the Blessed Virgin Mary is not at all the same as showing that such was the real intention of the Apocalypse authors.* We need to be most careful on this point, since, as we have already indicated, the passage is understood better if we abstract from Christ's historical mother. It is also possible that the Qumran hymn, which we quoted earlier, may supply us with an instance of a merely metaphorical mother of the real personal Messiah.

The twofold allusion to Isaias VII and to Genesis III: 15 inclines us to think that the author had in mind a mother of flesh and blood, a real mother, such as Mary, and not exclusively the personification of the people of God. However, this is hardly a decisive argument.[68] Although the LXX text of Isaias VII

---

67 This was the principal objection which the ancient writers raised against the marian interpretation. OECUMENIUS, who favors the marian interpretation of Apoc. XII, sees in the childbirth pains of the woman the moral pain which Mary suffered before Joseph was told by the angel that "that which is begotten in her is of the Holy Spirit" (cf. the text in LeFROIS, p. 45). L. CERFAUX considers these pains as merely an allusion to the ancient prophetic oracles (*Eph. Theol. Lov.*, 1955, p. 31). However, this does not explain the sacred writer's insistence on the sufferings in citing these oracle texts. Taking a purely biological point of view, A. MITTERER of the University of Vienna maintains that a virgin childbirth does not necessarily exclude the pains which ordinarily accompany a normal birth. (*Dogma und Biologie der hl. Familie, nach dem Weltbild des hl. Thomas von Aquin und dem der Gegenwart* Wien, 1952, pp. 119-124. Cf. Le Frois p. 313, note 2). Even so, it still seems impossible that this Apocalypse text should refer to the birth of Christ in Bethlehem, for all the reasons which we have given above.

68 Long before Braun and Cerfaux, Cardinal Newman had already used the text of Gen. III: 15 to justify the marian interpretation of Apoc. XII: "If the dragon of St. John is the same as the serpent of Moses, and the man-child is the seed of the woman, why is not the woman herself

speaks of the "virgin" (*parthenos*) who is to bear Emanuel, and while Matthew (I: 23) and Luke (I: 27-31) refer to the prophecy in this way in applying it to Mary, still the Apocalypse speaks not of the virgin but of the woman. The Qumran hymn, which also refers, perhaps, to Genesis III: 15 and to Isaias VII, still refers to a merely allegorical person.

Nevertheless, the Apocalypse is a Christian work. It is inconceivable that a Christian writer, much less the Apostle John, the author of the fourth Gospel, could have spoken of the Mother of the Messiah, without having a thought of Mary, the Mother of Jesus. As a matter of fact, in our opinion, the strongest justification for the Marian context of Apocalypse XII seems to be in its relationship to John's account of Mary at the foot of the cross, as P. Braun has shown well. It is imperative that we maintain the greatest care here in comparing these two passages.

The relationship of these two passages to each other would be much more in evidence if we could be certain that the fourth Gospel places Christ's Passion in relation to the Protoevangelium, as does the Apocalypse. But it is more difficult to establish this than we might wish to think: [69] merely to adduce such texts as VIII: 44; XIII: 2; 27 or I John III: 8 is hardly to prove the point. And it would certainly be a vicious circle to invoke the Apocalypse in order to place this element in John XIX: 25-27, if we are to make use of this fourth Gospel text in order to give a marian interpretation of Apocalypse XII. Given the unresolved state of this entire question, we consider it more prudent to refrain from invoking an unproven similarity between the fourth Gospel and the Apocalypse.

However, it is legitimate nonetheless to relate the Apocalypse to the Johannine tradition. Whatever position one may adopt with regard to the unity of the authorship of the fourth Gospel,

---

she whose seed the man-child is? And if the first woman is not an allegory, why is the second? If the first woman is Eve, why is not the second Mary?" (*Difficulties of Anglicans*, New York, 1930, vol. III, pp. 58-59). On this argument cf. D. J. Unger, *Cardinal Newman and Apocalypse XII*, in *Theological Studies*, 1950, pp. 356-367. If, as Unger shows, Newman sees the woman of Gen. III: 15 not as Eve but as Mary (cf. the above text), then certainly the argument is much stronger.

69 This is the principal criticism which most authors (Giblet, Van den Bussche) raise against Braun's attractive work. Their objections are reproduced in *La Mère des Fidèles*, 2nd ed., pp. 197-200.

of the Apocalypse and of the so-called Johannine Epistles, there is no doubt that these writings are of the same school, and that it is correct to explain one of them by the others. Christ is called the "Logos" nowhere in the New Testament except in the fourth Gospel, in I John and in the Apocalypse; the theme of "living water" is common to John's Gospel and to the Apocalypse, and is found only in these two works. The text of Zach. XII: 10, "They shall look upon him whom they have pierced," occurs also in John XIX: 37 and in Apocalypse I: 7, in a translation different from that of the LXX, and which occurs only in these two passages. The same phenomenon occurs in Apocalypse XII and John XIX: 25-27. This list could be lengthened, but these examples suffice to establish the point.

There are in John XIX: 25-27 three characteristics of the Mother of Jesus which do not occur in the other Gospel, not even in that of St. Luke, which is the most complete of them all on Mary: (a) the insistence with which the Mother of Jesus is called "Woman." This coincidence between the two scenes of Cana and of Calvary betrays an intent of the author which must be of the doctrinal order. Especially, as R. Murphy [70] observes, it is insofar as she is the Woman *par excellence,* that Mary is given to St. John as mother; (b) she has other children than Jesus; the Savior Himself gives her the beloved disciple to be her son; (c) Mary's spiritual motherhood is linked to the mystery of Calvary.

These same characteristics seem to apply to the Mother of the Messiah in the Apocalypse. She is called Woman, a fact all the more remarkable, we think, insofar as the author was thinking, no doubt, of the virgin of Isaias. She also has other children than the Messiah. Finally she is also associated with a metaphorical childbirth inseparable from the cross. Add to this the fact that the scene in Apocalypse XII: 9-12, with the defeat of Satan, his fall to earth and the heavenly voice heard to cele-brate the victory of God and of Christ recalls closely that of John XIX: 28-32 (a heavenly voice linked to the defeat of the devil and the glorification of Jesus), and it becomes indubitable that we have here also a basic johannine tradition, common to both the fourth Gospel and the Apocalypse.

Now we should look more closely at John XIX: 25-27.

---

70 Theological Studies, 1949, p. 571.

Gaechter [71] and Braun have both correctly attributed a profound theological meaning to this scene. This scene cannot be only a gesture of filial piety on the part of Christ toward His Mother: it is the beloved disciple who is given to Mary, not vice-versa, and this despite the probable presence of John's own natural mother at the foot of the Cross. The events surrounding this scene all have a messianic overtone, and fulfill the Scriptures, which leads us to believe that this scene is of the same kind.

It is not easy to determine to which Old Testament oracle the author intends to refer in this case. We mentioned above that we are not sympathetic to the hypothesis of a reference here to Genesis III: 15. However, Hoskyns [72] and R. H. Lightfoot [73] lead us in a different direction. Hoskyns sees Mary here as a figure of the Church, the spiritual mother of Christians, a most attractive interpretation. If it is true, as M. Dibelius [74] holds, that the beloved disciple represents the Christians who love Jesus and who keep His commandments, then it may well be correct to see Mary too as a representative type of person. And since the entire context of this scene refers to the Church and to the sacraments, which are to be the earthly continuation of the salvific actions of God's incarnate Son, the ecclesiological interpretation of John XIX: 25-27 may very probably correspond to the real thought of the sacred author.

R. H. Lightfoot leads us to the same conclusion, but by another route. He places this scene in relation to the woman who gives birth to a child in XVI: 21; both passages speak of a woman, of motherhood, and of the hour. And since XVI: 21 is itself a recollection of the metaphorical childbirth of Sion predicted in the oracles of Isaias (especially XXVI: 26-27 and LXVI: 7-9), it is tempting to conclude that in the mind of the evangelist these oracles are fulfilled when Mary at the foot of the Cross suffers fruitful pains, such as those of childbirth, and that Christ gives her all His disciples in the person of John. As the Sion of the prophetic texts, Mary here becomes the mother

---

71 *Maria im Erdenleben*, Innsbruck-Wien-München, 1954, pp. 201-226.

72 *The Fourth Gospel*, London, 1947, pp. 529-530.

73 *St. John's Gospel*, Oxford, 1956, p. 317.

74 Jn. XV, 13, *Eine Studie zum Traditionsproblem des Johannes-Evangeliums*, in *Festgabe für*, A. Deissmann, Tübingen, 1927, pp. 178-180. Origen sees in St. John given to Mary as her son, the representative of all Christians. Cf. *La Mère des Fidèles* pp. 101-102.

of offspring which she has not produced. In other words, it is in view of these same elements that Christ compares His Passion to a childbirth in XVI: 21, and that in XIX: 25-27 He gives His own mother the unusual title of "Woman," by assigning to her a maternity which is purely spiritual.

If this exegesis is correct, then there are the strongest links between John XIX: 25-27 and the Woman who bears her child in Apocalypse XII. Even if it is true that this passage has in view principally th people of God personified, it now seems to us to be all but impossible that the author should not have thought of Mary, since the fourth Gospel affirms that already at Cana, and above all at Calvary, John saw in Mary the Woman whose wonderful childbirth the prophetic oracles had foretold, (i.e., the ideal Sion of the messianic era).

In other words, the bond of union between the two works is in the texts of Isaias XXVI: 17 and LXVI: 7-9, referred to in John XVI: 21-22 and in Apocalypse XII: 6-7 (rather than Genesis III: 15, of which there is not the slightest trace in the fourth Gospel). Furthermore, these same Old Testament texts to which we referred in the first part of our study to show the metaphorical character of the messianic childbirth, now serve to justify best of all our application of Chapter XII to both Mary and the Church.

It is not too difficult to determine how these prophecies were transformed and joined together, in order to be adapted to the expression of a specifically Christian truth. In the little Apocalypse of Isaias (XXVI: 26-28) the post-exile community complains of having undergone in vain the pains of childbirth without bringing salvation to the world. Isaias LXVI: 7-9 speaks of the unexpected birth of a new people of God without the pains of childbirth. John, knowing that the birth of the new people of God is conditioned on Calvary, speaks in his Apocalypse of the terrible pains of childbirth which lead to the metaphorical birth of Christ and of Christians. He describes the Mother of the Messiah, remembering Mary, who was given to St. John as his mother by Jesus on the cross.

All of this indicates that John's marian doctrine (if we can give this title to what seems rather like a number of passing references) is set in a context which is essentially ecclesiological. His theological reflection on Mary's role in God's plan seems linked to the thought of the people of God in the Old Testament, and of the Church, which is the continuation of them.

The same seems to be true, if to a lesser degree, of the Gospel of St. Luke.[75] Thus, the announcement made to Mary in Luke I: 28-33, of the conception of the Savior of the world in her womb is based upon Sophonia's statement (III: 14-17) to the daughter of Sion that Jahweh her savior is in her midst (in her womb). The Magnificat is much more than Mary's hymn of thanks. Mary here is the incarnation of Israel; thus she gives thanks by choosing Old Testament expressions which refer to Israel (compare, for example, I: 46b with Hab. III: 18; I: 47 with Dt. XXVI: 7; I: 48 with Michea III: 11, I: 49 with Dt. X: 21); or by identifying herself with the collectivity of the poor and humble, the privileged portion of the chosen people (vv. 51-53), or in including the whole race, beginning with Abraham, the common ancestor. Perhaps we might also include in this sense the words of Simeon to Mary that, "Thy own soul a sword shall pierce" (II: 35), if it is true that this prediction, recalling that of Ex. XIV: 17: "If I brought the sword upon this country...", looks to Israel through Mary. "The Messiah shall be for the chosen people a sign of contradiction (I: 34) or a stumbling block. His word, like a sword of judgment, will divide Israel. The life of Mary, daughter of Sion, will be mysteriously affected by this piercing".[76]

Thus once again we are able to discover a relationship between the lukan and johannine traditions. There is also a remarkable difference between them; while St. Luke's infancy accounts place in relief especially the greatness of Mary's role in the mystery of the Incarnation, paradoxically St. John, the great theologian of the Incarnation of the Word, is concerned only with stressing Mary's part in the mystery of the Redemption. Apocalypse XII is no exception, because, as we have shown, the birth mentioned therein is related to Calvary.

It seems as if St. John wished to complete St. Luke on these points, and that furthermore he must have had at least some

---

75 The following data are taken largely from R. LAURENTIN, *Structure et théologie de Luc I-II*, Paris, 1957.

76 R. LAURENTIN, *Luc I-II*, p. 90. This exegesis is, of course problematic. We wonder whether it would not be better to explain the text of Luke II: 25-35 (which has a typically johannine style) primarily in terms of johannine theology. Simeon's words to Mary would be a prelude to John XIX: 25 ff.

undetermined amount of influence on St. Luke's gospel, especially on the infancy narratives.

Every careful reader of the Apocalypse is surprised at Chapter XII. Chapter V brings him into the presence of the immolated and glorified Christ, who undertakes to open the scroll of destiny. The septets of the seals and of the trumpets lead him to the end of the world and to the general judgment (cf. especially XI: 15-18). Now we see that Chapter XII brings the reader to the (metaphorical) birth and heavenly exaltation of Christ. As we have explained elsewhere [77] the reason for this new beginning, this apparent retrogression, is not a collection of different documents, which would have to be separated or distinguished from each other, but in the Apocalypse author's idea of the religious history of the world, a conception which is slightly similar to that of St. Luke, as H. Conzelmann has shown.[78]

As does St. Luke, John distinguishes two great stages in the religious history of man, which we might call the time of the Jews and the time of the nations, or, to use a terminology similar to that of Conzelmann, the time of Israel and that of the Church. The septets of the seals of the trumpets concern especially (although not exclusively) the Jewish race, whose destiny is described in the light of the catastrophe of 70, and then prophesied in its general outline for the last era, leading to the end of time. We refer here to the exegesis which we have already given for chapter XI.[79]

Wedged in between the sixth and seventh trumpets, Chapter X describes a new prophetic investiture and foretells a new series of events affecting the Christian Church, especially in its relationship with the nations and most particularly with the Roman Empire. These events begin in chapter XII, in which the glorified Christ is no longer greeted by such Jewish titles as "Lion of Juda" or "Scion of David" (v. 5), but now as

77 *Le Chapitre X de l'Apocalypse, son apport dans la solution du problème eschatologique du Nouveau Testament, Communication faite au Congres Biblique International de Bruxelles.* Cf. also ch. II of this part, above.

78 *Die Mitte der Zeit, Studien zur Theologie des Lukas.* Tübingen, 1957.

79 *Essai d'interprétation du chapitre XI de l'Apocalypse,* in *New Testament Studies,* April 1958, pp. 183-200. Cf. also Chapter III of this second part above.

he who is to beat the nations with a rod of iron. The woman whom the seer contemplates is, as we have said above, the ideal people of God of the Old Testament, who, after giving Christ to the world, becomes the Christian people, the Church. Her painful childbirth refers to Christ's Passion, the necessary prelude to His Resurrection and to the appearance of the Church. In our view, therefore, this vision is well situated; it marks the transition from the time of Israel to that of the Church.

The marian interpretation fits well into this total context. If it is true that in the fourth Gospel Mary, who is called "Woman" by her Son, is credited with the metaphorical and miraculous childbirth of the Woman-Sion, described in Apocalypse XII, then it is clearly obvious that this latter passage refers to Mary. Seen from the point of view of the general structure of the Apocalypse, she seems to take on a new meaning. St. Paul says, "When the fullness of time came, God sent his son, *born of a woman,* born under the law" (Gal. IV: 4). In God's plan of salvation, this woman plays an essential role, which the Apocalypse merely mentions without explaining it in detail, although later Christian tradition has abundantly clarified her part. In effect, the mystery of the Redemption, which is essentially a mystery of solidarity, supposes that the Son share our carnal nature.

Thus the woman who is Christ's mother is at the center of the history of salvation. This is the place which John gives her in Apocalypse XII. We see there how through her the transition takes place from the economy of the Law to that of Grace (to use a typically pauline vocabulary). These two economies are as distinct (not to say opposed) as are Israel and the Christian people, although the one is the perfect continuation of the other. It is precisely the Blessed Virgin Mother who assures this continuation, because she belonged first to the old economy of the Law before passing into the new Christian economy by giving the world its Savior.

Remarks

Because the pains of childbirth are incompatible with the joyful mystery of Bethlehem, we proposed above that the birth described in Apocalypse XII is a direct reference to Calvary. Still, strictly speaking, we could admit a double birth here, that of Bethlehem insofar as Mary is shown in her individual role as Mother of Jesus, and that of Easter morning insofar as Mary represents and is the incarnation of the body of believers. Here we think of the frequent Semitic practice of passing from the individual to the group, and vice-versa. The history of the community becomes that of its individual members, just as the deeds of individual persons of the past or present appear as having a relationship to the whole community. Thus an ecclesial exegesis of Apocalypse XII does not at all exclude a marian exegesis, as long as this latter retains the secondary and subordinate position which alone is proper to it.

ALBA HOUSE is staffed by the Pauline Fathers and Brothers. All the operations going into the making of this book were carried out by the Fathers and Brothers as part of their publishing apostolate. The Society of St. Paul was founded to work exclusively in communications. By this is meant that it was instituted to spread the teachings of Christ via the press, radio, motion pictures and television.

PAULINES reach thousands daily — by each book, pamphlet, production — multiplying the good message and at times carrying it into places almost impossible to reach. It is their job in the Church to staff editorial offices, publishing plants, film studios, etc., and to develop those fields of communications still comparatively un-touched for Christ.

PAULINES, aside from living a balanced religious life, perform their apostolic work according to their talents and training as: editors, designers, directors, proofreaders, writers, artists, photographers, pressmen, typesetters, binders, compositors, photoengravers and technicians of all kinds in the Communications Apostolate. The Vatican Council's decree on the media of social communications has been a great source of renewed energy for them.

INTERNATIONAL as the air-waves, the Pauline Fathers and Brothers are located in twenty-three countries, with headquarters in Rome. In the United States they are in New York City, Buffalo, Detroit, Boston and Youngstown.

A BROCHURE on the Society and its aims can be obtained for yourself, or any young man whom you feel might qaulify to become a Pauline Priest or Brother, by simply sending a card to: The Pauline Fathers and Brothers, Vocation Office, 2187 Victory Blvd., Staten Island, N. Y.